Business and Professional Communication

DAN B. CURTIS
JAMES J. FLOYD
JERRY L. WINSOR

Central Missouri State University

 HarperCollins*Publishers*

8-4-94

Dedicated to our wives,
Linda L. Curtis, Rebecca Wenske Floyd, Mary E. Winsor

Sponsoring Editor: Melissa A. Rosati
Project Editor: Susan Goldfarb/Brigitte Pelner
Cover Design and Design Supervisor: Jaye Zimet
Photo Researcher: Rosemary Hunter
Production Manager/Assistant: Willie Lane/Sunaina Sehwani
Compositor: BookMasters, Inc.
Printer and Binder: R. R. Donnelley & Sons Company
Cover Printer: Lehigh Press, Inc.

Business and Professional Communication

Copyright © 1992 by HarperCollins Publishers Inc.

Library of Congress Cataloging-in-Publication Data

Curtis, Dan B.
    Business and professional communication / Dan B. Curtis, James J.
Floyd, Jerry L. Winsor.
        p.   cm.
    Includes bibliographical references.
    ISBN 0-673-38095-5
    1. Business communication.   I. Floyd, James J., 1941–
II. Winsor, Jerry L.   III. Title.
HF5718.C87   1992
658.4'5—dc20   91-23713
                                                    CIP

91 92 93 94   9 8 7 6 5 4 3 2 1

Contents

Preface

OVERVIEW

You are about to begin a journey that will help you understand how to communicate more successfully in the business setting. No doubt you have skills, assets, experiences, and many other qualities that have served you well when you have been called upon to speak. Our goal is to help you maximize your abilities to become a more accomplished business communicator.

Textbooks for business and professional communication often attempt to cover too many concepts. In this book we focus on the preparation necessary for making successful presentations. We also discuss other important contexts of communication in order to prepare you for the variety of communication challenges that face business communicators.

You will need to work successfully in small groups, interview well for positions, and screen candidates for positions. You will need to listen effectively to superiors, peers, subordinates, and clients. Competence or effectiveness in interpersonal communication also is a key to ongoing success in the business world.

Every day, business executives, sales personnel, and other company and agency officials make "pitches" to persuade decision makers to "buy" ideas and/or products. Business presentations normally are made before a small number of influential people. The main goal for a business presentation is to persuade clients to purchase a product, adopt a service contract, or adopt an idea that will ultimately profit the organization.

Our design is a pragmatic one focusing on a carefully integrated approach to business and communication. We present theory where it is important for understanding. However, our main thrust is practical. The authors' years of experience in making presentations, teaching presentational skills to university students, leading business training seminars, and providing critiques to clients form the basis for the suggestions contained in this text. This is a "how-to" text that can be used by business presenters as well as university students in communication and business-related fields.

FEATURES

This text incorporates additional features: (1) It is comprehensive. (2) It is based upon classroom-tested concepts. (3) It includes ideas from the authors' corporate experiences in training, consulting, and active management. (4) It reflects a balance between communication/management theory and practice. (5) It has a strong business orientation. (6) It emphasizes the importance of ethical considerations in relation to communication effectiveness.

We will take you step by step through the process of conceptualizing, planning, developing, and implementing effective business presentations. We offer learning goals, examples, summaries, and activities in each chapter. Whether your instructor follows our organizational plan chapter by chapter, designs a course around part of the text, or improvises another organizational plan in reading or assigning chapters, we believe you will achieve a solid understanding of business communication and increased competency in making business presentations.

ORGANIZATION OF THE BOOK

Part One, "An Overview of Business Communication," explores the nature of business and professional communication and the basic interpersonal skills and concepts necessary for success.

Part Two, "Communication Skills," considers specific skills. In Chapter 3 we explore the importance of effective listening for business communicators. In Chapters 4 and 5 we focus on achieving competence in conducting interviews.

Part Three, "Group Management," discusses group management in business. In Chapter 6 we discuss the advantages of working in the group setting and identify the responsibilities of leaders and participants. In Chapter 7 we discuss how to plan, conduct, and review business meetings.

Part Four, "Planning for Your Presentation," is composed of Chapters 8 through 14. Here we discuss the planning process for successful presentations. We look at how to analyze your audience, inform and influence others, support your ideas, organize your points, work for proper style, and enhance your ideas through use of multimedia aids.

In Part Five, "Making and Evaluating Your Presentations," we provide guidance for good delivery and for addressing audience questions, and discuss ways to analyze the content, purpose, support, audience, and social context of the presentation. We believe that learning to analyze and evaluate your presentations both before and after their delivery will contribute significantly to your growing competence as professional communicators.

We would like to thank all those who reviewed the manuscript: Patricia Andrews, Indiana University at Bloomington; William E. Arnold, Arizona State University; Thomas J. Costello, University of Illinois at Urbana-Champaign; Samuel Edelman, California State University at Chico; Lois J. Einhorn, State University of New York at Binghamton; Carl Kell, Western Kentucky University; Gary Kreps, Northern Illinois University; Michael R. Moore, Purdue University–Calumet; Charles R. Newman, Parkland College; James E. Quisenberry, Morehead State University; Gary M. Shulman, Miami University; Barbara Strain, San Antonio College; and John L. Williams, California State University at Sacramento.

Special thanks to Ann Graves for editing an earlier draft of the manuscript, to Tricia Hansen for her assistance with proofing and cartoon selection, and to Joyce Hitchcock, our resident computer whiz, for her patience, advice, and expertise in loading and reformatting the latter revisions of the text.

Dan B. Curtis
James J. Floyd
Jerry L. Winsor

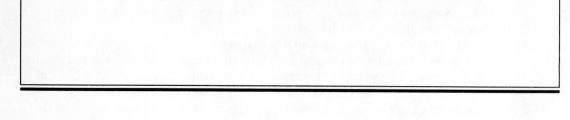

About the Authors

Dan B. Curtis

Dan B. Curtis has had more than 20 years of experience in helping people develop effective communication skills in a wide range of settings, including business, industrial, government, religious, and educational organizations. His clients and audiences have included such premier American organizations as IBM, TWA, the Future Farmers of America, and the Kansas City Chiefs. The U.S. Navy and Army have also utilized his consulting and training services. Previous to his teaching career, Dr. Curtis served as an assistant sales manager of a nation-wide photography firm and district sales manager of an insurance company.

He holds a doctorate in speech communication from the University of Missouri. Dr. Curtis is chairman of the Department of Communication at

Central Missouri State University, where he is a professor of speech communication. A coauthor of four books, he has published numerous articles in national and regional journals.

Dr. Curtis is the recipient of the highest teaching and research award granted by his university.

James J. Floyd

James J. Floyd has taught speech communication at the high school and university levels for 27 years. He has conducted communication training for a variety of business, professional, and educational organizations. He has also served on a board of education and on the boards of religious and charitable organizations. Dr. Floyd is the author of a textbook on listening improvement and has published articles in regional and national journals. He received his Ph.D. from Indiana University in 1972 and is currently a professor of speech communication at Central Missouri State University.

Jerry L. Winsor

Jerry L. Winsor has been involved in teaching communication theory, principles, and skills for over 25 years. Dr. Winsor received his Ph.D. from the University of Nebraska at Lincoln and his M.S. from Kansas State Teachers College. He has been chief executive officer of two corporations. He maintains a real estate license, has sales experience in insurance, and is an active trainer in business, industry, government, and education. He is now a professor of speech communication and graduate coordinator in the Department of Communication at Central Missouri State University.

Dr. Winsor continues to receive high ratings as a public speaker, trainer, and consultant. He is the author and coauthor of numerous articles published in national, regional, and state journals. He continues to make presentations for professional associations in communication and related disciplines. Dr. Winsor has been an NEH summer scholar.

Dr. Winsor has provided leadership in several organizations, including serving as president of the Mental Health Association in Missouri. Dr. Winsor has been nominated for various awards for achievement in teaching.

PART ONE

An Overview of Business Communication

Chapter 1

The Nature of Business Communication

After reading and reviewing this chapter, you should be able to . . .

1. Discuss the basics of the communication process.

2. Define *source, receiver, encoding, decoding, feedback, feedforward, channel, context,* and *noise.*

3. Describe and apply the following communication principles: (*a*) it is impossible to avoid communicating; (*b*) communication is largely nonverbal; (*c*) context affects communication; (*d*) meanings are in people rather than words; (*e*) communication is irreversible; (*f*) noise affects communication; and (*g*) communication is circular.

4. Apply the following concepts: creating common ground is essential, communication has effects, communication has ethical dimensions, and quality is more important than quantity in communication.

5. Describe an organization in terms of its communication networks and information flow while indicating what could be done to improve its communication effectiveness.

As he planned his first day as the new sales manager of the personal computer systems unit at American Computer Systems, Inc., Bob Trent realized he had much to learn. With his new department decimated by promotions, retirements, and transfers, Bob now faced the challenge of building his sales team. Sue Derkman, the previous sales manager, had given Bob an orientation prior to her promotion. He knew he would have to evaluate the remaining personnel and seek the kinds of people who would make the unit a continued success. Bob was happy for Sue and the others who had been promoted, but he was eager to assemble a vibrant, cohesive, and productive team. In reviewing the challenge before him, Bob realized that he had much to learn about effective and efficient business communication.

Although Bob had a good technical background, he was new to management. Communicating beyond a somewhat isolated technical work group would be a new experience. He realized he would need communication skills to help him select good employees and listen effectively to clients, employees, and managers. Additionally, his new responsibilities included participating in and leading group discussions, conducting meetings, and facilitating decision making. Furthermore, Bob needed to develop his own philosophy of management and to establish an appraisal and feedback system for his team members.

Bob realized that he had just earned a chance to prove himself, and he wanted to make the best of the opportunity presented to him by American's upper management. He was excited by the challenge. At the same time, he was apprehensive because he believed he lacked many business communication skills.

That afternoon, as Bob sat at his new desk reading his sales manual, his telephone rang. Over the phone, the sales unit secretary reminded him that the first applicant personnel had screened for his new sales force team would be coming for an interview on Monday at 10:00 A.M. Bob swallowed hard, realizing that this first important decision rested largely on his ability to select the right person for his new team. He reminded himself that in order to succeed, he needed to understand the nature and practice of effective business communication.

COMMUNICATION: EXCHANGE OF MESSAGES

When you *communicate,* you are generating, transmitting, and receiving messages. The *business communication setting* includes the sending and receiving of messages in an organization—between two people, or among a small group of people, or in a one-to-many setting, with the intent of influencing organizational behavior. The results of communication efforts thus may be *intentional* (one person deliberately attempts to influence another) or *unintentional* (one person's actions are perceived and interpreted by another). All business communication is ultimately persuasive in nature and represents an attempt to influence behavior in organizations.

What is a business presentation? In what ways does a business presentation differ from other forms of address? Business presentations are oral presentations made by a variety of people interested in selling ideas, processes, programs, products, and so forth to a variety of groups that have the power to recommend or make purchase decisions.

RATIONALE FOR COMMUNICATION

There are several reasons why communication takes place in organizations. One goal of communication is *to inform* clients, colleagues, subordinates, and supervisors. Another is to *be informed*. Behavior is altered through informing and being informed. Each communication interaction provides a little more data about other people as well as ourselves. Having information available increases the potential for productivity in a business organization. People tend to feel better about themselves when they are well-informed and granted access to information. Access to information is part of being trusted and feeling secure. Furthermore, communication is intended to *influence others*. Communication serves to stimulate interest, lessen hostility, and actuate people to complete a task or initiate a behavior.

Bob Trent is a case in point. Bob knows he must demonstrate his competence to his immediate superior, his peers, his sales team, and others. His job in the business organization primarily involves appropriately influencing others. Additionally, he will conduct sales meetings, make requests through the administrative structure, and interact with numerous people and groups of potential customers. In each case, he must demonstrate that he is a reasonable person with important ideas to express and relevant questions to ask. He hopes to be an effective communicator for his company and for himself.

Communicators in organizations also seek to *help others*. Bob Trent will need to counsel those who work with him as members of his sales team. He will help customers solve problems. He will strive to motivate others to achieve their career goals. Much of the satisfaction he will derive from working at American Computer Systems will come from helping others develop and grow.

Like Bob Trent and Sue Derkman, you have been communicating with others almost from the moment of birth, and you will do so until you die. You spend the better part of each workday communicating in one way or another in order to satisfy physical needs, ego needs, and social needs. The essence of effective organizational management is effective communication.

Yet despite the amount of time devoted to business communication, business people frequently do not communicate as well as they could.

Communication in a business organization is employed *to solve problems and make decisions*. It could be argued that the higher one goes in business, the more one depends on decision-making and problem-solving skills for success. Yukl (1981) indicates that technical skills are often more important for lower-level managers but that middle-level managers are likely to use both technical and conceptual skills. Yukl contends that upper-level managers utilize conceptual skills (making strategic decisions) most frequently (p. 87).

When two people come to you because they want to take their vacations at the same time, and you realize that only one can be absent if your production targets are to be met, you have a problem to solve (a human relations problem) and decisions to make. How will you handle this situation? Which employee needs the vacation most at that time? What is the best way to make and communicate such a decision? With a problem like this, you need sensitivity and communication sense in order to satisfy both employees.

Another purpose of business communication is *to evaluate behavior* effectively. Members of an organization need appraisal in order to know what they are doing well or when corrections are needed in their performance. Appraisals require sensitivity and communication skill.

COMMUNICATION COMPETENCE

Communication competence implies success in sending messages clearly, humanely, and efficiently. Competence is manifested also by accurately receiving transmitted messages. Communication competence refers to our understanding of the social aspects of the communication situation. A business communicator who keeps silent, recognizing that the managers present are not open to suggestions at that particular time, is reflecting competent adaptation. Competence is also demonstrated by recognizing whether or not a topic is appropriate, what amount of touching is acceptable, what physical distance is appropriate, and so forth. Competence is enhanced by developing a positive communication atmosphere for success in the future.

COMPONENTS OF COMMUNICATION

In order to achieve communication competence, each business communicator should understand the components of the communication process shown in Figure 1.1: *source, message, encoding, channels, feedforward, decoding, receiver, feedback, noise,* and *context*.

The *source* (business communicator) is the initiator of a *message*. *Encoding* is the process or act of selecting the symbols that stand for one's

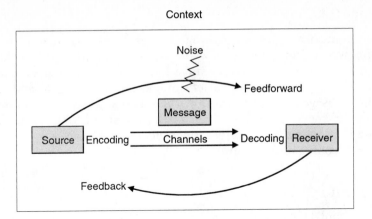

Figure 1.1 The communication process.

thoughts. A source chooses a *verbal or nonverbal* code, such as American English, and sends symbols through *channels* (such as sound waves and visual stimuli) that are intended to be understood by receivers. *Feedforward* is prefacing information about forthcoming communication, including verbal messages. *Decoding* is the process of assigning meaning to the received symbols. The *receiver* is the person who receives the symbols. *Feedback* is any verbal or nonverbal message sent back to the source in relation to the source's message. *Noise* is any factor that distorts or interferes with clear message reception. *Context* includes the physical and other conditions that surround the act of communication.

Source/Receiver

A *source* is an originator of a *message*. Since business communication involves people communicating with other people in an organizational setting, each person becomes a source of messages. Obviously, Sue Derkman, Bob Trent, and their team members will originate many messages. Sue and Bob will be involved in planning, organizing, staffing, directing, and controlling activities. These and other activities are major motivations for initiating communication in a business environment. This communication process is made more complex by the fact that each human source is a transceiver. A *transceiver* is a source that sends and receives messages at the same time. For example, while Sue Derkman briefed Bob during his orientation, she monitored the content of his questions, his posture, his facial expression, and, in general, his level of interest and understanding. Each source performs decoding (receiver) and encoding functions at the same time—that is, each person formulates and transmits messages while perceiving and comprehending messages.

Encoding/Decoding

In communication, the act of assigning symbols to thoughts—for example, deciding which words to say or write—is *encoding*. The process is the act of choosing symbols for thoughts. Since human beings are capable of using all five senses, encoders have a variety of codes to select from and combine in sending messages. Creating meaningful sound waves is an appropriate code, suitable for encoding by a source; translating sound waves into thoughts is decoding. As source and receiver functions are simultaneous, so are the functions of encoding and decoding.

Feedback/Feedforward

Feedback and feedforward often involve a combination of verbal and nonverbal messages. *Feedback* is composed of information about messages previously sent, while *feedforward* is information about messages that will be sent in the future. Feedforward messages are constructed to tell the listener something about the forthcoming content. Feedforward includes verbal statements, such as "Wait until you hear about this" and/or nonverbal indicators, such as change of mood. Sometimes, a furrowed brow signals a change in the tone of the communication. Feedback and feedforward may be interpreted positively or negatively. Successful business communication depends more on effectiveness in perceiving feedback than it does on extensive use and understanding of feedforward. In other words, feedback is essential; feedforward is optional.

Channels

Communication channels are the media through which messages are conveyed. Normally, more than one medium is used. When people communicate in the business setting, they usually combine vocal (auditory channel) and sight (visual channel) displays. Touch (tactile channel), odors (olfactory channel), and tastes (gustatory channel) are available in message channels in communication as well. Bob Trent, like most thoughtful business people, carefully chooses his cologne for positive effect. He does not want the smell to be so strong that it arrives before he does. Bob, a gourmet cook, sent cookies to Sue Derkman in appreciation for her helpful orientation, thus utilizing the less common channels of smell and taste in a business communication.

Context

All communication takes place within a context of some kind. The physical context includes the room, tangible objects, scenery, and so forth. Sociopsychological constructs of the context include factors such as the status of the people involved in the communication relationship, their roles, and their degree of sincerity. The timing or temporal dimension of the context includes the time of day and the perceived chain of events preceding the communication event.

Noise

Noise is inherent to communication. Noise distorts and interferes with message reception. It may be physical, psychological, or semantic. *Physical noise* consists of external sights and sounds, such as blurred print, distracting colors, machinery, and so forth. *Psychological noise* is caused by biases and distortions within the mind of the sender and/or receiver. It includes many intrapersonal variables, such as conflicting values, attitudes, and opinions. *Semantic noise* involves misconceptions of intended meaning, often because of insufficient and unfamiliar vocabulary or use of technical language or jargon.

Developing effective communication habits, like developing any skill, requires an understanding of both theory and practice. Just as simply understanding the theory of baseball playing alone will not produce a star baseball player, understanding the theory of communication will not automatically produce an effective communicator. Theory must be put into effective practice.

BASIC PRINCIPLES OF COMMUNICATION

All forms of verbal interaction involve basic principles of communication that business people must understand clearly. Bob Trent will need to understand and apply these basic concepts in his work-related and personal communication.

It Is Impossible to Avoid Communicating

A first principle of communication is that *it is impossible to avoid communicating.* In other words, there is no such thing as noncommunication. DeVito (1988) notes that communication is inevitable, that we cannot *not* communicate and we cannot *not* respond (p. 19). Some of the ramifications of this principle are obvious, and some may not be as clear. For example, it is impossible to follow the instruction to "not behave." You can drop your head and remain silent. However, someone may assign meaning to this behavior. Since it is not possible to avoid being on display, inevitably you become a source for communication (stimulus). Bob Trent and the members of his new team will need to understand this principle in order to minimize counterproductive behaviors. Bob wondered, "How can I deal with such a complex concept?" Upon reflection, Bob realized that he may have sent unintentional messages during his orientation by Sue. He recalled that he had used language from his technical background that Sue might not have understood, since her experience is in sales and marketing management. Bob recalled that he used the terms *interface, bytes,* and *bits,* which are technical jargon.

Some impressions are *intentional*—under the control of the communicator. Skilled business communicators consider the importance of first impressions as they plan for a presentation. They carefully observe the way confident people walk into a room; they consider appropriate dress (colors, textures, style, etc.); they note how even handshake techniques affect the impression. Additionally, skillful presenters manage the amenities of small talk and factors such as seating arrangements in an effort to make a favorable first impression. Bob Trent has a good example in his predecessor, Sue Derkman. Sue carefully avoids any dress or grooming practice that would focus undue attention away from the professional message she intends to communicate. She has good "stage presence": she walks into a room naturally and confidently, speaks with quiet assurance, and maintains good eye contact. One way Bob can apply the principle that it is impossible to avoid communicating is to pay attention to the way people like Sue behave in business and other settings.

Indeed, a "sharp image" may be planned and cultivated well in advance. One must "sell oneself" before offering an idea or a plan of action; this should motivate the communicator to consider communication variables that affect the success of the appeal. Factors such as the content and quality of written communication, dress, grace in attempting to put the other(s) at ease, and even the choice of time and place should be planned carefully.

Bob understands that while appearance and amenities of the situation are important, the message content of communication should be far more important. The content (words or verbal symbols) of communication carries a significant basis for decision making. Hence, it is the responsibility of the source to encode verbal symbols as clearly as possible in order to evoke the meanings intended. Bob should select language that is as precise as possible.

Other impressions are *unintentional.* While recognizing that such impressions are unavoidable, effective communicators will try to be as sensitive to unintended cues as possible in order to minimize potential distractions from an intended message. For example, if Bob, without thinking, folds his arms during a presentation, an unintended meaning may be perceived by audience members (this gesture is often thought to be a negative or closed-minded behavior). Bob may use feedback devices such as videotape recordings and/or oral critique sessions to look for some of his unintentional cues. Since it is impossible to account for all the stimuli to which a given audience member will be receptive and attach meaning, it is impossible to control all the stimulus potential (impressions) conveyed in a given communication situation. A good business communicator tries to minimize misunderstandings. Even the most sensitive persuader will have to recognize that much unconscious communication (communication below the threshold of awareness) and/or unintentional communication will occur during a given interaction.

Only a careful audit of the *feedback* behaviors of the audience members will give the business communicator clues as to the presence of such unintentional stimuli. Bob Trent might improve his communication style considerably if someone would make him aware of a few of his idiosynchratic behaviors. These include habits that only a very good friend would point out without being asked. For example, when Bob stands to speak, invariably he puts a hand in his pocket and rattles his keys and change. He tends to shift to one foot, he straightens his tie, and he habitually clears his throat. These are not big problems, but they can be annoying, and they do compete for attention with the messages he wishes to communicate.

Another example of unintentional communication might occur in the classroom. Perhaps your behavior in class appears, to the instructor, to convey indifference toward what is being covered in lectures. Unintentional behavior can send messages that are perceived negatively by the instructor. You, like any business communicator, need to learn from this principle that all behavior has the potential to be misinterpreted. You simply cannot avoid displaying stimuli that will be interpreted by others. Awareness is the beginning of stimulus management.

Communication Is Largely Nonverbal

The foregoing discussion leads us to a second principle of communication: *impressions are made largely in response to nonverbal cues. Nonverbal communication* is any communication other than words that serves to accent, complement, contradict, regulate, repeat, or substitute for the verbal message. To *accent* means to highlight or emphasize some part of the verbal message; to *complement* is to reinforce the attitude or tone of the verbal message; to *contradict* means to exhibit behaviors that discredit the verbal message; to *regulate* means to control or indicate a change in the direction of the verbal messages; to *repeat* is to reiterate the verbal message with nonverbal behaviors; and to *substitute* means to replace the verbal message with a nonverbal message of similar meaning (Eckman, 1965, chap. 13, p. 440).

If Bob Trent tells Sue Derkman that he appreciates her stopping by his office to see how things are going, but continues to thumb through the half-done projects on his desk while she is present, Sue is likely to conclude that Bob would rather work on his project than talk with her. Bob's nonverbal cues have contradicted his verbal communication. Instead, a pleasant smile, attentive and warm vocal tones would serve to accent and complement Bob's appreciative message.

Nonverbal communication is relatively primitive and emotional. Clearly, it has limitations. Consider how difficult it would be to communicate nonverbally such abstract concepts as truth, justice, ethics, and religion. The degree to which people are able to accurately interpret nonverbal codes varies widely. Many people overestimate their ability to do so. DePaulo and Rosenthal (1979) note that "people's perceptions of their own decoding skills and of their attentional biases do not correspond at all to their actual skills and biases as measured by our instruments" (p. 242). Bob Trent should remind himself that his decoding of nonverbal messages will give him little more than indications of what people actually feel and mean. He should look for consistency between verbal and nonverbal messages as he decodes. Inaccurate decoding of nonverbal cues can lead to embarrassment. For example, some people perceive others as attracted to them when, in fact, extra smiles and laughter may be a manifestation of nervousness or friendliness.

Mehrabian (1968) noted that as much as 93 percent of all meaning is transmitted nonverbally (p. 53). Birdwhistell (1955) found that no more than 35 percent of a speaker's total communication is conveyed in words (pp. 10–18). These researchers emphasized the importance of nonverbal communication, but it is important to recognize that the 35 percent (the verbal content) could be the essential content for influencing a business decision. A speaker who comes dressed in a rumpled suit, speaks in a high-pitched monotone, and appears to ignore the listeners might still convey information of extreme value to the audience.

It is difficult to confirm that 93 percent or 65 percent (or somewhere in between) of all communication is nonverbal. You should realize, however, that considerable attention is devoted to such behavior. Business speakers who know about these research findings regarding nonverbal communication analyze their own presentational skills. It is interesting to hear people recount exactly what they *said* without mentioning one word about what they *did* nonverbally. Such descriptions certainly underscore our collective tendencies to assume that verbal behavior is always the dominant message.

Understanding these two communication principles—that one cannot avoid communicating and that communication is largely nonverbal—is crucial to success in the business environment. One implication for the business communicator is that effective delivery skills are important. The way a message is spoken often plays a significant part in making the final impression and may, in fact, be a greater contributor to the presentation's success or failure than the actual words used.

Tone of voice, for example, may suggest that the business communicator is uncaring, is not interested in the audience, or is not impressed with the product. Recall the first time you heard your voice on a tape recorder. You may have said, "That's not me!" Others present probably answered, "Oh, yes it is—it sounds just like you." A speaker's unconscious negative *paralanguage*, or vocal inflection, may completely contradict the positive verbal content, leaving the presenter with no clear understanding of why his or her good ideas ultimately were rejected. Paralanguage spans a wide range of vocal characteristics, including pitch, range, resonance, rhythm, articulation, tempo, dysfluencies, and pauses. (See Chapter 15 for a more detailed discussion of these and other delivery variables.) The opportunity to improve your vocal tone is as close as an inexpensive tape recorder. Paying careful attention to such nonverbal behaviors can mean the difference between success and failure as a business communicator. For example, you can tape-record your voice when speaking in a business setting, then analyze the vocal tones later. You might decide to work for clearer articulation, fewer fluency breaks, a less nasal tone, or other changes.

Bob Trent realized that he had not monitored his telephone voice thoroughly. His wife said that he sounded tired and grouchy when she called him at work. That is not the image Bob wants customers and team members to have about his attitude toward them and their ideas. His wife's feedback motivated him to record his voice and become more aware of the energy he puts into his voice as he answers, "Personal computer unit sales department, Bob Trent speaking. How may I help you?"

It is important to recognize that all communication has relational aspects, which are communicated largely nonverbally. *Relational aspects* are indications of how the communicator feels about the topic and/or the receivers of the information. A communicator is likely to be viewed as having either positive or negative feelings toward members of the audience and/or the subject of discussion. These perceptions in the minds of the audience are derived from auditing cues the presenter sends (consciously and unconsciously) through nonverbal stimuli. For example, it is obviously important for a presenter to appear interested and caring toward both the audience and the topic of the presentation. It is also the receiver's responsibility to attend, to decode accurately, and to be responsive to the ideas presented.

Context Affects Communication

A third principle that has a direct relationship to successful communication is that the *context (environment) affects communication.* As noted earlier, *where* (under what conditions) ideas are presented makes a difference in how they are interpreted. Physical conditions are one aspect of context. It is unlikely that participants will attach a similar meaning to the same communication interaction held in a nightclub and in a church sanctuary. Less extreme contextual situational differences may not be as clear. One way business people control the context of communication is to take potential clients to dinner at a nice restaurant, then make their presentation in a room with a businesslike atmosphere. It often helps to be away from the clients' busy office, where constant interruptions compete for attention. *If you don't learn how to control the context* (at least the most negative aspects of it), *context may control the success of your presentation.*

Furthermore, any business communication has a psychological dimension. This dimension may be much more complex than the physical context. Each organization has unique characteristics and relationships—a *corporate culture.* As people interact, they form a culture. Corporate cultures have written and unwritten expectations (rules or norms) that influence their members. Pace and Faules (1989) write, "Implicit in the concept of culture is an appreciation of the way organizations are molded by unique sets of values, rituals, and personalities" (p. 63). Some climates are "work hard, play hard." Others may be "all work and no play." Still others are "laid back," where almost everything goes. The people in organizations develop norms of behavior; new members need to observe and analyze these norms in order to avoid violating important expectations and to be able to predict behavior with some degree of accuracy. For example, respect for status or position may be crucial in some organizations and of much less importance in others.

Norms are formed as people relate in an organization. In each situation, an astute communicator perceives subtle cues of friendliness or unfriendliness in the work setting. Is humor appropriate? Are games being played? The answers to these questions are indicators of norms within the business environment. An understanding of the situation and the corporate culture may be as important as knowing what your specific purpose is as a business communicator. In order to be successful, you must control the context or adapt to the existing environment.

You should also consider time as a component of context. Some people are morning people; others are not. Some students, for example, welcome every word of wisdom an instructor has to offer for the first moment of class to the last. Other students close their minds (even before their notebooks) several minutes before the end of the class. In the business setting, it is more appropriate at sometimes than others to address a grievance or to discipline an errant employee. Timing is an important aspect of context, and understanding timing is important to becoming a successful business communicator.

Context also includes the surrounding environment. The environment includes the physical properties of the setting (color, spaciousness, temperature, sound, light, etc.) and the psychological dimensions (mood, roles, games, friendliness, formality, norms, etc.).

Meanings Are in People, Not in Words

A fourth principle important to your success is that *meanings are in people, not in words.* Meanings are in the perception of decoders; people "mean," but words do not. The message remembered by people often is not what a communicator intended to say. The message remembered is whatever the listeners interpret it to be. Listeners have a least 50 percent of the responsibility. Suppose, for example, you say, "Your product has two features that none of the competition has developed." The listeners may process this information in ways that you could not predict by analyzing the wording of your message. For example, one listener may be stimulated by these words to wonder how many features the competition has that your product does not. If you have a chance to view the notes taken by clients during a presentation, you may be surprised to see how many varied reactions occur. These reactions may be quite different from those you intended.

Because meanings are in people, the successful persuader will restate major concepts more than once, using different language patterns. This process gives the audience members a clearer "fix" on the meaning actually intended. A ship's distress signal cannot be located with accuracy from one transmission, but additional distress calls could help the receiver plot an exact location. Similarly, expressing abstract ideas more than once with different words allows the receivers to clarify meanings more precisely. It may be impossible to communicate completely even the most simple, discrete information, but one can expect that the meaning most people take from the message is close to that which was intended. Normally, only important points need to be repeated or restated.

Communication Is Irreversible

A fifth important principle is that *communication is irreversible*. At one time or another you may have wished you could change what you have said or done. Unfortunately, that is simply impossible. You may give additional information or a rationalization for your previous actions, but you can only modify the impression you have already made.

"Sorry, Chief, but of course I didn't mean 'bimbo' in the pejorative sense."

Communication is irreversible. (*Source: The New Yorker*, vol. 3, no. 10 [April 27, 1987], p. 44.)

A related concept is that *a communication event or setting cannot be repeated*. Communication does not stop for anyone. Some impressions are fleeting in any situation. Even the same video recording produces at least slightly different effects of perceptions when it is played before the same audience at different times. The same person cannot step in the same river twice: the river flows on and the person never has the opportunity to perceive the event twice.

You can enhance your success in business communication by recognizing that communication impressions are easy to make but difficult to modify. *First impressions are largely irreversible.* An arrow once released is difficult to retrieve in flight; first impressions tend to be lasting.

Unfortunately, people do not always monitor first impressions in their business communication. It is impossible for a speaker to control all the impressions that are recorded by the auditors, but it is possible to control many. A business person who considers how to dress, how to walk into a meeting, how to greet people, how to work the opening statement, and so on is adapting positively to the principle that communication is irreversible.

Noise Affects Communication

A sixth principle of communication is that *noise is a factor in any communication situation.* Noise, as you will recall, is any factor that interferes with the clear and accurate transmission of a given message.

Bob Trent realized that he had "noise in his channels." He was trying to assimilate a mass of detail in a very short time. That made it hard to concentrate on some tasks at hand. He needed to learn to accomplish one goal at a time. He hadn't been getting rest, and he felt tired. (Other types of noise include hunger, the effects of drinking too much coffee, and so forth.) Bob realized also that each person who attempted to listen to him would have competing noise. He needed to minimize noise within himself, and he needed to compete effectively with the noise he could not control in his listeners.

Some noise can be reduced or eliminated—for example, by closing a door or turning off a stereo. Some noise simply requires compensation—perhaps by repeating the message and/or using more than one channel of communication to carry the message.

Everyone can profit from making more precise language choices. Precision in language reduces the damage potential of semantic noise. Nonverbal messages that are congruent with the verbal message being sent can improve the fidelity (minimize distortions) of the messages listeners receive. All these changes will help reduce the negative impact of noise. Bob Trent should try not to use technical jargon when discussing product systems with laypeople. He should avoid or clarify terms like "hard card," "interface," and "bytes" when he talks with people who have no frame of reference for them. Bob can reduce the damage potential of noise by pausing to explain any term that makes a client's brow furrow in puzzlement.

Communication Is Circular

A seventh principle is that *communication is circular, not linear.* This means that people send and receive communication simultaneously. It is misleading to say that the process begins when a sender encodes a message to send through channel(s) to a receiver. Even before the sender is stimulated to

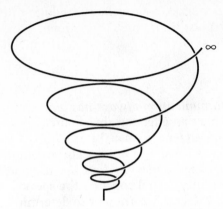

Figure 1.2 Human communication can be represented as a helical spiral. (*Source*: Frank E. X. Dance, ed., *Human Communication Theory*. New York: Holt, Rinehart and Winston, 1967.)

code a message, he or she may feedforward—indicate verbally or nonverbally just how important the forthcoming message will be to the receiver.

Because of its simultaneous aspects, the communication process could be considered a circle or spiral (see Figure 1.2) rather than a line. People process feedback while they speak to others, and they speak to themselves—think— while others are speaking. Business communicators who believe that they can simply lay out a message and get a particular response are likely to be surprised. Communication is a complex process.

In interviewing candidates for his sales team, Bob Trent needs to understand and adapt to the circular nature of communication. For example, he may not want to reveal a positive first impression: any clues he leaks may alter the candidate's natural responses to future questions. He should learn to watch interviewees' reactions as he asks questions regarding their sales experience and abilities. He will operate as a transceiver—sending and receiving messages at the same time—as he proceeds through the interview.

Creating Common Ground Is Essential

An eighth principle is that *communication is most efficient when the participants share a considerable amount of common experience*. *Common experience* is achieved by using shared symbols and speaking from a shared history. Misunderstandings are less likely in such situations. In a business organization, managers become more effective communicators when they make a conscious effort to see issues or ideas as their employees do. The greater the experiential differences, the more difficult communication will be. Bob Trent should make every effort to establish common ground with his co-workers and clients.

Special attention should be given to making people of different nationalities and cultures comfortable. Attention to such detail is important to business success. Each culture has some specific nonverbal codes; for example, beckoning with the fingers turned up may be the way to summon a dog rather than a person. Foreign visitors may realize you do not know this, but common ground can be enhanced if such behaviors are considered in advance.

Communication Has Effects

A ninth principle is that *communication always has an effect of some kind.* Even shouting at a wall can have an effect on the shouter. For every communication act, there will be consequences—usually for all parties involved in the communication. People can even feel a sense of accomplishment in a communication exchange in which a listener does not respond verbally. For example, if the listener shows interest and concern, the speaker may feel that being understood is a victory. It takes discernment to determine the effects of our communication and whether those effects are the ones sought. When a person in a business setting agrees to carry out a task you suggested, you are usually correct in thinking your communication has had a positive impact.

Knowledge of these nine principles can be of great help to people like Bob Trent. An understanding of each of these principles of communication can give a "rookie" manager like Bob some direction; he can maximize his chances of being a successful communicator. He can use this information to adapt his ideas to people and situations in the business environment. Although knowledge of these principles will not guarantee success, the business communicator who takes them into account can eliminate problems that could otherwise spell defeat.

COMMUNICATION ETHICS

Ethics are central to communication. *Ethics* are standards of conduct and moral judgment. *Communication ethics* is the consideration of the rightness or wrongness of a given communication act. Whenever anyone seeks to effect change in an organization or in a relationship with another person, there are ethical dimensions to consider. The following questions illustrate the issues involved:

- Is the request in the long-term good of the organization?
- Is the request in the best interest of the parties involved in the communication?
- Do all parties have the information and understanding they need in order to make an informed choice?
- Is the information correct/truthful?

In ethical communication, the answers to all these questions have to be "yes." These are among the ethical questions that are raised whenever a business communication is transacted. It is not ethical to lie or hide the truth when it prevents another person from exercising the right to choose from a full range of options.

There is an inherent relationship between ethics and communication. In addition to deciding what is efficient, effective, and desirable in a communication interaction, the straightforward business communicator will choose what is ethical. A more detailed treatment of ethics is presented in Chapter 10.

QUALITY VERSUS QUANTITY

More communication is not inherently better communication. Sensory or message overload paralyzes a business organization. Effective communication (quality) in the business setting may be more helpful than more messages (quantity). Moreover, the best possible communication will not solve all problems in a business organization. Some problems may occur because of a lack of resources, innovations by competing businesses, or philosophical differences that can be explored but not overcome through communication.

Now that we understand the inherent relationship between ethics and communication and realize that an increased quality of communication will not solve all business communication problems, we can explore communication structures in organizations.

COMMUNICATION NETWORKS

Business organizations contain formal and informal networks. *Networks* are patterns of communication in an organization. They are channels through which messages pass from one person to another. *Formal networks* are legitimate (authorized by management) and often are indicated by an organization chart that displays who answers to whom (see Figure 1.3). An organization chart shows the levels of authority within an organization and reflects the expected flow of information. Normally, each employee answers directly to only one person. Such formal networks indicate a unity of command. A higher-ranking company official who wants an employee under the authority of another to perform some task normally communicates the request through an informal network or asks the employee's immediate supervisor to see that the task is completed.

Informal networks are unofficial channels through which information passes in an organization. Formal communication networks contain more of the written, predictable, and routine communications; informal networks are faster, richer, and often more accurate, and communication is more likely to be face-to-face. Informal communication networks are not controlled by management. Sometimes people "leak" information to the informal network for the purpose of sending up "trial balloons" (ideas not ready for formal proposals). Conrad (1990) writes, "Because using formal communication networks takes so much time and effort, people may choose to not communicate at all if they have no informal channels available. Even 'gossip' and 'rumors'

American Computer Systems, Inc.

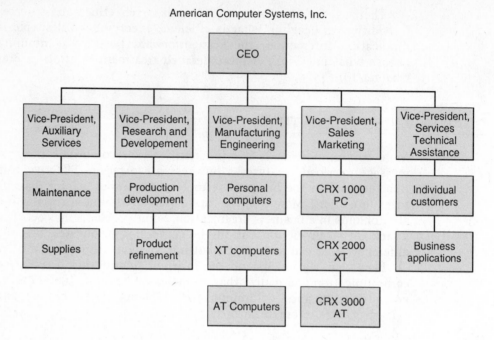

Figure 1.3 Organization chart of line and staff positions.

usually provide accurate information" (p. 172). Such networks are often called *grapevines.* They reflect patterns that employees develop when the formal channels are not clear, efficient, and/or respected. DeVito (1988) notes that the grapevine's "speed and accuracy make it an ideal medium to carry a great deal of the social communications that so effectively bind together workers in an organization" (p. 287). Informal channels of communication flow upward, downward, and horizontally, with little regard for designated positional relationships. Successful managers learn to "tap" the grapevine and alter the flow of formal communication appropriately.

Line and staff distinctions are important for business communicators. *Line functions* are usually essential to the successful operation of the organization. On an organization chart, line functions are usually connected by solid lines indicating the direction of authority. Line networks normally involve superior-subordinate relationships. *Staff relationships* between members of an organization are most often advisory in nature. It is possible for a given employee to have a line relationship with one group in an organization and a staff relationship with another. Bob Trent has a line relationship with his supervisor, who is directly above him in his line of command. Bob has a staff relationship with Sue Derkman, who held his position previously; he will look to her for much advice. Sue Derkman's encouragement of Bob Trent to call or drop by her office with his questions and her attentiveness to his needs for job orientation increase Bob Trent's chances of performing well in his new position.

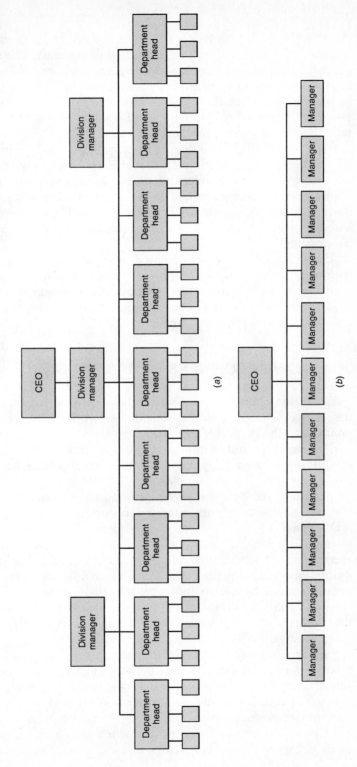

Figure 1.4 (*a*) Tall organizational structure; (*b*) flat organizational structure.

The *span of control* refers to the number of subordinates who are under the authority of an individual supervisor or manager. The smaller the span of control, the more communication access each employee will have to the supervisor. If employees are assigned similar tasks, the span of control may be somewhat greater. If employees perform complex and divergent tasks, then the span of control should be consolidated so access can be increased; otherwise, communication problems may result.

Tall organizational networks have multiple levels of management and supervision; *flat organizational structures* are broad-based (see Figure 1.4). Flat structures allow more independent action by employees and provide greater access to top management. Flat (or wide) structures have fewer third- and fourth-level supervisors. Communication tends to be freer in more broadly based (flat) configurations because there is a shorter chain of command to pass through with a given message.

Some organizations are operated in a task-oriented manner. Other organizations are more loosely disciplined. A relaxed communication network (normally found in flat structures) is more likely to support innovations than a tight or mechanistic one, because there is less delay in the communication flow and a less restrictive atmosphere.

INFORMATION FLOW IN BUSINESS ORGANIZATIONS

Organization charts do not indicate how all information travels, even in the best-managed organizations. Informal networks take the form of friendship groups and the grapevine of corporate gossip. In a well-run organization, formal channels should be more accurate. In many less effective organizations, the informal networks appear to be more accurate in reflecting what is really happening.

Another factor in business communication is the direction of communication. *Downward communication* occurs when a manager or supervisor sends a message to one or more subordinates. Downward communication is often designed to give instructions or to explain how a superior wants a task accomplished. Superiors send information about rules, policies, and minimum standards. Superiors also give information to appraise a subordinate's performance or to further motivate the subordinate.

Downward communication sets the tone for a business organization. If the majority of communication in a business comes from the top (vertical down) and generally is directive, the organizational style tends to be autocratic. If the majority of the downward communication is supportive and has a large element of concern for the subordinates, the tone set will be more supportive. Such communication will encourage collaboration between management and employees. Furthermore, it will encourage a full range of upward communication.

Upward communication occurs when messages flow from subordinates to managers or from supervisors to executives. Employees are expected to report their progress in completing tasks; what, if any, tasks are causing them problems; suggestions for product or procedural improvement; and, most important, how they feel about how things are going. Upward communication is important—managers need accurate feedback about whether their messages have been understood, how decisions are being accepted, and what problems are developing.

Horizontal communication (or lateral communication) occurs between people at the same level, or between people at corresponding levels in different divisions, within an organization. Effective horizontal communication can help people to coordinate projects, solve problems, provide for collation of information, resolve conflicts, and pave the way for business relationships.

All too often, horizontal communication is blocked because of jealousy, the barriers of technical specialization or separate locations, and because too much information flows for any one employee to process the data meaningfully. For example, people in a unit may feel that they are in competition with the production staff for all sorts of "perks"—bonuses, information, new positions, and so on—and they may seek to limit the amount of information that is shared. Insightful managers create an environment in which cooperation has more reward than competition; thus, they improve the communication environment of the entire organization. Recognizing and rewarding a group—a team—of employees is one way to encourage a cooperative spirit.

SUMMARY

- Business communication includes the sending and receiving of messages between two people, among a small group of people, or in a one-to-many setting, with the intent of influencing behavior in an organization.

- Communication competence means sending messages clearly, humanely, and efficiently. Competence also includes receiving messages accurately.

- The components of communication are the source, message, receiver, encoding, decoding, feedback, feedforward, channels, context, and noise.

- When communicating in a business setting, individuals seek to create and sustain a positive impression. Unintentional factors, such as nervous gestures or tenseness in the voice, may create unwanted distractions for the speaker.

- There are nine basic communication principles: (1) all behavior communicates something intentionally or unintentionally; (2) nonverbal communication affects perception greatly; (3) the context affects communication; (4) meanings are in people, not in words; (5) communication is irreversible; (6) noise affects communication; (7) communication is circular, not linear; (8) having a common field of experience helps ensure success in communication; and (9) communication always has an effect of some kind.

- Communicators are transceivers (that is, they send and receive messages at the same time).

- Ethical considerations are important in effective communication.

- Businesses depend on the flow of communication in networks. Formal networks are commonly represented in an organization chart. Informal networks reveal how communication normally travels outside the chain of command.

- More communication is not a panacea for solving business communication problems.

- Downward communication sets the tone of a business organization by revealing whether the type of management is directive or more participatory. Upward communication happens when messages flow from lower to higher levels in the organization. Horizontal (or lateral) communication generally occurs between equals within a unit or between complementary units.

QUESTIONS FOR REVIEW AND DISCUSSION

1. What is meant when we say that one cannot avoid communicating? What examples can you draw from your personal experience in communicating unintentional messages?

2. Explain the principle that communication is largely nonverbal.

3. What types of "noise" might be present in a business setting? What could be done to minimize or eliminate each of these distractions?

4. Define business communication and explain how it differs from other forms of communication.

5. Why is the study of ethics a consideration in business communication?

6. What is communication competence, and how can it be achieved in the business setting?

7. What are vertical and horizontal communication? What are the complications of overuse of downward communication?

ACTIVITIES

1. Write your own definitions of the terms *communication* and *business communication*. Compare your definitions with the definitions given in this chapter. Justify your differences.

2. Visit a service industry and observe employees' communication behaviors. Examine communication with customers, with peers, with management, and with subordinates. What components did you observe? What principles of communication were practiced?

3. Write a brief analysis of the communication flow within an organization. What are the vertical and horizontal communication patterns? What functions do the upward and downward communication patterns serve?

Chapter 2

Interpersonal Communication in the Business Setting

After reading and reviewing this chapter, you should be able to . . .

1. Understand the importance of a positive self-concept and recognize how to encourage self-esteem in others.

2. Recognize the importance of basic human needs (inclusion, control, and affection) in forming lasting relationships.

3. Identify levels of communication, from the most basic to those of greater depth.

4. Discuss supportive behaviors in organizations and behaviors that produce defensiveness.

5. Comprehend motivational theories and understand how to apply them in managing employees.

6. Evaluate management communication styles in given organizations and assess their appropriateness.

*I*n this chapter, we explore interpersonal communication as it applies in the business setting. We introduce several interpersonal constructs, including self-concept, interpersonal needs, and openness. In addition, we discuss applied interpersonal concepts, such as organizational communication styles, task and relationship dimensions, working climate, management styles, selected motivational theories, suggestions for effective feedback in business communication, and management of power and interpersonal conflicts.

Like Bob Trent, you will need to understand interpersonal relations in order to enhance your abilities as a business communicator. Some people are slow to advance or are dismissed from employment because they fail to get along with others. Improving interpersonal relationships is an important consideration for all of us.

INTERPERSONAL COMMUNICATION

Interpersonal communication has both qualitative and quantitative dimensions. *Interpersonal communication* is communication primarily between two or a few people (quantitative) that is genuine in nature and has promise of producing an ongoing, productive relationship (qualitative). *Intrapersonal communication* refers to the many messages people send internally (thought), often about themselves (self-evaluation). The sound, theory-based study of effective interpersonal communication encompasses skills applicable to the business setting. A national study of personnel directors found that interpersonal communication and human relations skills (followed by oral communication skills) were ranked the most important of 16 factors needed for success in job performance (Curtis, Winsor, and Stephens, 1989, p. 11). In this study, courses in interpersonal communication were ranked second in importance of 22 courses for entry-level management positions. The skill most important for the ideal manager to possess was found to be the ability to work well with others one-on-one (p. 12).

SELF-CONCEPT

One of the central components in any study of interpersonal communication is the self-concept. A large measure of Bob Trent's success or failure will be determined by how positively he views his abilities.

Most positions advertised are for people who are assertive, self-starting, team-oriented individuals. The component of interpersonal communication emphasized here is *self-assurance* or a *positive self-concept*. Myers and Myers

(1988) state that self-esteem is the feeling you can get when your actions match your self-image and when the particular image approximates an idealized version of what you wish you were like (p. 67). Goss and O'Hair (1988) indicate that self-concept refers to how you value yourself, how much you think you are worth as a person (p. 43). Self-esteem is more of a perception of public evaluation than self-concept. Self-concept is a more private evaluation. These internal messages about yourself (self-concept and self-esteem), in large measure, direct how you feel about yourself in relation to others. In this chapter we include the public sense of self-esteem when we discuss self-concept. The single most significant social determinant of how you relate to others in business communication and in private relationships is how you feel about yourself—your self-concept.

Some of the many things about Sue Derkman that impressed Bob Trent were her self-confidence, her ability to put others at ease, the way she encouraged each person she supervised to make innovations even at the risk of failure, and her willingness to admit when she had made a mistake. Bob reflected on just how important a positive self-concept trait was at American Computer Systems.

The development of self-concept is a relatively passive process. Essentially, you behave in a certain way and audit the reactions of others toward your behavior. This is not necessarily a thoughtful process; it happens pretty much by chance. Mead (1967) and Cooley (1983) believe that the self-concept is a reflection of the way others appear to respond to us. A person's self-image is a reflection of the way that person thought others reacted to him or her during childhood.

A small child can cry for attention and nourishment. At that point the world seems a good place to be. As babies begin to crawl, they are told "no" and may be called "bad boy" or "bad girl." They begin to internalize these messages and notice other things. For example, adults around them do not spill their milk—adults must be more able and valuable than the child. This message comes across even in the most nurturing families. In less caring homes, neglect or physical abuse can leave permanent damage that affects later behavior. Lessons learned at a most impressionable age tend to linger. Inadequate parenting often produces an adult who feels incapable or unworthy of a leadership role in an organization.

In essence, you act, either nonverbally or verbally, and then watch how others respond. Normally, you do not ask them directly how you are doing but interpret clues to gauge their response. This response will shape your own self-concept.

The view that you hold of yourself has changed over time. While the basic self-view may be difficult to change after adolescence, modifications are still possible. A successful salesperson may have a poor year and suffer a slump in self-evaluation. Managers, such as Bob Trent, can help employees see their value and their potential.

According to Cathcart and Gumpert (1986), self-image is formed primarily through interpersonal communication and is checked frequently by interacting with others (p. 92). People receive many different messages from others and make multiple determinations as to what they mean to the self-image. Myers and Myers (1988) claim that children begin to imitate without much understanding, then go through role-playing of familiar patterns of behavior they observe, and finally turn to symbolic role-taking: "What will mom or dad say?" (pp. 60–61). At that point the concept of the *generalized other* becomes operative (Mead, 1967). The child's behavior meets the expectations of other people in general.

Business communicators carry a relatively stable self-concept with them into business presentations, interviews, and other forms of communication. However, each person and each situation becomes an opportunity to slightly modify the self-concept. A negative self-concept is difficult to modify. Someone with negative experiences in processing the self-image tends to find negative cues in the environment; such a person does not believe positive feedback as readily as negative feedback. This tendency is called *the self-fulfilling prophesy.* An employee who does not feel respected will probably interpret others' responses as proof that his or her opinion is not valued.

When confronted with criticism, people with positive self-concepts believe they can improve their own behaviors. They adapt to feedback. Such people regularly seek indications of how they are doing from others and, as objectively as possible, evaluate their own performances.

In short, the self-concept is a filter of all information that comes to an individual. The more realistic and positive the self-concept, the more responsive the employee will be in seeking and attending to effective feedback. Of course, there will be times when it is appropriate for people to feel embarrassed by their behavior in business situations. Recognition of behavioral flaws is a part of a positive self-concept.

RELATIONSHIPS

It is important that the organizational climate be supportive. A sense of self-worth and a supportive climate are prerequisites for successful business relationships. Productive, professional relationships in the business environment are essential for effective teamwork and productivity. Kreps (1986) argues that "it is only through interlocked, coordinated activities that anything of consequence is accomplished in organizational life" (p. 162). Relationships help individuals to communicate and to influence the behavior of others. To be an effective business communicator, you will need to consider an essential component of business relationships—*satisfaction of interpersonal needs.*

Relationships are based, in large part, on mutual fulfillment of needs. William Schutz (1966) has identified three basic interpersonal needs: *inclusion, control,* and *affection* (see Figure 2.1). These needs underscore most of the relationship behavior you see in an organization; they are reflected in how people wish others to include, control, and show affection toward them and in the degree to which they wish to offer these to others.

	Inclusion	Control	Affection
Expressed			
Wanted			

Figure 2.1 The basic interpersonal needs. (*Source*: Adapted from W. Schutz, *FIRO–B*. Palo Alto, Calif.: Consulting Psychologists Press, 1977.)

According to Schutz, the need to be included is basic to all people. A person with a *high inclusion need* seeks recognition within an organization. This type of employee seeks multiple relationships. The person with a *low inclusion need* seeks fewer relationships and has less need for visibility. The person with low inclusion needs may be a capable, independent type who can work well when teamed with one or two others, but does not, on the whole, relish working in large groups. Both very high and very low inclusion types are motivated by the same concern: they fear not being recognized as the people they think they are. As Myers (1988) puts it, "The people with high inclusion needs will combat fear by forcing others to pay attention to them. Those with low inclusion needs have convinced themselves they will not get any attention, but that is the way they want it" (p. 85). A value judgment is not implied here. You may work very well by yourself, or you may be an excellent team player in an organization. An effective business leader is one who recognizes that the needs of employees may range from being *under-social* (relatively low needs to interact with others) to *oversocial* (relatively high needs to do things with others). People with high needs to include others may not be highly selective about fellow workers, but people with a low inclusion need may be very selective about people they will work with productively.

Each person seeks a balance of inclusion and independence. Needs are relative to the circumstances and do vary over time. You develop relationships in your work setting partly on the basis of the level of needs you feel and your perceptions of who responds to you at the level desired. Bob Trent has a strong desire to develop a sales team—a group that shares in successes and, if need be, in failures. Obviously, he will seek people with at least an average need to work with others. He will not select people who are uninterested in working directly with others. However, depending upon philosophy, another manager might seek very independent types who are competitive with each other and see the manager's role as coordinating their relatively independent activities.

The need for *control* relates to a wish for power, for a sense of being in charge and empowered to modify the environment. A person with a high need for control wishes to be in charge. This may be as simple as choosing where to have dinner or, in a business relationship, deciding which specific tasks will be done by whom. A person low in the need for inclusion and high in the need for control may learn how to manipulate others in order to get his or her way indirectly. A person high in both needs may seek to dominate the situation more directly. People who are low in the need for control and high in the acceptance of authority are often loyal followers. Such a person may not be highly effective in a leadership role.

The third need area provides a significant reason for choosing relationships—the need for *affection*. Affection is expressed by giving "strokes"—verbal and nonverbal indications that the employee's behavior is valued by others in the work group. People with a high need for affection seek warm and intimate relationships. They want others to recognize their value and give positive feedback (strokes). A person with a relatively high need to show warmth and caring may express it in extended touch during a handshake, appropriate pats on the back, extended eye contact, smiles, and so forth, as well as in words ("Hey, that was a great job" or "I want you to know I really appreciate your help with this").

Persons with a low need for affection often appear to be cold. They do not make friendships readily. They tend to be very selective in developing relationships. Business managers need to recognize that people less motivated to give positive strokes to others do not always mix well with people who have high affection needs when they are forced to work together in a continuing team environment.

As a business communicator, you must be sensitive to interpersonal needs in order to manage the dynamics of the work environment. It can be most helpful to recognize that every person you meet will have levels of comfort in including others, managing others, and giving strokes to others, and will have a level of comfort for such behavior from you. People's needs simply are that—their needs at the time. There are no better or worse needs. You can be a better organizational communicator by using these insights. Managers should take a few moments periodically to reflect on what individual needs are manifested in employees under their span of control. This analysis can be used to modify work assignments in order to enhance the work climate for all employees.

Openness

Strong and productive relationships are based on the mutual fulfillment of needs in interactions with others. Expectations must be made clear through effective communication. *Openness* involves disclosing to others, reporting your reactions to stimuli honestly, and "owning" feelings. Owning your feelings involves searching yourself to be sure you know what you feel, reporting the feeling accurately, and taking responsibility for any consequences of the report. You cannot expect others to be mind readers, nor should you assume that you understand what another wants or needs without "checking it out" through interpersonal communication. DeVito (1989) says, "We want people to react openly to what we say, and we have a right to expect this. We demonstrate openness by responding spontaneously and without subterfuge to the communications and the feedback of others" (p. 96). Many unhappy relationships are developed because people simply are not open in their communications with each other.

One aspect of openness is the way in which information is shared—the style of communication. Is information shared in a personal and caring way or an impersonal and unconcerned way? Another aspect is whether sharing is limited only to peers. Is it standard operating procedure for employees to share information with supervisors, managers, and people from other divisions? Is the communication channel legitimate (through regular channels) or through a grapevine system? How accurate or authentic is the communication in the organization? Is disclosure intentional or relatively forced? Is the tone of most communication positive and upbeat, or is it negative and critical? If serious issues need to be aired in the organization, can they be disclosed openly and constructively? These are some of the important questions you can answer by auditing the communication in your organization.

Levels of Disclosure

Powell (1969) suggests that there are *levels of depth* in communication between people. Productive working relationships have some substance to them. Shallow, superficial relationships dissolve quickly at the first encounter with stress.

Level 1, the most elemental level of communication, involves *routines* or *rituals*. We interact this way daily in surface communication, such as "How are you today?" or "Hey, what's new with you?" Through this beginning level of openness, we *affirm* others—we recognize that we are aware of their presence and that they are people in our environment. Unfortunately, many people, some of whom believe they relate to each other as friends, have exchanged only routine communication. This superficial level of communication cannot produce much depth in a relationship.

Level 2 communication involves *general information exchange*. This information is neither secret nor threatening to the person sharing it. In other words, no risk is taken. The information shared could have been obtained from other sources. Hence, there is little depth to the communication. This level of sharing takes place in the following exchange:

EMPLOYEE 1: Did you ever operate computer-aided drafting equipment?
EMPLOYEE 2: Yes, I worked as a drafter with Ruskin Manufacturing, where I used second-generation equipment.

This information could have been obtained from several sources besides the employee. It is relevant, but it has little depth. Again, knowing such information about another is not the basis for a lasting relationship, although many people who call each other friend have no greater depth than this level of communication between them.

Level 3 communication involves *disclosure of opinions, beliefs, and values.* Here risk is taken. This type of openness begins the process of bonding in relationships. It signals that trust is present in the sender. Risk is taken in that the receiver may not accept the sender (affirm the person) who makes the disclosure. The receiver may use the information to cause problems for the sender. Therefore, the prudent person shares only after trust is established. This level of sharing is the beginning of the relationship known as friendship. Any level of sharing less than this does not bring the dignity to the concept "friend" that this special designation deserves. In the business environment, such a level of trust is essential between supervisor and those supervised. If, for example, Bob Trent tells one of the engineers at American that he does not like all the changes in the new computer hardware they are designing, he runs the risk that the engineer may behave defensively. Bob will have to carefully analyze just how he explains his concerns, or he will risk the consequences. Bob will try to seek a proper context in which to ask some questions and present his concerns in a constructive, caring way:

BOB TRENT: You know, I am concerned about the process of making design changes. I think that it would be helpful in selling our products if someone from Research and Development would discuss planned changes with a representative of our sales group before production begins. Does this concern make sense to you?

ENGINEER: I believe I understand what you are saying. Having such meetings will take some time away from our design activity, but it may be well worth it from the company's standpoint. Is your group willing to commit the time for the discussions on short notice?

In this exchange, Bob shares an opinion and receives an appropriate response. The development engineer is understanding, yet cautious. The engineer, like Bob Trent, discloses a value: what is in the best interest of the company.

Powell indicates yet another level of communication: level 4 involves sharing of *feelings*. The notion of sharing personal feelings with another can be threatening. Consider the interpersonal needs discussed earlier. If a manager needs to communicate to an employee who has demonstrated a high need for affection, it is important for the manager to share positive feelings for the employee. The following exchange illustrates this level of communication:

BOB TRENT: Cindy, please come in. I invited you here because I want you to know how pleased I am with your work. I am happy to inform you that your probationary status is now a matter of history. I am very glad to welcome you to our firm.

CINDY: Oh, thank you very much, Mr. Trent. I want you to know it's been a challenging experience, and I still have a lot to learn. I've really appreciated everyone's support.

In this exchange, feelings are shared openly. It is just as essential that negative feedback be given openly, as illustrated in the next exchange:

Table 2.1   LEVELS OF COMMUNICATION AND THEIR FUNCTIONS

Level	Function
1. Routine communication	Acknowledge/affirm others
2. Exchange of facts	Give information
3. Disclosure of opinions, beliefs, and values	Display trust
4. Feelings shared	Interpersonal bonding
5. Intimacy	Full disclosure

SAM: You wanted to see me, Mr. Trent?

BOB TRENT: Yes, Sam. Please sit down. I want to share a couple of concerns with you. I noticed that you missed the sales meeting yesterday. Sam, I'm concerned because this has happened several times recently. I want you to know that I care about you, and I want to hear what is going on with you.

Assuming that these are authentic expressions, this is direct and clear communication combining level 2 interaction (facts) with level 4 (feelings). The information is "laid on the table," the value of the individual is affirmed in a feeling statement, and the employee has an opportunity to be heard.

Rarely does interpersonal communication in a business setting need to go deeper than level 4. Occasions when feelings need to be better expressed, the air cleared, relationships affirmed, and so forth, require skill at level 4 openness.

According to Powell, there is one more level of communication. Level 5 is reserved for special circumstances within special relationships. This level is termed *peak* or *intimate communication*. A "significant other" is one with whom you can share deep feelings upon many topics. Such relationships are rare in the work environment. Normally, this level of communication is reserved for marital partners, other members of the immediate family, or special relationships outside the family. Table 2.1 lists the five levels of communication and their functions.

STYLES OF ORGANIZATIONAL COMMUNICATION

Through their communication behavior, managers create a *climate*. Some managers are *democratic* and others are more *autocratic*. Some treat employees as equals and some do not. Some send as many requests for information as they do directives; others do just the opposite. Carefully analyze your own communication style in dealing with others in the business environment. The climate you create has a significant impact upon all with whom you work.

As you are aware, openness is important in effective business relationships. The climate created in a business can encourage or discourage openness, depending on the style of *downward communication.* As noted in Chapter 1, downward communication sets the tone for all other types of communication. Downward (or vertical down) communication is the means of communication that upper management uses to send messages to subordinates. Regardless of how management perceives this avenue, effectiveness in communication is determined by whether middle management and line personnel view the communication as appropriate.

Autocratic management depends on *autocratic communication* which is composed of numerous directive messages sent down the organizational channels. It is a style often adopted by highly directive parents for communicating with their children. This quasi-military style of communication may work with some people; however, it does not work well with many of us over time. In businesses, it may produce resentment and the outbreak of the negative aspects of the "rumor mill" (grapevine). The premise of this style of communication is that management has the answers and line employees must be told only what they "need" in order to do their jobs. Such a style is anything but open. Openness, of course, requires both a willingness to share information and a receptivity to feedback from others. A manager who clearly discloses demands but does not encourage discussion of directives given is not being open.

You might agree that emergency situations require decisiveness or that some decisions are so trivial that discussion is not warranted. However, most working relationships are improved by openness.

A much more appropriate style for most organizations is the democratic style. Here the premium is placed upon *relative communication equality.* What is communicated is the sense that each person has value and can make contributions. The pervasive attitude is that management may have a different (unique) function, but not an inherently higher or more important one. This communication style creates a context in which people can develop open and caring relationships. Ideas flow freely up and down (vertically) in the organization and across divisions (horizontally). Permission need not be sought before talking to others about ideas or asking questions.

Bob Trent would do well to consider this management style. If he wishes to have a close working relationship with his new sales team, Bob will need to analyze the climate he creates. He should analyze how he gives directions and solicits input from his new team members.

Tasks and Relationships

Every communication event includes both a task dimension and a relationship dimension. The *task dimension* includes such factors as job information, organizational procedures, marketing plans, and other information necessary to complete a service, sales, or manufacturing procedure. If a supervisor asks whether you are willing to be the team leader on a forthcoming production venture, there are both task and relationship dimensions in the communication. The task dimension, of course, is the assigned duty. The *relationship dimension* includes the facts that you are perceived as qualified to be the team leader and that the supervisor has placed trust in you. Further, note that this is presented as a request rather than a demand. A request indicates that you are free to say you do not feel comfortable with the proposal and that it would be appropriate to ask a number of task-related questions prior to making a commitment. Many proposals are better stated as requests rather than as directives.

All organizational communicators, especially management and supervisory personnel, need to consider seriously their use of task and relationship communication. A balance should be maintained. Not many of us are drawn toward loyalty and relationships to someone whose style is to allow task communication to dominate disclosures. However, people eventually lose respect for a manager who cares only for developing and maintaining relationships and does not consider the productivity of the unit.

Climate

Each working environment has an atmosphere. Relationships may be described in terms of the climate, or "weather forecast." Your subordinates will describe the atmosphere of their workplace in terms of the comfort levels that they perceive are created. Gibb (1961) has divided climates into two extreme categories—*defensive climates* and *supportive climates.*

Kreps (1986) says the organizational climate is "the internal emotional tone of the organization based on how comfortable organization members feel with one another and with the organization" (p. 228). The concept is based on the analogy between the condition of the business setting and the condition of the weather. Some working climates are warm and sunny: people are cared for and treated with dignity. Some climates are cold and stormy: there is a lack of respect, and hostility reigns in the workplace. The climate of an organization develops primarily out of the behaviors and actions of management and is advanced in the behaviors of specific organization members.

In defensive climates, people say that the atmosphere is "heavy" and repressive. In supportive climates, people feel respected and encourage each other as they attempt to accomplish their many tasks. Table 2.2 lists specific behaviors that reflect the climate of an organization.

Communication that appears to be evaluative, blaming, judgmental, and so forth tends to increase people's defensiveness. If you feel judged or criticized or that someone is evaluating you, your natural reaction is to feel threatened. When you feel threatened, you may blame others (displacement), evaluate others negatively (projection), or give reasons that are not the real reasons for your behavior (rationalization). You may combine these negative

Table 2.2   CHARACTERISTICS OF SUPPORTIVE
AND DEFENSIVE COMMUNICATION
CLIMATES

Defensive climates	Supportive climates
• Evaluation	• Description
• Control	• Problem orientation
• Strategy	• Spontaneity
• Neutrality	• Empathy
• Superiority	• Equality
• Certainty	• Provisionalism

reactions. Reflect on your internal state when you were reprimanded for something recently. Perhaps you provoked an instructor's ire by repeatedly coming to class late. If the instructor asked to see you after class, you would feel defensive enough without the instructor saying that your tardiness was offensive and would no longer be tolerated. The instructor might instead choose to ask you whether you were having a problem with which he or she could help. That would produce a climate more conducive to interpersonal communication.

People who manifest defensive behavior may exhibit stress, shown nonverbally in body squirms, strains in the voice, stomach problems, and so on. Internally, the person may question self-worth. Even simple questions may be perceived as trick questions or something more than they appear on the surface.

Managers who are aware of the importance of a supportive climate and have developed the skills necessary to create one are most valuable to the success of an organization. In this type of atmosphere, productive relationships can blossom and a full measure of trust is possible. Individuals feel valued for their unique qualities and experiences. Few individuals enjoy hearing an endless series of complaints, but people should be free to express their relevant concerns as well as joys. Openness is fostered through supportive behaviors. This style of communication is as contagious as the negativism of the defensive climate.

Each of the specific pairs of behaviors Gibb describes is worthy of attention. No one member of an organization is likely to exhibit all of either the defensive or supportive climate indicators. However, even one or two defensive behaviors can create a negative environment for many members of an organization. Hence, you must inventory your behaviors carefully and examine how you might cultivate each of the supportive skills listed in Table 2.2.

Evaluation/Description   Negative, evaluative behavior often promotes a defensive response. *Evaluation*—being judged by others—normally creates tension. Often negative communication blames others and involves what is termed a "you" message:

MS. KALTHOFF: (*In an angry tone*) Tom, what did you do to lose the Connors account? He was ready to sign with us last week! Were you being flippant again, or what?

TOM: (*Not wishing to accept the responsibility*) Ms. Kalthoff, it wasn't my fault. Dorothy Rickman and her people didn't have their act together. I did my best, but production couldn't promise delivery soon enough and Connors said he couldn't wait for us any longer. I . . . I think you should be talking with Dorothy rather than with me.

Clearly, Tom senses that he is being evaluated, and he feels threatened. He responds defensively. He displaces the blame on Dorothy Rickman and attempts to shift the total responsibility to her. Although this example may seem simplistic, it is typical of the way much organizational communication is perceived. A supportive alternative would go as follows:

MS. KALTHOFF: Tom, let's see if we can learn something from our difficulty with the Connors account. I know that you put quite a lot of effort into trying to close that deal. I am as sorry for you as I am for our company that it didn't work out. From your point of view, what should we have done differently?

TOM: Well, Ms. Kalthoff, I appreciate your concern. I think I may have made a few mistakes, and so did others. I was in a hurry to close with Connors so I could deal with the Smithson account. I should have been giving Connors my full attention. I learned a lesson. I wish you had been here Friday to help with some contract details. I didn't know how to handle the shipping delay. We have been keeping Dorothy Rickman's people pretty busy lately. If I had it to do over again, I would suggest some overtime for them. I think we could have completed the deal that way.

Compare this to the first exchange between Tom and his supervisor. Notice how Ms. Kalthoff, in this case, does not evaluate (blame) Tom in any way for the contract problem. In the first case, she gave Tom a "you" message—indicating that Tom was responsible for the loss of the account. This caused Tom to become defensive and seek to displace the blame to Dorothy Rickman. Tom did not feel strong enough emotionally to share his feelings with Ms. Kalthoff, to accept part of the responsibility, or to suggest creative alternatives for the future. In the second scenario, Ms. Kalthoff initiated a more descriptive and, hence, supportive approach. The results were much better. Tom may be totally at fault, or Dorothy may have dropped the ball completely, but little would be gained at this point if the manager were to berate either party. When Ms. Kalthoff was supportive of Tom, he was willing to accept part of the responsibility, to be supportive of Dorothy Rickman, and to indicate how the situation could have been improved. He even felt comfortable enough to suggest that the presence of Ms. Kalthoff might have helped—perhaps a mild bit of negative feedback to the supervisor. An analysis of the linguistic differences of the second interaction shows that both parties were using the "I" language of ownership—taking responsibility. Communication was much more open.

Description simply means that organization members focus their messages on observable events and minimize any reference to subjective or emotional reactions. In the second exchange, Ms. Kalthoff and Tom were free to give each other information. Neither appeared to threaten the ego of the other. It was a descriptive interaction. Ultimately, the organization will profit from such conversations; the organization might suffer from evaluative exchanges.

Control/Problem Orientation   To *control* means to attempt to manipulate another person, to impose an attitude or point of view on another person, or to stop an action another person or faction wishes to take. The person who seeks to control the actions of others assumes that the others' ideas are inferior. Such attitudes and behaviors cause a large measure of defensiveness.

In the first scenario between Tom and Ms. Kalthoff, you see control implied. Ms. Kalthoff appeared to assume that Tom should be disciplined for his failure to close the account. In this exchange Tom was defensive. He learned less from this communication strategy than from the alternative. Although there are elements of control in the second scenario (calling a conference, stating a concern, an implied employee-employer relationship, and so forth), the control factors are minimized.

Problem orientations are an antidote to controlling strategies in an organization. It is important to communicate a desire to find solutions rather than impose solutions, to collaborate rather than manipulate. A problem orientation suggests that management does not have a fixed position. Rather, managers want to discuss what is best for the organization: to seek information, suggestions, or guidance, and to test ideas. Obviously, this is a refreshing and encouraging communication behavior model for members of an organization.

Strategy/Spontaneity   Defensive behaviors are stimulated when members of an organization use strategies in communicating with others. *Strategies* involve manipulation of employees, perhaps by withholding pertinent information or engaging in subtle "behind-the-back" innuendos. According to Gibb's analysis, people can be tricked into making a decision that may have negative consequences later. However, someone who cultivates the surface appearance of having the interest of another at heart will be exposed over time. Many people would be surprised to realize that others see them as manipulators.

Gibb offers *spontaneity* as the alternative to strategy. To be spontaneous, as Gibb uses the term, means to be straightforward and "lay the cards on the table" with others in an organization. Spontaneous people seek to avoid any sense of deceiving; they seek to be honest and "up front" with others. These people "tell it as they see it," and their viewpoint is in the best interest of the organization.

Managers who say that they "have something down the road in mind" for an employee, without giving an indication of what or when, have a manipulative tendency. Spontaneous managers are open with subordinates instead of dangling an unknown before them:

> TOM: Ms. Kalthoff, do you plan to let me work with the Hitchcock account when the contract comes up for negotiation?
>
> MS. KALTHOFF: Tom, I have some things in mind for you, but I do not want your attention diverted from your other responsibilities right now.

In this example, Ms. Kalthoff is not sharing information she possesses. She implies that Tom is not capable of seeing a larger picture and giving input about his future assignments.

> TOM: Ms. Kalthoff, do you plan to let me work on the Hitchcock account when it comes up for negotiation?
>
> MS. KALTHOFF: Tom, I'm open to your doing that. I haven't made a commitment to anyone else. Do you think you would have the time to handle that, with your other deadlines?

In this exchange, Ms. Kalthoff indicates her willingness to consider all possibilities. She is open, revealing where she stands.

Neutrality/Empathy   Gibb states that defensive climates are characterized by *neutrality*—neutral behaviors that indicate little concern for the person to whom communication is directed. The individual addressed gains no sense of being special and does not feel appreciated. People do not feel rewarded for past contributions, nor are they given credit for learning from past failures. Neutral behaviors treat others more as objects ("its") than as human beings.

The opposite climate is *empathy*. The sincere attempt to understand the situation from the point of view of others is an important skill to learn. Empathy is more than sympathy (feeling sorry); it is *feeling with* another. Identifying with other people's values, attitudes, and opinions affirms and encourages them; they realize that they are not alone.

In the first communication between Tom and Ms. Kalthoff, there was a sense of neutrality. The supervisor cared only whether the contract was signed. Tom did not appear to be important to the supervisor. Tom did not feel important until Ms. Kalthoff took a supportive interpersonal approach.

Superiority/Equality   Inequality is an unfortunate image to create in an organization. Using the artificial leadership tool of power is a poor choice in most situations. It is easier to pull a string (to lead) than push it anywhere;

using power, with its inherent suggestion that the ideas of others are less worthy, is likely to yield defensive, counterproductive behaviors. An attitude of *superiority* is manifest by using position, authority, intellectual ability, wealth, physical strength, or attractiveness to gain assent. This climate is likely to encourage resentment, both interpersonally and organizationally.

In a climate of *equality*, "pulling rank" is reserved for special circumstances, as when dangerous behaviors must be stopped. Equality implies that there is a measure of unconditional respect for others in an organization. There is an attempt to minimize differences in power, intellectual prowess, and so on. Communicating a belief that each person can make a contribution to the success of the organization creates a sense of involvement and a desire to contribute (to invest oneself). Circumstances may justify a manager's use of power—in emergencies or in getting the attention of an employee who will not respond to more humane treatment. Tom, however, was responsive in the second scenario, when his supervisor asked questions as she would with an informed equal. Such strategies empower employees and enhance their self-esteem. In that second exchange with Tom, Ms. Kalthoff showed little or no evidence of being in a higher or superior position. She considered Tom a valued source of information. He responded by giving information, indicating what he had learned, and demonstrating a willingness to apply what he had learned to similar future situations.

Certainty/Provisionalism   Gibb argues that *certainty* (believing oneself to be correct and others incorrect) contributes to a negative, defensive climate. The rigid and dogmatic manager who acts like a teacher of less-informed others, or who attempts to correct others, will not produce a positive organizational environment. People who demonstrate certainty are not open to discussion or to additional information; rather, their minds are made up in advance. Managers who manifest certainty appear to see two ways of approaching organizational problems—their way and the wrong way.

Again, Gibb offers an alternative behavior designed to support people and organizational goals. He terms this position *provisionalism*. A provisional person is willing to be tentative in assessments as to what is best. Such people seek various points of view, as much information as is realistically possible, and they are open to changing their minds when situations dictate (unless the choice would violate an ethical position and/or principle). For example, a provisional manager might say, "Let's try it this way and get some feedback about how it is going. We can make changes if this doesn't work out." Such behaviors are encouraging to others.

In the first encounter, Ms. Kalthoff implied that Tom was wrong. That was probably a snap judgment. In the alternative communication, she might have gone on to say, "In any similar future situations, try calling Dorothy to see if you can find a way to guarantee at least a partial shipment. Do you think that would help us?" Here Ms. Kalthoff does not tell Tom how to handle his job now and forevermore, but gives him an alternative and asks for some feedback. She acted provisionally by implying that if this does not solve the problem she will try other methods later.

Corporate culture is essentially a communication climate. The climate reflects comfort levels within the organization. It is important to recognize the behaviors which encourage a supportive climate and minimize defensiveness that threatens the development of productive relationships in organizations.

INTERPERSONAL MANAGEMENT STYLES

McGregor (1960) presented what has become a classic dichotomy between what he termed *Theory X* and *Theory Y* management behaviors. McGregor, like Gibb, presents his theoretical constructs as polar opposites. These opposites represent extremes in assumptions regarding human nature.

According to McGregor, some people in supervisory positions (Theory X managers) convey by their behavior that they believe most people have an inherent dislike of work and will avoid it if they possibly can. These managers think that workers are lazy and irresponsible and cannot be trusted to work on their own and that "because of this human characteristic of dislike of work, most people must be coerced, controlled, directed, and threatened with punishment as means of forcing them to put forth adequate effort toward the achievement of organizational objectives" (McGregor, 1960, p. 34). Theory X managers believe their responsibility is to control, threaten, direct, and otherwise regulate the activities of subordinates.

McGregor suggests that some managers believe that the average person prefers to be directed, wishes to avoid responsibility, and has little ambition. Theory X managers believe that workers want security above all else and that employees are best motivated at the physiological and safety levels of the hierarchy of needs described by Maslow (1954). Theory X managers believe that employees are motivated by money (the carrot) and by fear of demotion or termination (the stick). Furthermore, Theory X managers think that most employees are not creative and have little capacity for solving problems.

In general, managers with a Theory X philosophy take a dim view of human nature. They do not trust the motives of line workers in an organization. They see their managerial role as controllers, writers of directives, and developers of rules, and they believe that lower-level employees must be told how to perform. This is an authoritarian style of leadership.

McGregor's Theory Y management style reflects a contrasting set of beliefs concerning human nature. Theory Y represents the most positive view of human relations in regard to effective organizational management.

Theory Y managers believe that if conditions are favorable, work is as natural as play or rest. They assume that one function of management is to provide favorable conditions. A challenging and satisfying job will encourage and motivate workers.

Theory Y managers also believe that external threats of punishment or other controls are not the best means for developing motivation toward organizational objectives. Kreps (1986) says, "This assumption suggests that the key to workers' performance lies in their level of commitment to a job, rather than in managerial control" (p. 89). Commitment is developed when management attitudes support a caring climate. If they are to be motivated, workers need opportunities to grow and accept challenge.

Theory Y managers recognize that motivation increases as self-esteem and self-actualization needs are met. The Theory Y manager helps employees feel good about themselves by giving them challenges that they are able to meet successfully. McGregor argues that workers can and do find satisfaction and motivation in the work itself.

McGregor's Theory Y manager believes that employees do not avoid responsibility; rather, they seek opportunities to lead. Theory Y managers believe that negative behaviors are conditioned by negative circumstances within organizations. People treated with indifference will demonstrate indifference toward work.

Theory Y managers believe that the capacity for creativity, ingenuity, and imagination in solving organizational problems is distributed widely in the work force. Programs such as *quality circles,* in which people from all levels of the organization meet to discuss how conditions and production could be improved, are an outgrowth of this view. Strict control by management too often restricts or discourages creativity. It hardly makes sense that only management-level personnel have creative ideas.

Quality circles also flow from so-called Japanese management models. Dwiggins (1986) described *Theory Z* (Ouchi, 1981): the transition from a top-down power structure to a structure in which power is shared at all levels. Joiner (1985) discusses the principles of Theory Z:

1. Long-term employment
2. Relatively unhurried evaluation and promotion processes
3. Wide career paths (several options)
4. Consensus decision making
5. Trust and equalitarianism (employees are treated as creative equals with managers)
6. Holistic concern for people (employees and customers are treated as management would like to be treated)
7. Participatory structure with discussion forums (quality circles)

According to Joiner, the Japanese-style Theory Z management system should be introduced in a series of steps:

1. Building a cohesive management team
2. Creating and communicating future directions
3. Establishing strong intracompany support systems
4. Creating a participative organizational structure (pp. 57–63)

All of these are lofty but worthwhile goals.

Managers should realize that one goal of management is to discover the hidden potential of each employee. The concepts of participative management stem from the notions of Theory Y and Theory Z.

MOTIVATION IN ORGANIZATIONS

Herzberg (1966) analyzed human motivation in organizations and introduced the *two-factor theory of motivation.* Herzberg recognized that the factors that often frustrate employees are not the same ones that lead to motivation. He noted two different kinds of needs that must be met in quite different ways in order for satisfaction and motivation to occur in a business organization.

Herzberg recognized that first, employees want and expect an adequate salary, job and personal security, good working conditions, status, and responsible company policies and administrative behaviors. If these basic *hygiene needs* are not satisfied, workers will look elsewhere for employment opportunities, absenteeism will increase, relationships will deteriorate, attitudes will suffer, and so on. Many managers think that satisfying these needs will increase motivation and production. However, this is not what Herzberg discovered. When hygiene needs are *not* met, employees are dissatisfied and cannot be motivated because they are preoccupied with meeting hygiene needs. Providing for these needs leads to satisfaction but not directly to increased production.

In contrast, higher-order *motivational needs* include opportunities for personal growth, achievement, recognition, advancement, responsibility, and enjoyment of work itself. In order to motivate an employee, according to Herzberg, the manager must first meet and minimally maintain hygiene needs. After this occurs, motivational needs become a priority.

Herzberg (1987b) also introduced a motivation-hygiene theory: employees throughout the world are motivated by their own inherent need to succeed at challenging tasks, not by more benefits, new status symbols, or higher wages (pp. 29–32). Thus, job enrichment is obviously necessary if the manager is to motivate employees.

Herzberg (1968) also offers some recommendations for providing work incentives. First, he suggests that managers reduce their administrative control while maintaining their accountability for performance. This will give a measure of freedom for individual creativity. Herzberg believes that management can increase employees' personal accountability for the quality of their work so they have more responsibility and recognition. (He believes that members of an organization should be able to complete an entire project or work unit in order to increase feelings of pride in their accomplishments.) Second, Herzberg recommends giving more job freedom, authority, and responsibility to workers. He suggests direct, periodic feedback, not requiring communication through a supervisor, in order to increase recognition. Third, he recommends providing workers with new and challenging job duties in order to increase their opportunities to learn and grow. Fourth, he suggests that managers help employees become experts in their specific job responsibilities in order to increase their sense of recognition, responsibility, and growth (pp. 109–120).

OTHER INTERPERSONAL MANAGEMENT THEORIES

Blake and Mouton (1964, 1991) suggest that managers can be categorized in terms of how they interact with employees regarding two central issues—*concern for production* and *concern for people*. These two concerns are pictured visually on the Leadership Grid® Figure (Figure 2.2) as nine-point scales, where *1* represents low concern, *5* represents an average amount of

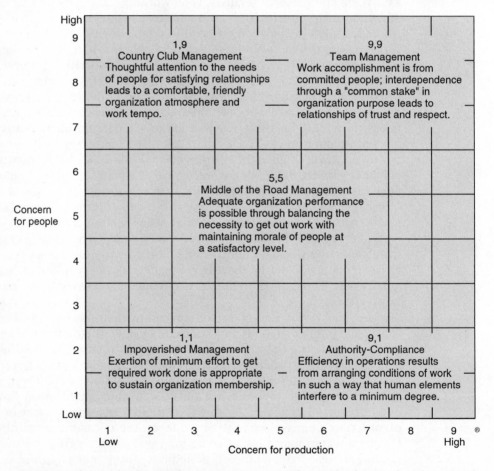

Figure 2.2 The Leadership Grid®. (*Source*: Figure, "The Leadership Grid®." from *Leadership Dilemmas—Grid Solutions* by Robert R. Blake and Anne Adams McCanse. Houston: Gulf Publishing Company, page 29. Copyright © 1991 by Scientific Methods, Inc. Reproduced by permission of the owners.)

concern, and 9 is high concern. These theorists identify five leadership styles, as determined by the degree of concern the manager has for either production or people. The five management styles can be described as "impoverished," "country club," "authority-compliance" (task-centered), "middle of the road" ("organization man") and "team."

A 1,1 score (low on both axes) reflects an *impoverished* style of leadership. This type of leader is not sensitive to the needs of people or the organization and abdicates authority to others. Leadership communication is largely absent. The manager who has little or no concern for other people or for accomplishing organizational tasks is an ineffective leader. Impoverished leaders are often the product of the seniority system, in which long-term employees are promoted to management without regard for their ability or interest. The impoverished leader can be expected to give only minimal effort to getting the work done. Such a leader demonstrates little concern for personal relationships and the human aspects of the job. This type of person might be characterized as unfriendly and lazy or grouchy and obstinate.

A 1,9 score (low concern for task, high concern for people) characterizes the *country club* style of leadership. This individual is greatly concerned with interpersonal relationships but shows no more interest in production than the impoverished leader. This manager is most concerned with keeping everyone satisfied. The country club leader attempts to avoid conflict as much as possible, using congeniality to win satisfying working relationships. Such a leader wants everyone to be happy and relies on others to accomplish organizational objectives. This person often is viewed as a social individual who is nice but a bit disorganized. The country club style of leadership does not work well when decisions have to be made that affect people in the work group. Decisions about promotions, merit pay, and transfers are difficult for this type of person.

Just the opposite is the 9,1 style (high concern for task, low concern for people). This *authority-compliance* style is concerned about efficiency in the operations of the organization. This type of leader relies on authority, rules, and order to get the job done. The view is that each employee is nothing more than another tool to use to accomplish the task at hand. Results are all that count. Any problems that interfere with production, especially human relations problems, are upsetting to the task-centered leader. This type of personality might include the coach who uses players to achieve personal career advancement, saying, "Dedicated team members will play even when hurt."

The *middle-of-the-road* position (average in concern for task accomplishment and in concern for people) is the niche for the compromiser (5,5). Leaders of this type attempt a juggling act between task and people needs. They usually get acceptable organizational performance; however, in the process of making trade-offs, some people and organizational goals get lost. Such leaders keep things going but do not initiate a large amount of organizational communication.

Finally, Blake and Mouton give us the ideal: the 9,9 style, *team* leadership style. The team leader is a person who has both high concern for people and high concern for production. The team leader is a good motivator. People working for this leader are committed to doing the job that needs to be done. This type of person is skilled at indicating that there is an interdependence between job satisfaction and the achievement of organizational goals. Kreps says:

> This leader is interested in making effective decisions that will help the organization accomplish goals and reflect the ideas and goals of organization members, wants to integrate organization members' goals with the organization's goals, and stresses the establishment of good working relationships through use of open lines of communication with organization members to gather information and feedback. (1986, p. 178)

Again, this is the ideal.

Obviously, this type of leader uses communication to establish effective relationships. This ideal leader is able to accomplish tasks because people recognize genuine interpersonal skills. This manager is a high-production achiever by virtue of working extremely well with people. The ideal leader gets to know employees—the manager's door is open and employees come by often. Such leaders appropriately recognize progress in team members. To achieve this ideal takes training and skill. Such people are rare and valuable.

The management positions represented by Blake and Mouton are important and useful tools for evaluating managers' concerns for maintaining interpersonal relations and accomplishing organizational goals.

POWER AND CONFLICT

The power issue is an important dimension of interpersonal communication in the business setting. Power is difficult to define, yet it affects everything. *Power* is recognized influence that one person has over another and is based on the other's dependency. In all organizations a balance of perceived power is important. Most successful business organizations need to have a balance between interdependence and self-sufficiency. Any form of total dependency is a negative process in the modern organization.

When there is competition for power within an organization, there is *conflict*. Some conflict is good and necessary in an organization. Managers design various contests to motivate employees. This is an attempt to create a level of conflict or competition. However, conflict over the use of power must be managed. Managers should not seek to resolve all conflict—only that conflict that is potentially destructive.

Filley (1975, pp. 4–7) identifies four major benefits of conflict:

1. Many conflict situations have the effect of "defusing" more serious conflicts. This is especially the case when the conflicts (perhaps more accurately described as competitive exchanges) are played out according to a system of rules. The disagreements that result often reduce the probability that more significant conflicts will arise.

2. Conflict situations lead us to acquire new information, new ways of looking at things. They energize our creativity and force us to explore new ideas and ways of behaving.
3. Conflict between groups functions to increase group cohesiveness. One of the most powerful ways to encourage members of a group to interact cooperatively and efficiently is to put them into conflict with another group.
4. Conflict provides an opportunity for individuals or groups to measure their power, strength, or ability, since it is in conflict situations that such qualities are mobilized to their peak.

Coercive power exercised through vertical down communication channels will create a defensive communication climate in most organizations. Too often managers consider their intent pure in this regard, but their messages are perceived as power communication. Power-based communication stirs resentment and defensive behaviors almost immediately.

Communication from management that is *elitist* in tone (that indicates that managers know better, know more, have a better position from which to carry out company goals, etc.) will be perceived as power-based and potentially coercive. Examine the following exchange:

DON: Have you completed the proposal for Acme Manufacturing Company yet? Remember, I told you that I would need it this morning.

TERRY: All but the final bid amounts. I think the markup should be cost plus 15 percent. I'm afraid that if we go with 21 percent again, we won't have a chance. This project is important to all of us.

DON: You aren't paid to make those kinds of decisions! I want that proposal on my desk by noon, and it had better have the 21 percent markup figures in it or I'll find someone else who will do it! You got that?

This type of coercive power communication creates much *dissonance* (mental conflict) for the subordinate. The use of power appears arbitrary and nonnegotiable. There is little room for open discussion. The subordinate experiences internal conflict (between values and beliefs and the manager's directives). The above example demonstrates a questionable use of power. The harvest of such power use is likely to be poor morale, absenteeism, time theft from the organization, searches for more creative employment opportunities, and so on. None of these will serve the organization well in any market, let alone a very competitive one.

One can argue that even the president of the United States has relatively little real power. The president's legitimate power comes from the ability to influence (persuade) others to use their skills to shape events.

Power legitimately can be used to make personnel changes that restructure an organization. However, all direct applications of power without consultation will have a cost in conflict. If managers wish to have good employee relations, they will involve employees in planning for change. Power applied in the short term may be less available in the longer term. The most powerful people in an organization may well minimize their use of power. They know how to manage conflict and interpersonal relations. They lead and encourage rather than trying to direct and control. Here is an alternative to the first dialogue between Don and Terry:

DON: Terry, how are you coming on that proposal that we agreed needed to reach my desk today? Do you need any help on it?

TERRY: I'm about finished with it, Don. I do have one concern that I would like to discuss with you. You suggested a 21 percent markup beyond the cost figures. As you know, we have lost the last two bids. I wonder if we ought to consider a 15 percent markup on this one. Our unit could use the work, don't you think?

DON: You're right, Terry; we need the work, and we have lost the last two contracts. Go ahead and use the 15 percent on parts 1 and 2. I would like you to figure it both ways on part 3. We underestimated that the last time, you may remember. How do you feel about that?

TERRY: Sounds reasonable to me, Don. I'll have it on your desk by early afternoon.

DON: Good, Terry. I'll see you this afternoon. Thanks for your suggestions. Give me a ring if something else comes to mind.

This is quite a different organizational communication climate or use of power, and it averts potential dysfunctional conflict. *Dysfunctional conflict* is any conflict that disrupts an organization. If employees are angry and frustrated within the organization, they may produce little of high quality. Heightened emotions suggest dysfunctional conflict.

Conflict Management

When conflict arises and interpersonal disagreements are sharp, management has a responsibility to manage the situation for the good of the organization. For example, if production supervisors are angry because salespeople are making promises production cannot meet, higher-level managers need to be able to call the supervisors together (use power) and lead in discussing the situation. Managers may need to support the aggressiveness of the sales staff, having the company pay overtime so production personnel can complete the tasks on time (thereby recognizing legitimate needs of production personnel). This can be a "win-win" situation. Knowing when to intervene and when to listen may not require the wisdom of Solomon; it does require patience and experience, along with communication skills.

DeVito (1989) describes a humanistic model of effective interpersonal communication. Five characteristics apply to conflict management: (1) openness, (2) empathy, (3) supportiveness, (4) positiveness, and (5) equality (pp. 344–347).

As discussed earlier, *openness* involves stating feelings and thoughts openly, directly, and honestly without attempts to manipulate others. Ownership of ideas is indicated by "I" messages, such as "I want . . . " or "I wish. . . . " The central issues in conflict are addressed directly. Listening carefully and openly to the others involved is essential to effective conflict management.

Again, *empathy* involves listening skills of a particular type. As an empathic listener, you attempt to feel what the other person feels, to view the situation the way the other does, while not minimizing differences and the view that you hold. Empathy includes validation of the feelings of others, using messages such as "I can see how you would feel that way" or "You must really be upset by that." Validation does not mean agreement; it simply means acknowledging the legitimate views of another.

The concept of *supportiveness* involves Gibb's notion of building a supportive climate while minimizing any arousal of additional defensiveness. A person who wants to build a supportive climate while in a conflict situation must be descriptive rather than evaluative, problem-centered rather than control-centered, spontaneous rather than strategy-centered, and empathic rather than denying the other has a legitimate concern. Supportive people treat others as equals rather than as subordinates and are provisional, when possible, rather than appearing to be certain their position is correct.

Positiveness is an attempt to set up a win-win situation. To successfully manage *interpersonal conflict,* you need to care about other people and their ideas as well as caring about yourself and the ideas you embrace. Both parties must care about an issue in order to have a conflict. This mutual caring can be viewed as a positive dimension. Positiveness involves the recognition that normally there is more than one legitimate point of view on an issue. A search for common ground or for points of agreement can reduce the hostile atmosphere of conflictive discussions. Sincere positive statements about opponents and their arguments or the legitimacy of their positions can reduce dysfunctional conflict. Additionally, it helps to be positive about the possibility that by working together, the parties can find solutions that are mutually beneficial.

Equality involves ongoing respect for others. Treating the other party involved in conflict as a person of equal value forms a basis for minimizing hostility and reaching a solution. Being able to summarize the concerns, arguments, and issues raised by the other party suggests that you value and affirm the other. Giving at least equal time for the other party to express concerns affirms equality.

Should conflict persist despite these suggestions, it may be necessary for the parties to submit willingly to third-party negotiation or arbitration. Submitting to third-party intervention can be viewed as a more positive conflict management means than continued disagreement without resolution.

SUMMARY

- A positive self-concept is important in successful business communication. What you tell yourself about yourself (intrapersonal communication) enhances or diminishes your self-concept. Feedback from others can be perceived as positive or negative.

- Relationships are important in business communication. Each person has ideal comfort levels for inclusion, control, and affection that they offer to others and expect in return from others. Open people share information regarding their needs with others. Disclosing people share information regarding their feelings, beliefs, attitudes, and so forth, as well as factual information.

- A communication style can be vertical or horizontal. The democratic style is more effective than the autocratic style. It is desirable to encourage the development of a supportive climate and avoid a defensive communication climate.

- Theory Y managers, who believe in the basic goodness of employees, are more successful than Theory X managers, who see employees as inferior. Theory Z managers also stress humane interpersonal principles. Leaders who merge the essence of Theory Y and Theory Z concepts strengthen their leadership with the majority of employees.

- Hygiene needs must be met before employees attend to their motivational needs. Managers too often demonstrate concern for accomplishing tasks rather than concern for people.

- Management can produce job enrichment by (1) removing some controls while maintaining accountability; (2) increasing employees' responsibility for their own work; (3) assigning tasks as complete, natural work units; and (4) helping employees become experts in their jobs.

- Power must be used to achieve organizational goals, but coercive use of power can make employees resentful and defensive.

- Conflict can be desirable in many situations: (1) defusing potential escalation or more serious future conflicts, (2) sharpening issues and nurturing creativity, (3) building group cohesiveness, and (4) providing a means to measure assets. Management should intervene when conflict in interpersonal relationships becomes dysfunctional. Conflict can be managed by application of the constructs of openness, empathy, supportiveness, positiveness, and equality.

QUESTIONS FOR REVIEW AND DISCUSSION

1. How important is a positive self-concept to success in business today? Why?

2. Describe the concepts of inclusion, control, and affection. What is meant by the "expressed" and "wanted" dimensions?

3. What are the major risks of being an open person in the business environment? Of being a closed person?

4. What are the different communication styles? What are the advantages of the democratic communication style discussed in this chapter?

5. Describe a defensive business climate. Describe a supportive business climate. Contrast a defensive climate with a supportive climate.

6. Discuss the views of a Theory X manager and contrast them with the outlook of a Theory Y manager. What do the Theory Y notions add to effective leadership?

7. Describe the team-centered leadership style. Contrast it with other leadership styles discussed in this chapter.

8. What is effective feedback, and how can it be achieved in an organization?

ACTIVITIES

1. Describe your view of yourself (self-concept). Ask a close friend to describe you. Compare the descriptions. What can you do to improve your self-confidence?

2. How would you rate yourself on the following scale?
   Very open $\longleftarrow$————————————————$\longrightarrow$ Very closed
   What could you do to be more open? Would that help you professionally?

3. Go to an organization in your community and observe the styles of leadership that you see in a work group. Make a list of suggestions for what might be done to improve the leadership style.

4. In a discussion group with your classmates, explore what motivates employees in a work setting. What can you do to improve motivation within a group to which you belong?

PART
TWO

Communication Skills

Chapter 3

Listening in the Business Setting

After reading and reviewing this chapter, you should be able to . . .

1. Discuss the importance of listening in the business setting.

2. Contrast listening with hearing.

3. Identify and explain the stages of listening.

4. Identify and explain the six reasons for ineffective listening.

5. Identify and explain some tips for effective listening.

6. Compare and contrast dialogic and monologic listening.

*L*istening is important in business because it is the communication skill most often used in human interaction. A person like Bob Trent will spend about 70 percent of the workday communicating in some way. Between 45 and 55 percent of Bob's communication time will be spent in listening to others (Nichols and Stevens, 1957, p. 6; Werner, 1975, p. 26). In short, listening will occupy more of Bob's time each day than any other activity.

If Bob, or anyone else, could conclude that this listening will be done effectively, there would be little need for further discussion of the topic. Unfortunately, however, listening is *not* a skill that most people perform well. Studies repeatedly demonstrate that people do not listen effectively. Nichols and Stevens indicate that on the average, people listen at only 25 percent efficiency (1957, p. ix). Their research was verified by other studies.

Undesirable listening habits become so established that people frequently fail to remember or understand what others say. This leads to such problems as message distortion and poor evaluation of messages. Interpersonal relations are adversely affected. Opportunities are lost. Valuable time is wasted. Patients are given the wrong medication and airline pilots misunderstand crucial instructions from the control tower (see Steil, Barker, and Watson, 1983, pp. 40–41). As a business communicator, Bob Trent knows that he and his colleagues cannot afford poor listening. It is simply too costly.

In business organizations, listening problems are particularly troublesome. Recognizing the neglect of listening in our schools, the Sperry Corporation developed an extensive training program to help employees improve their listening skills. Sperry officials realized that listening problems add up to huge losses: "With more than 100 million workers in America, a simple ten-dollar listening mistake by each of them would cost a billion dollars." As a result of poor listening, "letters have to be retyped, appointments rescheduled, shipments reshipped." Sperry also emphasizes that the failure of people to listen results in the distortion of ideas "by as much as 80 percent as they travel through the chain of command." This leads to a situation in which "employees feel more and more distant, and ultimately alienated from top management" (pamphlet, Sperry Corporation, p. 8).

THE IMPORTANCE OF LISTENING IN BUSINESS

The need for effective listening in business settings is unmistakable. In a survey of 63 companies, Johnson (1971) found that "industry relies heavily upon listening as an element of communication." According to this survey, "listening affects the understanding of a problem, the retention and attention of an individual and the morale of a group" (p. 297).

Becker and Ekdom (1980) summarized surveys concerning the demand for various communication skills. When 282 members of the Academy of Certified Administrative Managers were asked to rank the 20 skills most crucial for management ability, active listening was rated number one and was considered "supercritical" (pp. 14, 22). These managerial experts clearly ranked listening as a top communication skill in business.

Research conducted by DiSalvo, Larsen, and Seiler (1976) provides impressive support for concluding that people in business view listening as critical to job success. They surveyed 170 people in business organizations, asking respondents to describe the communication skills they considered most important and also to indicate which skills they wished they had been taught in college. In both categories, listening was the number one response.

Your ability to interact and work with other people will be an important part of your success in business. Learning to listen well can do much to improve your relations with others. As Rogers and Roethlisberger (1952) have said, "Good communication . . . , is always therapeutic." A major factor in communication is the ability "to see the expressed idea and attitude from the other's point of view" (pp. 46–47). When we recall the importance of feedback, working in groups, responding to objections, and other aspects of business communication, we see that the interpersonal part of listening is critically important.

THE NATURE OF THE LISTENING PROCESS

It is not easy to define listening, and people have different ways of doing so. Wolvin and Coakley (1982) point out that *the* definition of listening is still in the process of being developed" (p. 30). It may not be possible to provide a definition that everyone will accept.

In a very general sense, listening is defined as *"a receiver orientation to the communication process;* since communication involves *both* a source and a receiver, listening consists of the roles receivers play in the communication process" (Floyd, 1985, p. 9).

Scholars such as Weaver (1972) and Spearitt (1962) consider listening a singular activity (distinct from all others); but listeners perform a *variety* of related, intertwined activities in their attempt to fulfill the receiver function in the communication process. Specifically, listening is a process that includes *hearing, attending to, understanding, evaluating,* and *responding to* spoken messages (Floyd, 1985, p. 9). Note that this definition includes attention to and understanding visual as well as oral stimuli. Although it is technically true that one does not hear visual stimuli, they are included in this discussion of listening because of the extremely close connection between visual and oral stimuli. Imagine, for example, that you ask a friend to do a favor. Your friend *says,* "No, I don't want to," but winks as the words are spoken. To ignore the visual element would cause a serious misunderstanding of the message. Essentially, then, Floyd's definition treats the listener as an active participant in the communication process and implies that a person will become a better listener by learning how to perform these various parts of the listening process.

The only step that requires little effort on the part of the listener is hearing. Since hearing is a matter of receiving sounds, if your ears function properly, you hear. Of course, sounds can be drowned out by other sounds or blocked in some way, but there is little that keeps you from hearing. The absence of hearing problems in no way means that you are listening or that you are listening effectively. Hearing is basically a condition necessary for listening. The other steps of the process are not automatic. Improvement in them will make you a better listener.

REASONS FOR INEFFECTIVE LISTENING

Listening, as suggested earlier in this chapter, is a skill that we all perform, but usually not well. Indeed, we have been listening all our lives. During that time we have developed the listening habits that we use today. Unfortunately, these habits are frequently undesirable. Such habits are so well established that we perform them without thinking. Most of us need to be concerned about changing the poor, or undesirable, habits. A good way to begin the process of becoming a better listener is to become aware of the characteristics of poor listening.

Let's consider six reasons for much ineffective listening. These do not apply equally to all listeners, and the extent or degree to which they do apply will vary from situation to situation, speaker to speaker, topic to topic, and so forth. Nonetheless, they represent common and important reasons for poor listening: (1) talking rather than listening, (2) the entertainment syndrome, (3) giving in to biases, (4) uncritical listening, (5) giving in to distractions, and (6) fear of difficult material (Floyd, 1985, pp. 21–30).

Talking rather than listening occurs when we want to talk more than we want to listen. As Weaver says, "Most people do not really want to listen but to talk" (1972, p. 82). We too often love to hear the sound of our own voices, and we feel that nothing anyone else has to say could be as interesting or as important as our comments. So, rather than listening carefully to other people, we spend our time thinking of what we are going to say next and looking for the opportunity to say it. Even when we cannot respond overtly, we may keep up a running, internalized speech or argument with the person speaking. It keeps us from paying attention to and understanding the speaker.

The entertainment syndrome is a significant listening problem. Because we like to be entertained, it is easy to expect, or even demand, that speakers be interesting and entertaining before we will give them our time and attention. Certainly it is easier to listen to people who hold our attention through effective, dynamic delivery and content. No one wants to be bored.

In fact, one might argue that effective speakers have an obligation to adapt to their listeners, to make their subjects interesting. Unfortunately, however, this attitude does little to improve our listening. Not all people are interesting, dynamic speakers. At the same time, an uninteresting, even dull, speaker may have something important to say. You may benefit from listening even if the speaker isn't entertaining. In short, you may hurt yourself more than the speaker by not paying attention. It may pay to listen even if the content and delivery are not interesting.

Giving in to biases leads to ineffective listening by contributing to inattention, failure to comprehend speakers, and, subsequently, poor analysis and evaluation of others' messages. Everyone has biases, for we all have preferences, likes, and dislikes. When you observe a close friend in a competitive situation, you probably want him or her to win simply because that person is your friend. And you might very well perceive and interpret the performance on the basis of friendship rather than objective observation of the performance.

Although there is nothing inherently wrong with having biases, they do get in the way of effective listening. If you hear a speaker discuss ideas or use words that you don't like, you might stop paying attention to the message. Or, because of your biases, you might distort the message, thus failing to understand it. Consequently, your evaluation of the speaker and/or message could be unfair or in error. In order to listen more effectively, we have to learn to prevent our biases from getting in the way of attention, comprehension, and fair evaluation.

Another reason for poor listening is *uncritical listening*. This may strike you as contradicting much of what we have said about ineffective listening. If we urge you not to expect every speaker to be entertaining (indeed, we ask you to listen carefully to dull speakers), and if we ask you to keep your personal biases out of listening, then how can we say that you should listen critically? The point is that some speakers know that listeners like to be entertained. Some speakers know that listeners like to have their biases reinforced. So there are speakers who seem to fulfill all listener needs, make difficult issues simple and easy to understand, and basically tell their listeners what they want to hear. For example, a person running for a political office promises lower taxes, more jobs, better streets, and a significant reduction in fees for various city services. This message might sound so good that an uncritical listener would accept it at face value, without questioning how these goals could be accomplished.

Another reason we tend to be uncritical is that we may have been taught that it isn't good to be critical. The words *criticism* and *critical* are often viewed negatively; they suggest faultfinding, "putting people down," being nasty to people, and so on. We may come to believe that it is better to be uncritical of others.

Actually, criticism involves both praising and faultfinding. Even the latter can be helpful and constructive. Learning to listen critically is extremely important, as analysis and evaluation take us into the deepest and most important aspects of listening. Consequently, you should be careful to pay attention, to comprehend, and then to analyze and evaluate what speakers say. Too hasty acceptance of messages that tell us what we like and want to hear can lead to serious problems. The person who promises all kinds of desirable changes without having a means of paying for them may well lead an uncritical listener into real problems. Being too uncritical is an important listening problem.

Giving in to distractions is difficult to avoid. A distraction is anything that pulls your attention away from that which you want, or need, to pay attention to. There may be distractions in the environment, and there may be distractions within you, the listener. For example, as you sit in a meeting, listening to a report, you notice a painting on the wall and spend a few seconds or minutes thinking about it. You then turn your attention back to the speaker but soon begin to feel that the chair is uncomfortable. As you shift your position in the chair you wonder why anyone would select such uncomfortable chairs for a conference room. And while you are thinking about the painting, shifting your position, and thinking about the poor choice of chairs, you may miss important parts of a message.

A headache or stomachache might prevent you from attending to a speaker in spite of a strong desire to do so. Or perhaps you had an argument with a friend earlier in the day and can't stop thinking about it. Each time such experiences occur, you are being affected by distraction. To the extent you give in to them, they function as a major reason for ineffective listening.

Perhaps the most subtle reason for ineffective listening is what we call the *fear of difficult material.* Much of your listening involves situations and materials that are new, difficult, and challenging. You might be required to take inservice courses in subjects that you find strange and difficult. Or you might have to work with or for a person whom you find demanding and difficult. At other times you might have to attend meetings in which highly technical and/or detailed information is presented.

In such situations it is difficult to listen, particularly when you are not highly interested or motivated. Yet you know that you need to listen carefully. Very often you may respond by avoiding or rationalizing. In either case, your listening will almost certainly be affected adversely. A major reason for wanting to engage in avoidance or rationalization is the fear of failing. It is unpleasant to fail, and most people will try to find ways to avoid it.

There are a number of ways to avoid failure. You can simply refuse to pay attention and spend your time doing something else. This is a matter of giving up on the situation. If, as a result, you do not remember or understand the information presented, you can tell yourself that you didn't fail to understand it; you merely refused to deal with it. The results may prove detrimental, but psychologically, you did not fail to understand. Or you might conclude that you knew that the material would be too difficult, so there was no need to try. That too is failure avoidance.

Rationalization also helps people to avoid the reality of failure. One can declare the speaker and/or material dull and uninteresting. Or a person might give in to biases by declaring the speaker and/or material "wrong," "stupid," "unimportant," "immoral," and so forth. A closely related ploy is to hold

Table 3.1 IMPROVING YOUR LISTENING HABITS

Reasons for ineffective listening	Basic causes	Solutions
Desire to talk	Greater interest in our own ideas	Develop interest in others
Entertainment syndrome	Desire not to be bored	Listen for self-benefit
Biases	Our experiences	Set biases aside
Uncritical listening	Speaker says what we want to hear	Weigh and evaluate the message
Distractions	Distractions are always present	Remove, reduce, or listen past distractions
Fear of difficult material	Fear of failure	Accept failure as normal

someone else responsible for the consequences of not listening or understanding. One might say, "It's actually Ms. Robinson's fault. She makes me attend sessions that have little to do with my job." Regardless of the reasons or the means, avoidance of difficult material usually proves costly.

Table 3.1 summarizes the reasons people do not listen effectively.

LISTENING FOR EFFECTIVE COMPREHENSION

Comprehension means that you are able to understand the speaker. Speakers and writers do not broadcast thoughts, ideas, or meanings. Instead, they convey symbols. Symbols stand for something, but they are not actually the things they stand for. They *represent* thoughts, ideas, objects, and experiences but are not any of those things. Thus, when speakers send symbols—either verbally or nonverbally—listeners must receive those symbols and attach meaning to them. To the extent that the meanings attached to the symbols by the listeners are similar to the meanings attached to them by the speakers, the listeners have understood the speakers. But to the extent that listeners cannot attach meaning to a speaker's symbols, or attach meanings that differ significantly from the speaker's meanings, the listeners have failed to understand, or have misunderstood.

As a listener, the best position is to maximize your ability to understand, and, conversely, to minimize the chances for misunderstanding. This sounds easier than it is, for understanding speakers requires desire, knowledge, and practice. Let's examine some basic ways to improve our ability to understand speakers.

TIPS FOR MORE EFFECTIVE LISTENING

The first step toward more effective listening comprehension is paying *increased attention*. Attention is a matter of focusing on the speaker and message, then sustaining that focus. Attention is important because it relates directly to memory. Essentially, you must pay attention well enough and long enough to place the incoming verbal and nonverbal stimuli into your long-term memory. Then you can recall the information, compare it with new and old material, and so on. Verbal and nonverbal stimuli not stored in your long-term memory will be lost in a matter of seconds. There will be no way to understand it, because you won't remember it (see Murch, 1973; Norman, 1968; Treisman, 1969; and Tyson, 1982).

You can increase your attention by realizing that it is important to do so, avoiding the common tendency to daydream, fighting the tendency to give in to external and internal distractions, removing distractions when possible, and learning to listen over distractions. You can frequently get rid of distractions in the environment. For example, if the room is too hot, open a window. If there is material on the chalkboard, erase it. If it is difficult to hear, move closer or ask the speaker to talk louder. For the most part, these are common sense ideas, but like much common sense, they are frequently not practiced.

Not all distractions can be removed from a listening environment. And if they could be, the utter lack of any stimuli would probably be distracting. Thus, good listeners learn to attend to the speaker and ignore the distractions. Although no one can do this all the time, anyone can increase the ability to pay attention. One authority has stated that we have the ability to listen to and understand speech even when there are severe distractions (Moore, 1977, p. 239). Mostly, it is a matter of desire and motivation. Anyone *can* shut out both internal and external distractions through directed attention and concentration.

The second step in increasing your ability to understand speakers is *to understand the nature of nonverbal communication.* Nonverbal communication is any communication expressed not in words but in body motion; para-language (*how* something is said); proxemics (the use of space); artifacts (physical objects); or environment (Knapp, 1980, pp. 4–11). Nonverbal communication serves a variety of functions. Among these are to "repeat, contradict, substitute, complement, accent, or regulate verbal communication" (Knapp, 1978, p. 38).

You should remember that nonverbal communication is not automatically more important than verbal communication; it is a mistake to think that contradictory nonverbal communication is more reliable than the verbal content of a message. We offer the following suggestions for improving your ability to understand nonverbal messages: (1) study nonverbal communication; (2) always examine the context; (3) interpret verbal and nonverbal communication simultaneously; (4) use feedback to check your perceptions; and (5) guard against stereotyping.

Observe nonverbal communication regularly and carefully in a wide variety of situations. Read about nonverbal communication in works by scholars who study it objectively. Remember that much popular writing on it is careless and inaccurate. Many colleges have courses in nonverbal communication that offer excellent opportunities for you to obtain in-depth information on this topic.

In situations of all kinds, you can significantly increase your listening comprehension by attempting to discover and to understand the contextual factors that influence and alter meanings. Avoid assuming that nonverbal behaviors mean the same thing in every situation. For example, shouting in a crowded, noisy area is not the same as shouting to someone during an argument in a quiet place.

The ability to interpret verbal and nonverbal communication simultaneously is extremely important. The two are interrelated and should not be viewed separately. When they contradict each other, you should carefully attend to the total verbal message and to clusters of nonverbal messages. Understanding verbal messages will help you understand nonverbal messages, and vice versa. Feedback can confirm your impressions.

The use of feedback to check your perceptions is an excellent way to avoid mistakes in understanding another person's nonverbal communication. It is true that a person's nonverbal communication is often unconscious (Argyle, 1975, p. 8), but if you ask a speaker to explain his or her nonverbal behaviors you stand a good chance of aiding your ability to understand. Requesting other people to respond to your impressions of their nonverbal communication will help you check your interpretations. Imagine, for example, that a speaker talks loudly, gestures vehemently, and pounds the table. You might *assume* that the person is angry, but if you ask, you might learn that this kind of nonverbal behavior characterizes that person's speaking when he or she is excited and involved. When angry, that person is quiet. The feedback would prove quite valuable.

Finally, be careful to guard against stereotyping. Stereotyping involves careless generalizing about any group or class of people and behaviors. For example, if you assume that all members of a nationality, race, or cultural group behave in certain ways or share certain characteristics, then you have not considered their individual differences. Nonverbal cues are also subject to stereotyping. For example, someone might assume that the pitch or intonation of a person's voice means that person is "masculine" or "feminine." Making such an assumption on the basis of voice, without any knowledge of that person, is another form of stereotyping. We urge you to avoid such careless assumptions about people and their nonverbal communication.

A third important step toward more effective listening is to increase your ability to comprehend verbal symbols, or messages. The listener must attach, as closely as possible, the same meaning to the speaker's symbols that the speaker attached to them. Many listeners find it difficult to approach understanding as a listener obligation. Quite often people believe that understanding should result from the speaker's effort to be clear and meaningful. Without denying that speakers have such an obligation, we emphasize that since communication is a two-way process that requires both speakers and listeners, the listener has as much responsibility as the speaker. Failure to understand a speaker may be partially the speaker's fault, but it remains a failure of the listener to understand. Effective listeners make an effort to enhance their ability to understand all speakers they encounter. You can improve your understanding by (1) increasing the quality and quantity of your experiences, (2) learning to use context as a means of increasing your understanding, (3) keeping your biases from getting in the way of understanding, (4) controlling any fear of failure, and (5) improving your vocabulary.

In almost any listening situation, the person whose *experiences* provide some knowledge and understanding of the topic being discussed can enjoy a major advantage over the listener who has no idea what the speaker is talking about. For example, assume you are scheduled to attend a session in which a new marketing concept will be discussed. If you read as much as possible about the topic, ask people for their ideas and opinions about it, and even talk to some clients, you will be in a much better position to understand the speaker than if you do nothing to familiarize yourself with the topic area. If you make good use of them, all experiences—travel, jobs, memberships and participation in organizations, reading, hobbies, movies, plays, and so forth—will help you to understand other people.

When you find that a person's words and phrases are unclear or unfamiliar, the *context* in which such words and phrases occur can provide you with an important means of understanding. The *context* refers to the surrounding words and phrases as well as to the totality of the message you are hearing. It also involves such factors as time, place, audience, culture, and occasion. Consider a situation in which a speaker uses the word *precarious*. You may not know the word, but paying attention to the context can help you figure it out. What if the speaker says, "The recent settlement with Acme Industries over a threatened suit, combined with unexpected increases in utility costs, left us in a precarious position for the third quarter. If we are not careful, we'll show no profit and possibly a significant loss." Without really knowing the word, you could figure out—from the context—that *precarious* means at risk, or lacking security, or in danger.

We have discussed the problem of biases in relation to reasons for ineffective listening. The key is not to rid yourself of biases but to attempt to set them aside in order to understand what a person says, to avoid ignoring or distorting some or all of the message. A listener who decides in advance that a speaker has nothing important to say or that the speaker's position is wrong may fail to pay close attention, hear only what he or she expects the speaker to say, and so forth. Without abandoning your feelings and beliefs, make a strong effort to keep them from getting in the way of your understanding the speaker as well as possible.

Another reason for ineffective listening is the fear of failure. Again, we will sometimes avoid situations, refuse to try to understand, or rationalize our own failure simply because it is not pleasant to fail. We strongly urge you to realize that everyone fails, without exception. And we stress that there is nothing disgraceful about trying and failing. Indeed, failure can be an important form of learning. Discovering what you do not know or understand tells you what you can focus on in order to improve your understanding. Don't refuse to try simply because the material is difficult.

Expanding your vocabulary is an extremely important way to improve your ability to comprehend speakers' meassages. Obviously, if you are unable to attach meaning to a person's words, or if the meaning you attach differs significantly from the speaker's meaning, you have a problem in listening comprehension. Increasing your vocabulary will not solve all listening problems, as listeners must understand thoughts, ideas, and concepts as well as words. Still, it is true, as Rubin suggests, that "without an understanding of words, comprehension is impossible" (1983, p. 66). We offer the following specific ideas for increasing your vocabulary: (1) read, (2) study words, (3) vary your experiences, and (4) use a systematic approach to vocabulary improvement.

The major advantage of increasing your vocabulary through reading is that you can learn words from context. When you see how an unfamiliar word is used, you can often figure out its meaning. Also, reading enables you to see words in a variety of contexts. Through repeated exposure and seeing words used in various contexts, you can naturally increase your vocabulary. You can assist this process by looking up unfamiliar words that you encounter in your reading.

You can combine word study with reading to help you improve your vocabulary. Studying synonyms, antonyms, homographs, and homonyms will help. Also, studying word origins (etymology), prefixes, suffixes, root words, and figures of speech is a useful way to improve your vocabulary (see Dale, O'Rourke, and Bamman, 1971, p. 15). The important point is that becoming interested in words and how they work will definitely help you to increase your vocabulary. Discovering what you do not know or understand tells you what you can focus on in order to improve your understanding. Don't refuse to try simply because the material is difficult.

Earlier in this chapter we discussed the importance of varied experiences as a way to help you understand other people. Since vocabulary improvement is part of that process, it follows that varied experiences can help you improve your vocabulary. Through travel, getting to know people and their ideas and customs, and through the development of a wide variety of interests you will unavoidably hear words used in various contexts and situations. You'll also learn the special vocabularies for jobs, hobbies, and specific events.

It is important to approach vocabulary improvement *systematically*. We urge you to become more aware of words, looking for new words or for words used in unusual ways. When reading, try to figure out the meanings of words from their contexts. Use feedback as a way to seek clarification or better understanding of a speaker's words. Write down new words, look them up, and keep a notebook of those new words and their meanings. If possible, take courses in the history of English, semantics, lingusitics, creative writing, or foreign languages. And try to develop and maintain an interest in language (see Rubin, p. 92).

A fourth way to improve your listening effectiveness is to *listen in order to analyze and evaluate*. Once you have attended to and understood the speaker, you are ready to analyze and evaluate the message. Please keep in mind that you cannot properly evaluate the speaker's message until you really understand it. Always strive to suspend your judgment. A very common

Table 3.2   IMPROVING LISTENING COMPREHENSION AND ANALYSIS/EVALUATION

Comprehension

1. *Increase your attention:* fight daydreaming and distractions.
2. *Increase your understanding of nonverbal communication as it accompanies verbal communication:* study nonverbal communication; use context; interpret nonverbal communication along with verbal communication; use feedback; avoid stereotyping.
3. *Increase your understanding of the verbal content of messages:* increase experiences; use context; fight biases; control fear of failure; increase your vocabulary.

Analysis/Evaluation

1. *Suspend judgment:* understand before evaluating.
2. *Analyze the support:* examine factual and nonfactual support.
3. *Analyze the reasoning:* examine data, reasoning process, conclusions.
4. *Evaluate the support:* evaluate statistics, examples, and objects; evaluate appropriateness to audience.
5. *Evaluate the reasoning used by the speaker:* evaluate causal, analogy, example, and sign reasoning.

reason for ineffective listening is the tendency of listeners to judge before understanding.

When you analyze a message you are examining its components, or its parts. Analysis may be accomplished informally, or it may be more formal and systematic, as in the case of formal speech criticism. Evaluation is the rendering of judgment on a message. It is a matter of deciding the worth or value of the message or parts of the message that you have heard, attended to, and understood. The analytical and evaluative functions require you to examine a speaker's support and reasoning.

In Chapter 11 we discuss the concepts of support and reasoning. As a listener, it is your responsibility to apply standards of evidence and reasoning to the speaking of others. This is not for the purpose of faultfinding or unfair attacking of other speakers. You want your response as a listener to be intelligent and responsible. As you study and use the standards for support and reasoning in your own speaking, you are simultaneously learning to analyze and evaluate the speaking of others. Cathcart (1981) states, "Students bent on improving written and oral discourse need not become rhetorical scholars or professional critics. They do, however, need to be reasonably knowledgeable in the areas of speech and criticism" (p. 14).

A fifth suggestion for better listening is to *improve your interpersonal listening skills. Interpersonal listening* refers to the listening that takes place between spouses, parents and their children, friends, neighbors, and colleagues. By improving your ability to listen interpersonally, you can more effectively establish, strengthen, and sustain good relationships with the people you live and work with each day. Indeed, the attitudes involved in good interpersonal listening extend to all listening situations.

Essentially, effective interpersonal listening involves the way you think about and approach the speaking of other people (see Table 3.2). We discussed the tendency of people to talk rather than to listen. Effective interpersonal listening requires a different attitude and approach to listening. It requires that you take a genuine, honest approach to others, expressing and demonstrating an interest in others as people of worth who deserve to be heard and understood. Such listening can make a significant difference in your effectiveness in business settings. To help you in your efforts to improve such communication, we urge you to consider the differences between two fundamental approaches to communication—monologue and dialogue.

You may think of monologue as communication sent by one person while others merely listen without comment or direct interaction. You may view dialogue as an exchange in which speakers and listeners continuously switch roles in a give-and-take. But as we are using the terms, *monologue* represents communication that "seeks to coerce, manipulate, conquer, dazzle, deceive, or exploit" (Johannesen, 1971, p. 377). *Dialogue,* in contrast, is an attitude toward communication "characterized by such qualities as mutuality, openheartedness, directness, honesty, spontaneity, frankness, lack of pretense, nonmanipulative intent, and love in the sense of responsibility of one human for another" (Johannesen, 1971, p. 375).

The key to dialogue is that the dialogic communicator tries to recognize and minimize his or her tendencies toward manipulation, selfishness, and objectification of the other person. In contrast, the monologic communicator fails to consider the needs and rights of others or intentionally practices selfishness and manipulation. Frequently, we think of these contrasting approaches in relation to speakers, but they can just as readily apply to listeners. Let us, therefore, consider some major characteristics of monologic and dialogic listening—for the purpose of stressing the desirability of the latter.

A monologic listener does not attempt to identify or empathize with others. Instead, he or she views speakers as people to be used, to be taken advantage of for selfish purposes. Such a listener may view the speaker as someone to be manipulated or even ignored. Such listeners disagree and/or argue prior to understanding. They pretend interest, concern, and involvement in order to look good or to gain information to use against the other person, perhaps as a means of exploiting weaknesses.

In contrast, a dialogic listener enters communication situations with a genuine and caring attitude toward the other person. Johannesen (1971) lists the following essential characteristics of dialogue: (1) genuineness, (2) accurate empathic understanding, (3) unconditional positive regard, (4) presentness, (5) a spirit of mutual equality, and (6) a supportive psychological climate (p. 376).

Genuineness means that a person listens without deception. A person who does not listen genuinely presents feedback that is insincere, or pretends interest in another's feelings and ideas, or only *seems* interested in the other's activities and problems. A person who listens with genuineness responds honestly and avoids jumping to conclusions, judging the speaker, or using the speaker for selfish purposes. The genuine listener is what he or she appears to be.

To achieve *accurate empathic understanding,* you try to place yourself in the speaker's position. You avoid being detached, disinterested, or removed from the speaker. Such listening demands that you understand rather than judge or evaluate. An empathic listener makes extensive use of feedback; the speaker has the opportunity to agree with or correct the listener's understanding and is encouraged to try to communicate.

Unconditional positive regard is not an easy concept to accept. It means that, as listeners, we accept other people as having unquestioned worth simply because they are human beings. It does not mean that all people are equally good, kind, productive, fair, honest, or acceptable. It means, instead, that we respond to people as having intrinsic value as humans. Even those whom we dislike or disagree with are beings of worth and may make important contributions if we can learn to listen fairly and openly.

Presentness means that as a listener you actively attend to the person speaking. It is possible to sit next to someone but not really be present with that person. Your thoughts and attention may be elsewhere. You may nod and give meaningless feedback without really getting much of the person's message. Your relations with others will improve significantly if you can increase the degree of presentness in listening situations.

A *spirit of mutual equality* does not mean that you think all people are equal. It means, instead, that you attempt to listen to others from an orientation of equality, in the sense that all people have the right to communicate freely. If you let your biases determine that the other person's ideas are inherently inferior or superior, you will lessen your ability to identify with the speaker in any way. Essentially, this criterion asks that you consider all people as capable of expressing themselves and that you accept that everyone deserves to be heard.

A *supportive psychological climate* is a culmination of all the above criteria for dialogic listening. It means that you, as a listener, attempt to convey that you are for rather than against others. It suggests that you encourage them to communicate and that you will make every effort to listen genuinely, openly, and honestly. In such a climate, people feel encouraged to speak; they feel that someone cares about them and what they have to say.

Learning to listen dialogically will benefit you as well as those who work with you. It can enable you to grow beyond the limitations and restrictions of yourself by seeing and feeling from the other's perspective. As Rogers and Farson state in their discussion of active listening, you must be willing to take a risk: by opening yourself to the feelings and views of another person, you risk being changed, and this can be extremely threatening (1969, pp. 489–490). At the same time, you make it possible to realize unlimited benefits. We hope you'll take that risk. You will become a better listener, and other people will want to associate with you both in personal and business settings.

SUMMARY

- Listening is the communication activity that people practice more than any other, and yet most people do not listen effectively.

- Listening is a matter of hearing, attending to, understanding, evaluating, and responding to messages.

- People listen ineffectively because they want to talk instead of listen; they desire to be entertained; they give in to their biases; they listen uncritically; they give in to distractions; and they are afraid of difficult material.

- You can become a more effective listener by improving your ability to comprehend speakers and by doing an effective job of analyzing and evaluating speakers.

- You can strive to listen more effectively interpersonally by practicing dialogic rather than monologic listening.

QUESTIONS FOR REVIEW AND DISCUSSION

1. Why do people think that listening is automatic, as long as one's ears work properly?

2. Can you think of times when ineffective listening has proved costly to you or others?

3. Some people think that nonverbal communication is essentially unrelated to listening. Do you agree or disagree?

4. Why is it accurate to say that listeners and speakers share an equal responsibility for effective communication?

5. In what ways do you think interpersonal listening skills can enable you to have more friends and better relationships with others?

6. If most people lose their jobs not because of ability to do the work but because they cannot get along with others, how could effective listening decrease the problem?

ACTIVITIES

1. Interview a person who holds a position in a business or profession. Ask this person for his or her views concerning the importance of listening.

2. Choose a situation in which you think the speakers and/or topic will be dull and uninteresting. Attempt to pay attention from start to finish. Note the difficulties you encounter as well as any positive results.

3. Observe the nonverbal bahaviors of the people involved in a meeting. Then list or discuss your observations.

4. Listen to someone with whom you strongly disagree. Keep track of the times you tune out the speaker, get angry, want to argue, and so on.

5. For a specific period of time, make an effort to listen to your friends or co-workers with attention, caring, understanding, and empathy. Observe their reactions and responses.

Chapter
4

Gathering Information Through Interviews

After reading and reviewing this chapter, you should be able to . . .

1. Describe ten basic steps in planning a successful information-gathering interview.

2. Recognize how to prepare open, directed open, and closed questions in order to gain needed information.

3. Organize questions in funnel form.

4. Utilize probes to gain depth in an interview.

One of Bob Trent's first tasks is to select members for his sales team. Before he sees his first interviewee, Bob will need to gather a variety of information regarding the specific needs of his work unit. One way for him to begin is by reviewing the responsibilities assigned to his group. He will want to talk with other managers to get suggestions for selecting the best people. He will want advice on preparing clear job descriptions and developing questions that relate directly to an applicant's ability to do a given job. As Bob reflects on this task, he realizes that gathering information in order to make a decision will be one of the activities he performs most frequently as a business communicator. Many of Bob's attempts to gain information will involve interviews.

An *interview* is a task-centered communication between two parties. Two roles are assumed in an interview—the role of the interviewer and the role of the party being interviewed (interviewee). An interview may be conducted by more than one person. One person may question several interviewees, or different people may take turns questioning several interviewees.

Stewart and Cash (1988) indicate that there are two fundamental interviewing approaches—the directive and the nondirective. In a *directive interview*, the interviewer establishes the goals of the situation early in the interaction. (An aggressive interviewee may wrest control of the interview away from the interviewer later.) In a *nondirective interview*, the interviewer allows the interviewee to control the purpose, pacing, and subject matter of the interview. The nondirective style is chosen in settings such as counseling, performance appraisal, and problem-solving sessions. The directive approach is easier to learn; it is time-efficient; it provides for exchange of specific data; and it gives the interviewer more control of the interview. However, the directive approach is less flexible; it reduces the spirit of collaboration; and it limits the interviewee's response choices. The nondirective approach encourages the interviewee to give depth to answers; it can be more flexible; it encourages voluntary information (information not specifically requested); it often garners more information than a more directive approach; and it allows the interviewer to adapt to the interviewee. However, the nondirective approach can take much time; it requires considerable skill; it generates unnecessary information; and interviews are difficult to replicate. A combination approach is often most desirable (Stewart and Cash, 1988, pp. 7–8).

When time is of the essence, a majority of the interview may be directive by design. A particular interviewee may provide more useful information, however, if granted the greater freedom to respond in a nondirective format. The choice should be made by the interviewer after careful consideration of the purpose of the interview and the specific situation.

Table 4.1   BASIC TYPES AND FUNCTIONS OF INTERVIEWS

Type	Function
Information gathering	To gather information
Employment	To select and properly place personnel
Appraisal	To give feedback to employees
Problem solving	To make decisions among alternatives
Counseling	To help resolve personal problems
Disciplinary	To restore an employee to productivity
Grievance	To help employee(s) resolve disagreement with management or peers
Exit	To determine what types of employees are lost and why
Persuasive	To "sell" ideas and influence behavior

A party wishing to gather or share information initiates the interview. Initially, at least, this person (or party) attempts to guide the interview through the use of questions. Interviews, unlike other business presentations, involve the frequent exchange of the speaker and listener roles, and neither party has exclusive control of the communication situation. Interviews are more formal than conversations in that they are characterized by a higher degree of order, greater depth, and minimal digressions.

VARIOUS INTERVIEW SITUATIONS IN BUSINESS

Interviews occur frequently in the business environment. The first contact company personnel have with an applicant or a customer normally occurs in a question-and-answer format. Business interviews are conducted for information gathering, employment, appraisal, problem solving, counseling, discipline, grievance resolution, exit situations, and persuasion. Table 4.1 indicates the functions of each of these types of interviews.

In this chapter you will learn about the processes necessary to success in information-gathering interviews. Chapter 5 discusses employment and appraisal interviews, and Chapter 10 considers persuasive communication.

INFORMATION-GATHERING INTERVIEWS

Perhaps the most common communication in business organizations is the securing of relevant information through pertinent questions. Stewart and Cash (1988) note that interviews are "the most common form of purposeful, planned communication. Each day millions of people engage in sales interviews, informational interviews, job interviews, counseling interviews, health care interviews, survey interviews, appraisal interviews, and recruiting interviews, to name only a few" (pp. 7–8). And because information is essential in decision making and problem solving, an information-gathering or probing interview is a common means of discovering vital information for making an effective business presentation.

Planning the Interview

Step 1: Set a Clear Interview Purpose   Since you are seeking specific information, careful planning is essential. Arthur (1986) reminds us that as part of the preparation, you should determine exactly why you are conducting the interview. What are your objectives? Many business people find it helpful to write down a purpose statement before selecting whom to interview or composing questions of any kind. Bob Trent might write, "After talking with a company engineer, I want to know how compatible our equipment will be with the multiuser needs of my present client." Such a statement can be used both to select the appropriate engineering support staff to question and to develop subareas for questions.

Step 2: Do Your Homework   Bob Trent's second step in planning will be to read and review what he knows and has learned about the topic. (People being questioned appreciate your having done your homework prior to taking their time from other tasks.) Many of Bob's questions regarding multiuser interfacing could be answered by reading the available technical material. Only questions not covered in the technical material should be asked during the interview. This way the interview will be efficient and effective.

Step 3: Select Appropriate Sources   An appropriate source for an interview is a person who has the experience and training to really know about the subject of the interview. An appropriate source will be someone who is open—willing to share experience and knowledge of the topic. Bob Trent has a great source in Sue Derkman. She performed well in Bob's position and has indicated her willingness to help. Another criterion is that an appropriate source is a person who will be available when needed. The best sources will often be inaccessible when you need them most. Hence, the search for an appropriate source of information should be initiated early.

Step 4: Make the Appointment   Your approach to the appointment is similar to presenting your business card: you want the impression to pave the way for you. Attention to etiquette is important.

Many interviews are arranged by telephone, which is usually the most appropriate way to contact people. Your telephone conversations should include some important information. First, clearly identify who you are and what organization or division you represent. Second, state that you are asking for a specific amount of time (say, 20 minutes) within a specified period of time (the next week). Ask when would be the most convenient time for the other party. This is a direct and assertive method, as the following example illustrates:

BOB TRENT: Hello, Mr. Drake. This is Bob Trent of the sales department here at American. I would like about 20 minutes of your time, if possible, before next Friday afternoon to get some background information regarding the new CX-1000 line of personal computers. I would like to include the CX-1000 line in the updated sales manual I am preparing for my new sales team. When would it be convenient for you to visit with me?

This request is concise and reasonably complete. Assuming that the person agrees to the interview, Bob should close his conversation with a restatement:

BOB TRENT: Good, Mr. Drake! I look forward to seeing you next Thursday afternoon at 2:00 P.M. at your office. I appreciate your willingness to help me.

This "perception check" confirms the specifics of the appointment. Furthermore, the process demonstrates courtesy, brevity, and a professional attitude. Since Bob was considerate on the phone, the interviewee can expect that he will make good use of time during the interview.

Had Mr. Drake been unavailable, or had he suggested an alternative interviewee, Bob should then have asked if he could say that Mr. Drake recommended that he talk with that person. This added "leverage" might help to secure the interview.

As you wait for the day of the interview, there are things you can be doing. You should read any relevant material you can find on the topic of the interview. You should continue to inform yourself about the person you will interview. Many interviewees expect you to have read what they have published on the topic before you interview them. You also can begin to plan the order of topics you wish to cover in the interview.

It is proper to confirm an interview close to the appointed time. The best time for Bob to confirm his appointment would be Thursday morning. Confirmations serve to remind the other person and to avoid an unnecessary trip should the interviewee have been called away or become ill that day. Furthermore, confirming an interview is professionally courteous. Such calls include the same level of detail:

BOB TRENT: This is Bob Trent of the sales division. I'm calling to confirm my time with Mr. Drake this afternoon at 2:00 P.M. As you recall, I wished to speak with him regarding the CX-1000 line of personal computers as a background for updating a sales manual.

The confirmation call complements the positive, professional image developed in the initial call. An affirmative response from the secretary (as in this case) is an indication that the stage has been set properly. Should the interview be scheduled early in the morning, an afternoon call the previous day would be appropriate. (Our students have requested information-gathering interviews from hundreds of professionals, whose feedback reflects the positive impression created by the confirmation call.)

Step 5: Schedule Your Questions   The next step in the advance planning process is to finalize the questions you plan to ask. Normally, it is best to divide your information needs into two to four sections. Such a limitation is necessary in order to focus the interview and to use the interviewee's time efficiently.

Interviewers who plan not to deviate from their list of questions are using a *highly scheduled* format. People who prepare a solid, basic set of questions in advance, but grant themselves the freedom to depart from the schedule of questions as new information becomes available in the interview, are using a *moderately scheduled* format. Persons who do not prepare a specific set of questions in advance are using a nonscheduled format. (Many counseling interviews are *nonscheduled.*)

Later in this chapter we present a more thorough discussion of the types and techniques of questioning. We need to understand what open and closed questions are before we can order specific questions in a schedule.

Step 6: Make Positive First Impressions   In an employment interview, the first few moments are crucial to the applicant's success; in the same way, rapport building is important in the information interview. First impressions often begin with how well the interviewer handles the appointment process. As pointed out in Chapter 1, everything we do relates to communication, including the first impression we make on others. Impressions, once formed, are difficult to change dramatically. If you follow the suggestions regarding making the appointment, you should make a positive impression.

Try to arrive 5 to 10 minutes early. Arriving late or "just in time" creates a negative impression in the interviewee. If you were not able to choose the meeting place and this is your first visit to the location of the interview, take a few moments to consider the environment. For example, where would you like to sit in relation to the interviewee? Where could you place your tape recorder? Is there any furniture you may want to move?

Just as your arrival time makes an impression, so does your personal appearance. Your appearance should indicate that you are serious about your purpose. Although situations vary, one rule is to dress like the better-dressed people in the setting where you will conduct the interview. "Looking the part" means looking appropriate *in that context.*

Your initial actions and words establish that important first impression:

> BOB TRENT: Hello. My name is Bob Trent. I'm with the sales department. I believe Mr. Drake is expecting me at 2:00. As you may recall, I wish to speak with Mr. Drake regarding the information for the sales manual that I am planning for our new unit.

Note that, for the third time, Bob has indicated the basics of the appointment—who he is, what organization he represents, what information he is after, how the information will be helpful to him, and the specifics of the appointment. Normally, the approach is acknowledged by the receptionist and the interviewer is invited to have a seat.

Assuming that Bob has arrived a little early, he will have time to relax for a few minutes and adjust to the surroundings. This is a good time to observe the people in this unit. Often, items in the immediate environment will provide the perfect "small talk" openers. For example, tennis trophies with Mr. Drake's name on them suggest an opening gambit. Bob can provide Mr. Drake with an opportunity to talk about one of his interests—tennis. Such openers virtually guarantee that the interviewer will be received pleasantly.

After a bit of small talk, the interviewer can nonverbally signal readiness to "do business," by opening a notebook. Normally questions should be on the left side of the notebook (or legal pad); a place to record brief answers should be on the right-hand side. Opening a notebook has proved to be a good procedure for transition from the routine of small talk to the important questions you need to ask. It also serves to remind the interviewee that the interviewer will be asking most of the questions for the next few minutes.

The *orientation* stage of the interview is an overview of the agenda prior to asking the first question. The interviewer mentions the two to four main topics to be covered, asks for the privilege of taping the interview (if the interview is to be recorded), and, once again, clarifies how the information will be used. The orientation sets the stage for the interview and indicates the interviewer's expectations.

Step 7: Plan for Recording   There are three basic ways to record information. You can attempt to remember what the interviewee says, take extensive notes, or make a recording. Experience indicates that a recording is usually the best choice. Unless you have an excellent memory and are extremely poised during the interview, reliance on memory will not serve you well. Taking notes also poses problems. Unless you are a trained stenographer, you will slow the interview. This could result in a loss of rapport while you reduce the answers to writing. It is difficult to communicate responsiveness to the interviewee nonverbally (to indicate you are interested and listening) while looking ahead to the next question you intend to ask and writing at the same time, but you can improve with practice.

A small tape recorder is the best choice, if the interviewee is amenable. Usually, interviewees appreciate that the use of a recording enhances the probability that they will be understood accurately. However, courtesy demands that you get permission prior to using a recorder. Should the interviewee indicate hesitation, either verbally or nonverbally, then consider the answer to be "no." But all is not lost.

One way to minimize your need to write extensively is to plan for "downtime" after each interview. *Downtime* is a block of unscheduled time after the interview you can use to sit by yourself and enhance your sketchy notes while they are fresh. Reporters, who must achieve a high degree of accuracy, have learned this review technique. They can verify the accuracy of their quotations later, but once the notes become "cold" they are difficult to decipher and much of the information gathered, which was the reason for doing the interview, is lost. Planning for downtime can minimize this difficulty.

Step 8: Use Communication Sense   *Communication sense* means management of the pace and depth of the interview. It is paramount to know what information is most important, what information is new to the interviewer, and what knowledge cannot be obtained easily from any other source. Getting such information should constitute the focus of the interview. Knowing when to probe (go deeper into a topic) is also extremely important.

Experience teaches the interviewer when to stop pursuing a point. As you gain seasoning, it becomes easier to realize when you have a reasonable answer to your question; when you see that new information is not forthcoming, it is time to move on. Further, it is important to minimize the number of questions in areas where you have access to written or other sources of data. You ask only enough to discover whether there are "blind spots"—areas you know nothing about.

You also need to know when you have "worn out your welcome." When answers to your questions indicate that the interviewee has little or no additional information, it is time to quit. You waste time trying to make a nonproductive question (or interview) more useful.

Finally, it is valuable to know when you should confirm what you have heard from the interviewee. You may pause and reflect on what you have heard from the interviewee:

> BOB TRENT: Let me see, Mr. Drake. We have covered three ways to demonstrate the advantages of the CX-1000. First was compatibility. Second was desktop publishing capability. Third was interchangeability. Do I have this right?

This interview technique, known as "mirroring" or "perception checking," gives you a chance to confirm what you have heard. It also allows the interviewee to clarify any misperceptions.

Step 9: Close the Interview   The way you close an interview is almost as important as the way you manage first impressions. The concepts of *primacy* and *recency* mean that, all things being equal, people tend to remember first and last impressions best. Hence, attention to ending an interview (recency) will pay rich dividends.

After you finish your planned schedule of questions, you should offer the interviewee an opportunity to provide additional information:

> BOB TRENT: Well, Mr. Drake, can you think of anything you would like to add to what we have discussed today? Is there anything else you think I should know about the CX-1000 line?

This *summary question* signals Mr. Drake that Bob has finished his questions and is open to any further information. Bob also might request permission to call Mr. Drake should he think of additional questions.

After asking the summary question, complement the verbal message with a nonverbal cue—closing your notebook—to emphasize that you are ending the formal conversation. This is the time to exchange pleasantries with the interviewee. Bob Trent can return to the small talk regarding tennis. As you engage in small talk, rise and begin initiating obvious and appropriate leave-taking routines. One leave-taking routine would be to say, "I'll let you get back to your work."

As you move out the door, be sure to express appreciation. It is especially appropriate to mention something specific you learned from the interview that will be most helpful to you. These departing behaviors enhance the impression you leave with the interviewee. A positive impression is likely to mean an open door for future interviews.

Finally, a day or two later, you should send an interoffice memorandum, or even better, a personal thank-you card or note, to express appreciation for the interviewee's help.

Step 10: Evaluate Your Approach   It is a good idea to take some time soon after the interview to assess what you have learned and how you could improve your interview skills in the future. The process of regular self-assessment is vital for business communicators who wish to succeed.

First, if you were unable to use a tape recorder, complete the notes taken during the interview. While the material is fresh, take several minutes to "debrief" the interview. At this point, your memory will be at its freshest.

Second, think about what you might have done to improve your interview technique. Ask yourself questions: How did I do in making a positive impression? How did the small talk go? Were my questions on target—did they lead to the information I needed? What do I wish I had asked or inquired more about? How did I handle the closing? Have I developed the basis for continuing to interact with the interviewee? Did I remain in control and handle the pace of the interview well? Did my plan for recording the information work well? In general, how could I improve as an interviewer?

The single most important factor is to evaluate the accuracy and adequacy of the information obtained. In a 20-minute interview like the one described above, it is likely that no more than 10 to 15 percent of what you hear will be new or highly relevant. However, if you have done your homework well, that information will be valuable to you.

Decide what holes, if any, still exist in the material you need. Perhaps Bob Trent thinks he should have asked Mr. Drake for the name of another person knowledgeable about the applications of the company's product. He could have asked permission to use Mr. Drake's name when contacting the other source. Again, Bob could still call Mr. Drake if another question occurs to him.

Table 4.2   REVIEW OF STEPS IN ADVANCE PLANNING

Step	Function
1. Determine the purpose of the interview.	Decide what information is needed.
2. Do your homework.	Review what you know; do background reading.
3. Select sources.	Determine who is competent and who is available.
4. Make the appointment.	Show professional courtesy; save time.
5. Develop a schedule of questions.	Plan efficient questions.
6. Provide for a positive first impression.	Build rapport.
7. Plan for recording.	Ensure accuracy of data.
8. Use communication sense.	Cover topics efficiently.
9. Close the interview.	Leave-taking.
10. Evaluate your approach.	Self-assessment.

Most information-gathering interviews in business result in a written report. The outline of the presentation and/or the text of the account should be checked for accuracy prior to reporting ideas from the interview.

When you evaluate the success of a given interview, consider the following salient variables:

- The mood of the interviewee
- What the interviewee has just finished doing
- The interviewee's expectations regarding the interview
- Influences of the context (surroundings) of the interview
- The interviewee's desire (motivation) to be helpful to the interviewer
- The fatigue level of parties involved
- "Noise" (interference) in the channels of communication (sound, heat, inability to hear, interruptions, etc.)
- Perceived power (relative equality of the parties)
- Seating arrangement

These factors are important to the planning process. Additionally, each interview evaluation should include a note about how such challenges were met or could be better met in the future.

Table 4.2 reviews the steps in planning an interview. With these considerations in mind, let's go on to another important aspect of successful interviewing—effective questioning techniques.

QUESTIONING TECHNIQUES

One major indicator of success for an interviewer is the amount of effort that goes into planning the schedule of questions. Much more time should be given to preparing good questions than asking them. It is not unusual to spend at least ten minutes in preparation for every minute you plan to ask questions. This is another way of emphasizing that *planning your schedule of questions* is central to success. Downs, Smeyak, and Martin (1980) agree: "Questions are basic to most interviews, whether you are conducting a survey, selecting an employee, making a sale, or collecting information for a newspaper story. Consequently, the ability to use questions *effectively* is a key communication skill you should cultivate constantly" (p. 41).

Questions laid out in a planned sequence constitute a schedule of questions for an interview. (Meetings are centered around *agendas*, discussed in Chapter 7; presentations are powered by *outlines*, discussed in Chapter 12; and interviews are driven by *schedules of questions*.)

Recall that a 20-minute interview should be divided into no more than two to four main parts. Hugenberg and Yoder (1985) recommend that planning begin with a brainstorming session (see guidelines in Chapter 6) regarding questions. They put it this way: "During the preparation stages, the interviewer brainstorms a list of questions for potential use. Realizing the goals of the interview, the interviewer will prepare a list of questions which reflect specific goals and objectives" (p. 262). Let's consider the types of questions possible.

Open Questions

Open questions ask for open answers—that is, the interviewer does not know how the interviewee will answer. Generally, such questions are broad and nonspecific. Open questions can be either totally open questions or directed open questions.

Open question:

What can you tell me about yourself?

Directed open question:

What can you tell me about your sales experience?

Both of these examples are open questions, because the length and general direction of answers are up to the interviewee. The second question is directed because it requires more focused information for a satisfactory answer.

There are advantages to using open questions. They tend to produce more voluntary or novel information. After all, a major reason for conducting a business interview is to obtain data you do not have. The information is less "contaminated" by specific directions from the interviewer. Open questions give the interviewee more freedom to respond and, consequently, are more enjoyable for interviewees. Furthermore, the use of open questions allows the interviewer to learn how the interviewee thinks. Feelings and deeper levels of thought are expressed more freely when open questions are used.

Although the advantages of open questions are numerous and significant, such questions are not without limitations. Before you fill your schedule with such questions, you should consider how much time will be consumed if you ask only open questions. In most business settings, time is a major constraint. Open questions give much control to the person interviewed. Although it is true that you wish the interviewee to do most of the talking (about 70 percent), you should expect to control the direction of the proceedings. Another limitation to the extensive use of open questions is that they require much nonverbal skill on the part of the questioner.

The interviewer can use nonverbal means to maintain control: nodding to indicate understanding and interest, leaning slightly forward when the interviewee is most on target with answers and leaning away from the interviewee when such is not the case, and using paralinguistic sounds of approval ("ah," "umhum," etc.). *Paralanguage* cues are the vocal (but nonverbal) aspects of speech. DeVito (1988) says that paralanguage "refers to the *manner* in which something is said rather than to *what* is said" (p. 171). Withdrawal of positive nonverbal cues tends to shorten the length of answers to open questions. It takes experience and self-monitoring to learn the regulative function of these nonverbal skills.

Closed Questions

There are three types of *closed questions:* (1) *"fill-in-the-blanks,"* (2) *multiple choice,* and (3) *bipolar* (either/or) questions.

Fill-in-the-blanks question:

How many expansion slots does the CX-1000 personal computer have?

Multiple choice question:

Which of the following software products do you prefer: (*a*) word processing programs, (*b*) desktop publishing packages, or (*c*) integrated text and data processing systems?

Bipolar question:

Do we have more XT or AT models in our inventory?

Closed questions allow the interviewee relatively little latitude in framing answers. But using closed questions does have certain advantages. One obvious advantage is that, from the point of view of the interviewer, control is less threatened. Another advantage is efficiency. Time can be managed in such a way that many topics can be covered in a short span of time. Yet another advantage is that closed questions elicit specific information from the source. The interviewer can obtain important facts, statistics, details, and so on with a level of precision often lacking when open questions are asked. Also, it is easier to teach beginning interviewers to use closed questions effectively.

There are disadvantages to using mostly closed questions. One disadvantage is that answers are relatively shallow. In addition, such questions make it difficult to learn how the interviewee thinks. That the person is less likely to express feelings or to offer voluntary information and is more likely to become bored with the interview is obvious. One could consider a closed question as similar to a yo-yo in that answers come back pretty much as expected. Since open questions and closed questions each have strengths and weaknesses, often it is best to use both types.

Tunnel Technique

Customers in shopping malls are sometimes approached by a person with a clipboard who wonders if they would mind answering a few questions. Almost without exception, such encounters use the *tunnel technique*—a series of closed questions. The responses are marked on paper, and the interviewer moves on to another person in the mall. These are simple, efficient interviews. However, depth is sacrificed for efficiency. Research questionnaires often make use of tunnel techniques, as in the following example:

> What is your name?
>
> What is your age?
>
> Where do you reside?
>
> What is your occupation?
>
> What is your annual family income?
>
> Do you operate a personal computer?
>
> *(If operated)* How would you rate your satisfaction with your current personal computer: (a) very satisfied, (b) somewhat satisfied, or (c) neither satisfied or dissatisfied?

Interviews featuring a progression from open to closed questions provide the opportunity for more depth and variety.

Funnel Technique

In preparing a schedule of questions, a mastery of the basics of the funnel technique is requisite. The *funnel technique* uses a combination of open and closed questions. It attempts to have the best of both worlds while minimizing the disadvantages of both types of questions.

A funnel begins with an open question, proceeds to directed open questions, and ends with closed questions. Bob Trent is planning his schedule of questions for the interview with Mr. Drake and is completing his first funnel as follows:

> BOB TRENT: Mr. Drake, what are the advantages of our CX-1000 system over the competition?

Note that this gives Mr. Drake considerable freedom to respond. Bob's second question is more focused:

> BOB TRENT: Mr. Drake, how would you compare our system to the competition in terms of flexibility?

Again, this question gives much freedom to Mr. Drake. However, in this case, the question is more specific as to the parameters of information needed. This is a directed open question. A parallel question follows:

> BOB TRENT: What would you say, Mr. Drake, regarding the compatibility advantages of our CX-1000 line?

This is another directed open question. Bob is proceeding from the most open to the more directed questions. Furthermore, he is giving Mr. Drake every opportunity to offer volunteer information. The funnel technique is designed to stimulate recall without asking specific questions. Further directed open questions can form additional subdivisions of this topic:

> BOB TRENT: Mr. Drake, what would you tell a potential customer about our record of product reliability?

At this point, some specific data regarding the advantages of the product would be appropriate. The following closed questions might complete the body of the first funnel for Bob's interview:

What popular software lines will our CX-1000 handle?

Is our CX-1000 compatible with all the commonly used business programs?

What do you think is the best feature of our CX-1000?

How would you rate the reliability of the CX-1000 hard disk drive: (a) better than any of our competition, (b) as good as the competition, (c) a little worse than our competition, or (d) not a strong point in relation to our competition?

Each of these last four questions can be answered either with a "yes" or "no," by "filling in the blanks," or by making a choice between options. Each is a closed question designed to evoke specific details that Bob Trent can use in his presentation. His first funnel is complete.

Inverted funnels begin with closed questions and move to open questions, but this technique should be used sparingly. Such a sequence of questions is advisable only when interviewees are not open to being interviewed and need to be stimulated. A closed question or two may help focus the thinking of interviewees who may not believe initially that they have much information about a given topic. Closed questions may help to "prime the pump." People who are interviewed frequently may resist being questioned. Beginning with a carefully chosen series of closed questions may entice them to respond and, thus, serve as a stimulus for the interview.

The Funnel Technique

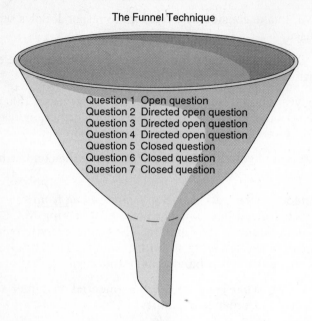

Question 1 Open question
Question 2 Directed open question
Question 3 Directed open question
Question 4 Directed open question
Question 5 Closed question
Question 6 Closed question
Question 7 Closed question

Figure 4.1 The funnel technique.

SCHEDULING OPTIONS

Interviewers are free to choose between *highly scheduled, nonscheduled,* and *moderately scheduled* formats. For most interviews, and for the information-gathering interview in particular, the moderately scheduled approach is best. Highly scheduled interviews do not allow the interviewer to deviate from the scheduled questions. The moderately scheduled format is a viable alternative. It provides the interviewer with the confidence of having a good plan to follow.

There may be good reasons to abandon the plan, even early in the interview. Suppose that Mr. Drake gives Bob Trent excellent, but unexpected, information. Using a moderately scheduled plan, Bob can depart from his schedule and take a *nonscheduled* approach (composing questions as he goes). After Bob pursues each item of voluntary information to his satisfaction, he can return to the flexible schedule. With the moderately scheduled format, Bob is free to probe for more depth whenever he receives an answer that indicates the interviewee has new information.

There is no magic number of questions for each funnel, but the format remains basically the same. Figure 4.1 will help you review the concept.

Bob Trent will close each funnel in his schedule of questions with a summary question.

BOB TRENT: Mr. Drake, is there anything else you can tell me about the advantages of our CX-1000 system over the competition?

At this point, Bob has completed one question pattern in the moderate schedule. Again, a moderate schedule of questions for a 20-minute interview may include a single pattern. Normally, the range is from two to four such patterns, with four being more likely in longer interviews.

PROBES

A part of the questioning process that separates the novice from the experienced interviewer is knowing when and how to ask follow-up questions or probes. Novices often fail to seek depth when additional valuable information can be obtained. Experienced interviewers know when to probe. *Probes* are secondary questions that maintain the topic and focus of the previous question (primary question) and are designed to ask for greater detail than the interviewer expects from the primary questions. Stewart and Cash (1988) emphasize the importance of probing: "The probing interview is the most common type of interview because it is used daily by journalists, lawyers, police officers, health care professionals, students, teachers, insurance claims investigators, supervisors, managers, counselors, and parents, to name a few" (1988, p. 81). A probe might be worded like this:

QUESTIONER: That's interesting! Could you tell me more about that?

This example is a verbal probe. The word *interesting* serves as a *stroke*—a brief, positive reinforcement (praise) as motivation for more detail. Knowing when to probe and when not to probe requires experience. You should probe whenever there is an indication that new information could be discovered. Such indications are called *flags*. When you perceive a flag, you have an opportunity to probe for depth:

BOB TRENT: What new directions do you see in personal computer development?

MR. DRAKE: In addition to refinements of the current lines, there are some technical developments in the works.

BOB TRENT: *(Responding to the flag—some technical developments in the works)* I would be interested in what you think the new technical developments will be. Please tell me more about this.

Additionally, silence, coupled with a questioning look, may qualify as a successful probe. Nonverbal probes are effectively used by experienced interviewers. Nods, appropriately timed, can increase the length and depth of answers an interviewee gives to a particular subject. A combination of probes can be effective in eliciting additional detail.

Specialized probes may be used when appropriate. A *hypothetical probe* involves (1) setting the stage and (2) asking a probing question:

BOB TRENT: Suppose, Mr. Drake, that you were going to make a presentation of our CX-1000 system to a company like the Santo Group. Which of the advantages would you discuss first, and *why?*

The first part of the question, which is narration (a story), is followed by the hypothetical question. Such probes can be used in all types of interviews, including employment and appraisal interviews.

A *confrontational probe* reminds the interviewer of something said earlier that appears inconsistent with the current answer. Confrontational probes can be abrasive, something like a police interrogation:

INTERVIEWER: Earlier I understood you to say that the most important factor in a good presentation is good preparation. Now I hear you saying that the delivery of the presentation is the most important. What is your position on this?

Questions like these can be used to test the interviewee's tolerance or adaptability to stress. Such questions should be used sparingly lest the relationship become antagonistic. An interview should not become an interrogation. Confrontive questions are rarely appropriate in information-gathering interviews, although a journalist may use a confrontive question or two to test the strength of a source's opinion before writing a news story based on some measure upon the source's information.

Another specialized probe is the *reactive probe.* Here the interviewer follows a primary question with a specific comment in order to learn about the interviewee's reactions. For example, Bob wants to know what Mr. Drake thinks of the competition:

BOB TRENT: *(Bob has been questioning Mr. Drake regarding claims by competitors)* Mr. Drake, I read our competitor's literature regarding their personal computer line. Their advertising claims their hardware has the fastest response time. How do you react to this claim?

As in the hypothetical probe, a narration is followed by a question. In this case, Bob uses the comments and materials of others to provide a springboard for the interviewee's comment.

Reactive and hypothetical probes contribute to the tools available to questioners, and they are challenging and motivating to interviewees as well.

LOADED AND LEADING QUESTIONS

You need to avoid some common problems when developing questions. First, consider the statement "All loaded questions are leading, but not all leading questions are loaded." The language in a *loaded question* gives a clue as to how the questions should be answered. Such questions are not neutral. Terms with *high value abstractions*, such as "mother," "the American Way," and "God," are examples of loaded language.

Loaded question:

Don't you think the time wasted fooling around with fads like computers could be better spent?

Answering "no" to this question would mean the interviewee opposes the use of computers. Here the word *fads* is linked with computers. This question is hardly neutral. It is leading the interviewee because it uses loaded language.

Leading question:

Don't you agree that the Pontiac Grand Prix is the finest motorcar built in America?

The language of this question is not loaded, but the preface of the *leading question* ("Don't you agree") indicates how the interviewee is expected to think. The interviewer is leading the interviewee.

Questions can and should be worded neutrally:

Neutral questions:

How would you rate the Pontiac Grand Prix as compared with other motor cars built in America: (*a*) superior, (*b*) better than average, (*c*) average, (*d*) worse than average, or (*e*) inferior?

Do you agree or disagree with the statement that learning to use computers is a waste of time?

In both cases the wording is neutral. Neutral questions are more likely to produce objective answers.

CONDUCTING INTERVIEWS

Equipped with the basics of developing a moderate schedule of questions by use of the funnel technique, business communicators should be ready to plan an interview. The following "blueprint" might be helpful in planning an interview:

2:00 P.M.	Greet the interviewee/small talk.
2:05 P.M.	Open the notebook; overview the topics to be covered (forecast/ preview); request to tape-record the interview; place the tape recorder, if permitted.
2:07 P.M.	First funnel (open questions, directed open questions, and closed questions). First funnel summary question.
2:17 P.M.	Second (and additional) funnel questions, with summary question(s).
2:27 P.M.	Final summary question. Close the notebook and remove the tape recorder (if used); rise and initiate leave-taking; express appreciation.
2:30 P.M.	Depart.
2:45 P.M.	Privately evaluate the interview.
Next day	Send thank-you note.

These are the basic components of the interview. Including a *time line* on your schedule of questions is recommended. If you know that your interview is at 10:00 A.M., you can plan to initiate the first funnel at 10:05, the second funnel at 10:15, and so on. Many factors may preclude adhering to a precise schedule, but having a guideline helps you cover what you wish to discuss in a limited period of time.

Adaptation is essential to conducting successful interviews. If the interviewee does not respond productively to one of the early open questions and you are anxious about the limited time you have for the interview, you need to adapt. One method is to skip some of the open questions. However, this can cause you to miss important information. You might try politely interrupting the interviewee:

> INTERVIEWER: Excuse me—I didn't ask a very clear question. Let me try again. What I meant to ask was . . .

This technique allows the interviewer to take the blame for the situation (even when he or she is not at fault). The question can be stated more directly and specifically, in order to elicit a specific response. Furthermore, the interviewer retains more control of the interview through this means.

The context can be managed positively. As discussed in Chapter 1, *context* is the environment which surrounds the communication situation. If you can obtain a conference room away from the interruptions of other personnel, telephones, and other distractions, you can maintain more control while conducting the interview.

You can arrange chairs and furniture to aid the interview. The distance between interviewer and the interviewee should be minimized; chairs of the same construction should be used (to promote equality and mutuality); and a small coffee-table-type piece of furniture can be placed between the two people.

SUMMARY

- The ten steps in planning an information-gathering interview are (1) write a clear purpose statement; (2) read appropriate background materials; (3) select sources that have information to give; (4) properly make the appointment; (5) develop questions for a moderately scheduled interview format; (6) make positive first impressions; (7) plan for recording the interview information; (8) consider pacing and other interview management skills; (9) close the interview; and (10) evaluate the success of the interview.

- A successful interview depends partly on questioning techniques. A moderately scheduled format is most desirable. Open and closed questions are basic to the funnel technique. Secondary questions (probes) include specialized types: hypothetical, confrontational, and reactive questions.

- Scheduled interviews follow a preplanned, specific agenda; nonscheduled interviews use questions composed at the time.

• Loaded and leading questions should be avoided in most interview situations. Such questions tend to suggest how they should be answered.

• A time line and "blueprint" help in preparing for an interview.

QUESTIONS FOR REVIEW AND DISCUSSION

1. Consider how many business communications are information-gathering situations. Give examples of such situations. What percentage of a business manager's job might be devoted to such activity?

2. Review in your mind the ten steps in the information-gathering process. What is involved in accomplishing each step?

3. What are the advantages of open questions? What are the disadvantages?

4. What are the advantages of closed questions? What are the disadvantages?

5. What are the three main types of questions, and how are they ordered for making a funnel?

6. What are the advantages of using a moderately scheduled set of questions in an informational interview?

7. Give three examples of specialized probes.

8. Give an example of a leading question that is not loaded.

ACTIVITIES

1. Watch a television interview program, such as "Donahue" or "Oprah Winfrey." Identify open and closed questions used during the program. How would you recast the questions to improve their clarity?

2. Go to your local courthouse and watch a courtroom trial. Note the use of probing questions by the lawyers. Identify examples of leading and loaded questions. Did the use of these techniques raise any ethical issues or damage the opposition's case?

3. Watch a television program, such as a "Barbara Walters Special" or "60 Minutes," and identify examples of hypothetical probes, confrontive probes, and reactive probes. What were the verbal and nonverbal reactions to these probes on the part of the interviewee?

Chapter 5

Interviews in the Business Setting

After reading and reviewing this chapter, you should be able to . . .

1. Discuss each of the ten steps in the employment process.

2. Develop a contemporary résumé.

3. Assess employment needs, write a job description, use probing questions to screen candidates for a position, and objectively assess candidates.

4. Follow affirmative action guidelines when selecting candidates.

5. Select an appropriate appraisal philosophy.

6. Determine which of the three basic appraisal approaches or combinations would be the most acceptable means of evaluating and/or motivating employees.

7. Apply the ten criteria for effective feedback to employees.

*B*ob Trent's first responsibility is the extremely important task of hiring good personnel to complete his sales team. Since some of the team will be new to Bob's sales unit at American Computer Systems, he will also need to prepare and conduct six-week and three-month performance appraisal interviews of these new employees. In addition, he will continue regular six-month appraisal interviews with existing employees.

Two of the most frequent reasons for interviews in business today are for screening or selecting job applicants and for appraising employees once they are hired. This chapter discusses the basic issues that relate to application for positions, the selection of candidates, and the motivation of employees through an appropriate appraisal process.

ASSESSMENT OF EMPLOYMENT NEEDS

Legal considerations regarding selection interviews may make business people reluctant to participate in the screening and hiring of personnel. Legal concerns aside, your recommendations regarding employee selection will put your professional reputation "on the line." Despite the deficiencies of the selection interview, it remains a central component of most organizational selection procedures (Avery and Champion, 1982, pp. 281–321).

Although screening and selection interviews are vital communication activities of business professionals, personnel selection remains an inexact science at best. People whose application materials appear to be "top notch" may interview poorly, and those who look mediocre on paper may interview well. Over time, managers necessarily refine their approach to selection, since they simply cannot afford to make poor choices. Good managers feel professionally and ethically obligated to conduct the best possible search for quality employees.

General Considerations

The first, and perhaps most important, step in the successful screening of candidates is the accurate assessment of employment needs. The nature of the climate (corporate culture) is one of the first considerations in determining the type of employee you need. For example, is the corporate culture "work hard/play hard" or is it "laid back"? Bob Trent decided that he would begin by reviewing the steps he might take if he were looking for a position with American. Since he realized that employers and potential employees need to understand each other, he thought this approach might help prepare him to interview candidates more sensitively and effectively.

Knowing that the employment interview is an extremely important 30 to 60 minutes for the potential employee, Bob wanted to understand how applicants think and how they decide which offer to accept. He wondered why so many people appear to take a cavalier attitude toward the entire employment process. Some people may believe that landing a job depends on luck, or that an agency (in business, industry, government, or education) "owes" them jobs because of the price they paid to secure their college degrees. A rude awakening comes when such applicants realize that a college graduate must compete with hundreds of other graduates each year for available positions.

Students often take elaborate measures in order to enhance their image in class, in courtship behavior, in order to make an athletic team, and so on. Why, then, are so many college students careless when they prepare for one of the most important presentations of their lives, that of selling their own skills and experiences? Just as many people spend years accumulating wealth but fail to spend a few hours preparing a will, many students spend 12 to 20 years in school engaged in exhaustive study, all with a hefty price tag, while neglecting to spend time learning how to market their skills and experiences in order to secure that important entry-level position.

STEPS IN THE EMPLOYMENT PROCESS

At least ten steps occur in the employment process. The actual interview is just one of a series of events that are shared by both parties. The employment process involves an ongoing series of *interdependent exchanges* between the interviewer and the interviewee. Let's look at a chronology of the employment interview process from the perspective of both parties.

The interview is only one important part of the total employment process. Recall that a *process* is a sequence of events that do not have easily recognizable beginning and ending phases. The total employment interviewing process consists of distinct, but interdependent, stages. In only one of these stages do the interviewer and interviewee engage in the mutual (face-to-face) exchange known as an interview. Obviously, impressions are formed by the communication that precedes the actual interview. For example, letters of application, phone inquiries, and calls to references contribute to the candidate's image. Furthermore, follow-up amenities, such as thank-you notes or phone calls of appreciation, along with the comments of additional references, can enhance or detract from the applicant's image.

Figure 5.1 shows the flow of events in the employment process. Success at each point is vital to success in the entire process.

Step 1: Assess Needs

Let us consider the first step in the process. *Assessing needs* demands that the employer carefully analyze the skills, relevant experiences, and desired conditions of employment. However, an applicant may have lost an opportu-

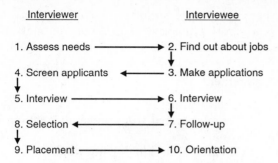

Figure 5.1 Ten steps in the employment process.

nity by waiting for employers to complete the first step. As a prospective applicant, you need to realize that waiting for an employer to finalize a job description before you apply lessens your chances of creating your ideal position. Many assertive employment seekers present themselves to decision makers *before* a job opening is announced. Applicants must first assess their skills, education, and pertinent experiences. Too often, applicants do not know themselves in relation to their interests, their skills, and their ability to convince employers that they will be useful to the organization. Such considerations are vital.

An employer's job description seldom matches your interests exactly. If there are great differences between the specifics of the employer's job description and what you are interested in doing, it is possible that the position is not for you. An alternative is to create a position for yourself.

If you have several genuine, accurately assessed *selling points*, and if you are familiar with the organizations that appeal to you, then try to *market yourself*. Begin by answering the following questions:

Self-analysis questions:

1. What am I trained to do?
2. What do I enjoy doing?
3. What do I do best?
4. What have I done to demonstrate my ability to do what I enjoy?

Questions about organizations:

1. What organizations would I like to join?
2. What would I like to do for them?
3. What do the organizations need?
4. Which of my skills could contribute to meeting their needs?
5. Who in the organization could best answer my questions and assess my strengths?
6. What do I need to know in order to present myself to the person I have identified?

After exploring these questions, summarize your answers. Perhaps the best way to do that is to develop positive "can do" statements of your abilities in relation to needs of the organization:

Sample "can do" statements:

1. I am a skillful communicator.
2. I am good at using computerized word processing equipment, including desktop publishing.
3. I am a highly motivated individual who works well with diverse people.
4. I can solve problems like those occurring within XYZ organization.

Applicants who realize that it is just as important for them to find the right position as it is for the organization to find the right person know how to ask appropriate questions prior to applying for a given position. Such an attitude of mutuality assures that both parties (employer and employee) will make the best decision.

How can a job seeker find answers to these questions and make a positive impression without having to apply for a specific job? This is a common question in interviewing classes. Some instructors send students to ask such questions of various organizational leaders. Prior to one of these information-gathering interviews, the student writes an ideal job description, a letter of application for the job described, a résumé targeted for the position, and a list of the basic questions an employer might ask a candidate interviewing for such a position. Then the student takes this material along to the interview. Comments on this activity have been extremely positive. Managers appreciate the opportunity to meet and evaluate potential candidates for positions without the pressure of an actual job interview. Candidates learn about the organizations firsthand, and the resulting interactions and written feedback help them to decide about their potential contribution. This model is useful for anyone who intends to seek employment.

Information-gathering interviews provide an invaluable means of learning to assess your strengths and skills. You can often avoid the frustration of taking a position that doesn't suit you if you learn about organizational expectations and corporate cultures in advance.

The opportunity to talk with responsible people in selected organizations will allow you to ask some important questions. The following are questions a sales applicant might ask Bob Trent:

1. How would you describe the corporate climate at American Computer Systems?
2. How do you view the growth pattern of your company?
3. How would you assess the financial future of your organization?
4. What opportunities are there for training and professional development within your organization?
5. Have there been layoffs in the past? If so, what were the basic reasons for them?

6. How would you describe the morale of the computer sales group at your organization?
7. What important qualities do you look for when hiring for the computer sales department?
8. Who are your main competitors?
9. From my research of your organization I understand your company makes products A, B, and C. Do you also make other products?
10. What suggestions would you make for someone interested in working for your organization?

Applicants can adapt these questions for use in other organizations. Appropriate thank-yous should be sent to the organizations' representatives when you inquire about job opportunities.

You should anticipate that as a job candidate, you will be asked certain questions. Though not all questions can be predicted, many questions can. And you can practice answers that you can adapt to the specific situation. You should be prepared to answer questions regarding your education, past employment, future plans, and personal interests. The following questions are typically asked in employment interviews:

Education:

1. Tell me about your educational background.
2. Why did you choose an organizational communication major?
3. Why did you elect a business marketing minor?
4. What courses did you like best? Least? Why?
5. What percentage of your college expenses did you earn? How?
6. What cocurricular activities were most rewarding? Why?
7. Do you believe that your education has prepared you for this type of work? How?
8. Do you think your grades represent your academic preparation for this position? Why or why not?
9. Is there anything else you would like to tell me about your educational background?

Past employment:

1. Tell me about your employment history.
2. Describe the positions you have held, including duties and responsibilities.
3. What were your greatest accomplishments?
4. What were your greatest limitations?
5. What responsibilities have you enjoyed the most?
6. Have you developed any special abilities? What are they?
7. What have you enjoyed most about previous work situations? Least?
8. What words would your supervisors use to describe your ability? What would they like you to do in order to improve?
9. Are there other things you would like to say about your work experience?

Future plans:

1. What can you tell me about your professional goals?
2. How will this position meet your professional goals?
3. What are your plans regarding continuing education?
4. What skills would you like to develop?
5. If you could design your ideal position, what would it be?
6. Do you prefer any particular geographic location? Where?
7. What are your financial expectations?
8. Why would you like this particular job?
9. What specific contributions do you think you could make to this position?
10. Are you looking for a permanent position or a temporary one?
11. What interests you about our products or services?
12. What do you know about our company?
13. What else would you like me to know about your professional plans?

Personal information:

1. Describe yourself as a person.
2. What kinds of things do you enjoy doing most? Least?
3. What kinds of people rub you the wrong way?
4. How much supervision is too much for you?
5. Do you enjoy routine work?
6. Do you handle pressure well?
7. What size city would you like to live in?
8. Are you willing to travel? How often?
9. Do you have any habits that irritate others?
10. What else would you like to tell me about yourself?

Once you have decided that an organization is attractive to you, prepare to *state your case.* "Writing your own ticket" is more than a cliché. You may be able to create your own position in a company if you are willing to state your case and support it effectively. The essence of the approach is, "I believe I would like to work with you. The research I've done concerning your company, coupled with what I have learned today, has convinced me. I believe I can contribute to your organization. While I'm here, let me tell you two reasons why I am confident that I can produce for you."

A created job is much more likely to motivate, challenge, and fulfill you, a pleasure not shared by 80 percent of American workers (Bolles, 1988, p. 118). The alternative to selling yourself is doing "their job," not necessarily "your job." Assuming that there is a reasonable match between what the employer needs and what you, as an employee, are capable of and interested in providing, both parties are winners. Before someone at the company starts writing a "help wanted" advertisement, you can be helping yourself.

Before announcing a job vacancy, the interviewer needs to develop a clear, concise job description. The following format is appropriate:

1. Name of company
2. General nature of products and services
3. Job title of position open
4. Major responsibilities of the position
5. Essential skills expected of employee
6. Essential experience expected
7. Special certification (if appropriate) expected/required
8. Education expected
9. Helpful experiences, skills, and/or training
10. Location/travel requirements
11. Working conditions
12. Salary range
13. Application procedure
    A. To whom
    B. By when (closing date for applications)
    C. What to include
       1. Salary history
       2. Portfolio of work samples (if appropriate)
       3. Letter of application
       4. Application form
       5. Reference letters and/or list of references

The items on this list provide a framework the interviewer can use to complete a job description and a position description. A complete job description that addresses the issues listed above provides an applicant with the information needed to decide whether the position is a close match with his or her abilities, preparation, and interests. The job description serves as a preliminary screening instrument. It should prevent needless applications and nonproductive interviews, a saving for both parties.

Step 2: Find Out About Jobs

Finding openings is a frequently misunderstood process. Conventional wisdom suggests relying on obvious sources, such as "help wanted" ads in a newspaper. Often, however, sending a letter of application and résumé to a blind box number is an exercise in futility. Some organizations use advertisements to attempt to satisfy affirmative action requirements for advertising positions or to determine market demand for the position in case of labor disputes during pending contract negotiations. Employment agencies may place such ads in order to gather new résumés or to compile a mailing list. Waiting for responses to applications for "nonpositions" can be quite defeating to even the most confident applicant. Jobs can, indeed, be found through newspaper want ads, reputable placement agencies, campus placement offices, trade journals, and so forth. However, in view of the low quality of many of these placements and the potential for wasting time, *there is no substitute for personal contact.*

Personal contact is the most productive way to find out about good positions. It takes dedication and planning to create or find the right position with the right organization. If you expect to work 40 hours a week on the job, then looking for work should be more than a pastime. A good plan would include researching organizations, discovering their strengths, and finding out how you might be able to make a contribution. It is also necessary to identify which managers in the organization have the authority to make a hiring decision. If you know what region of the country you want to work in and what organizations you would like to work for, you are ready to make plans for personal contact.

An interview is one means of making personal contact. It is usually easier to set up an information-gathering interview (as discussed in Chapter 4) than to secure a job interview when there is no announced opening. One avenue is to call the manager with a request for 20 minutes of his or her time to gain a perspective about the company. Assuming that you are genuinely seeking additional information and the manager is willing to provide the time, personal contact has been initiated in an ethical way.

After you indicate that you know a little about the history of the organization and the basic products or services offered, you can ask some specific questions.

1. What can you tell me about the working environment within your organization?
2. What business opportunities do you see for this organization in the future?
3. What are the things you enjoy most about working in this organization? Least?
4. What are your observations regarding the turnover of staff in your organization?
5. What skills and personal qualifications do you look for in applicants for your organization?
6. How do you further your employees' education and training?
7. What recommendations would you have for a person who would like to work for your organization?
8. What do you see as the biggest challenges ahead for your organization?
9. How open is the communication in your organization?
10. How would you describe the management style in your organization?

Questions such as these can be expanded through probes, as time permits. Caution: Do not exceed your time limit! Through the information-gathering interview you can gain much information while making a positive impression. Analysis of this data can help you decide which organizations offer the most opportunities that best match your interests, skills, and training.

Step 3: Make Applications

It is important to complete the application process carefully. Think of every step in the official application process as a sample of your work. Recognize that résumés and letters of application work best after personal contact has been established. The résumé and letter of application function as "calling cards"—items left for examination, in support of the personal image created.

Each potential position deserves a résumé and letter *targeted specifically* for the particular opening. General résumés simply do not work well for an applicant when compared to a targeted letter-quality résumé. Even the attractively printed general résumé does not provide the applicant the edge given by a résumé and letter of application that are adapted to the position. Moreover, new information cannot be updated conveniently on printed résumés. A word processor with a letter-quality or laser printer is an attractive alternative to the time-consuming typewriter. These work savers greatly simplify editing and rearranging blocks of information, and a professional look can be obtained.

The résumé shown in Figure 5.2 is strategic in that a career objective is stated and the body of the résumé gives evidence of the ability of the individual to accomplish the objective. The résumé begins with what the candidate has to offer (skills and abilities) and then describes the general nature of the type of position the candidate seeks. The career objective can be adapted to and focused for particular positions. In some situations, it might be better to place the work experience section ahead of the educational background. Since résumés are skimmed as often as read, having the strongest support for a particular position at the top of the résumé is an advantage.

Chronological résumés, which list dates for each professional development, are more suitable for personal promotional purposes—helping people write an introduction for a speaker, promoting a seminar leader, and so on. *Functional résumés,* which list qualifications, often in paragraph form, under various components of a job, normally are used for high-level managerial jobs.

Letters of application should be targeted carefully. A five-paragraph format is recommended. The first paragraph should indicate three important points: (1) the exact position for which you are applying, (2) what motivated you to write, and (3) a "hooker" (a reason to read on). Since a given organization may have multiple openings at a given time, you should state the exact position title in the first paragraph:

> Promotions Director Carmen Millan recommended that I apply for the position of Marketing Manager. Because of my five years' experience in marketing with a Fortune 500 company and my educational specialization, I believe I would be qualified for the position.

The first sentence clearly creates credibility, assuming that Carmen Millan is known and respected in the organization, and identifies the specific position.

John Doe
123 First Street
Anywhere, ST 12345
(000) 000-0000

CAREER OBJECTIVE: To use my skills in sales, communication, computer science, and computer-aided drafting in a position that would make a contribution to an organization and would have a potential for challenge and growth.

EDUCATIONAL BACKGROUND: Bachelor of Science of Power Technology, May 1992, Any College or University; courses emphasizing communication, computer science, and computer-aided drafting.

WORK EXPERIENCE: Maintenance Supervisor, Kentucky Fried Chicken, City, State, 1988 to present; responsible for a wide range of repairs, often while production is in process.

Laboratory Assistant for Power Technology Class at Any College or University, Fall 1988; hydraulics and pneumatics; developed a pneumatic logic control for a robot trainer.

Cook, Kentucky Fried Chicken, City, State, 1984 to present; responsible for production in a timely manner, customer contact, and the training of several employees.

ACTIVITIES/HONORS: Department Award, Power Technology Department, Outstanding Student, 1990; Dean's Honor List; 3.55 overall grade point average.

Member of Society of Automotive Engineers.

Elected President for Any County, State, student chapter of Vocational Industrial Clubs of America.

Youth Counselor, responsible for directing youth camps, communicating with parents, and working with other counselors.

PERSONAL: Willing to relocate; interested in music and in community work with youth; composer, singer, piano and keyboard player.

References available upon request; written references available upon request from Any College or University Career Planning and Placement Center, City, State, ZIP Code.

Figure 5.2 A strategic résumé.

It also explains the applicant's motivation. The second sentence functions as a "hooker"—a reason to continue to read the letter.

The second paragraph should present a brief overview of the applicant's qualifications:

> I expect to complete my M.B.A. degree in May. The enclosed résumé details my experience in promotions, marketing, and marketing management.

The third paragraph should introduce the most relevant targeted information to be detailed in the enclosed résumé:

> I was directly responsible for planning, implementation, and evaluation of the marketing promotion of product X. Completion of this assignment resulted in my being named the top production manager of the year. In my M.B.A. program, I have emphasized computer-aided marketing techniques, and I have adapted software programs for corporate telemarketing. Further, I have been given the responsibility of training interns and entry-level promotions personnel.

In this paragraph the applicant highlights experience in production, accomplishments, and human relations skills.

In the fourth paragraph, the applicant should indicate willingness to provide additional information and references and should state the desire for an interview:

> References and additional information will be provided upon request. I will call you early next week to arrange an interview at a mutually convenient time. I will check with you regarding the completeness of my application at that time.

Taking the initiative to telephone shows that the applicant is motivated and energetic. Also, the term *mutually convenient* indicates that the applicant values personal time as well as the interviewer's time.

The final paragraph should be a simple "thank you." This can be embellished by saying

> Thank you for your consideration of my application.

In a society where appreciation is expressed so rarely, surely no harm will come from basic courtesy.

If typed, the letter of application should be on bond paper, using clean, dark ribbon. If you enclose a résumé, type "Enclosure: résumé" at the bottom. This single-page letter should be in block or modified block style, carefully proofread, and styled for eye appeal.

Avoid dishonesty: do not "pad" your credentials in the résumé or letter of application. This stricture applies to all deception or misappropriation, from taking office supplies home (which is, after all, stealing) to using company letterhead in applying for another job. This is also ill-advised because it is a warning sign to the new employer.

A letter of application is shown in Figure 5.3.

Whenever possible in the application process, initiate personal contact before sending letters of application and résumés. Sending résumés and letters

Date

Mr. Joseph A. Bigg, Division Manager
Major Computer Products Division
Anycompany U.S.A., Inc.
1990 Future Drive
Wonderful, State 54321

Dear Mr. Bigg:

It was a pleasure to meet with you last month at your corporate
headquarters. After considerable research of major companies and
upon the recommendation of your computer sales department manager,
Ms. Roberta Yuppie, I wish to apply for the position of sales
associate. I am anxious to utilize my communication and human
relations skills at Anycompany U.S.A., Inc.

As you can see from my enclosed résumé, I will graduate from Any
College in May of this year with a degree in Communication and
Marketing. My cocurricular activities, part-time work experience,
and internship have given me experience in sales and computer
applications.

My internship experience with Blitz Computer gave me the opportunity
to work in a sales division and to have direct responsibility for
an inventory of over $750,000. While at Any College I was honored
by being named the Outstanding Communication Major and was
responsible for the budgeting and financial management of the
Speech Communication Society. I feel confident that my references
will confirm that I possess human relations and problem-solving
skills.

Further information is available upon request. I will call you next
week to check on the completeness of my application and to discuss
a date for an interview at a mutually convenient time. I look
forward to the opportunity to discuss the position with you.

Thank you for your consideration of my application.

Sincerely,

Jane Aspirant
Box 56789
Any College or University
City, ST 12345
(000) 000-0000

Enclosure: résumé

Figure 5.3 A letter of application.

of application and then waiting for the telephone to ring can be difficult at best. Prior personal contact can lessen the frustration. Also, remember that the résumé, any application forms, and the letter of application should represent your best work.

Step 4: Screen Applicants

Screening applicants is time-consuming. Unfortunately, some people take shortcuts. Skimming application materials too often takes the place of careful analysis. Few people take the time for preinterview calls to references. Interviewers should ask the applicant's references for names of additional references. Often a different story emerges when employers check references other than those furnished by the applicant. Managers should recognize that a hiring decision affects the company's costs and profits more than a major equipment purchase. It makes sense to scrutinize references.

Candidates may mistakenly view the screening period as a time to relax and wait for an interview call. The interview appointment may never materialize. Use this time instead to contact the potential employer and check on the status of your application. The ostensible reason for phoning can be to check whether your file is complete and to inquire whether the company needs more information. This call serves an additional purpose by bringing your name to the attention of the person who checks the file for completeness. This procedure is an important part of creating a positive image. You need to use courtesy and good taste on the phone. Furthermore, sending a letter, or arranging for an additional letter of recommendation to arrive during the screening process, is a good plan for one who wants to compete successfully in the job market.

Step 5: Interviewer's Considerations in the Interview

Interviewers, such as Bob Trent, face the serious responsibility of assuring that affirmative action and legal considerations are followed and that the best available applicants are selected. Managers who do not know or follow the law regarding employment practices risk significant fines and embarrassment for themselves and their organization. Furthermore, questions not based directly upon the specifics of a given position will not produce the best candidate for the position.

Some question whether interviews validly and reliably reveal the best candidates. Indeed, one study indicates that a typical interview has both low reliability and low accuracy in predicting future performance on the job (Karren and Nkomo, 1988, p. 88.) Job simulations and work sample tests may be viable alternatives to interviews in some cases. Other alternatives include reference checking, assessment center testing, and aptitude testing. The cost of adding these methods to the interview must be measured in time as well as money. Almost all Fortune 500 companies and most other organizations use interviews; that method remains the norm for selecting employees.

Managers sometimes fail to realize that the quality of the person conducting the interview is a significant factor in determining whether a well-qualified applicant will accept an offer. To the candidates, *the interviewer is the company,* and a bad impression of the interviewer means a bad impression of the organization. Even if Bob chooses not to hire an applicant, he wants all interviewees to be impressed positively with his company.

An effective interviewer must control the situation. This means proper preparation. Applicants have several complaints regarding interviewers. Many screening interviewers (1) do not have enough information about the job to answer questions, (2) fail to demonstrate that they are good listeners, (3) appear rushed, (4) fail to probe for any depth of understanding of the applicant's skills and experiences, (5) have biases, and (6) often interview when they appear fatigued (Downs et al., p. 137). Interviewers should accept the responsibility of knowing what the conditions of employment are. Even screening interviewers should be able to discuss job-related concerns: skills needed, responsibilities in handling customers, equipment operation, record keeping, the personalities in the work group, and so on. The interviewer who cannot answer such questions ethically is not prepared to conduct interviews.

Successful recruitment begins with a careful investigation of the skills needed for the position. Even if the position is not new, the employer must know what combination of training, personality, and skills would be ideal in the replacement employee. Again, should personnel employees be responsible for screening applicants and conducting screening interviews, they must know exactly what the priorities are for the position and how to respond to pertinent questions from applicants.

Managers need to have specific goals in mind when they approach candidate selection. For example, certain themes can be identified and prioritized:

1. *Mission.* Is there any indication that the candidate has an understanding of the goals of the organization and an orientation to accomplish them?
2. *Focus.* Do the candidate's goals appear to be in line with those of the organization?
3. *Performance orientation.* Does the candidate appear to be interested in the challenge of accomplishment?
4. *Pride.* Does the candidate show pride in self and the organization?
5. *Growth orientation.* Does the candidate have an interest in the future of the organization and an opportunity to grow in skills and contributions?
6. *Critical thinking.* Does the candidate have the ability to analyze and solve problems?
7. *Responsibility.* Does the candidate show interest in taking a leadership role and "ownership" of problems?
8. *Assertiveness.* Does the candidate speak up, ask questions, and present ideas in a constructive manner?
9. *Mastery.* Does the candidate show a willingness to work to become skilled at all phases of the job?

10. *Versatility.* Does the candidate have multiple abilities and a willingness to try new things to make contributions to the organization?
11. *Stamina.* Does the candidate demonstrate willingness to work the hours needed and any overtime that may be necessary to get projects completed?
12. *Relational skills.* Does the candidate demonstrate strong interpersonal skills, an ability to work with other employees and clients, and the capacity to handle direction well?
13. *Leadership ability.* Does the candidate know how to motivate and recognize the contributions of others?
14. *Customer relations skill.* Does the candidate recognize the need to be of service, have respect for others, and possess a measure of charisma?
15. *Social skills.* Does the candidate show interest in being around others, and would others enjoy working with him or her in completing projects?
16. *Organizing ability.* Does the candidate recognize that employees must be able to organize their approach to a task and coordinate their activities with others for the good of the organization?
17. *Ethics.* Does the candidate recognize and show concern for the image of the company? (Company officials have come to realize that the employees they hire *are* the organization.)
18. *Compatibility.* Does the candidate's personality fit well with other important "players" in the organization? (Adapted from Lunn, 1987, p. 45)

Bob Trent must understand the importance of such issues if he wants to achieve success in the screening process.

Past studies indicate that an employer's attitudes toward speech are important predictors of hiring decisions. In particular, observations of speech are used to judge competence and personality. Some employers listen to speech patterns to determine candidate acceptability. A candidate may present evidence of a university education and then contradict the impression of being well educated with careless speech (Hopper, 1977, p. 350).

Some interviewers or search committees develop weighted checklists to use in evaluating interviewees. For example, when ranking candidates for a teaching position, a committee might use a system like the following to evaluate applicants:

Bachelor's degree completed	10 points possible _____
Master's degree in progress or completed	5 points possible _____
Area of study matched to organizational needs	10 points possible _____
Flexibility in assignment	8 points possible _____
Ability to conduct research	8 points possible _____

A system like this should be agreed upon by all the people on the search committee.

Structuring the Interview Questions   The funnel format discussed in Chapter 4 will serve the interviewer well when constructing questions. Recall that funnels move from open questions to closed questions while focusing on a single topic area. The funnel patterns Bob Trent set up were (1) work history, (2) educational and training background, and (3) personal information relevant to the position in question. He divided personal information into such areas as current activities, self-assessment, goals, expectations, basic values, leadership potential, and orientation to people.

Bob reviewed the following generic interview plan and schedule of questions for an entry-level employment interview. He then adapted a plan for the needs of the specific position he wants to fill:

I. Amenities.

- Greeting to applicant.
- Seating applicant and small talk.
- Overview of procedures for the interview.

II. Work experience.

- Beginning with your present position, please tell me about the types of positions you have held.
- Why did you leave each position?
- Describe the relationships you have had with your supervisors.
- What did you like the most in these positions? Least?
- What accomplishments were attributable to your leadership?
- What were the most difficult challenges you faced?
- How did you go about resolving them?
- How do you feel about routine work? Overtime work?
- What professional goals have you been unable to achieve?

III. Education and relevant training.

- Why did you choose your college major?
- What went into the decision to choose the university you selected?
- What courses challenged you the most? Least?
- How does your grade point average represent the effort you put into college?
- What future plans do you have for continuing your education?
- Which were your favorite subjects? Least favorite? Why?
- In what cocurricular activities did you participate?
- What training opportunities have you experienced?
- Who influenced you most during your college years? Why?

IV. Personal information.

- How do you feel about what you have accomplished?
- What do you consider your personal strengths?
- What do you consider your weaknesses?

- Please describe your ideal supervisor.
- How would you describe your ideal level of independence?
- How would you describe your ideal position?
- What motivates you?
- What is your idea of an ideal community?
- How important are good community relations?
- Where would you like to be five to ten years from now?
- What two or three qualities about yourself do you like the most? Why?
- What two or three qualities about yourself do you like the least? Why?
- Do you prefer, on the whole, to work alone or with a team?

   V. Ask summary question: Is there anything else that you would like to tell me about your abilities?

   VI. Allow time for interviewee's questions by asking: What questions do you have for us?

   VII. Indicate what will happen next.

   VIII. Leave-taking and small talk.

While it is not necessary to follow this particular list of questions (or the list of questions for applicants to use in preparation, presented earlier in the chapter), it is important that some schedule of position-relevant questions be planned prior to the interview. Use these questions as a guide for the kinds of information you may wish to solicit.

Providing the Proper Environment   As managers, you will have a responsibility to provide the proper atmosphere for a job interview. Try to keep the environment free of distractions. Do not permit telephone calls or employee interruptions to interfere with an interview.

Provide a seating arrangement that gives equal status to the applicant. Make sure that the room has a comfortable climate: check for comfort and attractiveness, seeking to establish an informal and pleasant setting for all. A small coffee table between the interviewer and interviewee is better than a large desk. Fortunately for Bob Trent, his company provided a room designed for interviewing. All he had to do was reserve the room and ensure that the temperature was comfortable for the taste of his interviewing staff.

Legal Considerations   Some kinds of questions should not be asked in an employment interview. Such questions can have severe legal consequences for the person (organization) asking them. The law now extends beyond the job interview to encompass all conditions of employment, including promotion. The law is intended to prevent discrimination against members of racial minorities, women, ethnic groups, older workers, and so on.

Each state has other laws in addition to the federal employment statutes. Employers must know and adhere to specific regulations. More important, asking good questions helps to ensure fairness and lack of bias in hiring. Each question should relate directly to the job description of the position.

Prohibited questions may include the following:

Don't ask:

Have you ever been arrested?

Rationale:

Minorities often answer this question affirmatively. This may reflect racism or law enforcement bias rather than a higher rate of legal problems. Asking whether the candidate has a record of any convictions may be legal, especially if the position requires bonding.

Don't ask:

When were you born?

Rationale:

Answers to this question may lead to age discrimination. Such information may be obtained after employment, if needed.

Don't ask:

How many children do you plan to have?

What will your husband say if you accept a position such as this?

Rationale:

Questions of this type are not job-related. They are sexually biased.

Don't ask:

Do you own an automobile?

Rationale:

Owning an automobile rarely, if ever, is a job-related question. In some cases, *access* to acceptable transportation could be important and related.

All questions should be related to the specific job description and organizational goals.

Candidates who are asked such questions are advised to say, "I'm not sure how that question directly relates to my ability to do this job, but let me say this . . . " This language indicates that the interviewer is exceeding legal limits, in the candidate's perception, and that the candidate knows his or her rights.

Most organizations have an affirmative action officer and have filed affirmative action plans with the Equal Employment Opportunity Commission (EEOC). Each interviewer should understand the organizational procedures used to ensure protection of the rights of all. Clear documentation is the key to avoiding problems regarding hiring decisions. Documentation includes all applications filed for the position, the procedure for screening applicants, and the rationale for selecting the particular candidate.

Checking References   Do not "shortcut" the process of checking references. Too few are checked more often than too many. Each applicant should be asked to provide references that can be contacted in advance of any interview invitation.

Tell each reference the purpose of your call, that his or her name has been given by the candidate as a resource, and that a frank evaluation will be appreciated. Sketch the general nature of the position and the skills sought. Ask the reference to comment on the strengths and weaknesses of the candidate. Verify that items on the résumé are accurate.

Experience teaches that telephone conversations are more frank than written references. Some people are hesitant to be critical of others in writing. You can often get the name of another person who knows the applicant well but was not listed as a reference. That person might have a story to tell that the applicant would rather you not hear. Ethics and courtesy suggest that candidates be asked whether you may contact other people. The applicant may not wish the current employer to know about the job interview. The candidate should be given a chance to respond to any negative information obtained from secondary sources. Furthermore, confidences should be kept. Again, you cannot be too careful when checking references. From contact with the applicant's references and knowledge of the position, you can design specific, relevant questions for the interview. Always try to get a balanced and accurate perspective of the candidate and position prior to issuing an invitation to an interview.

Step 6: Applicant's Role in the Interview

Assume that an applicant is selected for the interview and a date and time are set. Both the applicant to be interviewed and the organization's representatives who will participate in the interviewing process should prepare carefully. Both parties should participate in mock interviews to sharpen their skills.

Interviewers tend to look for specific behaviors and facts in interviews. Failure to provide satisfactory responses may be a "red flag" or "knockout factor." Candidates would do well to observe their communication behaviors on videotape prior to an interview. Researchers conclude that *enthusiasm* and *oral communication ability* are the most important characteristics for an applicant to exhibit. Other important factors include leadership potential, self-confidence, assertiveness, initiative, emotional stability, writing skills, scholastic record, pleasant personality, and personal appearance (Downs, Smeyak, and Martin, 1980, p. 118).

Once selected for an interview, the candidate should practice for it (preferably on videotape), checking carefully for enthusiasm (positive personality projection); good communication skills, including nonverbal awareness (proper dress, posture, vocal stress, handshake, etc.); and listening skills. Honesty and directness are as important as content to most interviewers.

Step 7: Follow-up

After the interview, the applicant should remain an active part of the process. As part of the too often neglected follow-up period, the applicant should make a list of all people contacted, including secretaries, and should send each one a brief personal note on tasteful stationery. The follow-up period also is a good time for an additional letter of reference to cross the desk of the potential employer. Again, this helps keep the applicant's name in front of the interviewers. Consider the credibility of the reference and your knowledge of the corporate climate, as well as other factors, to decide whether additional written and/or oral statements would be helpful.

Step 8: Selection

While the interviewer reviews notes from the various interviews conducted for the position, the applicant should remain active. Even though the applicant really wants the position, an offer may not materialize. An effective job seeker never puts all eggs in one basket but continuously researches other possibilities. Remember, there may be scores of talented people looking for positions. Furthermore, an experienced person within the organization may have applied for the position. So, keep on actively seeking other positions.

Applicants should consider a number of factors before accepting an employment offer. Among these are the company environment (corporate culture), the company's financial soundness, the company's profit margin, the equipment and working environment, and the work itself. Is the work meaningful and challenging? Is it clear that the applicant can make a contribution? Applicants also should consider the future. Are there opportunities for challenge and growth? Will training programs be available? These and many other questions should be considered before deciding to accept an offer of employment.

Step 9: Placement

Assume that you are selected for a position you want. Contrary to popular belief, the process is not finished. Once you are hired, you can begin the process of advancing in the organization. New employees are seldom content to remain in an entry-level position; impressing the new employer by demonstrating a desire for effective orientation represents a first step toward possible advancement.

Ask the manager of your unit what you can do to get off to a good start. Inquire about training programs or regular meetings you might attend for a preemployment orientation. Such questions indicate that you are a person who cares. Meeting people at work to begin the process of networking (perhaps even identifying a potential mentor) can give you a distinct advantage over other new employees. Of course, you have to be careful not to appear overly aggressive.

Step 10: Orientation

Orientation refers to the process of learning your new job responsibilities and how to complete them successfully. Getting acclimated often depends on your own initiative. Ask questions: "Who has the information that I need to complete these tasks? Who can help in providing resources?" The people identified in answer to such questions become a part of your *network*, people who help you to meet the demands of the task before you. During orientation, you may discover an "older and wiser" individual who can help guide your career within the organization. This person can function as a *mentor.* Networking and finding mentors often help people become vertically mobile in an organization.

PERFORMANCE ASSESSMENT AND ENHANCEMENT

Once managers such as Bob Trent have selected the best candidates available, they face an additional responsibility—assessing and enhancing employee performance. Performance assessment and job enrichment are major responsibilities of managers in business organizations.

Once an employee is hired, oriented thoroughly, and beyond probationary status, the employer should provide feedback, evaluation, and further motivation. Infante and Gorden (1987) argue that encouraging independence runs "counter to most theories of administrative science and practice: hierarchy, bureaucratic chain of command, control systems, rules, and policies are designed for compliance rather than dispute" (p. 79). However, it is important that systems of management encourage such openness. The appraisal interview is one opportunity to encourage accurate feedback.

The managerial appraisal process has been called the Achilles' heel of management development, but it remains key. Koontz (1971) contends that if an organization, company, or business is to reach its goals effectively, "ways of accurately measuring management performance must be found and implemented" (p. 2).

Since the 1970s, the process of providing some form of appraisal to employees has become almost universal (Downs et al., 1980, p. 161). Former students indicate that the most difficult tasks they face are appraising subordinates and receiving feedback regarding their own performance. Interviewing classes often attempt to prepare students in these two areas.

The Appraisal Process

Appraisals typically include an analysis of employee performance and an interview (feedback session) in which the evaluation is communicated to the employee. Traditionally, the process culminates in a written report, which the employee reads and initials. This report remains in the employee's file.

Unfortunately, this process sometimes leads to "rope jumping": employees behave one way during the evaluation process and then revert to other behaviors after the appraisal sessions. Often managers behave similarly. Relieved that the annual process is completed, they go back to their usual activities. The process puts new data in the files for the record, but there is little change in behavior. Such systems become "games" that do little for morale or performance.

Approaches to Communicating Appraisal Assessment

Constructing an appraisal system requires value judgments. First, consider the goals that the system must meet. Among acceptable goals are the following:

To compliment the employee for good work

To indicate just how the employee stands in the eyes of the immediate supervisor

To indicate how the employee can improve chances for advancement

To set goals and time intervals for future appraisal

To motivate the employee

To find out what the employee is thinking about her or his work

To give the employee a sense of participation in the job

To get negative feelings out in the open in order to "clear the slate"

To indicate what must be done differently in order to prevent negative consequences—termination, demotion, loss of merit pay, and so on

To provide a written record as to what was communicated and when

Managers often neglect to develop goals for their appraisal systems. They fail to ask what they ultimately hope to accomplish. They do not consider whether the primary purpose is feedback or merely an annual evaluation. Actually, a combination of these goals is desirable. An effective ongoing system might couple positive feedback with evaluation and coaching at appropriate intervals (not longer than six months).

Managers also should decide upon methods to meet their goals. One approach is to identify the particular qualities, traits, or behaviors necessary for effective performance and then to appraise the employee relative to that profile. This is called the *rating method.* Another popular approach is to quantify objectives or goals and then to assess the employee's performance in regard to these mutually established objectives. This process, which renders a judgment that the employee either exceeds, meets, or fails to meet the objectives, is often called *management by objectives,* or MBO (Haynes, 1978). MBO is the most widely used model (Stewart and Cash, 1988). This approach can succeed when relevant behaviors can be quantified. One objective statement might be, "In the next six months, absenteeism on the assembly line will be cut 5 percent." At the end of six months the records can be analyzed and the performance standard assessed.

A combination of the rating method and MBO may work best. Managers must decide what standards to use when judging employees. Should the standards be individual, group-based, objective, or rational? Perhaps a clear job description will serve as a standard from which to develop ratings and objectives.

Managers also must decide who should be included in the appraisal process. In addition to the employee's immediate supervisor, peers, second-line supervisors, subordinates, and the employee may contribute to the process. You may agree that the design of the system should include peers and the immediate supervisor, but you might believe that subordinates and peers should be involved only in special circumstances when other reasonable means are not available (McEvoy, Buller, and Roghaar, 1988). Personnel committees composed of peers (peer evaluation) may be the best means of providing objective information on performance. The employee's privacy must be guarded carefully. *Field review* provides an alternative to peer review. It involves inviting an expert to appraise the employees as they work. The reviewer should be competent and objective. This process can be effective but is often expensive.

When sharing an appraisal with an employee, the manager should consider three approaches: the "tell-and-sell" method, the "tell-and-listen" method, and the problem-solving method (Maier, 1976).

The *tell-and-sell method* is often used, but it may not satisfy employee needs. In this process, an extended introduction covers a rationale for the forthcoming written evaluation; the written evaluation is presented; and, frequently, conflict ensues between the employee and the supervisor. The supervisor usually fails to listen to the feelings and concerns of the employee but attempts to defend the evaluation. Unfortunately, this process is characterized by too much emphasis on evaluation. Managers who approach the process with the best of intentions often get drawn into conflict. The interviewer usually talks a great deal during a tell-and-sell evaluation. Considerable training and practice are necessary for success.

The *tell-and-listen method* assumes that feelings are as important as facts. The manager believes that people will improve if the appraiser cares and understands. This approach relies more on intrinsic (internal) rewards than on extrinsic (monetary) rewards. Further, the interviewer remains open to influence, and the employee's responses are taken into consideration.

The manager who uses the tell-and-listen method spends most of the meeting time listening. As in the tell-and-sell approach, the manager presents a written evaluation, but in this case the manager encourages the interviewee to verbalize reactions.

The *problem-solving* appraisal interview often becomes a discussion of what can be done to improve job performance and working conditions. An objection to the problem-solving approach is that the goals of evaluation—informing the employee where he or she stands—may get neglected or lost.

Combining the tell-and-listen and problem-solving approaches may produce the best results. The manager begins by comparing the employee's self-appraisal and the supervisor's appraisal of that employee. The supervisor then listens to the interviewee's discussion of feelings regarding any differences between the appraisals; answers questions; negotiates, where possible; and turns the situation into a problem-solving activity. In this atmosphere, goals and intervals for future evaluations should be set (Maier, 1976). This plan has a good chance for success.

TEN SUGGESTIONS FOR EFFECTIVE SUPERVISOR FEEDBACK

The appraisal interview is not the only setting for feedback. In fact, good supervisors use feedback regularly. Bob Trent realized that one of the most important interpersonal skills he can develop is giving effective feedback. He summarized his thinking about employee appraisals in ten steps:

1. *Effective feedback is specific rather than general.* Managers may make sweeping and general statements, such as "You are really doing a good job" or "You folks need to shape up here." Both of these statements are relatively ineffective communication tools. Skilled managers will give specifics instead of easily discounted generalities. An alternative is "Julie, that model sales presentation was terrific! I especially liked the two visuals you showed that compared our product with the competition. They were really effective." Here you see that the manager has recognized Julie individually for specific strengths. Julie will find this more believable than a general praise statement.

2. *Effective feedback is initially given face-to-face.* At times, it is necessary to produce written information for records. Generally, feedback should be given in a personal manner first. Face-to-face feedback is crucial for negative information, which managers give in a private setting.

3. *Effective feedback is presented in a straightforward manner.* In discussing defensive and supportive climates, we noted that it is best to "lay information on the table." Managers should avoid using negative or positive feedback simply as a manipulative device. The

feedback should be genuine and should be communicated in a caring, personal way.

4. *Effective feedback is always well timed.* Good timing includes a consideration of when negative emotions are under control and when it is possible to find a private location to give the feedback. If feedback is to serve as a deserved recognition, it can be given in front of others. Good managers know that effective feedback is usually immediate but, more importantly, is always well timed.

5. *Effective feedback, when negative, relates to behavior rather than to the value of the person.* Disciplinary communication, for example, should be given in a manner that reflects the innate value of the person while directly indicating that certain behaviors are not acceptable. Parents often make the mistake of criticizing children whose behavior is not up to par. Managers do the same injustice when they imply that an employee is a problem person. Behavior may be a problem, but the person still has value, and that innate human value should be affirmed.

6. *Effective feedback is interactive.* Listening is an important part of effective feedback. Members of an organization should be encouraged and given every opportunity to respond to any feedback. Managers should provide an opportunity for people receiving feedback to clarify and respond to what has been said. In fact, in giving effective feedback, the manager usually spends more time listening than speaking.

7. *Effective feedback combines nonverbal and verbal communication in a complementary way.* All too often, positive things are said verbally but discounted by unintended nonverbal cues. Vocal tone, for example, can betray otherwise good intentions. Listening to yourself on a tape recorder or videotape can provide some feedback about your manner and style of communication, if you are capable of processing the feedback objectively and are able to identify inconsistencies between your verbal and nonverbal behaviors.

8. *Effective feedback is proportionate.* Organizational communicators should not be guilty of overkill—saying too much when a few clear, concise statements would suffice. Often, inexperienced communicators attempt to cover insecurities with a verbal onslaught. Managers should learn to apply an "80/20 rule"—spend 80 percent of the time on the 20 percent of concerns that will do the most good. Do not give an employee a "kitchen sink" full when a "coffee cup" amount would do nicely. However, the supervisor must provide enough information to enable the listener to grasp what is being said. Providing sketchy information may cause the employee to push the speaker to a deeper level of disclosure than is appropriate. Further, the employee may imagine that the manager has even more hurtful information held in reserve. Interpersonal feedback in

an organization should be focused on the most important issues and at the appropriate depth.

9. *Effective feedback is offered with appropriate intensity.* Anything that diverts attention from the message can easily distract a listener from accurate processing of information. An intense speaker who blows issues out of proportion will cause the receiver to focus on the medium rather than the message. At the same time, it is possible to be too "laid back" and appear uncaring. The sense that the supervisor seems to have no feeling or emotion about what is said will not add credence to the feedback that is offered. Feedback should be given in a personal, caring way.

10. *Effective feedback is not coercive.* Feedback should not contain an implied threat that the other must change. Effective feedback is descriptive and informative rather than threatening or manipulative. You communicate that you care and that you care enough to give information that others can use to monitor their behavior. You are not trying to impose behavioral change. Imposed change may be resented. Clear information, when presented in a caring way, is generally appreciated.

These suggestions for effective feedback should be helpful to personnel at all levels in an organization. Promptly and properly given, constructive feedback can significantly affect productivity, climate, and morale.

SUMMARY

- There are ten steps in the employment process: (1) assessing needs, (2) finding out about jobs, (3) making applications, (4) screening applicants, (5) and (6) interviewing, (7) following up, (8) selection, (9) placement, and (10) orientation. These steps involve both the interviewer and the interviewee.

- Two of the most frequent settings for personnel-related interviews are the screening or selection interviews utilized in hiring decisions and the employee appraisal interview. Both of these types of interviews take considerable time and are critical to success.

- Although the selection of personnel is an inexact science, there are some proven guidelines for interviewers: (1) assessment of employment needs, (2) a thorough understanding of the job description and job expectations, (3) manifestation of good listening skills, (4) an unhurried atmosphere, (5) exercise of effective probing questions, (6) objectivity, and (7) appearing alert and interested.

- The interviewer must (1) be well prepared with a carefully developed schedule of questions; (2) be knowledgeable about the training, skills, and personality desired in candidates for the position; (3) have clear criteria for selecting a candidate; and (4) understand the legal considerations affecting employee hires. A comfortable, attractive environment for the interview should be provided in a nonthreatening setting. Candidates' references should be checked carefully.

- Central to the performance appraisal is the opportunity for employee and supervisor to provide mutual feedback. The appraisal philosophy may include recognition of work well done, goal setting, and motivation for the future, as well as the evaluation of performance during the appraisal period. Three basic appraisal approaches are (1) tell-and-sell, (2) tell-and-listen, and (3) problem-solving. In most situations the tell-and-listen and problem-solving approaches are superior to tell and sell.

- Effective supervisor feedback (1) is specific rather than general; (2) is given face-to-face; (3) is straightforward; (4) is well timed; (5) relates to behavior rather than the value of the person; (6) is interactive; (7) combines nonverbal and verbal communication; (8) is proportional to the need for employee improvement, and considers the employee's self-esteem; (9) is expressed with the proper intensity; and (10) is not coercive.

QUESTIONS FOR REVIEW AND DISCUSSION

1. What is meant and implied in the statement "It is just as important for any applicant to find the correct position as it is for any manager to find the right person for a position"?

2. List all the things applicants can do to enhance their chances of finding a good position. What information in the chapter was new to you, and what would you add to what was mentioned?

3. What would you do as a business communicator to conduct a professional interview? What do you expect of others when you are being interviewed?

4. Recall a time when you received feedback regarding your work performance, and consider how you felt and how effective the interview was. What was discussed in this chapter that could have improved the situation?

5. Assume that you are given the responsibility to develop an appraisal system in an organization. What should be the primary purpose of an appraisal system? What human values should be reflected in the design of your system?

6. Explain the ten steps in the employment process. Indicate what you can be doing between each of the steps to maximize your chances of being selected.

ACTIVITIES

1. Develop a targeted résumé for yourself. Begin with a job description for your ideal job and target your résumé for that position. Ask a professional to critique your job description and to comment on your résumé.

2. Prepare a résumé and letter of application for a job description listed in your newspaper. Exchange with another person in your class. Critique your friend's materials and share your critiques.

3. Place yourself in the role of screening applicants for the position in Activity 2. Develop a series of questions in funnel form to be used in interviewing for the position. Ask a personnel officer to comment on your schedule of questions.

4. Conduct a mock interview for the position you chose in Activity 2. Serve as the interviewer for the position sought by your friend, and have the friend serve as interviewer for your position of choice.

5. Assume that you have been employed at a fast-food restaurant or held a comparable position. Role-play an appraisal interview. Act as the manager and have a friend assume the role of employee. First, role-play as a tell-and-sell appraisal interview. Next, role-play as a tell-and-listen appraisal. Finally, role-play a problem-solving appraisal.

6. Describe how you could have improved each of the appraisal interviews in Activity 5. Ask your friend for suggestions.

Group
Management

Working with Small Groups

After reading and reviewing this chapter, you should be able to . . .

1. Define a group.

2. Identify and explain the advantages and disadvantages of working in a group.

3. Identify and explain the two phases and six steps in the reflective thinking process.

4. Identify and explain the five rules for brainstorming.

5. Compare and contrast three types of public discussion groups.

6. List the characteristics of effective group members.

7. Define leadership.

8. Understand the traits, styles, and functions of leadership.

9. Identify and explain four styles of leadership.

10. Identify and explain three functions of leadership.

11. Discuss the meaning of the statement that a leader is a manager of information.

*B*ob Trent's excitement mounted as he considered the opportunity he had to build a cohesive and productive sales force. He knew that people are social beings who enjoy interacting and working together. Naisbitt (1984) observed that "citizens, workers, and consumers are demanding and getting a greater voice in government, business, and the marketplace . . . people must be part of the process of arriving at decisions that affect their lives" (p. 75). Participatory democracy thrives in the small group that provides information and recommendations to higher-level authorities.

Almost everyone participates in groups. Achieving membership in the "right" social group, high school club, college fraternity or sorority, or business association can be an important personal and social goal. One of the most telling signs of our need for group membership is the dread of exclusion.

As our society grows larger and more complex, effective group cooperation becomes more critical. Many of us have been involved in situations where the lack of cooperation resulted in catastrophe. For example, if savings and loan regulatory agencies had communicated effectively and had closely monitored loan activities, billions of taxpayer dollars could have been saved. If terrorists involved in bombings of embassies, airplanes, and other targets were to meet face-to-face with their antagonists, perhaps the pain, suffering, and mental anguish caused by these senseless acts of violence could be avoided.

Group communication, though at times simultaneously frustrating and rewarding, is one of the most effective means at our disposal in a democratic society for involving others in solving problems and making decisions that may dramatically affect their lives.

If you were to compile a list of all the groups to which you belong, either actively or casually, the length of the list would probably surprise you. In a lifetime, you associate with family groups, social groups, service groups, therapy and training groups, religious groups, and numerous work-related groups. Each of these groups has meetings of various sorts. The number of times you meet, the hours you spend, and the frustrations you encounter can be staggering.

This chapter focuses on improving your efficiency and effectiveness in working with task-oriented groups to solve problems and make decisions, with special emphasis on improving your effectiveness as a leader in the task setting. You spend a lot of time in these types of work groups. A sizable proportion of personnel budgets is spent on these functions. According to Seibold (1979), "Estimates suggest that most organizations devote between 7 and 15 percent of their personnel budgets to meetings" (p. 4). In an analysis of the work habits of managers, Mintzberg (1980) reports the use of five basic media: "the mail (documented communication), the telephone (purely verbal), the unscheduled meeting (informal face-to-face), the scheduled meeting (formal face-to-face), and the tour (visual)" (p. 38). He reports that "scheduled meetings consumed 59 percent of the manager's time" (p. 41). Doyle and Straus (1976) say that "middle managers in industry may spend as much as 35 percent of their work week in meetings." That figure, they note, "may grow to more than 50 percent for top management" (p. 4). It is not uncommon for a business person to spend most of the workday going from meeting to meeting. Many people dread such meetings, and they do not relish working with others in a group setting. But if you know what to expect in small group communication, group behavior, group characteristics, leadership, and the decision-making process, your work in groups can be more productive and pleasant.

THE NATURE OF SMALL GROUP COMMUNICATION

Small group communication occurs when *three or more people meet face-to-face, usually under the direction of a leader, to share a common purpose or goal and influence one another.* The essence of this definition is that people *interact*, they are *interdependent*, and they *influence* each other.

Groups Communicate Face-to-Face Effective small group communication requires you to interact face-to-face with others. For meaningful interaction to take place, communication must involve both speaking and listening in a common setting. With the introduction of new technology—computers, facsimile (FAX) machines, teleconferencing, and other forms of rapid communication—it is increasingly common for people to communicate and sustain relationships without being in one another's physical presence. However, the best group communication occurs when people can respond immediately and interpersonally to both the verbal and nonverbal communication of others. These important areas of communication are also discussed in Chapter 2, "Interpersonal Communication in the Business Setting," and Chapter 15, "Delivery of the Message."

Groups Have a Small Number of Participants Opinion varies as to how many people are needed to make a small group, but generally speaking, the outside parameters are 3 and 12 people. Size is determined in part by the group's purpose. If one purpose is to encourage individual input, a smaller number is desirable. If members are to be exposed to a variety of viewpoints, a larger group is preferable. The group should be large enough so that all the task-oriented and people-oriented functions necessary for accomplishing the job are present. Five to seven participants is generally a comfortable size for a work group. The group is neither too small to share a task nor too large to prevent free interaction among the members.

Larger groups may promote the formation of subgroups because it is difficult for all participants to share their ideas freely. With more than 12

A group interacting. (Joel Gordon)

members the group can become more like a public speaking setting, characterized by one or two people addressing the others rather than cooperative group interaction. Zarda (1982) says, "A person assembling a decision-making group will do well to restrict the group's size because give and take is more rapid and widespread in a small group than a large one" (p. 65–66). An odd number of members may be preferable so that there will be a majority if a vote must be taken. Disagreements are not inherently unhealthy, but a majority can overcome an impasse when a vote is necessary.

Groups Work Under the Direction of a Leader   Leadership is a significant dimension of small group study. Work groups can function with appointed leadership, leadership by virtue of office or rank, or emergent leadership. The important point is that *leadership acts*, or the collective acts that help the group achieve their purpose, are vital to the health, efficiency, and effectiveness of a group. It is generally more efficient to have one person designated in advance as chairperson, convener, moderator, leader, or facilitator of the group. When a higher authority does not appoint a leader, it is useful to elect someone to that position. Leadership is discussed in more detail later in this chapter and in Chapter 7.

Groups Share a Common Purpose or Goal   Several people are riding an elevator in an office building. One says, "It sure is a beautiful day. I wonder how the merger is going?" Met with silence and cold stares, the speaker sheepishly returns to her own thoughts about what a bunch of stuffy people she is riding with. Is this collection of people in the elevator a group? Not according to most definitions. To be a group, the members must share a common goal. Although the people on the elevator are engaged in the same activity—all riding the elevator—they are probably not going to the same floor, the same office complex, or the same destination. To be an effective team, a group must have a common identity demonstrated by common goals or purpose.

Group Members Exert an Influence on One Another   In order for people who are together to be a group, each member must be open to mutual influence—each person should engage in influencing and being influenced by each of the other members of the group. This spirit of reciprocity is essential to small group integrity. The behavior of each member is determined by, and determines the behavior of, the others. One person's very presence in a group can have a significant influence on the behavior and thinking of other members and on the total group process. Some people contribute ideas and raise questions; others keep the group focused on the task. A member can contribute to the group by breaking tensions, dealing with conflict, keeping on schedule, or serving as a record keeper. The leader is one person who influences the group, but any leadership act that aids the members in achieving their purpose is vital to the group's well-being. Each member can and should influence the other members and the group's decisions.

A critical factor of group participation is that each member must be open-minded and able to set aside personal ambition, "hidden agendas," and other behavior that may be detrimental to the group process and the final outcome.

ADVANTAGES OF WORKING IN GROUPS

Many people find working in a group setting challenging and fulfilling. They enjoy the camaraderie of working with a group. Awareness of the advantages of being in a group can help you approach the prospects with a positive attitude and foster a productive and pleasant climate for other members.

As the adage says, two heads are better than one. Generally, a group has access to more sources of information than a person acting alone. Unless the lone decision maker is an expert in solving a particular type of problem, a group has a greater chance of developing quality solutions to that problem than one person acting alone.

*"You take two of these at the first sign of the
onset of boardroom turbulence."*

Working with groups is not without costs. (*Source: The New Yorker*, 1985)

Group Synergy   The combined force of people thinking together produces a better product than could be devised by the best individual thinking in the group. This *synergistic effect* is one of the significant benefits of working in a small group (see Figure 6.1). Synergistic small group thinking cannot be achieved by individuals thinking alone.

Groups Are More Creative Than Individuals   Muhammad Ali said, "The man who has no imagination has no wings." The "wings" of imagination are more dynamic in the group setting. Besides having more information than a single individual, groups have more collective experience to draw upon. When people in groups can be freed from inhibitions, self-criticism, and the criticism of others, they can produce more imaginative ways to solve problems. Together, group members can provide more insights into problems, bouncing ideas off each other to help resolve the issues.

Figure 6.1 The synergistic effect.

Groups Learn More Than Individuals   The adage "Learn by doing" applies in work groups. You learn more by teaching a subject than by studying a topic on your own, and you learn more from one another in a group setting. Participants improve their comprehension of ideas in the give-and-take of group interaction.

Groups Carry Out Actions They Help to Plan   People carry out decisions they help to formulate. Group members are more likely to follow recommendations if they have a part in making them. Developing participatory decision making is an excellent managerial strategy for ensuring that employees support the recommendations made by the group.

DISADVANTAGES OF WORKING IN GROUPS

One barb you may hear is, "A camel is a horse put together by a committee." Another is, "A surefire way to kill a good idea is to give it to a committee ." People making such statements may be all too familiar with the problems, pitfalls, and disadvantages of working in groups.

Familiarity with the potential liabilities or disadvantages can help you address problems before they arise. Forewarned is forearmed.

Groups Take Longer Than Individuals   Many people dislike small group decision making because group work is time-consuming. The benefits of working in small groups are available only to people with the patience to invest the extra time it takes to get the desired results. When employees or students find they are expected to be part of a group project, they often express frustration, saying the process is slow, cumbersome, and frustrating. An all too typical comment is, "I'd rather do the job myself than wait for a dumb committee to discuss the problem and take action."

Groups May Be Dominated by Individuals   In the group context, there often are those who wish to dominate the discussion. Eager to take charge, they may discourage others from making potentially valuable contributions. Thus the group loses the input of those who may feel their ideas were squelched by overly zealous talkers.

Groups May Rely on One or Two Individuals to Do the Work   Working in groups can easily diffuse the feeling of responsibility. It is easy to blend into a group and contribute little or nothing. Few may want to do the work, but everyone wants to enjoy the benefits. When you participate in small group decision making, you will find that two of the most common frustrations are low attendance at group meetings and lack of participation of those present.

Groups May Pressure Individuals to Conform   In the group setting there is often pressure to conform. Janis (1972) discusses this phenomenon under the rubric of *groupthink*, which occurs when individuals agree because they value their membership and acceptance in the group more than the risk involved in conflict.

Although Bob Trent desires a cohesive sales force, a unit in which his people have a feeling of pride, loyalty, and commitment to the group, he does not want his salespeople to feel pressured to conform to his ideas or that they have no opportunity to challenge policies or procedures. Bob knows that disagreement can bring issues into focus and lead to better decisions. Hence, Bob plans to use the procedures listed in Table 6.1 to avoid groupthink.

Table 6.1   GROUPTHINK CAN BE MINIMIZED

1. One member of the group can be the "devil's advocate," or critical evaluator, to encourage disagreement and criticism of ideas.
2. The group leader should avoid revealing his or her preferences to the group at the beginning of discussions that will lead to critical decisions.
3. Different leaders can work independently on the same problems to provide different perspectives.
4. Group members can discuss the group's process with trusted friends and report their reactions to the group.
5. Outside consultants can be used from time to time as resource people. These consultants can be encouraged to disagree with the group's assumptions.
6. The group can spend extra time discussing issues which involve relations with rival groups (e.g., labor and management or advertising and sales), focusing on all warning signals from competing groups and considering alternatives the competitors can take.
7. A "second-chance" meeting can be held after preliminary decisions have been reached, so ideas can incubate. Other, possibly better decisions may emerge during the "incubation time."

Source: Adapted from S. L. Tubbs (1988). *A systems approach to small group interaction* (3rd ed., p. 177). New York: Random House.

SOLVING PROBLEMS IN GROUPS

A primary goal of some groups is to solve problems. And problem-solving discussions may also require the group to make decisions. There is considerable overlap between the terms *decision making* and *problem solving.* According to Barker et al. (1991), *"decision-making* refers to the process that a group follows in order to select among alternatives or chart a course of action" (p. 103). There may or may not be a problem. Problem solving is the process of overcoming obstacles to achieve a desired goal. The problem-solving process involves problem identification, problem analysis, solution appraisal, and the selection of and implementation of the best solution from among those proposed by the group. The group might ask, "How can we raise money for the railroad depot renovation?", "What can be done to improve the quality of education in our schools?", or "How can we secure a larger advertising budget to promote our products?" Each of these questions suggests there is an obstacle (lack of money) that must be overcome to achieve a desired goal (more local revenue, better education, a larger budget).

A systematic problem-solving approach called *reflective thinking* is one method of helping groups overcome obstacles to a desired goal. Based on ideas in a book by John Dewey (1910), the *reflective approach* is a prescription for rational problem solving, from a "felt difficulty" (problem perception) to implementation of a solution. Careful analysis and logical thinking lead to the solution ultimately selected by the group.

Although it is not necessary that every problem-solving discussion follow these steps, the process is useful for reducing some of the frustration and uncertainty every group experiences in solving problems. The six steps of the reflective thinking process can be divided into two general phases: the *problem description phase* and the *problem solution phase* (see Table 6.2). Within the problem description phase there are two steps; the first of these is to define and limit the problem.

Table 6.2   TWO PHASES OF REFLECTIVE THINKING

Problem description phase

1. Define and limit the problem.
2. Analyze the problem.

Problem solution phase

3. Generate possible solutions.
4. Appraise the suggested solutions.
5. Select the best solution.
6. Implement the solution.

Step 1: Define and Limit the Problem

The first step in reflective thinking is to identify the problem clearly by defining it so that all group members have a common understanding of the purpose of the meeting. Group members are more productive and better satisfied when a common understanding of the problem is reached early. To assist in this effort, the group may want to consider the following questions:

1. What is the specific problem we are concerned about?
2. What items, concepts, or ideas do we need to define?
3. Who is harmed by the problem?
4. When do the harmful effects of the problem occur?
5. What, if any, limitations should be imposed on the scope of the discussion?

Groups address questions that fall into three different categories: facts, values, and policies. Problem-solving groups should know what types of questions are being addressed. Factual questions are posed to inquire about events, happenings, and so forth, where existing conditions can be established or verified. Facts may need to be clarified or interpreted in order to assist the group in deliberation. The following are questions of fact: (1) What resources are needed by our department? (2) What is the purpose of the student advisory council? (3) When was the student government association established?

The value dimension of a problem concerns desirability. Value systems are derived in part from past experiences. The following are questions that call for value judgments: (1) Is it desirable for personnel costs to exceed capital improvement costs? (2) Is the university's system of grading fair? (3) Is it worthwhile to require a foreign language in a university studies program?

Many proposals made in the business setting focus on new policy proposals. Policy questions typically ask what should be done to remedy a problem or improve a situation. Well-worded policy questions are framed around a specific problem to be solved. Consider the following examples: (1) "What should be done to reform the tax base in our county?" (2) "What actions should be taken to balance the U.S. trade deficit with foreign countries?" (3) "What can be done to reduce date rape on our campus?" In addition to wording the question under discussion, the group needs to agree upon the boundaries of the problem, clearly establishing the limitations of the proposal.

Bob Trent attended a meeting to discuss the possible sale of personal computers to area universities. As the meeting began, Bob and several others in the group realized that progress would be made only if definitions were clear and a single issue was discussed until consensus was reached. After basic terms, such as *personal computer* and *hardware,* were defined, Bob suggested that discussion be limited to developing a brochure detailing how students' personal computers could be linked to the campus computer system. With this system, students could transmit an assignment to an instructor's computer terminal for critique. Had Bob not established this limitation, or parameter, the group would not have known whether to focus on hardware, services, or a host of other related matters. Bob might also have suggested that the group limit the discussion to certain kinds of target groups (students, faculty, staff, and administration). By raising questions of both definition and limitation, you can be more certain that everyone in the group understands and focuses upon the problems they are trying to solve. At this point, the group can begin to analyze the problem.

Step 2: Analyze the Problem

Analysis is the second step of the problem description phase. When you analyze a problem, you examine each of its facets. Like a physician probing the cause of a patient's pain, you must determine what is wrong and what is causing the problem. Analysis involves researching and examining causes, effects, symptoms, and history; establishing criteria that solutions should meet; and providing any other background information about the problem that will help the group arrive at a solution. The following questions are designed to get information for a thorough analysis:

1. What is the history of the problem?
2. How serious is the problem?
3. Who is harmed?
4. Where is the harm most serious?
5. What is the present situation?
6. What are the causes, effects, and symptoms of the problem?
7. What events or factors bring about these effects or symptoms?
8. What methods do we already have for solving the problem?
9. What are the limitations of these methods?
10. What are the obstacles that keep us from achieving our goal?
11. What are the efforts of the status quo?
12. What will happen if nothing more is done than is being done now?
13. Can the problem be divided into subproblems for definition and analysis?
14. Who has the authority and means to solve the problem?
15. What criteria should a solution meet?

Other questions may also occur, but this list suggests the kinds of issues important to the analysis.

Although it is more common for solution criteria to be developed as part of the analysis step, some researchers think that delaying generation of criteria until the appraisal process can enhance the production of creative ideas (Sattler and Miller, 1968). You are encouraged to establish criteria prior to developing solutions, as a logical and time-saving effort. Barker et al. noted, "If solutions are simply suggested without any basis for evaluation of completeness, it may take the group a long time to ferret out those solutions that will do the job" (p. 113–114).

Criteria are the standards of measurement or goals that a good solution must meet. Using these criteria, the group will recognize a good solution when it is offered. Without such guidelines, the group will have no "yardstick" to use to measure the acceptability of each possible solution. Typical criteria for solutions include but certainly are not limited to the following factors:

1. The solution should be implemented as soon as possible.
2. The solution should be attainable within the established budget.
3. The solution should be agreed to by all members of the group.
4. The solution should solve the problem.

After completing the two steps of the problem description phase, the group enters the second phase of the reflective approach to problem solving: the problem solution phase. The steps in this phase, which complete the six-step process, are generation of possible solutions, appraisal of the solutions, selection of the best solution, and implementation.

Step 3: Generate Possible Solutions

With the problem defined, limited, and analyzed, the group should now identify possible solutions. For this step to be most effective, the group must have a wide range of possible solutions to consider. Brainstorming is one creative tool which helps nurture ideas for possible solutions to a problem.

Responsibility for making brainstorming work effectively usually rests with the group leader, who must ensure that the flow of potential solutions is uninterrupted throughout the brainstorming process. The leader must also support and foster an atmosphere of acceptance for all ideas. In developing the process of brainstorming for use in his advertising agency, Alex Osborn (1957) appointed one member of his group to blow a whistle to interrupt participants who were being critical or were campaigning for particular ideas. The choice of technique for ensuring positive, uninterrupted brainstorming is left to the leader.

Table 6.3 lists a number of guidelines that can be used to secure the best results from a brainstorming session.

Suspend Judgment This rule protects participants' ideas from criticism. Criticism and faultfinding stifle creativity. Osborn regards criticism to be as counterproductive as driving a car "with your brakes on!" (p. 77). No one should be allowed to criticize a suggestion or to endorse a solution until the brainstorming session is brought to an end. If group members find it difficult to withhold evaluation, it may prove effective to have participants write their suggestions on paper and then share the ideas with the group.

Think Wild Any idea, no matter how extreme, deserves a hearing. Hearing one person's idea may trigger another member's thinking. Often the synergistic combination of one person's suggestion and another's adaptation leads to a solution.

Table 6.3 GUIDELINES FOR SUCCESSFUL BRAINSTORMING

• Suspend judgment.

• Think wild (think without restrictions).

• Piggyback (build on the ideas of others).

• Stress quantity rather than quality of ideas.

• Record ideas as they occur.

Practice Piggybacking   Expect someone's wild and crazy idea to trigger another idea from someone else. "Piggybacking" (or "hitchhiking") is basically the process of linking up with another's suggestion or combining two ideas. Extension, combination, and modification of ideas frequently result in truly creative solutions.

Stress Quantity of Ideas, Not Quality   Although this rule is covered in the first guideline, it cannot be overemphasized. Parnes (1967) discovered that the second half of a brainstorming session is often more productive than the first. When the prospects look bleak, the leader can read the suggested ideas out loud and try to pump new life into the process.

Make a List   Have a group member read all the suggested ideas. Participants need to see that their ideas are still being considered until a final selection is made. Keep the list on a chalkboard or flip chart, if possible, so that all ideas can be seen. The list is a tangible reminder that each idea is being treated equally during the actual brainstorming session. Having a visible list may also serve to generate further piggybacking.

Bob needs to remember that results, not the efficiency with which those results are generated, will measure the success of brainstorming. Some silence and many completely useless ideas should be expected. Certainly the process will challenge the group leader. Brainstorming does not work well when a group is under a tight deadline. The leader must determine, with the help of other members, whether enough time is available to use this potentially valuable technique.

After a set time has elapsed, the leader should call the brainstorming session to a halt. Using the guidelines for the next step in the reflective thinking process, the group can evaluate the suggested solutions.

Step 4: Appraise the Suggested Solutions

The leader should begin the appraisal of solutions with a review of the criteria any credible solution should meet. Using the agreed-upon criteria, the group can decide whether any of the proposed solutions will solve the problem. At this stage the group may discover the need to modify the criteria. The following questions often prove helpful in the appraisal process:

1. How does the proposed solution relate to the criteria established?
2. To what extent will the solution answer the question or solve the problem?
3. What are the advantages and disadvantages of the solution?
4. What would the long- and short-term effects be if this solution were adopted?

Step 5: Select the Best Solution

Once solutions have been evaluated, the group must select the solution the members think is best. If the group members have agreed upon useful criteria, maintained a spirit of objectivity, and honestly answered the appropriate

*"I still don't have all the answers, but I'm
beginning to ask the right questions."*

Asking the right questions is a key to successful appraisal of solutions. (*Source: The New Yorker*, 1989)

appraisal questions, there should be a consensus. *Consensus* has numerous meanings; it commonly implies implicit agreement without a formal vote. Sometimes a group will be unable to reach general agreement on the best solution. On such occasions it may be necessary to vote, with the majority prevailing.

Step 6: Implement the Solution

The group's work is not completed when the solution is agreed upon. The last step in the problem-solving phase of the reflective approach is implementation. The test for any solution is to try it out. Appropriate questions at this point include "How can we put the solution into practice?" and "What can we do to evaluate the success of our solution?" The solution must be put to the test and the results observed. Reappraisal and modification of the solution may be necessary. Plans and procedures must be in place for ongoing review of solutions, especially when serious and costly problems are solved.

PARTICIPATING IN SMALL GROUPS

Groups are sometimes criticized for "pooling ignorance," or reaching a lowest common denominator. Sometimes groups do fail to arrive at meaningful solutions, but this need not happen. To solve a problem intelligently, a group must depend upon the abilities of its members to make useful contributions. The following guidelines can assist members of a group to be more effective in making contributions:

1. *Effective group members seek to comprehend the problem and find an answer.* It is easy to describe how one feels about a topic, but thorough preparation is another matter. Each member should be prepared with sufficient current information and knowledge about the topic to make an intelligent and important contribution to the problem-solving process. Preparation is a joint responsibility. Without thorough research efforts, the group members will not be able to make a significant contribution to the problem being addressed. Everyone must make a genuine effort to research the topic.

2. *Effective group members secure and examine evidence that supports or contradicts opinions and assumptions.* Some claims may collapse when they are carefully measured against evidence, logic, and contradictory data. Some information comes from sources that are suspect, out-of-date, or in direct opposition to other sources. A group that reaches a consensus without weighing the validity of evidence is more likely to make a flawed decision. Some groups make good decisions and others do not; often the distinction lies in the ability of group members to scrutinize supporting data (Hirokawa, 1983).

3. *Effective group members avoid choosing a solution until the problem is thoroughly analyzed.* A "knife-happy" surgeon advises surgery

for every malady from headaches to ingrown toenails, without thoroughly analyzing the problem, asking for appropriate consultations, or discussing alternatives or probable results with the patient. The corporate world is result- and solution-oriented, but group members must resist the temptation to start suggesting solutions once the problem has been identified. The group must understand the causes, effects, history, and symptoms of the problem, analyzing it thoroughly before concentrating on solutions (Hirokawa and Pace, 1983).

4. *Effective group members maintain objectivity and avoid preoccupation with their own suggestions and proposals.* While total objectivity is impossible, group members should strive to maintain as much detachment as possible. One means of working toward this ideal is to view the contributions of each member as no longer the individual member's "property" but the property of the group. It requires a selfless attitude, a relinquishing of what you contribute, to allow your ideas to stand on their own merit under the tough scrutiny of the group.

5. *Effective group members work toward healthy relational goals as well as task goals.* In any group situation, there are dual goals at work—task goals and social goals. Our primary focus has been on the task dimension of the participant's responsibilities. The group's social goals are equally important. Social goals are intended to bring participants closer together as people who can relate to one another. Often, successful task achievement brings people closer together. Uniting people can also facilitate task accomplishment. Another way to encourage cohesiveness is for the group to recognize members' individual efforts and encourage them to continue. Stressing teamwork ("we are all in this together") fosters healthy relational and task goals. One of the skills critical to group participation is being a good listener. The listening skills discussed in Chapter 3 apply equally in work groups and in other family or social contexts.

In addition to understanding the messages of others, it is important that you respond courteously to them. This includes showing respect for views that are contrary to your own. Respect does not mean agreement. Keeping emotions under control minimizes tendencies toward defensive reactions which can cause group conflict.

Relational goals aim at nurturing healthy interaction so that a climate of trust and openness can prevail. By demonstrating that you are open to the ideas of others, you can nurture a spirit of reciprocity that discourages closed-mindedness and encourages positive interpersonal communication in group meetings.

6. *Effective group members make orientation statements.* To nurture cohesion, groups need to be productive in relation to both task and relational goals. Each member must feel free to express agreement or disagreement on various issues being discussed by the group. Likewise, each member should feel free to talk during the discussion pro-

"Obviously, some people here do not appreciate the gravity of our situation."

Healthy relational goals are important. (*Source:The New Yorker*, 1985)

cess, to ask "Where are we now?" or say "It seems to me we are off track." Comments about the discussion process are called meta discussion or *orientation* statements. *Meta discussion* literally means "discussion about discussion." One study suggests that meta discussion statements can help the group stay on target and enhance consensus (Gouran, 1969). Some group members may withhold comments concerning the process because they fear they may hurt someone's feelings or be perceived as trying to lead the group, but such reservations only serve to repress potentially serious group problems. Therefore, group members should work toward honest introspection of the process dimensions as well as the task and social dimensions of the group.

7. *Effective group members assist in managing conflict.* When people are sharing ideas and opinions about sensitive issues, it is likely that interpersonal conflicts will surface. Each group member should be prepared to help manage conflict when it erupts. *Substantive conflict,* or conflict about ideas, can be viewed positively as a means of focusing issues and as a sign of cohesion. *Interpersonal conflict,* however, can be detrimental. Such conflict may be related to role struggles or various personality factors (for example, one person may constantly belittle others or act on the basis of hidden agendas).

Tension can sometimes be resolved by using the following suggestions for conflict management:

- Deal with the source of tension openly and honestly.
- Discuss issues, not personalities.
- Explore ways to compromise rather than creating a winner and a loser.
- Seek to clarify misunderstandings about meaning.
- When in conflict, try to be descriptive rather than evaluative and judgmental.
- When making judgments, depend on facts rather than personal opinions.

As a step toward resolving conflict, the group should tell members when they are having a destructive effect upon other members or the group in general. Once informed of the negative impact, the individuals may change their detrimental behavior. Most group conflict can be dealt with openly, freeing the group to move forward toward meeting its goals. Group members who know how people in small groups behave and who can apply basic principles of effective participation will undoubtedly become valued members of the problem-solving groups in which they work.

PUBLIC DISCUSSION GROUPS

Public discussion groups are not normally considered problem-solving or decision-making groups, but they do serve useful functions in providing information, stimulating public opinion, or consolidating public support. Public discussion groups come in a variety of forms. The three most common forms are the panel, the symposium, and the forum.

The Panel

A *panel* is essentially a group of individuals who discuss a topic for the benefit of a listening audience. Panels may be highly structured or very informal. A structured panel may limit the length and scope of remarks; an informal panel may emphasize freewheeling, spontaneous interaction. Panelists are expected to prepare in advance for extemporaneous speaking and to have some knowledge or expertise as the basis for their comments, but formal speeches and long prepared statements are discouraged. Depending upon the topic of discussion, a panel's membership may consist of experts, interested lay people, or both. A basic criterion for a good panel discussion is interaction among its members. Through interaction, a variety of positions and ideas should be expressed, thus providing the audience with useful information. A moderator usually guides the flow of the discussion and encourages participation from all panel members.

The Symposium

A *symposium* consists of a group of individuals who each present a formal, prepared speech on a specific aspect or part of the discussion topic. For example, one member might present the history of a problem; another, recent trends; another, methods of solving the problem. An alternative form of symposium might have five speakers who each present a different solution to a problem. Symposia tend to be formal and so much like public speaking events that some authorities discount their use as public discussion. Members of a symposium do not usually interact with one another, like panel members, although some symposia evolve into a panel format after the speeches are presented. Both panel discussions and symposia are presented to an audience. An interesting variation of the symposium involves division of the audience into small discussion groups (see the discussion of "buzz groups" in Chapter 7) after the symposium speeches. In this variation, the symposium acts as a stimulus for audience involvement.

The Forum

A *forum* discussion involves a large group or audience which meets as the result of some other activity. Town hall meetings, public hearings, and open city council meetings are often forums used to solicit public opinion or to hear citizen complaints. Often, because they involve large numbers of people, forums seem disorganized and rambling, but they do serve a useful purpose in encouraging citizen involvement. In one kind of forum, often used on college campuses, two or more speakers deliver short position statements on opposing sides of an issue. After the speeches, a forum is opened to the audience, which discusses various aspects of the topic for a predetermined length of time. After the forum discussion, if appropriate, the audience votes, and a decision is made. Time may also be set aside for a forum after a panel or symposium discussion, to allow the audience to ask questions or offer opinions. Lack of adequate time is the main problem with forum discussions. Organizers often fail to allow enough time following the stimulus material (panel, symposium, or lecture, for example) for an adequate forum.

There are no clear-cut guidelines for determining which type of public discussion—a panel, a symposium, or a forum—best suits a given situation. Panel discussions tend to be more free-flowing and interesting to watch. Symposia cover specific areas of the topic in a highly organized, precise manner. Forums tend to be less organized than symposiums, but they involve the audience directly in the proceedings (Curtis, Mazza, and Runnebohm, 1979).

LEADERSHIP IN SMALL GROUPS

One approach to leadership attempted to distinguish leaders from nonleaders on the basis of differences in personal characteristics. Although many traits have been linked to leadership—size, age, physical attractiveness, intelligence, self-confidence, dynamism, originality, responsibility, verbal facility, dependability, and so on—the results have been largely inconclusive. The idea that leaders are born and not made has not stood up under careful systematic study (Fisher and Ellis, 1990, pp. 226–227).

The executives at American Computer Systems promoted Bob Trent because of his demonstrated leadership. American's top executives wanted a leader for the sales division who believed that both people and productivity are important. Moreover, the company wanted a person who could adjust management style to the needs of the situation. Bob Trent appeared to be such a person. He was group-oriented, flexible, caring, and sensitive to the needs of others. Bob was excited about assuming a position of leadership and was eager to demonstrate that top management's trust was well founded. He was ready to lead the sales team in the tradition of excellence established by Sue Derkman.

There are several facets of leadership that Bob Trent needs to understand in assuming his new responsibilities. Bob views leadership acts as behavior that helps the group achieve their goals. He realizes that one dimension is the style of group leadership he chooses to practice.

Several factors affect the overall quality, success, and effectiveness of the group problem-solving effort. Although leadership is only one of several factors, it is an important one. *Leadership* can be defined as the exertion of influence over the other members of the group. Any member who effects such influence can be viewed as a group leader. *Leadership acts* are those acts that help the group achieve its goals. Let's discuss the emergence of leadership, different leadership styles, and the functions of leadership.

Sources of Leaders

Leaders assume the role in a variety of ways. They may be appointed by someone outside the group; they may assume leadership because of office or rank; or they may emerge from among the members of the group. By virtue of his new promotion to sales manager, Bob Trent will need to function as group leader. In some situations, Bob may choose to designate a member of his team to assume temporary leadership, perhaps because of that person's expertise regarding a given project or process.

Situations in which leaders are appointed are quite common. If a business organization encounters a problem that cannot be solved by following the usual corporate procedures, an executive officer in the firm may select several subordinates, appoint one of them leader, and direct the group to solve the problem or make a recommendation. A mayor of a large city may appoint a prominent citizen to lead a group to come up with ways of assisting needy senior citizens in paying their utility bills. A university dean may appoint a group of faculty members to an ad hoc committee for the purpose of studying student retention problems and recommending a solution. The dean may appoint one of the faculty members as chair or convener of the committee (in order to allow them to select their own chairperson).

Leadership by virtue of office or rank is also fairly common. A person's position in the organizational bureaucracy may require group leadership. For example, a personnel director may serve, by right of office, as leader of the employees' benefit review board. The senior member of the Roman Catholic College of Cardinals, because of his rank, performs certain leadership functions when the college elects a new pope. The highest-ranking surviving officer in a battlefield serves as the commanding officer.

Emergent leadership is not as easy to determine or define as appointed or assumed leadership. Emergence of a leader within the group generally depends upon several factors: (1) willingness to work, (2) preparation, (3) contribution of ideas, (4) making a positive impression, (5) amount of participation, (6) verbal facility, and (7) seating arrangement. (See Table 6.4.) Obviously, other features are also important, but the group member who is able to use these variables as "leverage" can enhance the chance of emerging as group leader.

Willingness to Work   Some people who earnestly desire to be the leader of a group find themselves losing out to individuals who are ineffective, domineering, and perhaps less likable. Why does fate seem to deal such a blow? How is the more desirable person overshadowed? Perhaps this is because the leader who emerged possessed greater drive. Anyone who wishes to exert leadership must demonstrate a strong willingness to work.

Preparation   An emergent leader is not necessarily the most technically qualified member of the group. The leader often assumes that role because he or she is best prepared for the group meeting. Preparation may include familiarity with the topic, thinking of ideas to contribute, and, when appropriate, proposing a plan for collective action.

Table 6.4   CONTROLLABLE LEADERSHIP FACTORS

Factor	Applications
1. Willingness to work	Demonstrate initiative in completing tasks.
2. Preparation	Make recommendations; be informed; and provide resources for the group.
3. Contributions of ideas	Share helpful ideas.
4. Making a positive impression	Arrive on time; be flexible; and be open to the ideas of others.
5. Amount of participation	Contribute frequently and concisely.
6. Nonverbal interaction	Communicate with force and dynamism and express thoughts articulately.
7. Seating arrangement	Take a position central to group interaction.

Contribution of Ideas A group member with knowledge of the problem and a willingness to work certainly has an edge in leadership emergence. Also important is the group member who contributes ideas that shape factual knowledge and give direction to the resolution of problems. Since the ultimate goal is to make a decision leading to a solution, members who offer the ideas leading to such decisions often emerge as leaders. Participants must contribute ideas that are perceived by the other members of the group as being beneficial—not just any idea will suffice.

Making a Positive Impression Leaders often emerge through a process of elimination. To survive the elimination process, an aspiring leader must make a favorable early impression on the group. Bormann and Bormann (1988) suggest that about half the members of leaderless groups meeting for the first time are eliminated from leadership ranks, if they are quiet, "uninformed, ignorant, or unskilled at the task" (p. 130). During the "shakedown" of the group, any member who desires leadership must be careful to avoid being labeled as an undesirable choice.

Amount of Participation One factor in making a good impression is the quality of a group member's participation. A member who frequently participates, one who is verbally active, often emerges as the group leader (Fisher). A participant who contributes numerous comments, provided they are not considered inept, has a better chance of emerging as leader. When a group has more than one person who is exceptionally active verbally, competition for leadership generally surfaces. In this case, the act of participation alone will not guarantee the leadership position. Outtalking another garrulous person is not necessarily a clever strategy. The goals, values, and needs of the group should remain paramount over personal ambition. When group members have the choice between a potential leader who is obviously willing to make personal sacrifices for the sake of the group's goals and one who is driven by selfish ambition, the former should prevail.

Nonverbal Interaction Nonverbal communication contributes to the creation of a favorable impression (Fisher, 1980). Nonverbal facility suggests, according to Fisher, that "emergent leaders are fluent in delivering their contributions . . . [and] express their thoughts articulately . . . [The] leaders' participation is forceful and dynamic . . . an indication of their interest and involvement in the group task" (pp. 215–216).

Seating Arrangement Seating arrangement can also influence leadership emergence. If a group member is seated in a position that reduces or minimizes face-to-face interaction with others, both participation and leadership emergence are lessened. According to Sommer (1965), "in American societies, leaders tend to occupy the head positions at a table with their lieutenants at their sides" (p. 337). It follows that the group member who sits at the head of a table or in a position of prominence will tend to interact with others more

Table 6.5   HYPOTHESES ABOUT LEADERSHIP

1. Persons who actively participate in the group are more likely to attain a position of leadership than those who participate less in the group's activities.
2. Possession of task-related abilities and skills enhances attainment of a position of leadership.
3. Emergent leaders tend to behave in a more authoritarian manner than elected or appointed leaders.
4. The source of the leader's authority influences both the leader's behavior and the reactions of other group members.
5. Effective leaders are characterized by task-related abilities, sociability, and motivation to be a leader.
6. Democratic leadership results in greater member satisfaction than autocratic leadership.
7. Leaders tend to behave in a more authoritarian manner in stressful than in non-stressful situations.
8. The degree to which the leader is endorsed by group members depends upon the success of the group in achieving its goals.
9. A task-oriented leader is more effective when the group-task situation is either very favorable or very unfavorable for the leader, whereas a relationship-oriented leader is more effective when the group-task situation is only moderately favorable or unfavorable for the leader. (When the situation is favorable, the high task-oriented leader can be managing and controlling without arousing unfavorable reactions by the group because things are going well; when the situation is going poorly and the group is in jeopardy, then directive leadership is needed. However, if the situation is only moderately favorable, the group expects consideration so a permissive leader is more effective.)

Source: Group dynamics:The psychology of small group behavior, 3rd ed., by Marvin E. Shaw, pp. 343–344. Copyright © 1981 by McGraw-Hill, Inc. Reprinted with permission of McGraw-Hill, Inc.

often. Fisher supports that notion when he observes that "one absolute requisite for successful behavior for successful leader emergence . . . is verbal activity itself" (p. 215). Being seated off to one side suggests a desire for minimal interaction. Whatever the physical arrangement of the meeting place, an individual who wishes to exercise influence must sit in a position that facilitates interaction. Dominant people tend to choose positions in the center of the group.

Marvin Shaw (1981) discusses other communication-related factors that can help you understand and apply some important observations to your quest for leadership (see Table 6.5).

GROUP LEADERSHIP STYLES

Group leadership is an application of the general leadership styles discussed in Chapter 2. Group leadership style suggests how power is used—whether it is retained, shared, or yielded to the group. Style of leadership can also be revealed in how the leader interacts or relates with other group members. Some researchers identify a different number of basic styles; we will discuss four styles, progressing from the most to the least use of power: authoritarian, democratic, nondirective, and laissez-faire group leadership behavior. (See Table 6.6.)

Table 6.6   GROUP LEADERSHIP STYLES

Style	Identifying Behaviors
Authoritarian	Retains power; highly directive; makes assignments; controls group behavior.
Democratic	Shares power; participatory; seeks to guide, not direct group activities.
Nondirective	Invests power in group members; coordinates; facilitates; nurtures; encourages group members to exercise leadership.
Laissez-faire	Abdicates power; shows no interest in being a leader of people or in completing a task.

Authoritarian group leadership is most often associated with a high degree of control, structure, and direction. An authoritarian leader usually establishes group goals and objectives, assigns duties and tasks, monitors all phases of group activity, and makes or confirms the final decision. Traditionally, authoritarian leadership is cited as bad, or negative, leadership. Authoritarian group leaders are described as not trusting their fellows and of exploiting others through power and position.

To some extent, the criticism leveled at authoritarian group leaders is valid. Authoritarians fail to promote participation in decision making, interaction, open discussion, freedom, and creativity. Authoritarian leaders often exploit group members and abuse their own power and influence. However, authoritarian leadership sometimes best serves the interests of a group. For example, a group may find itself working against a deadline. Time pressure requires increased structure and direction, which can be provided best through authoritarian leadership. The authoritarian style might also be desirable in cases of conflict between group members; resolution of the conflict may rest upon an authoritarian decision when compromise or consensus cannot be achieved.

A leader relying on *democratic group leadership* seeks cooperation and participation from group members and seeks to guide, not direct, the group's activities. [Argyris (1964) noted that various researchers have used the terms *participative, collaborative, employee-centered,* or *group-centered* leadership (p. 214). The most enduring term, however, seems to be *democratic group leadership.*] Democratic leaders provide direction and structure as the situation requires, but they also encourage group members to develop or suggest procedures and methods of operation. Democratic leaders are open to conflicting ideas and opinions and strive to maintain free-flowing communication. Democratic leaders realize that group members will be more committed to supporting and following decisions in which they have shared, rather than decisions imposed by a leader. A democratic leader also conveys a positive attitude toward people. This attitude indicates to group members that they have worth, value, and ability and that, given the chance, they can be highly productive and successful.

Democratic leaders are active and involved in the group process; they exert influence, and group members seek their direction. Democratic leaders use their influence to increase member participation, involvement, and sharing to produce consensus.

A variety of labels, such as *nondirective, group-centered,* and *permissive,* are used to describe another style of leadership, in which the leader does not direct, guide, or control. In *nondirective group leadership,* the leader serves as a coordinator, facilitator, and sounding board. He or she attempts to maintain open communication channels between members of the group by asking questions, redirecting questions, and summarizing and reviewing the progress of the group. If the group expresses a need for direction and structure, the nondirective leader will ask questions of various group members, listen to their responses, and restate and reflect upon those responses, until the group charts its own direction and establishes its own controls. At no time does the nondirective leader impose his or her ideas or beliefs upon the group.

Nondirective leadership can be frustrating and at times difficult for group members. However, the goal of nondirective leadership is to develop a climate in which all members of the group exercise leadership and influence while the group makes decisions regarding procedures, objectives, division of labor, problem solving, and so on. The nondirective leader is both active and concerned with the group and its progress. A nondirective style is probably the most difficult for a leader. Nondirective leaders must maintain the belief and attitude that the group can direct its own course and achieve success. They must hold back their own feelings and ideas and avoid the temptation to assert control.

Laissez-faire group leadership is the opposite of authoritarian leadership. Laissez-faire leaders make little attempt to control, structure, or direct the activities of the group. Unlike the authoritarian, who appears not to trust group members, the laissez-faire leader appears not to care one way or the other about the group members or the group's task. Consequently, laissez-faire leaders may respond with indifference to requests for feedback, support, and direction. If there is an advantage to laissez-faire leadership, it might be that group members are free from close supervision. Given the right group composition, laissez-faire leadership can produce a very creative climate, along with high levels of member satisfaction. However, a group that requires structure and direction or one that works under stress or pressure would experience difficulty under a laissez-faire style of leadership.

Factors That Affect Leadership

The business of leading discussions has probably occupied the attention of group members and researchers more than any other aspect of the discussion process. The leadership role strongly affects the overall quality of the group discussion and its final product. How an individual acts in the leadership role often depends on the situation. Different types of leadership are most effective under different conditions. A successful discussion group leader will understand and recognize these differing situations and change leadership style as the situation dictates. A number of factors affect the group situation and thus the leadership style employed.

Environmental Factors   The environment or context within which the group operates affects leadership style. Time demands placed upon the group and the presence or absence of pressure or stress may call for alternative leadership styles. The leader of a newspaper editorial board may employ an authoritarian style in getting the group to decide upon the content of the next day's edition but not in planning feature stories for the next month.

Group Composition   The personality factors of the group members, their perception of appropriate leadership behavior, and their need for strong, moderate, mild, or nondirective supervision may affect the choice of leadership style. College instructors, because of their belief in academic freedom, often reject the authoritarian leadership style and may force their department chairperson and administrators into democratic leadership styles.

The Nature of the Task   The complexity or simplicity of the task and the limits or restrictions placed upon suitable solutions affect leadership style. For example, a department store chain might direct its marketing group to devise new ways of displaying merchandise to increase sales while maintaining optimum security against theft. In order to meet security requirements, the leader of such a group will need to shift from a nondirective leadership style intended to increase group creativity to a directive style.

Choosing a Leadership Style

What type of group leadership is best? No style is ideal for all situations. An effective leader must be able to recognize the best style of leadership for a given situation and must be flexible, adaptable, and able to adjust to the needs of the group, the context, and the task. For example, one condition affecting any group is the amount of time allocated for problem solution. An effective group leader will always consider the amount of time available when deciding upon the best type of leadership to employ. In general, the more time available for the group to transact its business, the less leadership control the group discussion process requires.

An American naval captain managing a European communications unit learned from the Pentagon of a multimillion-dollar computer installation planned for his command. At the weekly staff meeting he announced the project, along with the details that were available, to the officers who managed specific departments within the command. The captain explained some of the problems that might be anticipated in the coming months and suggested that the officers begin working on ways to overcome them. He also asked them to bring up any new problems and to report developments on the computerization project at each weekly meeting. Their overall goal was to insure that the new facilities be installed and in operation without disrupting vital European defense communications.

As the target date for the project's completion approached, the captain began to give more specific directions about which problems were to be given priority. The attention of the most talented subordinate officers was directed to these problems. Meetings were held biweekly, and frequently on weekends one would find the captain and other group members busily working on the installation. The night of the scheduled switch to the automated system, all members of the group were in attendance. The captain's directions now became commands. The situation which had existed months earlier, when control over the group's progress could be left in the hands of each member, was behind them. At the switchover, no time remained for discussion or speculation about how this or that problem might be handled. The captain controlled all the options, although the entire group actively participated in the actual switch. (Curtis, Mazza, and Runnebohm, pp. 129–130)

As this case study shows, the amount of time available and the amount of control exercised by the leader are usually related. (As the time for problem solving grew short, the captain began to take more control over the process. His changes in leadership style were necessary because of changes in the situation.) When time is short, an authoritarian style is most effective, because control of the discussion process is focused on the leader. The authoritarian leader directs the discussion and takes an active part in determining which points should be considered or discarded in order to speed the process.

An authoritarian leader is effective only to the extent that the group appreciates the conditions which lead to the exercise of control. The naval captain exerted different leadership styles according to the changing needs of the group. He did not maintain a single, uniform style of leadership. A leader adopting the authoritarian style must be candid about those conditions to avoid discouraging the other group members. A leader who asserts authoritarian leadership when it is unwarranted may be ineffective and may even be rejected by the other group members. Thus, authoritarian leadership requires a form of group consent.

The captain asked other group members for suggestions and gave them considerable latitude in working on the problem when adequate time was available. That is, he exercised democratic leadership, the type best suited to that occasion; he allowed each member of the group to contribute fully both to the group's operation and the overall task solution. Had he wished, he could have led the group throughout the installation process by using the authoritative style. His position as a naval captain permits his complete control of authority. From the beginning of the project he could have made assignments directed at solving each of the problems which came to his attention without soliciting any input from his officers.

Clearly, a senior naval officer has the authority to conduct the business of his staff meetings in any way he or she desires. This commanding officer chose a democratic leadership style when adequate time was available and an autocratic style when time was short.

LEADERSHIP FUNCTIONS

Thus far, we have explored leadership in terms of origin and styles. However, leadership can also be viewed as a series of specific functions performed by one or more group members. Fisher and Ellis (1990) suggest that focusing on functions "shifts the point of emphasis from the person to the communicative *behaviors* performed" (p. 233). Leadership functions are those procedural and coordinating communicative activities that aid or shape the organization and structure of the group discussion. Functional leadership duties support the group and its task and should not be used to control or force the group's behavior.

Functional leadership need not reside in one person. Functional leadership duties may be performed by any and all group members; as group priorities and needs change, so do the needs for functional leadership. The leadership functions may change hands several times during a single discussion, as various group members perform functions that place them in temporary leadership positions. A group member may satisfy an important group need regarding procedural requirements, for example, by initiating the discussion; monitoring the agenda; listing items to be discussed; and clarifying comments made by other members. Many groups share such functions; other groups delegate certain functions to an elected chairperson, to allow the group more time to concentrate on other concerns. In formal, structured groups found in business, industry, and government committees, leadership duties are incorporated into the responsibilities of the committee chairperson. Leadership functions can be divided into three broad categories: organizing, conducting, and concluding duties.

Organizing duties involve preparation that will aid the group during its discussion process. A chairperson appointed to a formal committee will need to develop a thorough understanding of the problem area and the committee's responsibility to the parent organization.

Other organizing functions include selecting a meeting place and informing the group of the time and location of the meeting. (See Chapter 7 for a complete discussion of this topic.)

Conducting duties are leadership functions performed during the actual group discussion. Depending upon the nature of the group, a formal group chairperson might assume responsibility for conducting duties, group members may share these duties, or individual members may share certain conducting duties on an irregular or as-needed basis. Typical conducting functions include providing a starting point for discussion, keeping the focus on the problem at hand, monitoring the agenda to keep track of the group's progress and digressions, keeping track of time if the group sets time limits or goals, providing internal summaries, enhancing the participation of others by reinforcing positive behavior, accepting expressions of feelings from others, and yielding to divergent points of view or opinions without prejudice. All are important conducting duties. (See Chapter 7 for additional "people skills," such as dealing with shy people, egotists, and idea squelchers.)

Members who perform functions that satisfy group needs gain respect from other participants, according to the quality and quantity of the contributions. The more respect an individual is accorded, the more that person's deviance from the group norm is tolerated. In other words, the participant who has provided leadership in facilitating the discussion will be able to defy the group's standards and beliefs more effectively and more often than the member who has contributed little or nothing (Fisher and Ellis, p. 270). The successful group member should remember, however, that deviating from the group norms diminishes the respect of other members. Thus, even a person who is well liked and has contributed much to the group effort may find other participants turning a "cold shoulder" if he or she persists in advocating an unpopular notion.

What we find, then, is a circular relationship between leadership functions and the group's task accomplishment. Since leadership is often viewed as behavior that supports the group and helps achieve its goal, and groups view individuals who perform those functions as leaders, people desiring leadership roles would be wise to perform functions that will facilitate the group discussion process.

Concluding duties provide a sense of closure or finality to the various portions of the group proceedings. Internal summaries are often overlooked, although they are useful as the group shifts from one area to another or after a decision has been accepted. Summaries at the end of a discussion session are also useful and fall into the category of concluding duties. Such summaries serve as a recapitulation (or "recap"), a review of the proceedings, which helps to refresh the group's memory of just what has taken place and what has been decided. In formal committee proceedings, the chairperson is responsible for seeing that a summary is made and that a written copy of the summary is sent to each group member. In less formal group discussions, one or more group members can provide functional leadership by offering to summarize what the group has accomplished.

THE LEADER AS A MANAGER OF INFORMATION

Likert, an advocate of the democratic style of leadership (participative decision making) in organizations, believed that management invites serious problems when workers are not involved in decision making. He stressed that worker participation is critical to the successful functioning of an organization. The leader, he stated, "strengthens the group processes by seeing that all problems which involve the group are dealt with by the group" (1961, p. 171). A key, he noted, is the promotion and development of supportive communication between workers and management. The leader "shares information fully with the group and creates an atmosphere where the members are stimulated to behave similarly" (p. 167).

Kreps (1990) points out that it is the responsibility of managers "to promote participative management by channeling worker messages up the hierarchy and leader messages down the hierarchy." In this way, the manager "acts as a communicative conduit" for including employees in the activities of the organization (p. 88). The manager "links" organizational units by communicating information back and forth to members of various groups.

The leader also has the responsibility of facilitating internal organizational coordination and enlisting cooperation between various units. Thus, leaders must gather background data to identify sources of conflict, suggest procedures for conflict prevention, and provide strategies for resolution of conflict between various individuals and units. Effective information managers are adept at preventing destructive personal conflict and at using constructive conflict to improve productivity and cohesion.

SUMMARY

- Whether you view working in groups as a painful necessity or as one of your most fulfilling activities, you will spend a sizable portion of your life working with others in groups. Small group communication occurs when three or more people communicate face-to-face, usually under the direction of a leader; group members share a common purpose or goal and influence one another.

- Working in groups to solve problems and make decisions has several advantages over working individually. As a whole, the group has more knowledge, more creative ideas, greater opportunity for learning, and greater satisfaction. However, working in groups has some disadvantages. Group work generally takes longer, is subject to domination, and can suffer from diffused responsibility, and participants are vulnerable to pressures to conform.

- A useful way to organize problem-solving group discussions is to follow the reflective thinking process. The process can be divided into two phases—problem description and problem solution—with a total of six steps: (1) definition and limitation of the problem, (2) analysis of the problem, (3) generation of possible solutions, (4) appraisal of suggested solutions and/or criteria, (5) selection of the best solution, and (6) implementation of the solution.

- For effective brainstorming, participants should (1) suspend judgment; (2) think wild; (3) practice piggybacking; (4) stress quantity of ideas, not quality; and (5) make a list of ideas suggested.

- Researchers have identified several characteristics of effective group members. Effective participants are prepared, carefully analyze evidence, avoid choosing a solution too soon, maintain their objectivity, work toward relational goals, make orientation statements, and assist in managing group conflict.

- Public discussion groups include the panel, symposium, and forum. Panels tend to allow more free-flowing interaction between and among panel members. Symposia cover specific areas of a topic in an organized, precise manner. Forums, while less organized than symposiums, involve the audience in a more direct fashion.

- Leadership is one of the most important roles in group problem solving. The success or failure of the group discussion process often hinges on the nature of the leadership present within the group. Leadership may be defined as any act or behavior that affects the group's climate, procedures, and effectiveness in problem solving and decision making. Efforts to describe group leadership focus upon various styles and functions. Efforts to identify leaders on the basis of their inherent personality traits, however, have been generally unsuccessful.

- Leaders are often appointed to authority; in many cases, however, a leader emerges from within the group itself. A group member who is willing to work, prepare, contribute ideas, make a good impression, participate actively, monitor nonverbal communication, and take a prominent position in the room can emerge as the group leader.

- A leader's behavior and attitude toward the group and the group process constitute leadership style. The authoritarian leader exerts a high degree of control, direction, and supervision. The democratic leader seeks cooperation and participation from group members. Democratic leaders provide direction and structure as required but encourage the group to develop or suggest procedures, operational methods, and free-flowing communication patterns. The nondirective leader attempts to stimulate the group toward self-direction. A nondirective leader does not impose his or her ideas or beliefs upon the group. Laissez-faire leaders exert little control or direction over the activities of the group. Group members serving under laissez-faire leaders have a high degree of freedom but may not accomplish the task at hand as quickly as groups under the first three kinds of leaders.

- Successful group leadership involves procedural and coordinating functions, as organizing, conducting, and concluding discussions. The object of functional leadership is to facilitate the group process, not to control the group members.

- The leader is a manager of information. A leader links organizational units by communicating information between groups and individuals. The leader enlists cooperation between groups and attempts to prevent or work through conflict for the sake of organizational unity and productivity.

QUESTIONS FOR REVIEW AND DISCUSSION

1. What are the characteristics that define a group?
2. Discuss the advantages and disadvantages of working in a group.
3. List and describe the two phases and six steps in the reflective thinking process used for solving a problem as a group.
4. Discuss the five rules for brainstorming.
5. Identify and describe three types of public discussion groups.
6. What are the characteristics of effective group members?
7. How would you define leadership?
8. Discuss the personal traits, management styles, and group functions of a leader.
9. Compare and contrast the four leadership styles.
10. Identify and explain the three functions of leadership.
11. What does it mean to say that a leader is a manager of information?

ACTIVITIES

1. Identify six groups to which you belong. How does each group meet the definition of small group communication presented in this chapter?

2. Develop a sample policy question for each of the following topics:
   • AIDS testing
   • Corporate takeovers
   • Employee health benefits
   • Accommodating handicapped employees

3. For each of the policy questions you developed for Activity 2, identify criteria that any solution to the problem must meet.

4. Working with a group of colleagues, use the brainstorming method to generate possible solutions for the following problems:
   • Lack of parking for employees
   • Employees moonlighting for extra income
   • Employee apathy
   • Safety problems at work

5. Observe a group problem-solving session. Identify and discuss the style of leadership demonstrated by the chairperson.

6. For the meeting observed in Activity 2, identify and discuss helpful behaviors of group participants.

Chapter
7

Group Meetings

After reading and reviewing this chapter, you should be able to . . .

1. Identify and explain the three dimensions of a meeting the leader must oversee.

2. Explain the five purposes for which meetings are held.

3. Explain the steps in planning a meeting.

4. List and describe the two management concerns in conducting a meeting.

5. Compare and contrast the task and social leadership functions important to a successful meeting.

6. Explain seven strategies for managing the people during a meeting.

7. Identify and explain seven errors the leader of a meeting should avoid.

8. Identify the typical way a group reports recommendations to superiors.

9. Compare and contrast four special problem-solving techniques used beyond the boundaries of regular problem-solving meetings.

*I*n his new position, Bob Trent soon will learn that meetings are a fact of life. They can be the source of many worthwhile ideas and decisions. Business writer Kent Davies (1988) says that "meetings can be very effective in gaining active participation and acceptance. They can be a vehicle to get information on the table and generate useful feedback. Meetings allow people to contribute personally and they help to generate a feeling of camaraderie that can be invaluable in implementing a new project or product" (p. 13). Mosvick and Nelson (1987) note three emerging trends in the "contemporary business scene" that affect the "frequency and importance of efficient business meetings." The factors include "(1) the need to adapt to accelerating changes in the business environment; (2) the need for greater coordination of increasingly interdependent business and governmental units; and (3) the movement toward participative management, particularly in the widespread quality circles movement" (p. 25).

Effective business communicators conduct and participate in productive meetings. A *meeting* is "any kind of purposeful coming together of people to carry out the business of the company" (3M Meeting Management Team, 1987, p. 2). Meetings are a way of life in our country. Perhaps as many as 11 million meetings take place in America each day (Doyle and Straus, 1976, p. 4). Seibold (1979) notes that "news media reports abound of decisions emanating from civic bodies, boards of directors, blue ribbon commissions, juries, legislative subcommittees, school boards, church groups, task forces, councils, local agencies, and bargaining units" (p. 4). If you attend "just four hours in meetings per week," you will "sit through more than 9,000 hours of meetings during your lifetime" (Doyle and Straus, 1976, p. 4). Add up the hours invested; the salaries of the participants; the payroll taxes and fringe benefits; the general overhead; the expenditures for photocopies, slides, printing costs, and secretarial costs; and the cost of a meeting becomes significant. The 3M Management Team provides a tool for calculating meeting costs (see Table 7.1).

Bob Trent has a challenge before him. Not only will he be attending many meetings; as a manager, he will conduct a significant number of those meetings. There are a number of ways Bob can improve the quality of meetings he will be expected to lead.

PLANNING MEETINGS

Bob Trent needs to plan, conduct, and follow up the meetings *he chooses to convene* in the fulfillment of his responsibilities. Note that the stress is upon the meetings Bob chooses to convene. Why have meetings, anyway? A great

Table 7.1 COST OF MEETINGS TO NEAREST DOLLAR PER HOUR

Annual salary	Number of participants									
	10	9	8	7	6	5	4	3	2	1
$50,000	481	433	385	337	288	240	192	144	96	48
$40,000	385	346	308	269	231	192	154	115	77	38
$35,000	288	260	231	202	173	144	115	87	57	28
$30,000	240	216	192	168	144	120	96	72	48	24
$20,000	192	173	154	135	115	96	77	58	38	19

Source: "Cost of Meetings to Nearest Dollar per Hour," from *How to run better business meetings* by the 3M Management Team, p. 14. Copyright © 1987 by McGraw-Hill, Inc. Reprinted by permission of McGraw-Hill, Inc.

many matters can be decided by a single individual; by holding an interview; by reading the organization's policy and procedure manuals (to acquire information that might eliminate the need for a meeting); or by practicing good listening habits when interacting with others. Numerous meetings could be eliminated (1) if managers chose to make unilateral decisions instead of depending upon others to share the responsibility, (2) if managers took responsibility for errors in the decisions they make, and (3) if managers obtained more of the information they need on a one-to-one basis. But when meetings are necessary, it is important to remember that just as fire prevention is more energy-efficient than fire fighting, planning a meeting is more cost-effective than "fixing" the results of a meeting that is ineptly planned or not planned at all. When asked how meetings can fail, professionals gave hundreds of examples. (Table 7.2 lists the 16 most common problems, which accounted for

Table 7.2 THE 16 MOST COMMON PROBLEMS IN MEETINGS

- No goals or agenda
- No premeeting orientation
- Starting late
- Poor or inadequate preparation
- Getting off the subject
- Taking too long
- Disorganized
- Inconclusive
- Ineffective leadership
- Irrelevant information discussed
- Time wasted
- Interruptions
- Ineffective at making decisions
- Rambling, redundant, digressive discussions
- Individuals dominate discussions
- No published results or follow-up action

Source: From *We've got to start meeting like this* by Roger K. Mosvick and Robert B. Nelson. Copyright © 1987 by Roger K. Mosvick and Robert B. Nelson. Published by HarperCollins.

90 percent of the total.) It is probably safe to say there is a direct correlation between a judicious amount of planning and the productivity and satisfaction growing out of a meeting. Whether the meeting is held so that corporate executives can review a new product or so that a fraternity or sorority can plan strategy for rush week, the same guidelines should be followed. So where do you begin?

Clarify the Purpose

Planning for an effective meeting begins with determining the purpose of the meeting. Meetings you plan may be for one or a combination of purposes: (1) training or educating participants, (2) disseminating information, (3) obtaining information, (4) solving a problem, or (5) making a decision. Determining the purpose of the meeting allows you to sharpen your planning focus by anticipating the results you want from the meeting. Meetings held for different purposes will have different desired results.

Anticipate the Results

The results sought from an education and training meeting might be new behaviors, skills, or techniques. Suppose that your student organization wants to conduct a "phone-a-thon" to raise money for a project. Training in telemarketing techniques would be essential to success. Your meeting might also focus on team development, role clarification, providing feedback, and support for the participants.

In other situations, meetings provide data, awareness, enlightenment, or rumor control. For example, if your campus was experiencing a problem with date rape, it would be wise to hold an information distribution meeting to provide safeguards against this crime. In addition, an information-gathering meeting might be held in order to secure facts, opinions, ideas, perspectives, or feelings. A problem-solving meeting might seek to identify a problem and to analyze, appraise, select, and implement solutions. The student government might convene a meeting focusing on "What should be done about date rape on our campus?" A decision-making meeting might produce plans, recommendations, and action. A successful problem-solving meeting might lead to a decision-making meeting with the vice-president of Student Affairs, to finalize plans and implement a campus wide course of action to protect students from date rape. After a determination of anticipated results, the next step is the selection of a plan to achieve those results.

Select a Plan of Action

A training and education meeting might include presentations, structured activities, demonstrations, applications, open discussion, simulations, and role playing.

An information dissemination meeting may include presentations and questions. An information-gathering meeting might be used to present issues and questions intended to secure reactions and comments. An action plan for a problem-solving meeting could encompass the reflective thinking approach presented in Chapter 6. A decision-making meeting might clarify alternatives, project outcomes, and work toward consensus.

At many of his sales meetings, Bob Trent will obviously have several purposes. A given meeting can move through phases for training, information dissemination, information gathering, problem solving, and decision making (see Table 7.3). Each purpose calls for different approaches to achieve the desired results. Problem solving and effective decision making depend on securing accurate and timely information to assist the group in overcoming obstacles and in selecting courses of action.

Develop an Agenda

The 3M Meeting Management Team (1987) reports that every meeting, "like every ship, needs a steering mechanism," and that "that mechanism is the agenda" (p. 58). A good agenda is the "blueprint" for a successful meeting. As a steering mechanism for the meeting, an agenda should identify the topics that need to be addressed in the meeting and the order in which they should be discussed. An agenda should not appear so formidable that group members dread attending the meeting.

A single meeting might achieve the five purposes listed in Table 7.3, although most agendas are not that thorough. As topics are being developed for the meeting, it is important that group members who will have reporting responsibilities be notified. Provide adequate lead time, preferably a week, so

Table 7.3   MEETINGS: TYPES AND OBJECTIVES

Purpose	Objectives	Plan
Training and education	Role clarification; behavior changes; develop skills; cohesion; feedback; new techniques; team development; support	Presentation; demonstration; applications
Information dissemination	Distribute data; enhance awareness; enlightenment; rumor control	Presentation; answer questions
Information gathering	Get facts, opinions, ideas, perspectives, feelings	Present issues; ask questions; get reactions
Problem solving	Identify and describe problem; analyze problem; suggest solutions; appraise, select, and implement a solution	Reflective thinking approach
Decision making	Make a decision; make plans; get recommendations; take action	Clarify alternatives; project benefits

that people with significant responsibilities can plan how best to address upcoming discussion and topics and organize materials for the meeting (Doyle and Straus, p. 201).

The ordering of items on the agenda is important. Tropman and Morningstar (1985) suggest a "bell curve agenda," arranging topics from simple to complex to simple (see Figure 7.1). Meetings should begin with agenda-relevant matters, informative announcements, and less controversial items. The more difficult matters should appear during the middle portion of the meeting, when members are at the peak of their energy levels. During the last third of the meeting time, the focus can again be on easier discussion matters. The meeting ends on a positive note because several quick items have been addressed. The "rule of the agenda bell" allows the group to "keep pace with the psychological and physiological energies of the group." By arranging items in "ascending and then descending order of controversiality" (so that more group energy can be focused on the more critical items), the chairperson can provide time for "decompression and release" during the last third of the meeting in order to achieve the positive ending desired (Tropman and Morningstar, 1985, pp. 53–63).

The leader of the meeting should code agenda items with an appropriate heading: "for information," "for decision," "for approval," or "for problem solving." This lets participants know the purpose of each item on the agenda. Agenda distribution is a leadership function assumed by the chairperson or convener of the group. Agendas should be issued at least a day in advance—

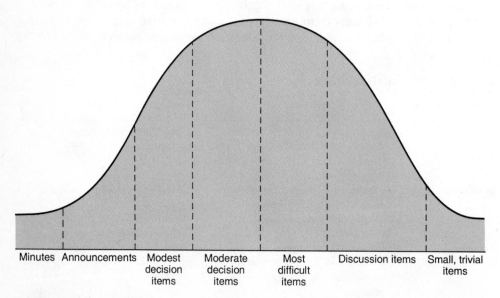

Figure 7.1 The agenda bell. (*Source: Meetings: How to Make Them Work for You*, p. 56. Copyright © 1985 by John E. Tropman and Gershom Clark Morningstar. Reprinted with permission from Van Nostrand Reinhold Company.)

two or three days is preferred. If study materials are complex and/or volumi-nous, a week's lead time may be in order.

Time Considerations

It is a good idea to announce starting and estimated finishing times on an agenda (see Figure 7.2). As a professional courtesy to busy people, the leader should end the meeting when the group has achieved the objectives of the meeting. Doyle and Straus (p. 204) suggest that meetings should last from an hour to two and a half hours. In meetings shorter than an hour, a large por-tion of the time is spent just getting started and building momentum. Meet-ings should start on time regardless of whether all participants have assembled. When chronic lateness is not rewarded by delaying the start or by summarizing what has been covered, stragglers will learn quickly to arrive on time. At the same time, latecomers can't follow through on assignments or contribute meaningful ideas, so be judicious in deciding whether an on-the-spot update is justified. An acknowledgment to the latecomer is appropri-ate. Bob Trent might say, "Welcome, Bill. Please have a seat and and join our

```
                         M E M O R A N D U M

      Date:   January 16

      To:     Communication faculty

      From:   Chairperson

      Re:     Bimonthly department meeting


      A reminder that our next faculty meeting of the Communication
      Department is scheduled for January 23 in Martin 128. The meeting
      will convene at 3:15 p.m. and end at 4:15.
```

Agenda items	Person responsible	Approach	Purpose	Time
1. Placement office update	Alewel	Presentation/ Q&A	Informative	15 minutes
2. Review of cable proposal	Minor	Discussion	For approval	15 minutes
3. Computer lab policy	Beynon	Written report	For approval	5 minutes
4. Faculty guest	Rodenberg	Itinerary	Informative	10 minutes
5. Job targets	Burke	Written report/Q&A	Informative	15 minutes

Figure 7.2 A sample agenda.

Table 7.4 MEETING CHECKLIST

1. Secure a room that is isolated and as soundproof as possible.

2. Find out how to adjust the heat, lights, and public address system.

3. Make sure you have good, even light that is not too dim or glaring.

4. Check the temperature; 68 to 74 degrees Fahrenheit is a good range for working and saving energy (remember, bodies give off heat, too).

5. Make certain that needed multimedia devices are hooked up correctly and functioning.

6. Avoid distractions. Face chairs away from windows, shut doors, hold calls, and so on.

---

meeting. We're into a discussion of our new sales campaign. Betty, will you continue, please?" Note that with his neutral but friendly language, Bob neither rewards nor punishes Bill for arriving late.

Other Planning Considerations

The chairperson should prepare or delegate the preparation of handouts needed during the meeting. Printed materials may take considerable time to prepare. Someone needs to reserve a meeting room, designate a person to keep minutes, ensure that appropriate accessories are present, and properly arrange tables and chairs, media aids, and so on (see Table 7.4). Refreshments, if provided, need advance preparation and timely delivery.

MANAGING THE SUBJECT MATTER

The chairperson of a meeting has two basic tasks: management of subject matter and management of people. The leader's ability to handle both the content and the social dimensions of meetings is critical for fulfilling the organization's mission.

The leader will manage the subject matter of the meeting by following the agenda, which was developed to further the meeting's purpose, results, and strategies. For example, Bob Trent held a meeting to discuss and set yearly sales quotas for his unit. For background for the decision-making component (setting goals all members think are appropriate), Bob thought it would be appropriate to review the goals and results from the previous year's meeting (information dissemination). He used this part of the meeting to find out what the sales team thought about the previous year (information getting). Bob might conduct a sales skit (training and education) to illustrate how sales goals can be reached and to provide strategies for addressing obstacles that might seem to block achievement (problem solving).

Task Roles

There are a number of leadership task roles that members of the group should assume. The chairperson may expect individuals with special skills to assume some of the following task roles:

1. The *initiator* proposes new ideas or approaches to group problem solving.
2. The *information seeker* asks for clarification or suggestions and can also ask for facts or other information that will help the group deal with the issues.
3. The *opinion seeker* asks for clarification of the values and opinions expressed by group members.
4. The *information giver* provides facts, examples, statistics, and other evidence that helps the group achieve the task.
5. The *opinion giver* offers opinions about the ideas under discussion.
6. The *elaborator* provides examples to show how ideas or suggestions would work.
7. The *evaluator* makes an effort to judge the evidence and the conclusion the group suggests.
8. The *energizer* tries to stimulate the group to greater production. (Benne and Sheats, 1948, pp. 43–44)

All these group task roles are valuable in addressing the meeting's objectives. Not all of these roles need be taken for a group to achieve its goals, but in successful meetings, most of the task roles will be assumed. Indeed, "no matter how conscientious and alert" the chairperson may be, the "responsibility for the success or otherwise of the meeting rests squarely with everyone in the group" (*Royal Bank Letter*, 1984, p. 4). When important task roles have been fulfilled, the chairperson may want to thank the participants for making vital contributions to the meeting.

Overview of the Agenda

The chairperson should review what is expected of the group when each agenda item is introduced. Is the group to make a decision? Does the chairperson expect the group to explore the issue further after the meeting? The chairperson should also make certain the group understands the issue and why it is being discussed. It may be necessary to give a progress report or history of the issue, as such background may have a significant bearing on how the group addresses the item. Sometimes background information is needed because the issues have ramifications with regard to personnel, company politics, policies, plant renovations, or future development.

Procedural Elements

The chairperson should be familiar with and make available company documents and procedures—a constitution, bylaws, handbooks, employee grievance procedures, and so on. A working familiarity with *Roberts' Rules of Order* or another appropriate parliamentary procedure guide is essential for dealing with various procedural issues (see Table 7.5). In discussing small committees, Ewbank (1968) notes that the behavior of members is bound

Table 7.5 CLASSIFICATIONS OF MOTIONS ACCORDING TO PRECEDENCE

	Second needed?	Amendable?	Debatable?	Required[1]	Interrupt speaker?
Privileged motions (in order of precedence)					
Fix time of next meeting	Yes	Yes	No[2]	½	No
Adjourn	Yes	No	No	½	No
Recess	Yes	Yes	No[3]	½	No
Question of privilege	No	No	No	Chair[2]	Yes
Subsidiary motions (in order of precedence)					
Lay on the table	Yes	No	No	½	No
Previous question	Yes	No	No	⅔	No
Limit debate	Yes	Yes	No	⅔	No
Postpone to a certain time	Yes	Yes	Yes	½	No
Refer to committee	Yes	Yes	Yes	½	No
Committee of the whole	Yes	Yes	Yes	½	No
Amend	Yes	Yes	[1]	½	No
Postpone indefinitely	Yes	No	Yes	½	No
Main motions (no order of precedence)					
Main motion for general business	Yes	Yes	Yes	½	No
Take from the table	Yes	No	No	½	No
Reconsider	Yes	No	[1]	½	Yes
Rescind	Yes	Yes	Yes	⅔	No
Make special order of business	Yes	Yes	Yes	⅔	No
Incidental motions (no order of precedence)					
Point of order	No	No	No	Chair[2]	Yes
Appeal from decision of chair	Yes	No	[1]	½	Yes
Suspend rules	Yes	No	No	⅔	No
Object to consideration	No	No	No	⅔	Yes
Parliamentary inquiry	No	No	No	Chair	Yes
Request for information	No	No	No	Chair	Yes
Withdraw a motion	No	No	No	½	No

[1]Debatable only when the motion to which it is applied was debatable.

[2]Requires only chair's decision; majority vote if appealed from chair.

[3]Original motion not debatable; amendment debatable.

Note: ½ means one more than half of those voting (simple majority); ⅔ means two-thirds of those voting.

Source: From *Essentials of parliamentary procedure*, 3rd ed., by J. Jeffrey Auer, p. 58. Copyright © 1959 by Appleton-Century-Crofts, Inc. Reprinted by permission of Prentice-Hall, Inc.

more by traditional rules of etiquette than by formal rules of order; however, certain procedural elements are necessary for efficient group meetings. Some essential parliamentary considerations are stating the motion to be voted upon, informing members what the outcome of the vote will mean, providing clear instructions for signaling "in favor" or "not in favor," taking a negative vote even when the affirmative seems to have carried, and stating clearly whether a motion carried or lost.

At the end of the discussion of each agenda item, the chairperson should provide a brief and clear summary of what the group has established or agreed upon. This will assist the person keeping minutes. Any person charged with the responsibility of implementing action should be so reminded in the summary statement, and that person's name should be mentioned in the minutes with the action he or she is to undertake.

MANAGING THE PEOPLE

It is important for meetings to start on time. It is also important for the chairperson to provide a role model and to nurture a climate in which members fulfill the needs of the group. A landmark study suggested that the following group maintenance roles are essential to group success:

1. The *encourager* offers praise, understanding, and acceptance of others' ideas.
2. The *harmonizer* mediates disagreements between other group members.
3. The *compromiser* attempts to resolve conflicts by trying to find solutions acceptable to disagreeing group members.
4. The *gatekeeper* encourages participation of less talkative group members and tries to limit lengthy participation by other group members. (Benne and Sheats, 1948, p. 44)

The chairperson can also facilitate these functions. It is important that members of the group engage in social-emotional leadership acts as well. Anthony Jay (1976) suggests some helpful strategies for managing the social aspects of meetings: (1) control the overly talkative; (2) draw out the reticent; (3) protect the newer and junior members; (4) encourage contention about ideas; (5) discourage idea-squelching tendencies; (6) work up the ladder of seniority; and (7) close on a positive note.

1. *Control the overly talkative.* Some people take a lot of time to say little. The chairperson has the responsibility to control such people. Sometimes an interrupting phrase, such as "Can you please get to the point?" or "That is interesting, but could you please distill it, as we are on a schedule?" will make the point. It is important to be polite but firm in heading off the garrulous.
2. *Draw out the reticent.* Some people say very little in meetings. This may be appreciated by other group members. If the person is silent because he or she disagrees with an item under discussion, has no contribution to make, or is waiting for various positions and issues to be aired, the chairperson should not intervene. However, it is especially important to invite input if (1) the person has salient ideas that

should be aired, or (2) the person is upset about some dimension of the process (the chairperson's behavior, the procedures being followed, etc.). An invitation to share—"Jerry, you seem to be bothered by something we are doing, do you care to comment?"—may help defuse a problem before it gets more serious.

3. *Protect the new and junior members.* The newer and/or junior members of the group sometimes are reluctant to enter the discussion, out of deference or because they fear their colleagues. Sometimes, in subtle or even overt ways, those with seniority squelch contributions from those of lower rank. Such behavior can weaken the meeting. Recognizing the contributions of younger and newer members of the group can be an important source of encouragement to these people as well as a statement to the "old guard" that the chairperson values meaningful input regardless of status.

4. *Encourage contention about ideas.* The leader should encourage contention *about ideas* but not between participants. Debate clarifies issues, and out of good arguments compelling points usually emerge. Additionally, if group members are not challenged to look for flaws in thinking, they may make poor decisions. Critical observers, experts, or people with conflicting points of view can challenge groups to new planes of thinking so that the best ideas emerge. But remember, the leader is encouraging members to disagree (if they legitimately do) over issues of substance, not over what Fisher and Ellis (1990) call affective conflict, which ordinarily stems from "selfish or personal issues" (p. 258).

5. *Discourage idea-squelching tendencies.* Jay (1976) notes that in nearly "every modern organization it is suggestions that contain the seeds of future success" (p. 56). Suggestions and ideas may be more vulnerable to disparagement than facts or opinions. Unless a group member has a lot of confidence and feels very secure, fear of ridicule may cause that person to avoid expressing what could be some excellent ideas. Add the further pressure of status differences, and the climate is right for a moratorium on ideas. An astute chairperson can use the germ of a good idea to encourage the piggybacking technique outlined in Chapter 6. The leader can also discourage idea squelchers by asking them, on the spot, to produce a better thought.

6. *Work up the ladder of seniority.* It is often useful to begin by asking for ideas from less senior members of the group. Be careful, however, not to put a fledgling member of the group on the spot by asking him or her to begin discussion of a volatile agenda item. Junior members should always be asked for input within their domain of experience and knowledge. For example, the chairperson could ask, "Steve, I believe you were involved in that public relations campaign. What observations did you have?"

7. *Close on a positive note.* The chairperson should always conclude the meeting on a positive note. Focusing on achievements rather than

failures, the group gets a "lift" and will be more likely to be "up" for future meetings. If a later agenda item was unresolved or ended on a sour note, the leader can refer to an earlier matter that was resolved. In closing the meeting, the leader should summarize the decisions reached and the responsibilities assigned. Finally, the chairperson should thank all for attending and should establish the time and location of the next meeting.

SELF-MANAGEMENT

The leader can commit a number of errors that detract from his or her personal effectiveness and from accomplishing the objectives of the meeting. Auger (1972) lists some distracting "sins": (1) domination, (2) poor preparation, (3) letting the meeting run away, (4) resenting questions, (5) allowing comic distraction, (6) harassing group members, and (7) tolerating interruptions (pp. 64–65).

1. *Do not dominate the meeting.* If you (as chair) dominate the meeting with your thoughts on every issue, resentment is likely to surface. In the view of the participants, you are autocratic and a "know-it-all." This behavior undermines the dignity of the members and destroys group cohesion.

2. *Prepare well.* If you come to a meeting poorly prepared, the fact will be evident. The group will notice you shuffling through papers, groping for catchwords, and making vague references to the subject matter. The meeting will meander like a ship without a rudder while you waste the time of those present. They will resent this, and the results may be disastrous.

3. *Control runaway meetings.* A meeting can get sidetracked, like a train without an engineer or conductor. Do not allow members to ramble on; intervene when comments are not germane to the issues being addressed. Meetings that end an hour late without apparent results, or end on time with little accomplished, are a big waste of time.

4. *Do not resent questions.* Do you resent questions or comments which appear to challenge your ideas and suggestions? Do you convey the message (intentionally or unintentionally) that there will be retribution if your words are questioned? Resentment is likely to surface in the group. You may also destroy the initiative of the members to be productive team players.

5. *Do not allow comic distraction.* Group leaders who feel they must tell funny stories or "off-color" jokes are most likely assuming a destructive role. A good story that is germane to the discussion may occasionally relieve tensions and make a point. But too much of a good thing can undermine the tone of a business meeting.

6. *Never harass participants.* If you publicly chastise members of the group, you are not being discreet. Picking on specific individuals and subjecting them to ridicule and harassment suggests you have a serious problem with your own feelings of security or self-esteem. Generally, criticism should be given only at private sessions for discipline or constructive feedback.

7. *Avoid interruptions.* If you permit interruptions to meetings (except in emergencies), you are inviting resentment. Taking a phone call during a business meeting (unless it is important to the objectives of the meeting) wastes the valuable time of the other participants. It is inappropriate to allow a secretary to bring in letters, memos, or other documents for your review while the meeting is placed on hold. Others should be informed that only emergency situations justify interruptions.

MEETING FOLLOW-UP

As Yogi Berra said, "It ain't over till it's over." Meetings are not over until several essential follow-up functions are completed.

Evaluate the Meeting Always evaluate the success of a meeting. Bob Trent might do this in several ways. He might send each person attending the meeting a simple critique form, asking what the participant liked best and least and inviting suggestions for improvements (see Figure 7.3).

On the evaluation form, Bob might also include a series of questions focusing on such factors as the purpose of the meeting and how successfully task and social dimensions were addressed. Another means for assessing a meeting is to assign someone to be a critical evaluator. That person can be charged with the responsibility of critiquing the meeting on a subjective basis. Finally, Bob can poll a few individuals for candid assessments and constructive suggestions. Figure 7.4 shows a useful form for participants to complete.

You can also judge a meeting by asking two simple questions: (1) What happened? and (2) How did the meeting go? In evaluating what happened, it is useful to review what problems were solved and what decisions were made. If the results of the meeting will have a positive impact on the future of the company (profits, services, member satisfaction, etc.), then the meeting was probably successful. A review of how the meeting went should focus on the process of the meeting. Did the group work well together? How did participants feel about the meeting? If the people attending had a good time, were stimulated and challenged, and built upon one another's ideas, then it was probably successful. If egos were battered and members felt frustrated by the meeting, the process was probably not successful.

1. How do you feel about today's discussion?

   Excellent_____   Good_____   All right _____   So-so_____   Bad_____

2. What were the strong points of the discussion?

3. What were the weaknesses?

4. What changes would you suggest for future meetings?

(You need not sign your name.)

Figure 7.3 A postmeeting reaction form. (*Source*: From John K. Brilhart and Gloria Galanes, *Effective Group Discussion*, 6th ed., p. 345. Copyright © Wm. C. Brown Publishers, Dubuque, Iowa. All rights reserved. Reprinted by permission.)

Distribute Minutes   Minutes should be issued promptly after the meeting, while the experience is still recent. The minutes should be concise and should include

- The time, date, and location, and the name of the chairperson of the meeting;
- The names of all members present and absent;
- Agenda items discussed and decisions reached;
- Names of people who are to complete assignments;
- The time at which the meeting ended; and
- The date, time, and place of the next meeting.

See Figure 7.5 on page 169 for a sample of meeting minutes.

The secretary distributing the minutes should have the chairperson review them for accuracy and should distribute them within 24 hours of the meeting.

Report Group Recommendations   Problem-solving and decision-making groups often need to report the results of their discussion to superiors. The

Instruction: Circle the number that best indicates your reaction to the following questions about the discussion in which you participated.

1. *Adequacy of communication.* To what extent do you think members were understanding each others' statements and positions?

| 0 | 1 | 2 | 3 | 4 | 5 | 6 | 7 | 8 | 9 | 10 |

Much talking past each other;   Communicated directly with each other;
misunderstanding   good understanding

2. *Opportunity to speak.* To what extent did you feel free to speak?

| 0 | 1 | 2 | 3 | 4 | 5 | 6 | 7 | 8 | 9 | 10 |

Never had a chance to speak   All the opportunity to talk I wanted

3. *Climate of acceptance.* How well did members support each other and show acceptance of individuals?

| 0 | 1 | 2 | 3 | 4 | 5 | 6 | 7 | 8 | 9 | 10 |

Highly critical and punishing   Supportive and receptive

4. *Interpersonal relations.* How pleasant and concerned with interpersonal relations were group members?

| 0 | 1 | 2 | 3 | 4 | 5 | 6 | 7 | 8 | 9 | 10 |

Quarrelsome; status   Pleasant; empathic;
differences emphasized   concerned with people

5. *Leadership.* How adequate was the leader (or leadership) of the group?

| 0 | 1 | 2 | 3 | 4 | 5 | 6 | 7 | 8 | 9 | 10 |

Too weak (   ) or dominating (   )   Shared, group-centered, and sufficient

6. *Satisfaction with role.* How satisfied are you with your personal participation in the discussion?

| 0 | 1 | 2 | 3 | 4 | 5 | 6 | 7 | 8 | 9 | 10 |

Very dissatisfied   Very satisfied

7. *Quality of product.* How satisfied are you with the discussions, solutions, or learning that came out of this discussion?

| 0 | 1 | 2 | 3 | 4 | 5 | 6 | 7 | 8 | 9 | 10 |

Very displeased   Very satisfied

8. *Overall.* How do you rate the discussion as a whole, apart from any specific aspect of it?

| 0 | 1 | 2 | 3 | 4 | 5 | 6 | 7 | 8 | 9 | 10 |

Awful; waste of time   Superb; time well spent

Figure 7.4 A postmeeting questionnaire. (*Source*: From John K. Brilhart and Gloria Galanes, *Effective Group Discussion*, 6th ed., p. 346. Copyright © Wm. C. Brown Publishers, Dubuque, Iowa. All rights reserved. Reprinted by permission.)

MEMORANDUM

Date: January 24
To: Communication faculty
From: Chairperson
Re: Minutes of meeting of January 24

Chairman Burke convened the meeting at 3:15 p.m. in Martin 125.
The following agenda items were discussed:

1. Teresa Alewel, activity director of placement, was introduced by Chairman
   Burke. Alewel gave an overview of the new services of the Placement
   Office after announcing their plans to move to the third floor of the Student
   Union in October. She mentioned a subscription to The Liberal Arts Newsletter
   This news source promises information about benefits of hiring liberal arts
   graduates. Alewel reported that plans are under way to host a panel of
   employers who show preference toward liberal arts graduates on November 16th.
   The panel will include employers of communication graduates. In October, a
   survey (based on phone and mail survey) of recent grads will be available for
   review. Alewel indicated a willingness to work with the department in
   establishing a departmental placement service.

2. John Minor discussed possible plans to provide programming on a cable channel.
   A feed would be placed in the Martin television studios and the journalism office.
   Ralph Bard inquired about the copyright implications and said he would read the
   franchise statement of the company.

3. Don Burke discussed the visit of John Beynon and distributed a draft of the
   itinerary. He also has an undergraduate catalog for faculty to peruse. A page
   from the catalog, which described course work in the department, was distributed
   to faculty. Burke encouraged the faculty to provide ideas about how best to
   make a reasoned decision concerning the desirability of a faculty/student
   exchange. He suggested that the personnel committee, the curriculum committee,
   the student affairs committee, and the professional relations committee discuss
   the matter. An opportunity will be provided for faculty to interview Dr. Beynon,
   and a short department meeting will be called to discuss the department's concerns
   about establishing an exchange.

4. The computer laboratory by the journalism ad hoc committee was reviewed and
   approved by consensus.

5. Burke provided a brief review of departmental goals for the coming year.

6. Burke expressed alarm about copy machine costs. He noted that the department
   use for less than one month was 26,626 copies at a cost of $525. At this rate,
   the annual cost could exceed $5,000 and would consume a major part of the
   operational budget. Faculty were encouraged to use the duplicator when more
   than 25 copies were needed. Burke requested that examinations be reused whenever
   possible and urged judicious use of the duplicating machines.

7. Burke announced that a meeting has been scheduled with academic advisors
   at 4:30 p.m. on March 19. The purpose is to educate the advisors about our
   policies and procedures and to recruit majors. Any issues faculty want aired
   should be passed along. Interested faculty are invited to attend the meeting.

The meeting was adjourned at 4:30 p.m. with a reminder that the next meeting will
be held on March 20 in Martin 128.

Dawn Swain, Secretary

Figure 7.5 Sample minutes.

Table 7.6 MEETING PREPARATION STEPS

Step	Activity
1. Planning the meeting	A. Clarify the purpose.
	B. Anticipate the results.
	C. Select a plan of action.
	D. Develop and distribute an agenda.
	E. Delegate other planning considerations.
2. Conducting the meeting	A. Managing the subject matter.
	1. Task roles.
	2. Overviewing the agenda.
	3. Procedural elements.
	B. Managing the people.
	1. Control the overly talkative.
	2. Draw out the reticent.
	3. Protect new and junior members.
	4. Encourage contention about ideas.
	5. Discourage idea-squelching.
	6. Work up the ladder of seniority.
	7. Close on a positive note.
	C. Self-management.
	1. Avoid dominating the meeting.
	2. Prepare well.
	3. Control runaway meetings.
	4. Avoid resenting questions.
	5. Avoid comic distraction.
	6. Avoid harassing members.
	7. Avoid tolerating interruptions.
3. Follow-up	A. Evaluate the meeting.
	B. Distribute minutes.
	C. Report group recommendations.

format can be oral, written, or a combination of the two. A standard format for reporting group deliberations and recommendations is the written report. Special discussion formats (such as the symposium, forum, and panel, discussed in Chapter 6) may also be adapted for reporting purposes.

Table 7.6 summarizes the steps in preparing for a meeting.

WRITTEN MEETING REPORTS

A written report should summarize key issues addressed by the group, with emphasis on final recommendations. One way to organize the report is to follow the reflective thinking steps discussed in Chapter 6. The report can begin with the "felt difficulty" or problem description. It can include the problem analysis; identification of viable solutions (it is probably unnecessary to list all brainstorming ideas generated); the criteria a solution must meet; the best solution; and suggestions for implementation. For the sake of clarity, it is helpful to use headings and subheadings throughout the report. The length will vary depending upon the complexity of the problem and length of time spent in deliberation. Reports might conclude with a bibliography of sources that were of assistance in reaching the group's conclusion.

SPECIAL MEETING FORMATS

Several special problem-solving procedures can serve as vehicles for structuring discourse during extended meetings or as means for solving problems outside the scope of regular meetings. These special problem-solving procedures include the buzz group, the nominal group technique, the Delphi method, and quality circles.

Buzz Groups

A *buzz group* is a small group selected from a larger unit. The buzz group meets to discuss an assigned issue or question for a specified period of time, then reports the answers to the larger group. Generally, several buzz groups work on the same question concurrently. The technique was developed by J. Donald Phillips, president of Hillsdale College. It has been called the "Phillips 66 buzz group technique" because groups of six people discussed a topic for six minutes. The buzz group technique is a good way to instill life into a stale meeting. Buzz groups can generate questions for a panel, identify problems or issues that grow out of a situation, and brainstorm a list of solutions to a problem. Buzz groups are an excellent technique for reducing the feelings of anonymity in large groups. Students and corporate executives alike are encouraged to try buzz groups to generate enthusiasm and a sense of involvement.

Nominal Group Technique

In the *nominal group technique* (NGT), a small group of people brainstorm silently in one another's presence to generate ideas, pool the ideas through interaction, clarify the ideas, then evaluate the ideas (often using a ranking system). *Nominal* is a key term because the group is, in some respects, a group in name only; much of the time is spent in individual work. However, participants do alternate between interacting with one another and working alone. NGT works as follows: (1) participants silently list ideas; (2) the people interact as a group; (3) the group selects a recorder; (4) each person reads his or her list; (5) the recorder lists the ideas on a chart; (6) members evaluate ideas critically; and (7) the group reduces the list until a satisfactory solution emerges. Delbecq, Van de Van, and Gustafson (1975) report that the technique was developed to accrue the advantages of group discussion without the disadvantages. They say that the nominal group technique is better for long-range planning than for routine meetings. Seibold (1979) summarizes a benefit of the technique: the procedure "generates a basis for group discussion which reflects all members' views, views carefully considered while working alone and expressed without intimidation from more powerful or talkative group members" (p. 11).

The Delphi Method

Like the nominal group technique, the Delphi method restricts the interaction between group members (typically a panel of experts) in order to minimize commitment to one point of view, domination by vocal members, and the pressure of majority opinions. The *Delphi method* can be defined as "a method for the systematic solicitation and collation of judgments on a particular topic through a set of carefully designed sequential questionnaires interspersed with summarized information and feedback of opinions derived from other responses" (Delbecq, Van de Van, and Gustafson, p. 10). Seibold describes the steps of the process: (1) Group members complete a questionnaire framed to solicit their opinions about a problem, policy, recommendation, or issue. (2) After a break, the panel of experts receives a second questionnaire listing the ideas of their fellow experts. Each is asked to evaluate the ideas, using specified criteria as standards of judgment. (3) During the next session, a third questionnaire reports the second-round ratings, mean scores, and areas of agreement. Members are asked to revise their earlier ratings in view of the means or areas of consensus. Those who still disagree are required to justify their minority views. (4) A final questionnaire reports all the ratings, areas of concern, and holdouts for divergent views, and members have a last chance to revise their positions. Sometimes, all the data gathered is forwarded to an independent group of decision makers. Or, the experts may be asked to interact face-to-face in an effort to arrive at a final recommendation. The liabilities are obvious. The task of assembling a panel of experts, the time spent in collating and recollating data, the stymied interaction, and the cumbersome nature of the entire process render the procedure inefficient. However, the process has been used effectively by numerous groups. Goldberg and Larson (1975) note that "groups consisting largely of 'non-experts'" might find the method inappropriate (p. 148).

Quality Circles

A *quality circle* is a small group of company employees who meet regularly on company time to discuss work-related matters. Since their start in Japan during the early 1960s, quality circles have become a very popular management tool for increasing productivity, morale, worker involvement, and the quality of products and services (Ross, 1989). (In Japan they are called quality control circles.) Usually employees meet for one hour a week, but the time varies from company to company (Brilhart and Galanes, 1989). As discussed in Chapter 2, each quality circle consists of people from a department or other unit designation who solve problems they or management identify. The leader may be appointed or elected. In order for the group to be effective, all changes proposed by quality circles must be considered seriously by managers, who must provide a quick response. It is also important that returns from implementing these suggestions be shared with employees as well as with management and stockholders. When employees are subjected to Theory X management (see Chapter 2), quality circles are not likely to work well.

SUMMARY

• Meetings are part of the workday in business, industrial, social, governmental, and educational agencies. Each agency has numerous meetings. Some meetings are effective, but many are poorly planned, poorly conducted, and poorly followed up.

• Planning a meeting involves clarifying the purpose, developing an agenda, strategically ordering the items of discussion, appropriately allocating time, preparing handouts, alerting members who will be responsible for reports, making meeting room arrangements, and planning refreshments.

• Conducting the meeting involves management of the subject matter and management of the people. Subject matter or task management focuses on nurturing various leadership task roles: initiator, information seeker, opinion seeker, information giver, opinion giver, elaborator, evaluator, and energizer. The chairperson should be familiar with the basics of parliamentary procedure. Traditional rules of etiquette are also important in maintaining dignity and decorum in a meeting.

• The management of people is an extremely critical component of an effective meeting. The social climate of the meeting depends on important leadership roles: encourager, harmonizer, compromiser, and gatekeeper. The chairperson must control the overly talkative, draw out the reticent, protect the junior members, encourage contention about ideas, discourage idea-squelching tendencies, work up the seniority scale, and close the meeting on a positive note. The chairperson should avoid committing several personal "sins" that can hamper a meeting: domination, poor preparation, allowing a runaway meeting, resenting questions, permitting comic distraction, harassing participants, and tolerating interruptions.

• Meeting follow-up includes evaluating the meeting, distributing minutes, and reporting group recommendations. A standard format for reporting meeting results to superiors is the written report, which can follow the steps of reflective thinking to summarize the group's deliberations and recommendations.

• There are special problem-solving procedures that can serve as tools outside regular problem-solving meetings, particularly when extended time is needed. They include the buzz group, the nominal group technique, the Delphi method, and quality circles.

QUESTIONS FOR REVIEW AND DISCUSSION

1. What three dimensions of a meeting must the chairperson oversee?
2. What are the five purposes for which meetings are held?
3. List the steps in planning a meeting.

4. What are management's top two concerns in conducting a meeting?

5. What task and social leadership functions are important to a successful meeting?

6. Discuss the seven strategies leaders can use to manage the social aspects of a meeting.

7. Describe seven errors the chairperson should avoid in a meeting.

8. How do groups typically report recommendations to others?

9. Discuss the four special problem-solving techniques used outside regular problem-solving meetings.

ACTIVITIES

1. After a group meeting, identify the task or social roles you assumed as a participant (use the following list).

   Group task roles:

   Initiator

   Information seeker

   Opinion seeker

   Information giver

   Opinion giver

   Elaborator

   Evaluator

   Energizer

   Group maintenance roles:

   Encourager

   Harmonizer

   Compromiser

   Gatekeeper

2. List five groups you belong to that have regular meetings. Evaluate the purposes of the meetings and determine whether they fit within the five categories identified in this chapter.

3. Do any of the groups you listed in Activity 2 fulfill more than one purpose in a given meeting? If so, what different purposes do they fulfill?

4. Design a form to use in evaluating the effectiveness of meetings. Attend a business meeting as an observer and use your form to evaluate its effectiveness.

FOUR

Planning for Your Presentation

Chapter
8

Preparing for Business Presentations

After reading and reviewing this chapter, you should be able to . . .

1. Explain the advantages of delivering your ideas in an oral presentation as opposed to a memorandum, a written report, or a letter.

2. Compare and contrast presentational speaking with public speaking.

3. Compare and contrast the purpose statement (objective) and the central idea statement (thesis) of an oral presentation.

4. Explain the use of a storyboard as a media planning tool for a presentation.

5. Define a "murder board" and explain its use as a presentation planning tool.

6. Identify and explain the steps in planning an oral presentation.

As Bob Trent sat at his new desk in the sales department, reading through his sales manual, the telephone rang. The unit secretary was calling to remind Bob of his appointment with the Sento Group on Thursday at 2:00 P.M. Bob knew that his predecessor, Sue Derkman, had struggled to secure this opportunity to explain their company's products and services to Sento. He realized that he alone would represent American Computer Systems, Incorporated, as he met the members of Sento's board of directors. He knew, too, that he would face stiff competition from the sales agents of rival companies.

Bob pulled the sales file on Sento, which Sue had prepared while developing this important contact. The information was largely statistical—Sento's total gross sales potential was estimated to be initially in excess of $175,000, with additional service contracts to follow. The long-range possibilities for American could be significant.

A problem suddenly came into focus for Bob. What, exactly, would he say on Thursday afternoon to a group granting him a maximum of 20 minutes? What materials should he take along? He began to panic. Sure, he knew the product line from his days in the manufacturing division, but he did not know how he could present the information in the most effective way.

Bob is about to make a *business presentation*. Thousands of people face this challenge every day in business, government, education, and industry. Their basic concerns are similar, even though their situations vary considerably. They face the challenge of presenting information regarding an idea, product, or service in the most effective style and manner for a specific audience. They, like Bob, will come to realize the meaning of the cliché that "everything is marketing," from the initial impression to the required service follow-up.

Bob needed some advice. By company standards, the Sento account was not exceedingly large, but it was *Bob's* account now, and he wanted to put forth his "calling card" as a person who does his best when representing American Computer Systems. But what was his best? What makes a really good sales presentation, anyway?

Bob put away the sales file and walked into Carmen Garcia's office. Carmen was sales manager and, hopefully, Bob's new mentor as well as immediate supervisor. Although she was obviously busy, Carmen greeted the fledgling sales team leader warmly. "How's it going, Bob?" she asked.

During the next few minutes, Bob explained his concern about making a good impression with Sento on Monday. He asked for advice. Carmen was impressed with Bob's concern about doing well in his first major presentation; she suggested that he spend the afternoon thinking about the salient features of the product lines, sketch some ideas by Tuesday, and then make a practice presentation to her early Wednesday morning. With this agreed-upon timetable, Bob thanked Carmen and headed back into his office.

Back in his office, Bob felt he was on the right track. He knew his product line well, and now he was ready to start preparing a quality business presentation. He would master the process in the same way he had learned about computer hardware and software—one component at a time. Bob knew that to be a successful corporate representative, he would need to perfect his ability to make effective presentations. For the first time he regretted not taking a presentational speaking course in college.

Unlike Bob Trent, you have the good fortune to be taking a business communication course that includes instruction in presentational speaking. You may find the overview in this chapter a bit frustrating because you will often be referred to later chapters for the details. The purpose of this chapter is to provide the broad strokes, an overview of the steps in planning a presentation. Just as it is not necessary to examine every thread of a tapestry in order to understand the design, you do not need all the details to understand how presentations are planned.

THE IMPORTANCE OF ORAL PRESENTATIONS

Bob Trent's situation is not uncommon. In an increasingly service-driven, "high-tech" society, proposals must vie with numerous alternatives in a competitive marketplace. The difference between making and not making the sale may depend largely on an oral presentation. Why choose oral presentations? Because there are obvious benefits to delivering ideas in person instead of placing them in a memorandum, a written report, or a letter.

1. *Efficiency.* In the long run, presentations can save time. We all have experienced the frustration of unanswered correspondence. Who has not waited days, weeks, or months for a response to an important proposal or request? The proposal gets buried, and time is wasted. With an oral presentation you can receive an instant response. Or, if there is delay in feedback, at least you know the presentation was given a hearing.

2. *Effectiveness.* Communicating face-to-face allows you to observe verbal and nonverbal feedback. As the presenter, you can see those raised eyebrows when you quote a cost figure the auditor views as questionable. You can note the nods and smiles when your point strikes home. You can draw upon additional information to clarify or amplify your point when the listener looks confused, and you can mention evidence to support your position. When members of the audience begin looking at their watches, you can draw the proposal to a close.

   In addition, you and/or audience members can raise questions, providing a chance for you to respond to potential objections or give more detail when information was not clear. The recipients of a written proposal may or may not call or write for a response to their concerns about the report. Since oral presentations are interactive, you can be assured that important questions will be raised by one or more parties involved in the exchange. Chapter 16 provides guidelines for managing questions in an effective and efficient manner.

3. *Influence.* McLuhan (1964) says, "The medium is the message" (p. 7). The oral medium offers leveraging opportunities when you attempt to influence an audience. For example, most people find it more difficult to say "no" in person than in a letter or memorandum. It is even easier to say "no" over the phone than in face-to-face exchange. Whether you are selling memberships in the chamber of commerce, asking for an additional line or staff position, or angling for an increase in your budget, an oral presentation is likely to be more successful than other means. Moreover, enthusiasm, appearance, vocal cues, and other factors can enhance the advantage of the oral medium for more persuasive impact (see Chapter 15).

CHARACTERISTICS OF BUSINESS PRESENTATIONS

Frank E. X. Dance (1987) compares and contrasts public speaking and presentational speaking (see Table 8.1). He notes that the differences between the terms *public* and *presentational* are "differences not of the genre but of the situation or setting" (p. 266). One attitude, "decentering," is not commonly discussed in the speech communication literature. It "relates to the degree to which the speaker/presenter is expected to make a serious effort to take the conceptual point of view of the audience members" (p. 269). In the presentational arena, the audience members (decision makers) expect the presenter to "demonstrate an effort to address their specific points of view and needs overtly" (p. 270).

A successful business presentation is a form of oral communication carefully planned for the purpose of selling ideas, products, or services to a decision-making person or group. Although presentations have much in common with public speaking, an understanding of their unique qualities is essential.

Business presentations are proposal-oriented forms of communication, given in a business setting to relatively homogeneous (more alike than different) audiences of various sizes. They function to provide information and influence decision making. A variety of multimedia aids are typically used, and an interactive mode of delivery is normally employed (that is, source and receiver interact verbally). Presentations are often assigned by a superior, who expects the employee to make the best possible impression on a decision-making body. The presenter is expected to utilize, in a cost-effective manner, all the human and physical resources available to maximize the chances for success. An effective presentation is expected to be a polished effort.

Table 8.1   EXPECTATIONAL DIFFERENCES BETWEEN PUBLIC SPEAKING AND PRESENTATIONAL SPEAKING

Factor	Public Speech	Presentation
Setting	Anywhere, inside or outside.	
How is topic chosen?	Flexible. Committee or program chair.	
Orientation of topic	Broad. Audience may easily support some deviation from announced topic.	Usually quite specific. Task-oriented. More technical job, task, business work goals and objectives. Ranges through staff briefings, marketing, teaching, reports, and so on. Audience usually expects close adherence to announced topic.
Time constraints	Tight timeline.	Tight timeline.
Audience composition	Self-selected. Usually a one-time event. May have broad topic orientation.	Audience usually designated to attend. Usually an ongoing relationship exists among audience members. Audience often has background information concerning relationship of topic to business. Closely focused on topic.
Expectation of audience participation	Latent interaction. Silent audience participation/feedback.	Overt interaction. Often vocal participation. Audience may feel free to challenge presenter.
Focus of responsibility for activity	Responsibility placed upon speaker. Audience expects manifest intent upon part of speaker.	Responsibility placed upon presenter. Audience shares focus of intent. Intent usually skewed toward management goals.
Expected degree of speaker expertise and preparation	Speaker is expected to have earned the right to speak. Expertise is anticipated. Speaker is expected to be fully prepared.	Presenter is often viewed as first among equals but is expected to be specifically prepared.
"Decentering"	Latent but present.	Present and manifest.
Degree of perceived spontaneity	Illusion of spontaneity expected.	Some illusion of spontaneity, but to a smaller degree than in a public speech.
Use of audiovisual aids	Seldom.	Usually.
Question-and-answer period	Sometimes entirely omitted. If used, almost always at end of speech.	Often ongoing, interactive, and continuous.

Source: After F. E. X. Dance, What do you mean presentational speaking? *Management Communication Quarterly* 1(2): 268.

Informational presentations may use entertainment as an interest factor. But presentations are generally designed to be audience-activating. Public speakers seldom utilize multimedia aids; presenters, however, rarely construct messages *without* integrating visual aids. Public speeches are generally designed to provide authoritative information, fulfill ceremonial or inspirational functions, improve public relations, and/or present various kinds of stimulation to an audience. A business-related public speech may be written by someone other than the speaker. For example, a speech writer may be employed by the chief executive officer (CEO) of a major corporation. Presentations, however, are usually prepared by the presenter, with the assistance of other agencies in the work environment—marketing, audiovisual support, and so on. Presentations are given in order to elicit change (often at the time of presentation), to support specific actions, and/or to encourage a group or person with some authority to make a particular decision. Hugenberg, Owens, and Robinson (1988) specify five areas in which changes are proposed in organizations: (1) changing the *product*; (2) changing the *process* by which the product is made; (3) changing the *plant*; (4) changing *policies* (the rules and guidelines the organization follows); and (5) changing the *personnel*, either by hiring new people, deleting existing jobs, or transferring people (p. 31).

Obviously, business people give public speeches and talks for many reasons, including positive public relations and personal ego satisfaction. As Bormann et al. (1982) explain it, "You will be giving the presentation to offer yourself, a sales proposal, a program, or an important budget or organizational change to others who have the power to accept or reject the substance of your message" (p. 196). A presentation may be accepted or rejected on the spot or within days, so the stakes are almost always high. Table 8.2 summarizes the differences between a presentation and a public speech. Obviously, these differences are relative in a given situation. These distinctions may be nonapplicable or overlapping.

Adapting a presentation to the audience and the specific circumstance of the moment is a prerequisite for all effective communication. Basic elements in a presentation are presentation of self; an analysis of the problem; a clear statement of recommendations (proposal); satisfactory answers to questions

Table 8.2 GENERAL DIFFERENCES BETWEEN
PRESENTATIONAL AND PUBLIC SPEAKING

Presentational speaking	Public speaking
Smaller audience	Larger audience
Multimedia use standard	Limited multimedia use
More homogeneous audience	More heterogeneous audience
Business setting	Varied setting
Topic predetermined or assigned	Topic often negotiated
Interactive (verbal) communication	Less interactive (verbal) communication
Proposal-oriented	Varied purposes
Image is critical	Image is less critical
Immediate results	Delayed results
Message is tested	Message is not tested
Assisted by content specialist	Sometimes prepared by speech writer/staff

(overcoming known obstacles); and a proposed course of action. Knowledge, practice, and skills in all these areas are essential to success.

Normally, business presentations are made in situations in which the outcome of the decision will have a major financial impact. (Smaller, less costly items or ideas may be handled more efficiently through informational interactions.) The relationship between the speaker and audience in a presentation is that of a professional with a client or potential client. The relationship is fiduciary in nature. For example, an architect might speak to a board of directors engaged in deciding which firm will design a new building; a salesperson like Bob Trent might speak to a group interested in a major purchase of goods or services for their organization; a consultant might make recommendations to the members of an organization that needs to implement a program to increase managerial efficiency.

Presentations are often reviewed by a superior in advance. Specialists in content and multimedia aids may help the presenter get ready. The audience for a presentation may consist of one key person or a small decision-making group. Audience interaction is expected.

"Backdoor" presentations are made by representatives of one unit to another unit within the same firm; "frontdoor" presentations are made to people who are not part of the same organization. Often presentations are a *team effort* in that more than one person has a major part in making the presentation. For example, one person may present the background information regarding a proposal; a second may discuss the technological capabilities of the equipment; and a third may present the service and pricing information.

Presentations increasingly make use of videotape. For example, people who market time-share or interval property ownerships often use videotape to "soften" the listeners' sales resistance prior to a tour and sales presentation. A polished person of "star quality" can appear on tape as a prelude to almost any presentational format. The taped message establishes a climate for questions and discussions. "Openers" like "What did you think about the tape?" and "Did you have any idea how much the cost of an average vacation had increased?" pave the way for the personal presentation.

Imagine a presenter using a videotape made by the instructional resource center of a college. In it, the presenter indicates how important a student exchange program can be. The videotape serves to legitimize what the presenter will say later discussing the benefits of the exchange plan and explaining the application procedures.

Successful presentations take careful planning. Poor planning is easy to detect, and the presenter will pay dearly for it. No presentation is perfect. However, the difference between a superior presentation and an average one is like the difference between whipping cream and skimmed milk. The difference results from thorough preparation and maturing of your ideas. Careful planning yields success.

PLANNING THE PRESENTATION

Review Your Objectives

Each of you, like Bob Trent, should begin preparation by reviewing the objectives of the presentation. Reviewing the objectives may be as simple as checking with the person who asked (or permitted) you to speak, to make sure the two of you are "on the same wavelength." You may want to put the objective(s) in writing for endorsement by all parties. When you are the initiator of the proposal, it might be wise to contact someone in a position of authority within the department or agency where you plan to make your presentation in order to confirm your understanding of expectations. For example, a consultant wrote the director of customer relations at a major airline to confirm expectations about a training proposal. The director outlined some budgetary constraints. The consultant had to modify the proposed training program extensively to keep costs down. The sale was successful. Had the consultant not contacted the airline, the proposal would have been dismissed as being unrealistic.

Reviewing the objectives forces you to determine precisely what you want from your listeners. In other words, what response is desired? For example, you may want $100,000 in funding from the board of directors of your company for a research and development project, or approval for a new advertising campaign, or a 10 percent increase in your budget for additional personnel. Such objectives should be written out in simple, clear, and brief sentences that meet the following criteria.

1. *Be descriptive.* The objective should be stated in a way that identifies the reaction wanted from the audience. Mager (1962) calls this "identifying the terminal behavior" desired from the subjects you are seeking to influence. If you simply state, "I want to demonstrate to my audience the benefits of a centralized computer climate control system," you have a problem. Why? The statement, as worded, does not reveal the response sought from the audience. If, instead, your objective were worded "I want the board of regents of Central University to approve the purchase of a central computer climate system from American Energy Foundation," you could assess the success of your proposal.

2. *Be specific.* A good objective statement is simple, clear, brief, *and specific.* A good objective statement asks the standard journalist's questions (who, what, when, where, why, and how) about your goal as specifically and precisely as possible. These points are discussed in more detail in Chapter 12.

3. *Be realistic.* Unrealistic goals can lead to frustration. It is not feasible to expect support for every proposal you make. A salesperson calling on a purchasing agent for the first time would be lucky to be offered a tour of the plant or an invitation to return for a presentation to department heads. A university department chairperson requesting

funds for a journalism laboratory outfitted with state-of-the-art word processors might actually receive funding to purchase manual type-writers and a one-year repair contract. Setting realistic goals can lead to more success and avert certain disappointment.

Examples of Specific Objectives

I want the board of directors of the Sento Group to authorize the purchase of 75 personal computers, the interface system to link the network, and appropriate business software from American Computer Systems.

I want the dean of the College of Arts and Sciences to authorize five graduate teaching assistant positions for the Department of Communication.

I want the board of directors of Southern Biochemical Corporation to authorize the purchase of 3 acres of land adjacent to the property currently owned by the corporation.

I want the plant manager of Rival Manufacturing Company to authorize a six-hour time management training session for the engineers of the Clinton plant.

Analyze the Audience

The presenter must understand the nature of the decision-making body. The process of audience analysis is explained in detail in Chapter 9. For our purposes here, a brief overview of audience analysis should suffice. The essential point is that your preparation will be easier from the start if you focus attention on the listeners.

Just what should you consider? What do you need to find out? It is impossible to learn everything about the audience, but the answers to the following questions should serve you well:

What is the name of the group (or person) you will address?

What are their decision-making functions?

Who will make up the group? What are their job responsibilities? How much influence will each have in the decision?

What does the group know about you?

What is the group's image of the firm or department you represent?

What experience do the decision makers have with the proposed idea, product, or service?

Have other members of your unit made presentations of a similar nature to the body? How long ago?

What was the response to previous proposals?

An audience analysis may be enhanced by using other in-house resources. For example, if someone in your organization has made a presentation to the agency before, that person may have learned invaluable lessons. Moreover, you can examine any multimedia aids utilized in an earlier presentation to determine whether any might be useful again.

Develop a Central Idea

Concurrent with the initial development of objectives and audience analysis, it is important to develop a central point, or theme, for the presentation. This objective is always audience-centered. Your specific objective is the goal, and your central idea is the means of reaching that goal. Returning to the sample objectives identified earlier, a possible central idea for each specific objective:

Examples of central ideas:

The purchase of American Computer Systems personal computers, network interface, and appropriate business software will provide the Sento Group with the most cost-effective and efficient equipment in the industry.

The Department of Communication needs five graduate teaching assistants to carry out the department's instructional mission.

The purchase of 3 acres adjacent to Southern Biochemical's property would make it possible to expand the physical plant.

Time management training is needed so the engineers of Rival Manufacturing Company will be more efficient and effective in their work.

A good central idea is succinct and direct. It is a condensation of the entire presentation into one declarative sentence. This central idea statement should match the objective statement by serving as a vehicle for achieving the goal of the presentation.

Develop Main Points

The next step in preparation is to develop the main or key points which form the backbone of the message, blocking out the principal subdivisions. Chapter 12 presents detailed guidance for setting up these main ideas.

Each main point should support, illustrate, or clarify the central idea of the message. Since it is extremely important for the listener to remember and understand key points, you must phrase them in simple, brief, and clear language. The main points can follow a chronological, topical, climactic, spatial, causal, problem-solution, or motivating sequence order. After selecting one of these organizational patterns, you need to develop two or three main points to constitute the body of the presentation. This, in essence, becomes the first stage of outlining.

Consult Information Sources

The next step in message preparation is to consult available sources of information to supplement your basic knowledge. After considering your *own* knowledge and experience, list those points on which you need no additional information. Then list points which will require research. After determining what information you need, undertake a thorough investigation to secure it. Useful data comes in a variety of forms and from numerous sources. Chapter 11 provides a thorough discussion of the use of evidence.

You may be able to delegate the information-gathering task to others. To get information yourself, converse with informed people within or outside your organization, arrange interviews with representatives of organizations that have had experience with similar proposals, or collect data at a public or university library. Often, you can locate the needed data in an education or training department in your own company.

Record Data

As you gather information, it is essential to record the data in an accurate and systematic form, so you can return to the source for verification or future reference. It is wise to collect considerably more material than you will actually need to use in the message. A rule of thumb is to gather at least two or three times as much material as you plan to use. This additional information will give you resources to draw from if you are challenged by a member of the audience during or after the presentation. As you collect information, you will begin to see relationships between this data and your main points. You can then select the subideas—evidence, explanations, and so on—using your audience analysis as a guide to what should be emphasized and what should be deemphasized. Chapters 9 and 11 discuss audience analysis and the use of evidence and reasoning in detail.

Outline the Presentation

After collecting and cataloging materials, you should begin putting the materials in a logical order. Outline all the materials in the form you find most helpful for wording and delivering the presentation. Some speakers find a key word outline helpful; others prefer a full-sentence outline. Chapter 12 presents a more detailed discussion of outlining.

After developing the body of the outline, you need to plan the conclusion and, finally, the introduction. At this point, you must review the entire outline, looking for gaps and inconsistencies. Any weak spots should be strengthened with additional data gathered by reviewing your sources and/or by finding new ones.

Examples of informational and persuasive presentation outlines are at the end of the chapter.

The Storyboard: An Alternative to Outlining

It may prove useful to prepare a storyboard in planning your presentation. A storyboard merges narrative and visual aids on a single sheet. Storyboards are easy to prepare by using sheets of paper (preferably gridded) divided in half horizontally (see Figure 8.1). Typically, the top half is reserved for the visuals and the bottom half for the narrative, which is a commentary about the visuals. Storyboards are often used for planning television commercials and slide/sound audiovisual presentations. A rough sketch of each visual is drawn on the top half of the page and the narrative written on the bottom half. In addition to "wedding" visuals and the narrative, the storyboard helps in timing the presentation. For example, half of a sheet of $8\frac{1}{2}$-by-11-inch paper accommodates 120 to 150 words. Hence, it will take about a minute to present each storyboard. So now you have a system to tie visuals with narration and to monitor appropriate pacing of your presentation. A modification of the traditional storyboard is the audio/video storyboard. Figure 8.2 illustrates an adaptation of the storyboard which includes audio copy and video instructions for planning a multimedia presentation.

Storyboards can be evaluated and reviewed in a meeting. Tape them to the wall, arranged in proper sequence, and measure their effectiveness by testing the flow of information. Do narrative and visuals combine in a smooth, consistent, and logical presentation that utilizes all the available means of persuasion?

Use of Notes

Not all speakers use notes. Generally speaking, presenters tend to use more notes than are necessary, and they look at the notes too often. People who are thoroughly familiar with their materials probably do not need notes unless they want to refer to complex statistical reports or detailed handouts. Multimedia aids often replace the need for notes at important points in a presentation.

The use of notes necessarily breaks contact with the audience and hurts the overall effectiveness of the presentation. You should experiment to see what works best for you, but try to limit the use of notes. Do not attempt to hide the use of notes from the audience. Notes are more effective when used openly and only when necessary.

Practice

Practice is the next step in the planning process. You cannot overpractice— but avoid letting the presentation become stale and memorized. You should go over the material both silently and orally. It is helpful to tape-record or videotape the message for analysis and review. Often the machine captures behavior or sound that you would not otherwise be aware of. After reviewing the tape, experiment with significant changes in the organization, delivery,

Storyboard for _____ _____

(Concept)   (Page number)

```
┌─────────────────────────────────────────┐
│                                           │
│                                           │
│                                           │
│                                           │
│                 (Visual)                  │
│                                           │
│                                           │
│                                           │
│                                           │
└─────────────────────────────────────────┘
```

Narrative _____

_____

_____

_____

_____

_____

_____

_____

Figure 8.1 A storyboard form.

VIDEO-Storyboard	VIDEO Instructions	AUDIO (Script for Anchor & Audio)
NEWS UPDATE from WOOD 17	LS Anchor on Left & KEY CG Page #1 right CG - #1 NEWS UPDATE from WOOD 17	(Cart-wailing vessel UP Full for :07 sec, then fade under & out for ANCHOR) (ANCHOR) IN TODAY'S HEADLINES...... THE EAST COAST ECONOMIC SLOWDOWN GETS WORSE, GOVERNOR CUOMO SAYS NEW YORK STATE HAS A HUGE BUDGET DEFICIT, LATEST POLLS SHOW CONTINUED HIGH SUPPORT FOR THE PRESIDENT, AND THE PHILIPPINE PRESIDENT WILL STEP DOWN... THIS IS THE WOOD 17 NEWS UPDATE WITH REPORTING.
	Key out & Zoom in to a MCU of anchor KEY CG Page #2 Anchor Name on bottom	FIGURES RELEASED TODAY BY THE COMMERCE DEPARTMENT SHOW THAT ECONOMIC GROWTH ON THE EAST COAST HAS ALMOST STOPPED AND THE AREA'S UNEMPLOYMENT RATE IS BEGINNING TO RISE. THE ECONOMY GREW AT A ZERO-POINT-TWO RATE, ALMOST NOTHING, WHILE UNEMPLOYMENT JUMPED FROM FIVE TO EIGHT PERCENT. ECONOMISTS BLAME BANK CLOSINGS AND MANUFACTURING CUTBACKS FOR THE VIRTUAL STOP IN ECONOMIC GROWTH. IN ALBANY, NEW YORK, GOVERNOR CUOMO SAYS THE STATE WILL HAVE ITS LARGEST DEFICIT EVER, OVER SIX BILLION DOLLARS. CUOMO SAYS THE FALLING ECONOMY IN THE EAST HAS DRASTICALLY CUT STATE TAX COLLECTIONS WHILE RISING UNEMPLOYMENT CLAIMS AND WELFARE PAYMENTS HAVE DRAINED THE STATE TREASURY. CUOMO SAYS THE BUSH ADMINISTRATION IS IGNORING DOMESTIC PROBLEMS TO PAY FOR THE GULF WAR.
NEWS ANCHOR	Key Out	
WHY	TAKE Gov. Cuomo Picture Full screen	

VIDEO-Storyboard	VIDEO Instructions	AUDIO (Script for Anchor & Audio)
HARRIS POLL GULF WAR 85% DOMESTIC 48% IMPROVES 12%	LS Anchor on Left & KEY CG Page #3 right HARRIS POLL GULF WAR 85% DOMESTIC 48% IMPROVES 12%	A POLL CONDUCTED BY THE LOUIS HARRIS GROUP FOR A-B-C NEWS SHOWS THE VAST MAJORITY OF AMERICANS THINK PRESIDENT BUSH IS DOING A GREAT JOB IN THE PERSIAN GULF WAR. EIGHTY-FIVE PERCENT OF THOSE CALLED THOUGHT HIS GULF POLICY WAS THE CORRECT WAY TO FIGHT THE WAR. BUT LESS THAN HALF- 48 PERCENT-THOUGHT BUSH WAS DOING A GOOD JOB AT HOME. EVEN FEWER-12 PERCENT- THOUGHT THE ADMINISTRATION COULD MAKE ANY IMPROVEMENT IN THE ECONOMY THIS YEAR. OVER 4 THOUSAND PERSONS WERE CALLED BY THE HARRIS GROUP. BUT IN SPITE OF THIS, PRESIDENTIAL NEWS SECRETARY MARLIN FITZWATER SAYS GEORGE BUSH STILL FEELS THE ECONOMY WILL GET BETTER AS SOON AS THE GULF WAR COMES TO A SUCCESSFUL END. FITZWATER SAYS EXPERTS PREDICT THE WAR WILL END PROBABLY BY SPRING AND THE PRICE OF OIL SHOULD REMAIN AT ABOUT 20 TO 25 DOLLARS A BARREL. FITZWATER SAYS THAT THE ALLIES WILL PICK UP 75 PERCENT OF THE COST OF THE WAR. ALSO IN WASHINGTON, THE HOUSE COMMERCE COMMITTEE SAYS CONTINUED SUPPORT FOR THE CONTROVERSIAL "T-V MARTI" (Mar-tee) PROJECT IS FADING. T-V MARTI BROAD-CAST T-V PROGRAMS TO CUBA FROM A BALLOON ANCHORED IN THE FLORIDA KEYS, BUT THE BALLOON BLEW AWAY.
	TAKE Fitzwater Pix Full Shot	
NEWS ANCHOR Wood 17 News	TAKE MCU Anchor KEY CG Page #2 Anchor Name on Bottom	

Figure 8.2 Sample storyboards. In the "Video Instruction" column, *LS* stands for "long shot," *CG* stands for "character generator," *MCU* stands for "medium closeup," and *BG* stands for "background." (*Source:* Special thanks to Mr. Ralph Bardgett, Assistant Professor of Mass Communication, Central Missouri State University.)

VIDEO-Storyboard

VIDEO-Storyboard	VIDEO Instructions	AUDIO (Script for Anchor & Audio)
	MCU Anchor (Continued)	"T-V MARTI," MODELED AFTER THE SUCCESS OF "RADIO MARTI," STARTED FIVE YEARS AGO AND WAS BEAMING TELECASTS INTO CUBA WHEN HIGH WINDS BLEW THE BALLOON OFF ITS MOORING AND SENT IT CRASHING INTO THE EVERGLADES.
	TAKE Full Shot Corazon Aquino	PHILIPPINE PRESIDENT CORAZON AQUINO (Ah-KEY-no) SAYS THIS IS HER LAST YEAR IN OFFICE. SHE WILL NOT FILE FOR RE-ELECTION NEXT YEAR FOR A THIRD TERM. SHE WAS SWEPT INTO OFFICE AFTER FORMER PRESIDENT FERDINAND MARCOS WAS ACCUSED OF RIGGING THE ELECTION AND HAD TO FLEE THE COUNTRY. ACQUINO SAYS NEGOTIATIONS WITH THE UNITED STATES ABOUT RENEWING THE LEASES FOR CLARK AIR BASE AND SUBIC BAY NAVAL BASE ARE ALMOST FINISHED. THE US WILL STAY FOR ANOTHER SEVEN YEARS.
	MCU Anchor	LOCALLY, THE WEATHER FORECAST FOR THE NEWS 17 AREA READS LIKE THIS.....
FORECAST Cloudy and Cold Chance of Snow LOW 25 HIGH 45	KEY CG Page 4 over Blue BG Color — FORECAST Cloudy and Cold Chance of Snow LOW 25 HIGH 45	CLOUDY AND COLD TONIGHT AND TOMORROW WITH A SLIGHT CHANCE—ABOUT 25 PERCENT— OF EITHER LIGHT SNOW OR RAINY DRIZZLE. THE LOW TONIGHT SHOULD DIP TO ABOUT 25 DEGREES AND THE HIGH TOMORROW SHOULD BE A COOL 45 DEGREES. ALL IN ALL A COOL BUT STILL COMFORTABLE DAY TOMORROW FOR THE NEWS 17 AREA.
	MCU Anchor	

VIDEO-Storyboard	VIDEO Instructions	AUDIO (Script for Anchor & Audio)
	MCU Anchor	AND FINALLY, CABLE SUPERSTAR TED TURNER MAY HAVE LOST A TON OF MONEY ON THE GOODWILL GAMES IN SEATTLE LAST YEAR BUT HE'S MAKING IT ALL BACK THIS YEAR.
TNT	TAKE Turner Pic Full	TURNER LOST MILLIONS LAST YEAR WITH THE GOODWILL GAMES WHILE HIS TURNER NETWORK TELEVISION AND SUPERSTATION W-T-B-S MADE MONEY. TURNER'S CABLE NEWS NETWORK MADE A GOOD PROFIT. THIS YEAR, C-N-N'S POPULARITY WORLDWIDE BECAUSE OF THEIR PERSIAN GULF COVERAGE HAS CREATED A HEAVY DEMAND FROM ADVERTISERS TO BUY AIR TIME ON C-N-N. THE CABLE NET HAS BEEN SOLD OUT FOR THE PAST MONTH AND IS INCREASING THE RATES THEY CHARGE ADVERTISERS. THEY'RE EXPECTED TO TURN A LARGE PROFIT THIS YEAR. AND THAT'S
	MCU Anchor	THE NEWS UPDATE FOR NOW. JOIN US TOMORROW AT THIS SAME TIME ON WOOD 17.
NEWS UPDATE from WOOD 17	Zoom out for LS & KEY CG Page #1 Put Anchor on left & CG Page on right — NEWS UPDATE from WOOD 17	UNTIL THEN THIS IS _____ SAYING GOODBYE AND HAVE A NICE DAY.
	FADE TO BLACK ON CUE	(Cart-wailing vessel UP Full to time, then fade)

Figure 8.2 (continued)

support, or wording of your ideas. The suggestions in Table 8.3 will help you to rehearse effectively.

Solicit Feedback

After carefully practicing the presentation, you are now ready to invite a group of friends or colleagues to hear a "dry run." The cooperation and guidance given by these people can be critical to your success as a presenter. Ideally, the group should act as a *murder board*, a tough but objective group of reviewers who evaluate the merits of your evidence and arguments as well as your arrangement of ideas and visuals. A good murder board is armed with an understanding of your client and is able to role-play the kinds of questions and responses the decision maker(s) is likely to provide. The tougher the questions your colleagues can provide, the better prepared you will be for a savvy buyer or board of directors (see Chapter 16 for a complete discussion on answering questions). A presenter who has rehearsed in a warm climate of nurture and deference may not be properly armed for the boardroom, where some people love to pulverize novices who are untested in the real-world arena.

Table 8.3   SUGGESTIONS FOR EFFECTIVE REHEARSALS

---

1. Finish drafting your outline or storyboard at least two weeks before your presentation date. The more practice presentations you can give, the better.

2. Revise your presentation as necessary to meet time constraints.

3. Prepare your speaking notes, audiovisual aids, and handouts (or ensure that the appropriate agencies have prepared them for you). Some speakers use a storyboard or pictorial symbols. Others use complete sentences or key words. Use whatever system works best for you.

4. Rehearse your presentation standing up, so you can practice your gestures, platform movement, and vocal delivery. Do not try to memorize your presentation. At most, memorize main points only. Do not plan your use of gestures; instead, rely on spontaneity. As you rehearse, be prepared to modify your speaking notes to reflect changes you or others decide to make.

5. Present your speech to a pilot audience. Seek constructive feedback from this "brain trust." Ask the audience to respond to your delivery and the content of your message.

6. Tape-record and/or videotape your presentation during the rehearsal stage so you can observe your presentation and make improvements. Some speakers find it useful to practice their physical delivery before a mirror.

7. In final rehearsal, attempt to create the speaking situation you will face. This "dress rehearsal" should include all audiovisual aids and handouts, as well as introductory events leading up to your presentation. If possible, use (or at least inspect) the conference room or office where the presentation will be made. If your listeners will be seated at a table or in a semicircle, then use that arrangement for the "set" on which you rehearse the presentation. Hold a tough question-and-answer period afterward. Obviously, the more realistic the rehearsal, the more confidence you should gain.

Integrate Appropriate Feedback   After the dry run, you should incorporate useful suggestions. At the very least, clarify areas of confusion and strengthen or delete weak arguments. Revise or eliminate any visuals that do not serve their purpose. Also, make sure you know how to operate any "hardware" or electronic devices you plan to use.

Final Rehearsal

Using the same groups of critical evaluators as before, give your narration and visuals one last trial run. Time the presentation and fine-tune it as necessary.

SUMMARY

- Oral presentations offer several advantages over written presentations: (1) efficiency, (2) effectiveness, and (3) influence.

- Business presentations are commonly proposal-oriented. They are always audience-centered and are often interactive. Multimedia aids are often used. Presentations are sometimes informational, but they are more often persuasive in purpose. Speakers often propose organizational changes regarding (1) products, (2) processes, (3) plants, (4) policies, or (5) personnel.

- A really fine presentation is founded on a careful review of the purpose or objective and the audience. An objective statement is descriptive, specific, and realistic. The audience will accept the objective only if it is based upon a solid idea which is developed logically, well supported, clearly organized, carefully worded, well outlined, and thoroughly rehearsed.

- The storyboard is an alternative to a key word or full-sentence outline as a planning tool. The storyboard merges narrative and visual aids on a single sheet of paper so the script and visuals will coordinate.

- Carefully picked colleagues who can accurately voice the concerns and objections of the prospective audience can help the presenter fine-tune the message. Rehearsal before such a group can pay huge dividends in preparing a successful presentation.

QUESTIONS FOR REVIEW AND DISCUSSION

1. What are the benefits of delivering your ideas in an oral presentation instead of a memorandum, a written report, or a letter?
2. What are the differences between presentational speaking and public speaking?
3. What is an objective statement? What is a central idea statement? Contrast the two.
4. Describe the use of a storyboard. What are the benefits of this planning tool?
5. What is a "murder board"? How can such a group be used effectively?
6. Identify and explain, in the proper sequence, the steps in planning a presentation.

ACTIVITIES

1. You have been called upon to make a business presentation. Explain in a group setting how you would analyze the decision-making body.

2. Role-play being a member of a murder board for a colleague who is planning a presentation.

3. Describe to the class the essence of a recent presentation you heard. In your opinion, why was the presentation successful or unsuccessful? What would you do to improve the presentation?

APPENDIX: A CAREER BRIEFING AND A PERSUASIVE PRESENTATION

Educational Public Relations (Career Briefing)*

Purpose: After my presentation, I want my audience to be able to identify and explain aspects of a career in educational public relations in terms of responsibilities, preparation, advantages, disadvantages, and employment outlook.

Central Idea: Educational public relations offers the practitioner an opportunity to explore many facets of the public relations profession and to work in a unique environment conducive to personal and professional growth.

Pattern of Order: Topical.

Introduction

I'm Jill Davis, and I want to introduce you to a unique area of public relations practice. Educational public relations is a field that merits special attention in light of the problems that have plagued American education in recent years. In 1983, a critical report, *A Nation At Risk,* sparked an awakening of national concern over the quality of our public schools. Violence, drug and alcohol abuse, busing, student rights, low test scores, "educational malpractice" lawsuits, defeated bond issues, and a host of other problems have cast public schools into an unflattering limelight. (Cutlip, Center, and Broom, 1985, pp. 598–609)

Higher education, too, has had its share of problems. Government funding has not kept pace with costs; the value of a college education was questioned in Caroline Bird's 1975 report, *The Case Against College*; students are making greater demands; society, in general, is changing. Parents, students, alumni, and other taxpayers are becoming more aware of the academic world and are demanding that the academic veil be lifted. (Cutlip, Center, and Broom, 1985, pp. 630–654)

Despite the problems, society still wants to believe in education. To believe, people must be aware of the positive things that are happening. A strong

(*Special thanks to Jill Davis, a student in presentational speaking class at Central Missouri State University.)

public relations effort is vital. Managing the negative while stressing the positive—this is the focus of educational public relations.

Today, I want to talk to you about this area of public relations, in terms of responsibilities, preparation and skills needed, advantages, disadvantages, and employment outlook.

Body Outline

I. Educational public relations responsibilities vary greatly with the institution and include a wide variety of activities.
    A. A primary responsibility is media relations.
        1. Getting to know media professionals is essential.
        2. Honoring deadlines and complying with established formats and procedures will enhance relationships.
        3. Understanding what the various publics want and need to know and disseminating that information promptly and clearly is vital.
    B. Another area of responsibility is community relations.
        1. Practitioners promote mutually beneficial relationships between the business community and the institution.
        2. Practitioners involve themselves in civic organizations and activities.
        3. Practitioners may be the "eyes and ears" of the community. (Landes, 1989)
    C. In higher education, a major responsibility is publications production.
        1. Brochures, posters, and other promotional pieces are produced by public relations departments in colleges and universities.
        2. Catalogs, semester class schedules, and annual reports may be partially or completely produced by public relations departments in colleges and universities.
    D. Advertising functions are included within the public relations department.
        1. Practitioners should be able to write advertising copy for both print and broadcast media.
        2. Knowledge of layout and photography is helpful.
        3. Knowledge of video production is helpful.
    E. Internal public relations is often a function of the practitioner.
        1. Producing a newsletter or other employee communication vehicle may be expected.
        2. Coordinating employee recognition activities may be a responsibility.
        3. Planning special events is a function of the public relations department.
        4. Acting as a liaison between the various internal publics and the administration is an important responsibility.
        5. Reinforcing a sense of pride in education professionals is important.
    F. Oral presentations are a major area of responsibility. (Landes, 1989; Ness, 1989)
        1. Most presentations are made to external groups.
            a. Practitioners present general information about the institution.
            b. Practitioners explain specific programs.
            c. Practitioners gain outside support for institutional activities with some presentations.

2. Most presentations are informational, although some are persuasive.

3. Enthusiasm and sincerity are vital to the presentation.

II. There is no single "correct" educational or experiential background for educational public relations, but certain skills and personal qualities are desirable. (*Public Relations Career Directory*, 1987, pp. 87–88)

A. Professionals in the field come from various educational backgrounds.

1. Public relations majors practice in this area.

2. Journalism provides a strong background.

3. A liberal arts degree may be the best preparation.

4. Courses in English, journalism, speech communication, advertising, business, and the social sciences should be included in any curriculum.

B. Good communication skills are essential.

1. The ability to write clearly and effectively is important.

C. Creativity is an important consideration.

D. The ability to gather and evaluate information is necessary.

E. Organizational skills are needed so the practitioner can establish priorities and complete tasks.

F. Strong interpersonal skills are imperative in this people-oriented career.

G. Specific personal qualities enhance the probability of success.

1. Flexibility is an asset in this dynamic environment.

2. Initiative is expected in a field where practitioners normally have little supervision.

3. Enthusiasm motivates others and "sells" ideas.

4. A strong commitment to education is vital.

5. A sense of humor reduces stress.

H. An internship or student employment in public relations office or a related area is a bonus.

III. Educational public relations offers unique advantages to those entering the field.

A. The academic environment fosters personal and professional growth.

1. Educational institutions are "idea factories."

2. Information resources are plentiful.

a. Instructors in all disciplines are accessible sources of information.

b. Libraries are convenient.

c. Academic courses are available.

3. Physical surroundings are generally pleasant.

B. The product (education) is worthwhile.

C. Personal satisfaction comes from seeing the institution benefit from public relations efforts.

D. The variety of duties provides a broad base of experience.

IV. Educational public relations also has disadvantages.

A. Salaries are somewhat lower than those in corporate public relations.

1. Entry-level salaries may range from $14,500 to $27,000. (*Careers, Inc.*, 1987)

2. Earnings of experienced directors in educational public relations average $31,250, while their corporate counterparts average $45,667.

B. Financial constraints limit some public relations activities.

C. Paperwork can be tedious.

D. People in academia may be skeptical about public relations.

V. The outlook for educational public relations employment is good.

    A. Employment of public relations workers is expected to increase much faster than the average for all occupations. (*Occupational Outlook Handbook*, 1988–1989, p. 181)

    B. Colleges and universities have increasing needs for recruitment, fundraising, and institutional advancement.

    C. More public school systems are recognizing the need for an organized public relations effort.

    D. Many entry-level positions will be created as a wider variety of activities are included under the umbrella of public relations.

Conclusion

This specialized area of public relations is for the person who likes a variety of responsibilities, has a strong liberal arts background and good communication skills, is people-oriented, and enjoys the stimulation of the academic world of public relations.

If you would like more information about the field, I have copies of a career summary from the placement office. Are there any questions?

References

A Nation at Risk: The imperative for educational reform. A report to the nation and the Secretary of Education, U.S. Department of Education, by the National Commission on Excellence in Education. April 1983. 65 pp. U.S. Department of Education, Washington, DC 20208.

Careers. Inc. Largo, FL: Revised 1987.

Cutlip, S. M., A. H. Center, and G. M. Broom. (1985) *Effective Public Relations.* 6th ed. Englewood Cliffs, NJ: Prentice-Hall.

Department of Labor. Bureau of Labor Statistics. *Occupational Outlook Handbook.* 1988–1989 ed. Washington, DC: U.S. Government Printing Office.

Fitzpatrick, Thomas F. Assistant director of public relations, Central Missouri State University. Interviewed Jan. 20, 1989.

Landes, Barbara, Coordinator of academic achievement, Blue Springs School District. Interviewed Jan. 19, 1989.

Ness, Bryan D. Public information specialist, Longview Community College. Interviewed by phone Jan. 20, 1989.

Public Relations Career Directory (1987) 2d ed. Hawthorne, NJ: Career Press.

Adopting an Affirmative Action Policy (Persuasive Presentation)*

Specific Purpose: After my presentation, I want my audience, the department managers of our company, to adopt my affirmative action policy proposal and to set aside a time for developing our specific affirmative action plan.

(*Special thanks to Melissa LaFollette, a student in presentational speaking class at Central Missouri State University.)

Central Idea: Affirmative action acts as a preventative tool against equal employment court action, resulting in the various benefits for our company.

Pattern of Order: Problem/Solution

Introduction

One of my areas of responsibility as a recruiter is making you, the department managers, aware of equal employment opportunity (or EEO) laws and their requirements. As you will see, these laws are quite complex. They are important to you, because as managers you make final hiring decisions. If someone were to sue under these laws, our organization would most likely be in trouble, due to the fact the court action sways toward the individual rather than the business. Right now, I'm going to outline for you what can happen to our organization if we are sued under any of these laws, along with the options we have in preventing these occurrences. First of all, let's look at the laws that deal with EEO.

Body Outline

I. Many laws affect the concept of equal employment opportunity.
  A. Title VII of the Civil Rights Act of 1964 applies to EEO.
    1. Title VII protects employees against discrimination that is based on five variables.
      a. Employees are protected from discrimination based on race.
      b. Employees are protected from discrimination based on color.
      c. Employees are protected from discrimination based on religion.
      d. Employees are protected from discrimination based on sex.
      e. Employees are protected from discrimination based on national origin (*Equal Employment Opportunity*, 1974, vol. 1, p.11)
  B. The Age Discrimination in Employment Act of 1967 prohibited the discrimination of individuals aged 40 to incapacity.
  C. The Equal Employment Opportunity Act of 1972 expanded the powers of the Equal Employment Opportunity Commission (EEOC).
    1. The EEOC assists with voluntary compliance.
    2. The EEOC investigates charges of discrimination.
    3. The EEOC acts as a conciliator.
    4. The EEOC files suits.
      a. These suits may result in costly litigation.
      b. These suits may result in awards of back pay.
      c. These suits may result in court-imposed goals.
      d. These suits may result in a damaged reputation for the company.
II. Affirmative action is a series of steps, procedures, policies, and programs designed to overcome the present effects of past discrimination against members of minority groups.
  A. Affirmative action is a preventative action not required by law.
    1. A goal is an element of an affirmative action plan.
    2. A quota is not an element of an affirmative action plan.
  B. There are four elements to an affirmative action plan.
    1. The first element is a written policy.
    2. The second element is self-evaluation to identify deficiencies in minority hiring and/or promotions.

      3. The third element consists of corrective steps on a timetable.

      4. A fourth element is accountability by senior management.

III. Affirmative action is a positive tool against the negative effects of prosecution under EEO.

   A. Affirmative action discourages discrimination.

   B. Data collected under affirmative action guidelines is admissible in courts.

      1. Affirmative action plans make it more likely that businesses will win cases.

      2. Affirmative action plans put the EEOC on the company's side.

IV. Affirmative action has added advantages.

   A. Affirmative action increases productivity.

   B. Companies with affirmative action plans qualify for government contracts.

   C. Affirmative action will help our company get through the labor shortage of the 1990s.

Conclusion

As you can see, EEO laws are extremely complex, and without prevention, we leave ourselves wide open to court action. With affirmative action, we not only avoid prosecution problems—we also reap several advantages, such as higher productivity, which make you, as managers, more successful. We are open to government contracts, which makes us, as an organization, more successful. So what I am asking you to do is to commit to an affirmative action plan that states our organizational commitment to abide by equal employment opportunity and affirmative action policies. I'll pass out copies of the relevant part of this policy now. We'll meet again next Wednesday. At that time I hope you will agree to implement this policy, and we can begin to work out the logistics of our specific plan. Are there any questions?

References

Dwyer, P. (1986, July 14). Clearing the confusion over affirmative action. *Business Week*.

Reed, L. (1981, January 11). Spirit of affirmative action lost in hassle. *Kansas City Star*.

Trippett, F. (July 14, 1986) A solid yes to affirmative action. *Time*.

U.S. Equal Employment Opportunity Commission (1974). *Equal employment opportunity and affirmative action: A guidebook for employers* (Vols. 1 and 2). Washington, DC: U.S. Government Printing Office.

U.S. Equal Employment Opportunity Commission (1976). *Know your rights*. Washington, DC: U.S. Government Printing Office.

Chapter 9

The Audience in the Business Setting

After reading and reviewing this chapter, you should be able to . . .

1. Explain why audience analysis is necessary *before* preparing a presentation.

2. Explain why it is important for a presentational speaker to understand individual differences between listeners.

3. Identify how people behave when participating in group activities.

4. Explain how you can gain valuable information about your listeners by asking questions or conducting a survey.

5. Explain the statement that certain needs are shared by all listeners.

6. Identify when a speaker should begin carefully observing potential listeners.

7. Explain how an understanding of decision-making processes will help you to analyze an audience.

*T*he success of any presentation depends on the speaker's ability to adapt to the audience. Regardless of purpose, setting, or topic, the speaker's first obligation is to analyze the audience as thoroughly and accurately as possible. The speaker's knowledge, concern for the organization and the issues involved, and dedication to a proposal or course of action will not take the place of successful adaptation to the audience. Hugh Duncan (1968) states, "Since all forms of address involve an audience, the relationship between speaker and audience has much to do with success or failure in such address . . . the *structure* of the relation between speaker and audience determines motivation because it determines *how* we address each other and thus how we affect each other" (pp. 288, 290)

As a speaker, Bob Trent may believe that the proposed policy he advocates is the correct approach. In his mind, the facts supporting his position are clear and undeniable. He has devoted long hours to studying the issues involved, and it seems natural to him that anyone hearing what he has to say will understand his proposal, accept it, and agree to its immediate implementation.

Actually, Bob's listeners may not view his ideas and information as he does. The one statistic that, for Bob, makes the proposal's desirability obvious may have no impact whatever on a listener who has other concerns. Assume, for example, that Bob has discovered a strong connection between training in telephone use and increased sales. It seems clear to him, therefore, that a program of training staff members to use the telephone more effectively will pay off in higher sales. Yet one of his listeners thinks that too much attention, time, and money are devoted already to staff training. She thinks it is time to do more for the advertising department, where investment will really pay off in sales increases. Unless Bob adapts his proposal to her concerns and interests, he may anticipate little chance of success with that listener.

Another listener worries that his chances for a promotion are not good. He views Bob as an upstart who is trying to attract the attention of upper management. Another successful project for Bob will only lessen the listener's chances of moving ahead in the organization. As he sits there, seeming to listen to Bob's explanations and statistics, he is actually paying little attention to the message. Given his insecurity, lack of involvement as a team player, and dislike of Bob's success, the chances that Bob will persuade him are slim indeed.

THE LISTENER IN THE BUSINESS CONTEXT

Perhaps no other aspect of presentational speaking is more important and challenging than audience analysis and adaptation. Since every listener at every presentation is a unique individual, each message will be filtered through his or her experiences, needs, attitudes, beliefs, values, and so on. A speaker like Bob Trent must realize that each listener is unique and cannot be thought of or treated only as a member of a group, department, or organization. Given the small size of the audience in presentational speaking, it is important that Bob Trent understand and adapt to each person in the audience. In this chapter we discuss specific ways to accomplish this critically important task.

Successful adaptation is not just a matter of adapting to *individual* listeners. People also belong to and participate in a variety of groups and organizations. In spite of the differences between people, there are also important similarities. Thus, Bob also needs to realize that part of successful audience analysis and adaptation is a matter of understanding how groups of listeners function together and what collective factors will help him to tailor the presentation to a group of listeners. Kiefer and Stroh (1983) explain the importance of this concept: "it is possible to achieve the highest levels of both organizational performance and human satisfaction." In such cases, "we find employees energetically operating as part of a larger whole." These people have not sacrificed "their personal identity for an organizational identity." For such employees, "who they are, in a very meaningful sense, is inextricably linked to a higher purpose to which the organization is committed" (p. 27).

Bob may also encounter less idealistic listeners who *have* given up many of their own needs and ideas in order to survive in the organizational structure. In this situation, "the nature of the corporation is incompatible with the requirements of true creativity." Furthermore, "in matters of corporate creativity, tenure is directly related to willingness to compromise" (Beiswinger, 1979, pp. 60–61). One might conclude that "their acceptance of the organization's formal and informal norms put them where they are" (Grossman, 1982, p. 64). These people succeed by conforming.

All of this suggests that an effective presenter must understand and adapt both to individuals as listeners *and* to groups of individuals within the organization. Dutton (1972) indicates that "team effort and the use of task forces to solve problems seem to be looked upon by management with increasing favor." Nevertheless, he reminds us, "it must be recognized that . . . most inventions and innovations have been the products of people working in isolation from others" (p. 818). Thus, Bob needs to consider both individual and group factors when attempting to understand the nature of his listeners.

THE INDIVIDUAL LISTENER

As we have seen, in a general sense audiences are composed of individuals, and each individual is unique. An effective presenter must attempt to discover as much as possible about each listener. Although it is not feasible to describe all the individual variables, the following are important factors to consider when analyzing individual listeners. The speaker might consider whether the listener is (1) sensitive to problems, (2) flexible or rigid, (3) curious or not, (4) self-confident and daring, (5) fearful of failure or free of such fear, (6) highly motivated or merely driven to succeed, (7) persistent, (8) tolerant of ambiguity and complexity, (9) selective, (10) in possession of a good memory, (11) able to allow an incubation period for new ideas, and (12) able to anticipate times of productive energy (see Raudsepp, 1983, pp. 14–26).

It is also important for Bob to be aware of different ways in which people in his audience process information. Again, he should not assume that merely providing accurate or, from his perspective, quite useful information will affect all listeners in the same way. Grossman reports that "people tend to learn differently when presented with new information. . . . some people derive much of their understanding of their environment through spatial and visual communication (i.e., graphs and pictures). . . . [some people] internalize best through written sentences or paragraphs that are precisely structured. . . . [and other people achieve] 'true understanding' only if they can find some verbal 'analogies' that express ideas to them in a totally different context" (pp. 65–66). Grossman's point is an important one: individual audience members listen and learn differently. Regardless of exterior concerns over such matters as "production lines and cash flow," it is important to remember that "crucial in every single aspect of what [managers] do is the brain and its perceptions and shapings and influences" (Lynch and Gorovitz, 1982, p. 63). Thus, understanding individual thinking processes and perceptions is extremely important to Bob's success in securing approval of his proposal for training in effective telephone use.

Bob can analyze his listeners' perspectives relative to the organization and its functions. To some extent, individuals will be dedicated to the organization and to their part in its successful operation. At the same time, they have personal needs and ideas that might conflict with the purposes of the organization or call for change in that organization (see Dutton, p. 821). These needs will, of course, vary considerably from one person to another, and so Bob—as a presenter—must make every effort to understand the thinking of those individual listeners.

Reactive Listeners

Although it is usually dangerous to place individuals into categories, it might be useful for Bob to consider that his individual listeners may be analyzed as roughly belonging to one type or another. Charles Watson (1983) says, for example, that managers can be characterized as "Type R" or "Type S." He states that "managers with reactive (Type R) mind sets neglect the process of formulating purposes and the methods of achieving these purposes before taking actions." Such people, Watson contends, believe that "one's life, to a great extent, is in the hands of fate, with success or failure being determined largely by chance." Thus, they are people concerned with "exercising their authority instead of identifying and making important contributions to benefit their organizations." As such, they attempt to avoid being blamed when things go wrong. These people are "risk avoiders, and do not want to be overruled by superiors on decisions or make errors." They often look to their superiors "for guidance and approval," and they tend to insist "that every rule and procedure be followed in detail" (p. 24).

Structuring, Pro-Action Listeners

In contrast, the Type S managers see the world as "filled with a variety of exciting opportunities and inviting challenges." These are people who have power and control over their lives. Furthermore, they are people who "learn from their mistakes instead of rationalizing, covering them up, or blaming others." They have the capacity to act after having thought through what they want to achieve (Watson, pp. 25–26).

As a means of better understanding the difference between these two personality types, imagine a situation in which a Type R person is talking to a Type S person:

TYPE R: You know, Smith, if you keep making careless errors, the boss is going to come down on us. And hard! I don't want to suffer because you're so careless.

TYPE S: I know what you mean, Davis. I have a tendency to get careless when I'm in a hurry. It's something I have to watch. I really don't want you to get in trouble because of me.

TYPE R: Well, I certainly hope not. I can't afford that kind of trouble. If you don't do better, I'll have to report you.

TYPE S: Right, Davis. I promise to be much more careful in the future.

This example illustrates differences between two extremes. Obviously, as a presentational speaker, Bob Trent would approach these people differently. Actually, most people are probably not entirely either Type R or Type S. On some days, in some situations, we all exhibit characteristics of each type. Communicating with an audience would be easier if all your listeners were Type S people. Unfortunately, they are not, but understanding Type R characteristics may provide additional insight into the nature of audiences and audience members. Bob can expect to find both types in the business settings where he will be a presentational speaker.

GROUP CONSIDERATIONS

The demands on individuals in today's business organizations are considerable. Managers are increasingly pressured to develop intellectual and imaginative abilities in order to keep their jobs (Rehder and Porter, 1983, p. 53). Not infrequently, the individual struggles to maintain a sense of personal identity as well as a sense of belonging to a group. The people in Bob's audience are engaged in an ongoing effort to reconcile their individuality with membership in one or more work-related groups. The need for getting along and fitting in becomes intense, and "the individual becomes almost afraid to think or act until he learns what his peers are thinking . . . " (Holleran and Holleran, 1976, p. 131).

Clearly, a person does not behave the same way in a group and in isolation from that group. Poole and Hirokawa (1986) quote an "anonymous British statesman" who said, "I may seem to know a man through and through, and still I would not want to say the first thing about what he will do in a group" (p. 15). This does not mean that a person's behavior in a group is either "better" or "worse" than it would be apart from the group. It merely suggests that important differences exist.

Bob tries to keep in mind, therefore, that "there is a world of difference between making a decision alone and making a group decision." At its best, a group effort can pool the thinking of individuals, "creating a resonance of ideas and a synthesis of viewpoints." At its worst, "a different chemistry" works within a group. It can "stop the reaction and contaminate the product with erratic reasoning or low commitment" (Poole and Hirokawa, p. 15).

On the positive side, membership and participation in groups offer advantages over individual effort. Participating in a group allows for a pooling of ideas, knowledge, and experiences. This, of course, enables a group as a whole to know more than any of its members individually (Galbraith, 1968, p. 73). The effective combining of people into groups can lead to sharing of concerns, identification of common goals, sharing of information, finding solutions to problems, and development of courses of action (see Patton and Giffin, 1978, p. 196). And as McGinnis and Ackelsberg (1983) suggest, creativity is enhanced when an "array of individuals" come together, "each of whom possesses a wide range of experiences in his/her background" (pp. 64–65).

There are problems to consider when you must work with groups. Social pressure, "valence of solutions," individual domination, and conflicting secondary goals can make it difficult for groups to function effectively and for speakers to adapt to them (see Goldhaber, 1983, p. 274). It is possible that when some members of a group are satisfied that all procedures and solutions are "shared by the members," conflict and dissatisfaction may actually exist. The listeners, as group members, may feel personally dissatisfied, dehumanized, or machinelike (Patton and Giffin, p. 194).

Remember that one condition Bob Trent should understand when communicating with groups, especially when the members of the group are highly cohesive, is "groupthink," a principle developed by Irving Janis. As discussed in Chapter 6, *groupthink* refers to "a deterioration of mental efficiency, reality testing, and moral judgment that results from in-group pressures" (Janis, 1967, p. 9). This means that members of a cohesive group tend to fall in line with the thinking of the majority. For example, if a member of Bob's team thinks that there are serious ethical problems with a plan to increase sales, he or she may say nothing, out of fear that the other group members will become angry. This person may fear that saying something contrary to the group's enthusiastic agreement on the plan will violate the group's togetherness and norms. "The greater the threats to self-esteem [of individual group members] ... the greater will be their inclination to resort to concurrence-seeking at the expense of critical thinking" (Janis, p. 206). You need to remember that such groups have a tendency to believe their decisions are free of errors. People in groups exhibit a tendency to rationalize, an unquestioned belief in the group's morality, and a tendency to stereotype outsiders. The group expects that individual members will cooperate. There is often a feeling that decisions are truly unanimous; people will warn others not to "rock the boat" (Janis; Patton and Giffin, pp. 246–251).

In order to clarify the potential problems that groupthink may pose for a presentational speaker, let's consider the following example. A task group in the marketing department has spent considerable time and energy studying reasons for poor sales in an important market sector. The group has arrived at a set of proposals for improving sales in that sector. Bob Trent, as director of sales, reviewed their findings, and he wants to speak to the group about altering some of their proposals. Some group members may immediately reject his thinking as that of an outsider who knows nothing about the situation. A member of the group who agrees with Bob's ideas may be extremely reluctant to say so, for fear of rejection by the other people in the task group.

We have seen that in order to persuade individuals and groups, a presenter needs to do a careful analysis of the audience. And in order to adapt to the listeners, the speaker must have some knowledge of the individual characteristics of audience members *as well as* an understanding of ways in which group dynamics affect the listeners. You can see that knowledge and understanding of the listener in business contexts is both important and challenging.

THE COMMUNICATION CLIMATE

Individuals and groups of listeners do not exist in a vacuum. One important factor in analyzing and understanding your audience is the work climate, or atmosphere. Businesses today face major challenges and difficulties. As you might suspect, "with an increased rate of technological change, coupled with social and economic instabilities in the marketplace, as well as new challenges from foreign competition," modern businesses and their employees frequently work in a pressure-packed climate (Grossman, p. 62). In the automobile industry, for example, demands for greater fuel efficiency and better pollution control, higher interest rates, and the popularity of foreign cars have provided constant challenges. It is clear that survival depends on smart thinking. Therefore, effective speakers try to understand the conditions—the pressures, problems, and demands—that listeners are dealing with when trying to do their jobs.

We cannot discuss the particulars of all climates here, but presenters should try to understand the climate in which listeners must operate. Climate factors interact with the audience characteristics discussed in this chapter. Indeed, the presenter's understanding of individuals and groups can be enhanced by an understanding of climate. Conversely, an understanding of individuals and groups can help the presenter understand the climate in which they function. As Folger and Poole (1984) explain it, "managers, labor leaders, and politicians observe an 'air of conflict' or 'a mood of compromise' among their employees, colleagues, or opponents." In addition, it is common for "planners and consultants" to "assess the 'climate for change' in the organization or groups they try to influence. . . . All of these people are responding to the general, global character of their groups and organizations, to what has been called the *climate* of the situation" (p. 81).

One approach to climate is to consider the differences between open and closed systems. Open systems "exchange materials, information, and energy with their environment." Closed systems, in contrast, "do not utilize these offerings from their environment, but rather operate as self-sufficient entities." Closed systems are "characterized by what is called *entropy*, a term borrowed from the second law of thermodynamics. . . . in essence . . . a closed system eventually becomes disordered and incapable of performing work" (Mettal, 1977, p. 57). When describing a closed system, Mettal discusses "a rigidly controlled bureaucracy that does not exchange information or energy with its environment" (pp. 57–58).

As an example of a closed system, consider an old, well-established company that operates under the strict control of its longtime owner. This company was once successful, but its owner has failed to adjust to significant changes in the society and in manufacturing procedures. The company is losing business, but the owner refuses to change the way the company operates, rejecting advice from workers as well as from people in the industry.

In contrast, a modern and highly progressive company may have leaders who are well aware of changes in the business environment. The executives of this company work side by side with the newest employees. They listen carefully to their people, who have graduated from leading universities and are up to date on the latest technology and methodology. This open system readily adapts to changes and to new information.

Applying these concepts to business organizations, you might suspect that open systems are more receptive to and make greater use of creative, innovative thinking than do closed systems. Indeed, Mettal states that creativity represents "the necessary dimension." He says that noncreative organizations and people use such phrases as *"standard operating procedures, prescribed ways of doing things,* and *following the manual."* In contrast, open organizations and people use "feedback methods and procedures (loops) to monitor: (1) the nature of the task; (2) the number and kind of people involved; (3) new research development . . . ; (4) unexpected contingencies; and (5) other changes in the environment" (pp. 61, 63). Authorities such as Beiswinger go so far as to assert that "the nature of the corporation is incompatible with the requirements of true creativity." Beiswinger contends also that "today's corporate entities . . . are major employers of artists," who do not react well when faced with "corporate restrictions." He says that some are simply enslaved by the need for compensation and others work for a short time, quit, and work elsewhere. At the same time, he acknowledges that some companies make "accommodating concessions" to creative thinkers (pp. 60, 61).

Another analysis is based on the functional differences between the two hemispheres of the brain. The left hemisphere seems to "process information in a logically analytic fashion," whereas the right hemisphere processes information in a "holistic or spatial" manner. In business, "both kinds of thinking are absolutely crucial." Too many companies make the mistake of punishing or failing to reward those people who think creatively (Lynch and Gorovitz, p. 64). (The same point is expressed somewhat differently by Rehder and Porter, p. 54.)

People in organizations sometimes insist on "agreement," which "tends to deal only with the mechanics of goals and objectives." In other cases, people are "aligned" and there is a greater concern with "the more inspirational aspect of an organization." People in aligned organizations are more likely to have a "common purpose" and "to keep their agreements with each other" (Kiefer and Stroh, p. 32).

Dutton contends that "the employee must feel that his work will eventually be implemented" (Dutton, p. 821) and that people should reasonably expect to be recognized and rewarded for their contributions. Nonetheless, one survey found that "93 percent of American workers believe that if they work harder or better, somebody else gets the payoff." Companies like "Marion Laboratories [now Marion Merrell Dow Inc.] or Motorola, which share ownership and profits with all their employees and contributors," are "more productive organizations than their competitors, who are still locked in the old models of rewards and incentives." The point is that a healthier climate is created in companies where employees truly believe that their efforts and contributions are rewarded (Schuster, 1987, p. 12).

It is important for presentational speakers to realize that when they understand the atmosphere, or climate, in an organization, they increase their chances of understanding the individuals in the audience. Employees' attitudes, methods of operating, and ways of listening and responding are affected by the environment in which they work.

THE PROCESS OF AUDIENCE ANALYSIS

To a large extent, a discussion of the nature of the listener in the business setting is simultaneously a discussion of audience analysis. This is true simply because the analysis of an audience, or of particular audience members, is a matter of understanding as much as you can about the people whom you are addressing. Their personal needs and attitudes, their view of themselves in relation to the company they work for, the ways in which they interact with others, and the climate in which they function are all extremely important factors. In short, then, audience analysis is a matter of examining all observable factors relative to your listeners, for the purpose of acquiring an understanding of them as recipients of your message.

There are a number of specific procedures that you can follow in order to analyze an audience or listener. As you examine these methods, keep in mind the basic differences between presentational speaking and public communication, discussed in Chapter 8. Also, keep in mind that the audience for a presentation is usually small and that you must adapt the presentation directly to individual listeners. There is some overlap between analyzing an audience for a public speech and analyzing one for a presentation, but the size of the group is a critical difference.

PROCEDURES FOR AUDIENCE ANALYSIS

Observe   Since most presentations involve people you work with, it is reasonable to utilize observation as a means of understanding your potential or actual listeners. What kinds of questions do various people ask? How do they perform under pressure? How do they interact with their superiors, co-workers, and/or employees? In meetings, what specific areas of interest and concern do various people express? What are their attitudes regarding issues of importance to you? Even though observation is an informal means of audience analysis, it is highly useful and should not be overlooked.

Ask Questions   One of the best ways to gain information is simply to ask questions. Talk to people who work with and know members of your audience. Try to discover listeners' major interests, concerns, attitudes, pet peeves, favorite ideas, and so on. And if you have informal contact with audience members, you can, of course, ask them questions about themselves and their attitudes. In more formal situations, it is sometimes appropriate to make appointments with audience members and seek their ideas and input before preparing your presentation.

Survey Your Audience   One way to obtain information about your audience is to prepare and administer a questionnaire. Formal questionnaires are used for surveying large numbers of people; they would not ordinarily be used to analyze an audience for a presentation. If possible, however, you should try to do an informal survey of listeners or potential listeners. Nadler and Lawler (1982) discuss use of "some structured method of data collection, such as a questionnaire" as a means of finding out what people want and value (p. 105). You could simply provide listeners or potential listeners with a set of questions and ask them to respond. There are various approaches that you may take, and in this respect the informal questionnaire can follow the same basic formats used in formal research. The listener may respond as he or she wishes to open-ended questions, such as "What do you think of subliminal advertising?" The response to closed questions, such as "Do you agree with the new retirement policy?" may be limited to particular choices. The respondent *must* make a decision when asked a forced-choice question, such as "Would you spend more funds for the marketing department or for the advertising department?"

There are different types of questionnaires, including Likert-type scales, semantic differentials, checklists, and multiple-choice questionnaires. A Likert scale asks a series of questions and allows respondents to indicate a degree of agreement or disagreement. Thus, a question might ask:

How do you react to the mandatory retirement policy proposed by the company?

$\longleftarrow$ $\longrightarrow$

Strongly agree   Agree   No opinion   Disagree   Strongly disagree

A semantic differential presents a series of bipolar adjectives and asks the person to respond. For example, a question might ask:

How do you react to mandatory drug testing for all employees of this company?

Calm	1	2	3	4	5	6	7	Excited
Cold	1	2	3	4	5	6	7	Hot
Good	1	2	3	4	5	6	7	Bad

A checklist might request that a person simply check appropriate items.

In what ways would you describe your work habits?
_____ Dedicated _____ Lazy _____ Involved _____ Team player
_____ Ambitious

Multiple-choice questions ask the respondent to choose the best, or most applicable, responses from sets of alternatives. One might ask:

Once you have rejected an idea for a new product, will you change your mind?
_____ Never _____ Sometimes _____ Frequently

(The foregoing discussion of questionnaire types is based on Goldhaber, p. 406.)

Consider Human Characteristics   All listeners are human, and as such they share basic needs and wants common to all people, regardless of circumstances. When satisfaction of such needs is either lacking or threatened, listeners tend to be receptive to proposals that will secure satisfaction of these needs. Parnes (1977) urges that we "consider instincts, such as hunger and sex, as data—whether it be pain, lust feelings, drives, or anything else we may inherit or learn." These factors, he contends, are "data" that accumulate from the totality of human experience (p.1). More specifically, "needs can be thought of as groups of outcome that people seek." They "are arranged in a two-level hierarchy." The lower-level needs are "existence and security needs." At the higher level are "social, esteem, autonomy, and self-actualization needs." Needs, "except self-actualization," are "satiable," meaning that they decrease in importance as they are satisfied. Finally, a person "can be motivated by more than one need at a time and will continue to be motivated by a need until it is satisfied or satisfaction of the lower-order needs is threatened." (See Lawler, 1982, pp. 79–99; Maslow, 1968, 1970.)

As a presentational speaker you may assume that all listeners, as humans, share such needs. Where your analysis of the audience and the setting reveals that these needs may be threatened, you can assume that listeners can be motivated to act against such threats. A proposal which will help to secure satisfaction of a need or avoid a threat to it will be motivational to any listener. Chapter 10 discusses how such connections are made.

As Mettal suggests, when discussing the role of creativity in problem solving, "objectives may be achieved through a variety of approaches and strategies rather than in a given prescriptive way" (p. 60). This also applies to the challenging task of audience analysis. You should utilize all ethical means of gathering information and knowledge about your listeners. Your chances for success in presentational speaking depend on it.

ADAPTING TO THE AUDIENCE

Audience adaptation is critically important for effective persuasion. It means that you are able to use the information acquired, through careful audience analysis, for the purpose of presenting ideas and proposals in ways that make them acceptable and desirable to the listeners. As discussed at the beginning of this chapter, it is not enough for a speaker to believe that his or her ideas or proposals are valuable, worthy, necessary, and so on. Even if they are, the speaker's task is to convince the audience to agree and to act in accordance with the speaker's ideas. Analyzing the audience is the necessary first step. But even the most careful and thorough analysis and subsequent understanding of the audience are not enough. You must then adapt your message and purpose to that audience.

Successful audience adaptation is the essence of persuasion. Without it there can be no persuasion. Chapter 10, "Presentational Speaking as Influence," discusses audience adaptation as central to the persuasive process. You should make every effort to understand and appreciate the nature and importance of audience analysis, for without it, adaptation cannot be accomplished.

THE NATURE OF THE DECISION-MAKING PROCESS

The members of your audience, both as individuals and in groups, must ultimately make decisions regarding the various proposals that are made to them. As an effective presentational speaker, you will want those decisions to be favorable to you and to your proposals as often as possible. To increase the likelihood that will happen, another important factor in understanding your audiences is knowledge of how decisions are made by individuals, groups, and organizations.

Let's consider three different sorts of decisions. (1) *Optional decisions* permit free choice between various independent options. As Littlejohn (1983) explains it, "farmers, for example, may grow any kind of corn they wish, regardless of the practice of their neighbors." (2) *Collective decisions* involve the interaction of decision makers. Deciding whether to institute water fluoridation is an example. (3) *Authority decisions* are decisions made by force. Littlejohn (1983) contends that authority decisions are fastest, but rapid decisions can be made through optional decision making as well (p. 276). By implication, of course, collective decisions can be expected to be the slowest.

Numerous organizations in the United States place a strong reliance on authority decisions. As Ouchi (1981) explains, "the department head, division manager, and president typically feel that 'the buck stops here'—that they alone should take the responsibility for making decisions" (p. 36). If you, as a presentational speaker, encounter situations in which one or a few people make decisions that everyone must follow, you have to analyze and adapt to those listeners and to those listeners alone. Similarly, if the members of your audience are able to make optional decisions, you must understand these individuals and the kinds of decisions that they might be influenced to make.

As we have discussed, some decisions are collective. Again, Galbraith (1968) has called into question the belief that decisions in today's corporations can be made by individuals, arguing that instead they increasingly result from collective efforts (pp. 71–72). Similarly, Ouchi (1981) acknowledges that divisions of labor and subsequent decision making were once the rule in U.S. companies, but he says that more recently, "some organizations have adopted explicitly participative modes of decision making in which all of the members of a department reach consensus on what decision to adopt" (pp. 39, 36). Modern organizations, "capable of inspired performance," share some important characteristics. There is "a deep sense of purpose," frequently "a vision of what the organization stands for or strives to create." There is also an alignment "of individuals around this vision." And while these factors suggest collective decision making, there is also a strong emphasis on "personal performance and environment that empowers the individual." Essentially, there seems to be a *combination* of collective and optional decisions (see Kiefer and Stroh, 1983, p. 28).

As you consider the coming together of individuals in collective (group) decision making, keep in mind that "any task group is confronted with two types of problems: task obstacles and interpersonal obstacles." Group members will probably deal simultaneously with each type. Thus, *both* factors must be taken into account when analyzing group problem solving (Littlejohn, p. 221).

The interaction of people trying to accomplish tasks will inevitably lead to differences of opinion. Putnam (1986) says that these differences are usually "surface manifestations of more basic beliefs, values, and goals." As a result, conflicting group members may "coalesce around preferred decision options." This usually constitutes an effort to "determine the majority position," and the coalition "may use communication tactics aimed at inhibiting the power of other factions" (Putnam, p. 194). You should consider such processes and conflicts in your analysis of an audience.

The important consideration in understanding how decisions are made in groups is to realize that conflict is "based on interaction." Conflicts occur as individuals in the group behave in various ways, and as they react to each other. Conflicts can be overt but are often subtle: "often people react to conflict by repressing it." They fear conflict and the "possible changes the conflict may bring about." Or they may simply think that an issue "'isn't worth fighting about'" (Folger and Poole, p. 4). Again, as a presentational speaker, you need to analyze your listeners in an attempt to understand how conflicts affect the decision-making process.

In order to accomplish this difficult task as effectively as possible, keep in mind that decision-making groups are involved in an "integrative process." Such groups must conduct a "review and adjustment of relational conditions; review and adjustment of perceptions; review and adjustment of attitudes; problem definition; search for a solution; and consensus decision" (Folger and Poole, pp. 194–195). As Poole and Hirokawa indicate, "decisions are assumed to be discrete events, clearly distinguishable from other group situations." As such, "almost every decision involves a series of activities and choices rather than a universal choice." They remind us that "defining the beginning and end of a decision process is also difficult" (pp. 24–25).

As a presenter, you should not be too discouraged even when the decision seems to go against you. If you have spoken well and adapted effectively to your listeners, future decision making may take the group in the direction you initially suggested. A few years ago a speaker attempted to make a case for a specific approach to employee evaluation. After considerable discussion by the group, the speaker's proposal was rejected. However, the ideas in the proposal made people think, and with additional events and experiences, the same group later adopted the proposal first introduced by that speaker.

Perhaps the best way to maintain a perspective on individuals functioning in groups is to remember that participants are dealing with the task *and* with other people. At times the interpersonal factors get in the way of group decision making; at other times they enhance the process. Ultimately, the group's success depends on the participants' communication skills. When the group takes advantage of each individual's contribution, the result is superior to the work a single individual can produce.

SUMMARY

- Effective audience analysis and audience adaptation are critical to success for the presentational speaker. Each presentation is directed to individuals. Thus, it is crucial to understand the listeners' individual characteristics. At the same time, individual listeners are also members of groups. Presentational speakers should thus be aware of group processes and characteristics and the ways in which individual behaviors are altered by group membership and participation.

- The effective speaker also needs to consider how the climate, or environment, of an organization affects its procedures as well as the roles of individuals within the organization. In open systems, there is an exchange of energy and information. In closed systems, there is little or no exchange.

- When doing audience analysis, the speaker should (1) observe, (2) ask questions, (3) survey the audience, and (4) consider human characteristics. These procedures enable the speaker to gain information to use in adapting the presentation to the listeners.

- Speakers should be aware of the ways decisions are made in organizations. Sometimes people are free to make decisions. Many organizations rely on authority decisions; others rely more on collective decisions. When individuals try to accomplish tasks through interaction with one another, there will be differences of opinion. The effective presenter needs to be aware of how conflicts are handled.

QUESTIONS FOR REVIEW AND DISCUSSION

1. Why should you do an audience analysis *before* preparing a presentation?
2. Why does a presentational speaker need to understand how individual listeners differ?
3. In what ways do people behave differently when participating in group activities?
4. Why would a presenter ask questions or conduct a survey of a prospective audience?
5. What does it mean to say that some needs are shared by all the people in an audience?
6. When should a presenter begin the process of carefully observing potential listeners?
7. In what ways will an understanding of decision-making processes help you to analyze an audience?

ACTIVITIES

1. Survey the members of your class in order to elicit their attitudes toward a controversial issue. Present your results and ask the class to respond.
2. Study an effective presentation or speech. Analyze the ways in which the presentation or speech reveals the speaker's analysis of the audience.
3. Determine a friend's attitude toward a specific topic. Then try to change your friend's mind by arguing against that attitude without trying to accommodate it. Discuss the results.
4. Find examples of attitude surveys. In a group or class meeting, discuss what you consider their strengths and weaknesses.
5. Survey and analyze your class, or another audience. Prepare and deliver a presentation in which you use your audience analysis.

Chapter 10

Presentational Speaking as Influence

After reading and reviewing this chapter, you should be able to . . .

1. Explain how presentations function to influence others.

2. Distinguish between informative and persuasive presentations.

3. Identify the three types of informative presentations.

4. Prepare and deliver informative presentations that are clear, relevant, interesting, and accurate.

5. Explain the nature of persuasion.

6. Use audience analysis in order to adapt your purpose to your audience.

7. Use effective persuasive techniques ethically in presentations.

*P*resentations attempt to influence the thinking and decision making of others. "The ultimate test of practical leadership is the realization of intended, real change that meets people's enduring needs" (Burns, 1978, p. 461). At times presenters provide specific, attractive answers or solutions to problems. At other times they produce change by presenting less specific, even visionary, ideas (see Kiefer and Stroh, 1983, p. 31).

Regardless of the specific approach or strategy employed, the presentational speaker must understand human motivation in order to effect change. Chrysler's Lee Iacocca states, "In addition to being decision-makers, managers also have to be motivators." He goes on to say that "the only way you can motivate people is to communicate with them" (1984, pp. 52–53).

PRESENTATIONS AND CHANGE

As a presentational speaker, you need to understand that communication and motivation are complicated concepts. Above all else, remember that *the change you attempt to produce through presentations must take place in the audience.* Your belief in a proposal is not enough. Your desire, or need, for others to do as you intend will not produce the change you want. To be an effective speaker, you must exert "a form of influence that predisposes, but . . . does not impose." Instead, your influence produces change by affecting listeners' "judgments, and not just their behavior." Your influence appeals to "their sense of what is true or false, probable or improbable," and affects "their evaluations of people, events, ideas, proposals; their private and public commitments to take this or that action. And, perhaps too, it may affect people's basic values and ideologies" (Simons, 1986, p. 22).

More than 30 years ago, one expert declared that persuasion constitutes "the dominant decision-making process in modern free societies" (Minnick, 1957, p. 9). That assessment appears no less true today, whether we consider leadership as a political, business, or interpersonal function. In his popular book *Megatrends* (1982), John Naisbitt emphasizes that we must reject the idea that strong leadership is desirable. Such leadership, he warns, "is actually anathema to a democracy." The "new leader," Naisbitt contends, "is a facilitator, not an order giver" (pp. 101, 188). A presentational speaker seeks to influence those who "are capable of being influenced by discourse and of being mediators of change" (Bitzer, 1968, p. 8). The presenter should therefore try to produce change in the audience not through force, power, or coercion but through effective communicative strategies.

Note that receptiveness to change depends on the audience, not the speaker. Chapter 9 discusses the nature and importance of audience analysis.

Table 10.1   STEPS IN AUDIENCE ANALYSIS

Step	Procedure
1. Consider the individuals.	Analyze the individual listeners and their roles in the organization.
2. Consider the group.	Understand the nature of groups and how individuals behave in group settings.
3. Consider the communication climate.	Analyze the atmosphere in which your listeners work.
4. Analyze the audience.	(A) Observe; (B) ask questions; (C) survey the audience; (D) consider fundamental human needs.
5. Make the decision.	(A) Choose optimal, (B) collective, or (C) authoritative style of decision making.

This chapter stresses the importance of using such analysis effectively, and appropriately, in the process of audience adaptation. Competent analysis of an audience will provide you with at least two kinds of vital information. First, it will help you understand the circumstances and attitudes of the audience in relation to your position. Second, it will help you determine the degree to which you can expect to accomplish change in that audience as a result of your communication with them. Table 10.1 lists the steps in audience analysis.

Gerard Hauser (1986) helps to explain uses and limitations of audience analysis when he outlines four situations that a speaker can face (see Table 10.2). In the first situation, the audience has *both* the ability to produce a change and an interest in mediating change. In such a situation, it is indeed appropriate for the presenter to attempt persuading the audience to change. The speaker's success with this audience depends on successful adaptation.

In the second situation, the audience is able to bring about a change but lacks an interest in doing so. In this case, the speaker can succeed only by "kindling an interest" in the audience to do something about the situation.

Table 10.2   APPROACHING DIFFERENT AUDIENCES

Audience	Approach
The audience has ability and motivation to change.	The sales force is concerned that sales are down and seeks a new approach. The speaker proposes changes.
The audience is able to change but lacks motivation.	The speaker shows listeners that failure to act could lead to staff reductions and pay cuts.
The audience desires change but lacks ability to change.	The speaker shows how changes may eventually be possible.
The audience lacks motivation and ability to change.	There is little the speaker can do.

Source: Adapted from *Introduction to rhetorical theory* by Gerald A. Hauser, p. 41. Copyright © 1986 by Harper & Row, Publishers, Inc. Reprinted by permission of HarperCollins Publishers.

Adaptation to this audience differs from the first situation. The speaker must first produce interest in the proposed change, or the effort at persuasion will fail.

In the third situation, change is even more difficult. In this case the audience desires a change but lacks the ability to bring it about. Obviously, the speaker accomplishes nothing by urging these listeners to do something that they are clearly incapable of doing. The speaker can instead address possible *future* changes, under circumstances different from those presently encountered by the audience.

In the fourth situation, the audience has neither interest in making a change nor any ability to bring such change about. In this condition, any attempt at persuasion would be inappropriate and fruitless (see Hauser, p. 41).

We have concluded, then, that speakers produce change when they effectively analyze and adapt to particular audiences and situations. In this way, presentational speaking is influence: "it functions to define problems" as well as to discover "ways to process and resolve those problems" (Hirokawa and Poole, 1986, p. 158). In the remainder of this chapter, we discuss presentational speaking as influence through informing and persuading audiences.

INFLUENCING BY INFORMING

Even though all presentations are persuasive in the sense that they attempt to alter the behavior of listeners (see Chapter 5), some situations in business call for presentations in which informing is the speaker's primary goal. Thus, you can influence an audience by providing important, useful information. In one way or another, informative speaking attempts to increase listeners' knowledge. The speaker might present information the audience does not know about, might add to their understanding of information they already possess, or might provide instruction which will help them to use information effectively.

Informative presentations can consist of *briefings*, *reports*, or *instruction*. These can overlap, but there are basic differences between them, resulting from the demands placed upon presenters in a variety of business situations.

A briefing may be either public or internal. A *public briefing* occurs, for example, when a company representative "briefs" the press. Perhaps two companies have decided to merge, and a spokesperson briefs the press on the details of the merger. An *internal briefing*, in contrast, involves a speaker and an audience within the same organization. Bob Trent might brief his superiors on the essentials of a new sales campaign for American Computer Systems' newest product line.

In a briefing, the audience already possesses a basic knowledge of the subject under discussion. The speaker's task is to analyze what key information the listeners need to know. In doing so, the speaker should take care not to make careless assumptions regarding the listeners' background and depth of knowledge (see Berko, Wolvin, and Curtis, 1983, pp. 227–228).

Reports, which may be formal or informal, usually accomplish one of three purposes. The speaker may first, supply data requested by whoever assigned the report; second, analyze and interpret the data; and third, recommend some action on the basis of known data (Rosenblatt et al., 1982, p. 317). When preparing a report, you need to know what you are expected to accomplish. Usually, the information that you provide in a report will help the audience to understand a problem or to make a decision. After carefully researching the problem and gathering necessary information, you might present a report in the form of an outline, including an introduction, a discussion of the problem, conclusions, recommendations, and any supplementary material, including multimedia aids (see Fellows and Ikeda, 1982, pp. 283–286). For instance, Bob Trent was assigned to determine why sales had decreased significantly in one region of the country and to suggest a remedy for this problem. Bob carefully studied the situation. He discovered that one major customer was about to go out of business and that one of American's competitors had increased its sales staff and overall efforts in that region. Thus, in his report to his supervisor and other executives, he presented these two facts and proposed that American increase contacts with two potential customers. He also suggested that two salespeople be transferred to that region.

Instructional presentations may involve training and/or orientation of new employees, updating the training of all employees, or explaining a new procedure or method. Bob Trent will conduct a session to introduce his staff to some new ideas about dealing with difficult customers. His purpose is to provide information that his staff can use to deal more effectively with difficult situations. Ultimately, such information may lead to increased sales.

When you make any type of informative presentation, you will attempt to realize two basic goals. You will want your listeners to *understand* the information presented, and you will want them to *retain* the information for their future use and application. In order to accomplish these two fundamental purposes, you should strive for *clarity, relevance, interest,* and *accuracy* in any informative presentation.

In order to achieve clarity when presenting information, Bob Trent strives to be specific and concrete. He tells his listeners exactly what he wants them to know so they will understand the scope of a problem. Saying "There are quite a few people who haven't done as well during the last quarter" is not nearly as clear as "In the last quarter 65 percent of the sales force witnessed a decline in their sales. This led to a 10 percent drop in total sales for the quarter."

You can also achieve greater clarity through the use of comparison. Essentially, this means that you present the unfamiliar in terms of the familiar. Sir James Jeans, a British scientist, once explained why the sky looks blue by asking his readers to think of light waves as ocean waves striking a piling that supports a pier. The large waves part and come back together, but the small waves, or ripples, scatter once they strike the piling. Jeans went on to explain that the large waves represent red light and the small waves blue light. When light travels through space and strikes dust particles, the long red waves come together, but the blue light scatters. This makes the sky look blue (Keast and Streeter, 1956, pp. 177–178).

By varying your support material, you can help listeners to maintain interest and attention. You may need to present large amounts of factual data; adding an occasional story, quotation, or analogy can help the audience enjoy the presentation while they learn what they need to know. Bob Trent might say, "The burden of having a new competitor is heavy; it's like that straw that broke the camel's back. But we just have to be a stronger camel with a stronger back."

Clarity can also be achieved by *personalizing* information, making it meaningful to the audience. Pointing out the efforts and contributions of specific people helps to personalize the information. Explaining the impact of a problem or a solution to the people most immediately affected makes it more personal. When listeners feel directly involved, they usually pay more attention. One authority on attention calls this "pertinence value" (Norman, 1968). Bob Trent might point out that a new proposal will probably lead to larger commissions for everyone in the department.

Relevance is another goal in preparing a presentation. When you personalize information, you make it more relevant to your listeners. Relevance means that you focus on the problem or issue under consideration and avoid presenting unrelated information or getting off on other topics. If Bob is assigned to report on his analysis of a problem involving angry customers, his listeners will not want to hear about a problem he is having with office equipment. They expect the report to be relevant to the assignment.

Accuracy is essential in any presentation. Informative presentations are intended to increase audience knowledge and understanding—and you will not effectively influence your listeners by providing inaccurate material. Be sure to check and double-check all information, making certain that you have interpreted and recorded it correctly. If you quote anyone, be certain you report exactly what the person said. When you use sources for locating information, give credit to these sources and cite that information correctly. Bob Trent knows that accuracy leads to both effective informative presentations and respect from his listeners.

You will need to provide clear, relevant, and accurate information in persuasive presentations as well as informative ones. Keep that in mind as you consider the nature and functions of persuasive speaking in the remainder of this chapter.

INFLUENCING BY PERSUADING

In ancient times, Aristotle thought that persuasion was a matter of discovering all the possible ways to produce a desired change in an audience. He viewed persuasion as a matter of learning how to select and develop effective strategies for achieving a goal (Aristotle, pp. 24–25).

Kenneth Burke, an important modern theorist, argues similarly that "a speaker persuades an audience by the use of stylistic identifications." Identification is important because it suggests that people attempt persuasion when there is division, or separation, between the speaker and the audience, and that persuasion reduces or eliminates division. As Burke (1969) expresses it, "identification is compensatory to division." He believes that divisions between people provide opportunities for communication that will reduce or eliminate separation (pp. 46, 22).

You might think of persuasion as a matter of one person asking others for cooperation (Weaver, 1971, p. 70). Or you might think of it as a communication process in which the speaker tries to modify, or change, others' judgments (Simons, p. 24). This means, essentially, that the persuasive speaker attempts to make the speech interesting and meaningful to the audience (Minnick, p. 242). Basically, this comes down to the vitally important business of "adjusting people to ideas and ideas to people" (Bryant, 1953, p. 413).

But even if we agree that persuasion consists of the speaker's effort to overcome separation from his or her audience through the presentation of a message that successfully enlists listeners' cooperation and agreement, what is the nature of the process by which one accomplishes that goal? Your understanding of the persuasive process and strategies for persuasion should provide you with a valuable starting point for making effective persuasive presentations.

Gary Cronkhite (1969), a major authority on the nature of the persuasive process, has defined persuasion as "the act of manipulating symbols so as to produce changes in the evaluative or approach-avoidance behavior of those who interpret the symbols" By "evaluative or approach-avoidance behavior," Cronkhite means attitudes. So, essentially, a persuasive speaker attempts to change people's attitudes. Since we have no way to measure attitudes except by observing overt behavior, it is also accurate to say that persuasive speakers attempt to change audience members' behavior (pp. 9, 12, 15).

It follows from Cronkhite's analysis that an effective persuader must carefully analyze and understand the audience in order to produce the behavioral changes desired. As Cronkhite states, "the persuader must rely on the experience of the listener in order to gain acceptance of the proposition that any one concept is related to any other" (p. 84). In short, there can be no persuasion until the speaker has effectively analyzed the listeners and adapted the message to them.

Bob Trent thinks that American's sales training program would be much improved by adding instruction in how to listen effectively. In his own work Bob has felt the need to listen, and he was impressed when Lee Iacocca said, "A good manager needs to listen at least as much as he needs to talk. Too many people fail to realize that real communication goes in both directions" (p. 54).

Bob began by discussing his concerns with his predecessor, Sue Derkman. Sue agreed with Bob and eventually arranged for him to make a 15-minute presentation to Tony Morris, the vice-president for sales; Martha Adkins, the director of training and development; and Martha's two assistants. Bob realized that the effectiveness of his presentation would largely determine whether listening would be addressed in American's sales training.

In the process of analyzing his audience, Bob discovered that vice-president Tony Morris is a no-nonsense person who wants clear information and appropriate supporting data. He has little patience for long, involved arguments and emotional pleas. As a pragmatist, Mr. Morris is motivated by what will work.

Bob knows that Martha Adkins is a dedicated professional who takes great pride in the comprehensiveness and smooth functioning of her training program. Ms. Adkins wants employees to feel that their training has been both personalized and useful. She strives for employee satisfaction. Her assistants, Robert Jones and Patricia Bennett, share Ms. Adkins's dedication. Robert, however, tends to view new ideas cautiously, even skeptically; Patricia is much more open to new ideas. Both assistants have considerable influence on Ms. Adkins's thinking.

Through informal discussions and by questioning people who know his four audience members, Bob also learned something about their attitudes toward providing listening training for employees of the company. He discovered that Tony Morris believes that training in listening would be a waste of time unless it can be shown to relate directly to productivity and profits. Bob learned that Martha Adkins thinks listening is important but that it is a matter of one's attitude toward the speaker and/or subject—that it is mostly a matter of making sure one *decides* to listen. Robert thinks that listening is pretty much automatic; he is against adding it to the training program. Patricia, in contrast, is more open-minded and willing to learn more about listening. She believes that it is very important to listen effectively, and she can see why a training program might include some instruction in listening.

At this point, Bob has a pretty good idea of what he must accomplish in order to persuade his listeners. He must convince Tony Morris that better listening by employees will reduce costs and increase profits. He must persuade Martha Adkins that merely deciding to listen does not engender effective listening. He must get her to see that training is necessary. He must show Robert Jones that listening is anything but automatic and that the effectiveness of the training program also depends on listening. Finally, Bob must strengthen and reinforce Patricia Bennett's generally positive attitude by providing solid support for her position and by acknowledging that her general attitude supports American's training program.

In this example, we can see that persuasion involves much more than merely telling someone what we believe or think is true. It is not enough to believe strongly in a position. And it is not enough to discover and present factual support for a position. Instead, successful persuasion requires that speakers succeed in producing changes in listeners' attitudes. Persuasion does not represent what the speaker does to an audience; it relies on what the speaker is able to get the listener to do.

Cronkhite's Model

In order to understand how the persuasive process actually functions, let's consider Gary Cronkhite's model of the persuasive process. This model contains two basic components. The first is the *object concept*, which is, essentially, the speaker's goal or purpose. For example, Bob Trent wants to change Robert Jones's attitude regarding listening training to a positive one. It could be said that *the importance of training in listening* is Bob's object concept, or that *the importance of training in listening* is "the object of persuasion" (Cronkhite, p. 75).

The second basic component is the *motivational concept*. This is a complex concept, but it can be understood in relation to the object concept. The speaker might begin by selecting a concept, or "stimulus," which the listener views positively. The speaker then attempts to get the listener to see a "positive relationship" between that concept and the speaker's object (Cronkhite, p. 75). For example, Bob Trent discovered that Robert Jones cares about employee satisfaction with the corporate training program. Bob might attempt to convince Robert that listening instruction is always viewed favorably by employees who have had it as part of corporate training programs.

The speaker might also attempt to show the listener that there is a "negative relationship" between the motivational concept and the speaker's object (Cronkhite, p. 75). For example, Robert Jones has a negative attitude toward upper management's dissatisfaction with employee training programs. Bob Trent might therefore stress that when listening training is not included in sales training programs, upper management complains more often and more angrily that employees do not follow procedures. Robert might be persuaded to view training in listening differently (more positively) in order to avoid a highly undesirable negative consequence.

It is also possible for a speaker to persuade a listener by showing that "there is *no* relation between two stimuli" (Cronkhite, p. 76). For example, Bob Trent discovered that Robert Jones thinks listening instruction would cause employees to ignore other important aspects of their training. Bob will attempt to show that there is no relationship at all between training in listening and ignoring other aspects of employee training. In fact, the trained listener knows *not* to ignore what is heard.

A third component of Cronkhite's paradigm of persuasion involves the establishment of a relationship between the object and motivational concepts. As Cronkhite expresses it, "the individual who wishes to persuade another must choose motivational concepts which consistently elicit strong behaviors from the listener, *and* he must demonstrate that these motivational concepts are clearly related to the object concept" [emphasis added] (p. 75). These statements suggest the importance and role of evidence and reasoning in persuasive speaking. In order to demonstrate the connection, or

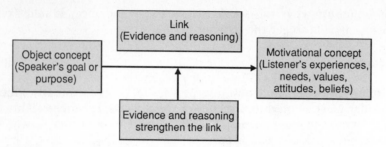

Figure 10.1 Cronkhite's paradigm. (*Source*: After Gary Cronkhite, *Persuasion: Speech and Behavioral Change*, Indianapolis: The Bobbs-Merrill Co., 1969)

link, between the object and motivational concepts, it is often necessary for the speaker to use reasoning and support. These subjects are discussed extensively in Chapter 11, which continues the discussion of persuasion.

The nature of the persuasive process is best summarized by stressing two points. The first is that it is seldom sufficient for the speaker merely to tell the listener that he or she must change. Indeed, that would prove effective only if the persuader functions as the motivational concept (see Cronkhite, p. 79). The speaker may have all the facts, the truth, the best solution possible, and so forth, but persuasion is not automatic. The second important point is that successful persuasion depends on the speaker's ability to analyze and adapt to the audience. Listeners are not blank pages. Instead, they reflect their past experiences, beliefs, values, needs, and associated attitudes. They are going to be persuaded to the extent that the persuasive speaker succeeds in understanding them and in *linking* the proposal to their motives and experiences. As Cronkhite states, "the success of the persuader will depend upon his having a complete and accurate catalog of his listener's attitudes toward a large number of . . . concepts" (p. 76). Figure 10.1 shows the relationships between the components of Cronkhite's model.

Strategies for Success in Persuasive Presentations

When developing a persuasive strategy, you must begin by learning as much as possible about the audience members, both as individuals and as members of groups. (Chapter 9 discusses the process of audience analysis.) Without such analysis it will be nearly impossible for you to adapt your presentations successfully to your listeners. This means that you should utilize observation, ask questions, survey listeners, and carefully consider the human characteristics of your audience in order to discover and understand your listeners' attitudes.

Bob Trent knows, as a result of his audience analysis, that one listener (Morris) wants practical results and hard data. Of the three dedicated members of the training department, one (Adkins) is motivated by a desire for smooth functioning of the program and for employee satisfaction. A second (Jones) is cautious and skeptical of new ideas. And a third (Bennett) is open to new ideas and is supportive of listening instruction. Bob is also aware that there is considerable interaction among the three trainers and that both assistants influence the director. While Mr. Morris has the power to institute a training program, Bob also realizes that it will not work well unless the leaders of the training department are supportive.

Strategies for Enhancing Ethos

Bob wants all four listeners to recognize that he respects their positions, problems, needs, and so forth. He wants them to perceive him as knowledgeable, trustworthy, sincere, and concerned about his audience (see McCroskey and Young, 1981). This character Bob wants to exhibit is his *ethos* or *source credibility*. The important point is that ethos is not something that the speaker has—instead, it is given to the speaker by the listeners (see Table 10.3). As a persuader, however, Bob can attempt to impress the audience as having those "manifested intellectual, moral, and emotional qualities" that listeners will accept and respect (Hauser, p. 105).

In one sense, Bob Trent or any other persuasive presenter can best impress an audience as being a highly credible speaker simply by striving to possess the qualities and characteristics that listeners respect and admire. In short, Bob's best bet is to make certain that he knows his subject and that he is well informed and accurate. He can exhibit confidence in himself as an effective speaker who is well prepared, concerned about his listeners, trustworthy, and sincere. This is what Richard Rieke and Malcolm Sillars (1984) refer to as *indirect credibility*. It means that the speaker "uses no specific statements from someone else or direct personal statements about his or her personal character." Instead, the presenter develops credibility by developing, supporting, and presenting arguments. Essentially, "the more effectively you argue the more credibility you gain" (p. 136). So, if Bob analyzes his audience, carefully prepares his presentation, knows what he is doing, presents it effectively, and so on, he stands an excellent chance of being perceived positively by the listeners.

Table 10.3 WAYS TO ENHANCE ETHOS

1. Know your subject. Be well-informed, accurate, and generally competent.
2. Make honest statements about yourself that tell listeners about your abilities, skills, and experiences.
3. Refer to your knowledge of and interaction with people whom your listeners respect and admire.
4. Appeal to the needs, values, and attitudes of your listeners, remembering that people want to feel appreciated and respected.

It is also possible for a persuader to use more specific strategies for enhancing credibility with the audience. Rieke and Sillars refer to one such strategy as *direct credibility*—the speaker makes "direct statements about himself or herself" (p. 135). For example, Bob Trent might relate an experience in which his own knowledge and practice of good listening skills were significant factors in an important sale for the company.

A third strategy for enhancing ethos, or credibility, is called *secondary credibility*. In this approach, the speaker "uses another person's credibility as the basis for the argument" (Rieke and Sillars, pp. 135–136). In using this technique, Bob might share a conversation he had with the company president, in which the president agreed with Bob that listening is of critical importance to personal success.

Bob can also take advantage of his careful audience analysis. He realizes, for example, that Tony Morris will consider Bob credible if he comes across as "no-nonsense" and confident of his facts. The three members of the training department will be favorably impressed if he shows concern for employees and for the value and importance of the present training program. In short, Bob Trent can do much to ensure the success of his presentation by creating a favorable image of himself in the minds of his listeners.

Strategies for Persuading Specific Audiences

It is important to keep in mind that presentational speaking differs in some important respects from public speaking. As mentioned in Chapter 8, the audience for a presentation is small, and the presentation must be adapted to members of that audience. In this respect, the challenge to the presenter is to tailor the presentation to those individuals rather than merely adapting to a general audience. Herbert Simons's discussion of rhetorical strategies and rhetorical problems can readily apply to the presentational speaker. Simons indicates that "rhetorical strategies we humans devise generally reflect *trade offs* among conflicting requirements; seldom are we able to reconcile them completely." He goes on to say that "not only do we play multiple roles, we also confront multiple and conflicting pressures in the same role." Examples of the kinds of pressures that Simons is talking about include "cross pressures" that are "at once dependent and independent, flexible and consistent, conforming and individualistic, cooperative and competitive" (pp. 90–91).

Simons's point is an excellent one. It has considerable importance in presentational speaking. The presentational speech, in particular, is a response to "the demands of the situation and the pressures on us with respect to them" (Simons, p. 90). Bob Trent is facing four people, who each have individual interests, needs, beliefs, and attitudes. Bob is asking these people to agree with his position and to make an investment of time and money to activate his proposal. He realizes that, to a large extent, he is putting himself on the line. Failure of his presentation and/or proposal will reflect adversely on him. Thus, he must be able to adapt to each member of the audience in one brief presentation.

Remember that success in the persuasive process depends on the ability of the speaker to "rely on the experience of the listener" (Cronkhite, p. 84). Let's return to Cronkhite's persuasive paradigm and examine the five strategies the speaker can use to link object concepts to motivational concepts: (1) contingency, (2) categorization, (3) similarity, (4) approval, and (5) coincidental association (pp. 81–84).

A *contingency relationship* expresses what is often called causality and sign. Thus, for Tony Morris, Bob might present evidence for Tony which demonstrates that training in listening can actually reduce losses and increase profits. For Martha Adkins, he might emphasize that employees who receive training in listening express greater satisfaction with training programs than those who do not.

In *categorization relationships*, the speaker wants the listeners to view, or understand, one idea as including another. One might say, for example, that being in the category "human being" includes the attribute "mortality": thus, to be human is also to be mortal. Bob might stress to Robert Jones that listening is an integral part of the communication process and that it should not be excluded. Thus, it is not a "new" concept. Bob might argue further that listening is not automatic when one is merely hearing. Hearing without other behavior isn't listening.

The *similarity* relationship depends on a close relationship between two concepts and on the listener understanding that similarity. Thus, it is a comparative relationship. Bob Trent discovered that Patricia Bennett believes *thinking* clearly is extremely important and must be included in an effective training program. Bob will therefore emphasize that the deepest levels of good listening are quite similar to good thinking—that one is much the same as the other.

The *approval* relationship links the listener's attitude toward a particular person or institution and with approval of an idea or concept. Bob knows that Robert Jones has great respect for Lee Iacocca, head of the Chrysler Corporation. Bob can expect that if he quotes Iacocca (someone of whom Jones approves) as being strongly in favor of training in listening, Jones will view the subject more favorably. Cronkhite distinguishes between what he calls "rational" and "irrational" approval relationships by stating that such a relationship is rational when the person approved of is an *"authority"* on the matter being discussed and irrational otherwise (p. 83). That distinction is not always easy to make. One might argue that Iacocca is an authority on automobiles, not on communication. As a highly successful manager, however, he might be considered an authority on communication in relation to business. At any rate, the approval relationship requires that listeners approve of an idea because they approve of the person or institution presenting it.

Coincidental association is another relationship that can be established between the speaker's object concept and the listener's motivational concept. In this situation, the speaker attempts to get the listener to make an association between two items merely on the basis of context. If the advertiser of a candy bar repeatedly showed healthy-looking people doing healthy physical activities, the viewer might come to *associate* the candy bar with good health and physical activity. In coincidental association, the *mere association* of words and ideas is all that happens in the listeners. There is no causal relationship. In general, it is advisable to avoid this approach to persuasion. However, a speaker might use it linguistically, perhaps using negative words for an undesirable concept and positive words for a desirable concept. For example, when discussing companies that do not provide listening training, Bob Trent might use words such as unprogressive, held back, or unsatisfactory. When talking about companies that provide such training, he might use words such as *profitable, happy,* or *healthy.*

Additional Strategies for Persuasion

In Chapter 9 we mentioned that all people share certain types of needs simply because they are human: "existence and security needs" and "social, esteem, autonomy, and self-actualization needs." As all of these needs except self-actualization are satisfied (met), "they decrease in importance" (see Nadler et al., pp. 79–99; Maslow, 1968, 1970).

In relation to Cronkhite's paradigm, it follows that a speaker can assume that all listeners have these needs. He or she can then demonstrate that the lack of a policy, or the acceptance of a policy, will avert various threats to such needs. Let's assume that the four members of Bob Trent's audience are interested in economic security. Assume too that they feel no immediate threat to their security need. As a persuader, however, Bob might point out that poor listening by employees is an increasingly serious threat to company survival and that American Computer Systems, like other companies, may have to make cuts in management positions. This way he ties the listeners' security needs to the problem of poor listening.

If Bob succeeds in creating a feeling that his listeners' economic security is threatened, he has reached an important human need and has demonstrated that it is threatened. This makes his listeners more receptive to ideas that lessen the threat or secure their economic futures. If he can show how employee training in listening would do that, the link between his object (a positive attitude toward training in listening) and the listeners' motives (economic security) will be made successfully. This, of course, goes back to our discussion of contingency relationships, but the focus is on fundamental human needs.

Additional strategies for persuasion are discussed by Charles Larson. In his book *Persuasion: Reception and Responsibility* (1989), Larson discusses seven persuasive tactics that can be used by speakers: the "yes-yes technique"; "Don't ask if, ask which"; "Answering a question with a question"; "Getting partial commitment"; "Ask more, so they settle for less"; "Planting"; and "Getting an IOU" (pp. 317–319).

With the "yes-yes" technique, the persuader attempts to evoke a series of affirmative responses from the listeners, whether such responses are overt or internal. The speaker asks a series of questions the listeners will obviously answer with a "yes." Then the speaker asks the audience a less easily agreed-upon question. For example, Bob Trent might ask whether his listeners want a successful company, happy employees, effective training. He might then ask them to agree that listening training is necessary.

With the "don't ask if, ask which" tactic, the speaker takes away the opportunity to decline. Instead of asking "Do we want listening in our program?," the speaker might ask "Do we want two hours or three hours of listening instruction?"

In less formal speaking, such as presentational speaking situations, the speaker often has the opportunity to interact directly with the listeners and can use the technique of "answering of a question with a question." One of Bob Trent's listeners might ask him whether there is time to add listening to an already crowded training program. Rather than arguing directly with the questioner, Bob could respond, "How can we *not* afford the time to teach employees effective listening?"

"Getting partial commitment" is a strategy that can be used in numerous ways. For example, a salesperson might ask a potential customer to take out a one-month trial subscription. Bob might attempt to get his listeners to agree to try a program in listening for one year and then see how it is working. That way the listeners can agree without making a total commitment.

The "ask more, so they settle for less" technique is commonly used in presenting budget requests. Typically, people request far more than they expect to receive, hoping that the final budget, after cuts, will be what they need. In his presentation, Bob might ask for more training time than he thinks the listeners will agree to, hoping for a compromise that will get the desired training into the program.

"Planting" is the technique of using listeners' senses to relate to a product or idea. In a commercial for tourism in a western state, an old cowboy might discuss his fond memories of the beauty of a desert sunset. The idea is that people will think of such a beautiful scene when they think of that state. Bob Trent might use this technique by asking the listeners to visualize the facial expression of a customer whose time has been wasted by an employee who didn't listen.

Finally, the persuader might use the "getting an IOU" approach, attempting to get listeners to feel indebted to him or her. If someone is willing to do something for you, then you may feel obligated to respond favorably to his or her request. If Bob promises the listeners that he will donate time to sharing his experiences about the importance of listening, the audience members may feel obligated to consider his proposal seriously.

Table 10.4 summarizes Larson's techniques.

Table 10.4 LARSON'S SEVEN PERSUASIVE TECHNIQUES

Tactic	Speaker's strategy
1. Yes-yes technique	Ask a series of questions that are certain to evoke positive responses. Then ask for acceptance of your proposal.
2. Don't ask if, ask which	Provide alternatives that involve acceptance of your proposal. The alternatives do not allow rejection.
3. Answering a question with a question	Instead of answering a hostile question directly, ask a question that invites the other person to respond to the issue.
4. Getting partial commitment	Suggest a trial, or temporary acceptance of your proposal.
5. Ask more, so they settle for less	Ask for more than your listeners will give. Then back down to what you can accept.
6. Planting	Associate your proposal with something important or valuable to your listeners.
7. Getting an IOU	Get the audience to realize that you have made contributions to them.

Source: After C. Larson (1989). *Persuasion: Reception and responsibility.* Belmont, CA: Wadsworth Publishing Co.

THE ETHICS OF PERSUASION

We have discussed the importance of communication as influence, its nature, and various techniques and strategies for persuasive success. Each presentational speaker must also consider the ethical implications of persuasion. As noted in Chapter 1, this means that we must consider value questions that go beyond the immediate success or failure of a persuasive speech. These issues include such matters as the *morality* or *immorality, rightness* or *wrongness, justice* or *injustice* of our persuasive efforts.

Persuasion is a powerful tool. The techniques of persuasion are not restricted to "good" people, or to those who always have the best interests of the listeners at heart. It is your responsibility to make every effort to persuade as ethically as possible. Speakers who ignore or dismiss ethical questions and issues are potentially dangerous—to themselves, to the audience, to the business community, and to society.

Unfortunately, however, there are no easy answers to questions about ethics in communication. Because individuals and groups have differing ideas and standards, there are no universally accepted ethical standards. This lack of agreement in no way lessens the importance of ethical issues. Speakers should consider whether their purposes and methods are right. Each presenter must make ethical choices.

Probably the best approach is to urge each speaker to be concerned about the ethics of persuasive speaking and to examine various standards carefully.

Table 10.5   MINIMUM STANDARDS FOR ETHICAL PERSUASION

1. Avoid presenting false or distorted information or evidence to your listeners at any time.
2. Never speak without informing yourself and without careful preparation.
3. Openly admit what you do not know.
4. Avoid knowingly or intentionally misleading your listeners with weak, illogical reasoning.
5. Be open to new information, new ideas, and criticism of your position.

Each person must decide which standards he or she finds most acceptable. These choices can, and probably should, be modified throughout one's life.

Richard L. Johannesen presents an extensive discussion of such perspectives in his book *Ethics in Human Communication* (1983). Ethics based on *political concepts* relate to fundamental principles of our political system. One might conclude, for example, that it is unethical in a democracy to keep crucial information from the public. *Human nature standards* regard the determination and upholding of uniquely human attributes as most important. A speaker who denies freedom of choice to his or her audience denies the listeners' human ability to reason and choose. *Dialogical perspectives* reject the idea that listeners are mere objects to be manipulated. You would not, for example, pretend to be someone's friend merely to obligate him or her to do something for you. *Situational perspectives* treat each communication situation as unique and accept standards of ethics that change from one situation to another. It might be all right to stretch the truth about a fishing trip, but it would be wrong to stretch the truth when reporting an important incident to the boss. *Religious perspectives* use religious beliefs as an ethical guide. The Golden Rule—"Do as you would be done by"—is a religious principle that can guide persuasive communication. *Utilitarian perspectives* value the greatest good for the greatest number of people. In making a decision to reduce staff, a corporate executive might decide that letting a few people go will be best for all the other employees and the organization itself. *Legal perspectives* equate legal codes with ethics. If an action is illegal, it is also unethical. Reporting a safety violation in a plant would be ethical because it is required by law (Johannesen, 1983, pp. 11–89).

Regardless of the perspectives that you decide to adopt and to follow, we urge that you consider the minimum standards set out in Table 10.5.

SUMMARY

- Presentational speakers influence listeners in two important and closely related ways: by informing and by persuading. Informative presentations consist of briefings, reports, and instructions. In order to achieve each of these purposes, the presenter should strive for clarity, relevance, and accuracy. Persuasion is designed to influence and change others in business settings.

- Persuasion involves the speaker's ability to understand and adapt to the listeners. In Cronkhite's model of persuasion, a successful persuader must analyze the audience and then link the persuasive purpose to the listeners' motives.

- Specific persuasive techniques are used for enhancing speaker ethos and for persuading particular audiences. Factors that enhance ethos include indirect credibility, direct credibility, and secondary credibility.

- The speaker can use contingency relationships, categorization relationships, similarity relationships, approval relationships, and coincidental relationships to link the object of the presentation to the listeners' needs and values.

- Larson's seven persuasive strategies are the "yes-yes" technique; "don't ask if, ask which"; answering a question with a question; getting partial commitment; "ask more, so they settle for less"; "planting"; and getting an IOU.

- Speakers must consider the ethical implications of persuasion.

QUESTIONS FOR REVIEW AND DISCUSSION

1. Why is it important for effective business communicators to produce change in others?
2. How does informing differ from persuasion?
3. In what ways do informing and persuading overlap?
4. What is likely to happen to an informative or persuasive speaker who fails to understand the listeners?
5. Explain how evidence could help a speaker strengthen the link he or she has made between the object concept and the motivational concept in a presentation.
6. Why is it important for successful persuaders to enhance their ethos, or credibility, with the audience?
7. Explain why knowing the facts and strongly believing in your position are not enough to persuade an audience.
8. What are communication ethics, and how do they relate to the process of persuasion?

ACTIVITIES

1. Talk to someone who works in sales, management, personnel, or public relations. Ask this person to discuss the importance of persuasion in that occupation.
2. Make a list of persuasive techniques and practices that you believe are inherently wrong. Compare and contrast your list with the lists of others in your group or class.
3. Analyze a written or recorded speech that you think is effectively persuasive. What are the reasons for its success?
4. Survey your listeners' attitudes toward a topic, then present a five- to seven-minute persuasive speech in which you try to change the thinking of most listeners. Survey their attitudes again afterward.
5. List your goals for a successful career, and estimate the role of persuasion in your attempts to reach those goals. Share and discuss your list with others.

Chapter 11

Support and Reasoning

After reading and reviewing this chapter, you should be able to . . .

1. Describe the nature of support and reasoning in presentations.

2. Distinguish between factual and nonfactual support material.

3. Use factual and nonfactual support in presentations.

4. Apply the tests for support and reasoning.

5. Avoid fallacies of reasoning.

Bob Trent wants to understand the nature and functions of support and reasoning. He has decided to examine them separately. Bob realizes that they are closely related concepts. He has observed that speakers reason *with* various types of support in order to establish their positions, or conclusions. He knows, therefore, that after studying the two concepts separately, he will need to understand how they actually work together in presentations.

THE NATURE OF SUPPORT AND REASONING

Support is anything that a speaker uses to back up or strengthen his or her assertions. Support material may be either factual or nonfactual. Facts are difficult to define, but Douglas Ehninger (1974) has stated that facts are things that people "believe to be the case, either because they have experienced them firsthand or because they are regarded as the truthfully reported experiences of others" (pp. 51–52). Nonfactual support, in contrast, is support used to clarify factual support, add interest to it, make it believable, or reinforce it.

Factual support consists of reports of direct observation (testimony), statistics, examples, and actual objects. Nonfactual support consists of stories, hypothetical examples, literary quotations, analogies, and so on. Nonfactual support is not necessarily inferior to factual support. However, the ways we use and evaluate these two forms of support differ significantly. Freeley (1981) explains that factual support is used "to establish a high degree of probability" or "logical proof," whereas nonfactual support can be classified as "ethical or emotional proof" (p. 119).

The *source* of a speaker's support material, whether factual or nonfactual, is the place where the support is found. Sources of support may be books, magazines, corporate reports, interviews, one's own observations, and so forth. It is expected that speakers will report sources of information to their listeners; it is also necessary, at times, for speakers to *qualify* their sources—that is, to explain why the sources are reliable.

Rieke and Sillars (1984) explain that support material, both factual and nonfactual, comes in three forms. First, support may be in the form of *evidence*, such as examples, statistics, and testimony. Second, support may be in the form of "the *values* [emphasis added] held by the persons receiving the arguments," the audience members. For example, if you think it is highly desirable to find a good job, and a speaker promises that reading a certain book will greatly enhance your ability to find the right job, that speaker will have attempted to support the desirability of reading the book by using a value that you hold. Third, support may be in the form of *credibility* (see

Chapter 10). A speaker's credibility can enhance the acceptance of his or her ideas (see Rieke and Sillars, pp. 90–148).

Both values and credibility may be supported by either factual or nonfactual material. Both factual and nonfactual support may be used along with value and/or credibility support. For example, if a speaker argues that because employees are not happy they should be given additional benefits, the supporting value is that it is bad for employees to be unhappy. This speaker might present factual support to explain why employees are not happy. He or she might also present factual or nonfactual support for the value that it is bad to have unhappy employees.

Bob Trent might relate his own experiences in order to convince the listeners that he is a competent person. Bob's experiences provide factual support. But they also serve as credibility support: favorably impressing his listeners by mentioning relevant experiences will increase the chances that Bob's listeners will accept his ideas or proposals.

Reasoning is a matter of arriving at a conclusion that follows from your data. Assume, for example, that you want your listeners to agree with your conclusion that the company will suffer a significant decrease in profits. You cite evidence, or support, that employee morale is extremely low. Thus, you are reasoning that low employee morale causes a decrease in profits. That conclusion is based on the *assumption* that whenever morale is low, profits decrease. As Infante (1988) suggests, the speaker presents a *claim*, or *conclusion*, that he or she wants the listeners to accept. Then the speaker presents *evidence*, or *data*, in support of the claim. And, finally, the speaker *reasons* from the data to the claim (pp. 57–58; see also Toulmin, 1958, pp. 94–145). In this case, reasoning leads to the conclusion that because of low morale, profits will decline. The assumption that declining morale hurts profits is the generalization on which the conclusion is based.

THE ROLE OF SUPPORT AND REASONING IN PRESENTATIONS

Cronkhite's paradigm of persuasion stresses that in order for persuasion to take place, the speaker must succeed in establishing a link between the object and motivational concepts (see Chapter 10). Indeed, as Cronkhite (1969) stated, the speaker must be able to "demonstrate that these motivational concepts are clearly related to the object concept" (p. 75). In order to demonstrate that link, it is often necessary for the speaker to use support and reasoning.

As a result of audience analysis, Bob Trent realizes that his listeners are motivated by efficiency; that is, they value efficiency and have highly positive attitudes toward ideas that work well while saving time, energy, and expense. So, in the presentation, Bob stresses that his product will save time, energy, and money. Bob realizes, though, that merely saying that his product is efficient may not persuade his listeners. Unless Bob's credibility is extremely high, or his listeners are willing to accept anything they are told, he needs to use support and reasoning to enhance his persuasive effort.

Thus, Bob presents two specific studies showing that American Computer Systems' computers are 25 percent more efficient than any others currently on the market. Additionally, he reveals that two independent efficiency experts have stated that the product is the most efficient available. In presenting the experts' statements, Bob also provides information to show that these experts are knowledgeable, reliable, and unbiased.

Bob is using support and reasoning as means of establishing, or strengthening, the link between his object (the product being sold) and the listeners' motives (a strong desire for efficiency). He uses three types of support. First, he supports the product's desirability by linking it to an audience *value* (efficiency). Second, he offers two *specific studies* concerning the product's efficiency. And third, he presents *testimony* by authorities who state that it is an efficient product. In addition to the value support and the two pieces of evidence, Bob could decide to back up his claim with credibility support by mentioning his years of experience working with a top researcher in computer efficiency.

Bob's reasoning is implied rather than stated directly, but it is present in the arguments. The value support makes it possible to conclude that since the listeners value efficiency, and since his computer is efficient, the listeners should value the product. The studies support the efficiency conclusion as long as the listeners believe that the studies were conducted objectively, accurately, and so forth, and as long as they are not contradicted by other studies. The listeners may thus conclude that the product is efficient.

The reasoning related to the expert testimony is based on the assumption that these two people are indeed experts and that their opinions can be trusted. If so, then the listeners have reason to conclude American Computer Systems' computers are efficient. These assumptions must be held by the listeners in order for the link to be established as a result of the evidence.

If Bob attempts to increase his credibility by discussing his years of experience working with a top researcher, then the audience might have been further persuaded that the claim of efficiency is true. Knowledge that Bob had worked with a top researcher would support the assumption that he is knowledgeable and competent and would enhance the claim that American's equipment is efficient.

EVALUATING FACTUAL EVIDENCE

The forms of factual support commonly used by presentational speakers include testimony, statistics, examples, and actual objects.* Let's examine each

---

*Tests for statistics, examples, and actual objects are based on Ehninger, 1974, pp. 55–60, and Eisenberg and Ilardo, 1980, pp. 43–50.

as a means of helping you evaluate these types of evidence for your own speaking and when listening to the speaking of others.

Testimony, as factual evidence, consists of reports of observed phenomena. The person who made the observation is the witness. When witnesses are authorities, the evidence is often called *expert testimony*. In order for the evidence to qualify as factual support, the witness must report only what he or she observes. If testimony consists of opinion or is interpreted by the witness, it is not factual. One test for testimony is the *accuracy* or correctness of quoted material. As a speaker, you must quote others' statements accurately, without error, distortion, or violation of context. It is also important to determine the *qualifications* of the witness. Is the witness honest, competent, without bias, and capable of testifying accurately? Was the witness actually present? Is he or she mentally and physically able to testify accurately? Can the witness testify soon after making the observation? (See Sproule, 1980, pp. 121–127.)

To illustrate the kinds of factors involved in using testimony, let's assume that an accident has occurred on an assembly line. The person in charge of investigating the accident hears testimony from a witness who claims that the injured employee was not paying attention and was careless with the equipment. Additional investigation reveals, however, that the witness was angry with the injured employee and wanted the employee to be blamed for the accident. This, of course, calls the testimony into serious question.

Statistics are often presented as evidence. Karlyn Campbell (1982) has stated, "A statistic is a numerical or quantitative measure of scope or of frequency of occurrence" (p. 178). Statistics may be numerical representations of facts (e.g., "The total labor force in the community is 750,000. Of those people, 720,000 are employed and 30,000 are unemployed.") Numerical facts may also be stated as percentages. ("The unemployment rate is 4 percent.") Statistics may also express central tendencies, or averages. (The *mean* is the average determined by summing scores and dividing by the total number of scores. The *median* is the middle score in a series—half fall above it and half below. The *mode* is the score that appears most frequently.) Statistics are also used for comparing one situation or group with another and for establishing probability. For example, a researcher might attempt to discover whether one procedure increases production more than another; probability estimates tell how likely it is that the difference is due merely to chance factors instead of to the differences in procedures.

Tests for statistics include a consideration of the objectivity, ability, motivation, methods, and accuracy of the person who compiles the statistics. For example, if a researcher reports that the results of an experiment could have been due equally to the treatment or to chance, you should be suspicious if he or she goes on to assert that the statistics show a trend.

It is important to consider the sample from which the statistics are derived. For example, a person doing marketing research concluded that 80 percent of all people surveyed like frozen orange juice better than fresh orange juice. But the people surveyed all work for a company that sells and distributes frozen orange juice. This researcher can hardly justify the conclusion that most people prefer the frozen juice. The sample is not *representative*. In a representative sample, the individuals or items making up a selected portion of a total population are *typical* of the larger group. The researcher cannot examine the entire population—in this case, consumers of orange juice—but should interview a sample that fairly represents the entire population.

There are two important factors to consider when testing examples. First, are the examples drawn from a large enough sample? If one researcher interviewed 100 managers in a large corporation while another interviewed only 20, the evidence based on the larger number of instances would be preferable.

Second, since an example represents a larger population, it is important that samples be *typical* of the population they represent. People tend to accept "facts" as somehow beyond question. How often do you hear statements like "The facts speak for themselves" or "You can't argue with the facts"? A speaker may present a number of examples that are clearly factual, meaning that they are verifiable, repeatable, demonstrable, agreed upon by observers, and so forth—yet these examples may be completely unrepresentative of the population. For example, someone who hears that three hair dryers have defective heating units might unfairly conclude that the manufacturer is producing dryers with poor quality heating units. Even though the examples are factual, they may be the exceptional cases. They do not prove that all dryers made by that company have defective heating units.

Using *real objects* as evidence makes it difficult to deny the truth of a claim. The object serves as tangible proof. For example, a metallurgist testifying that an airplane part failed because of a flaw in its construction might actually produce the part in question and show where the weakness occurred. The manufacturer of the part might point out, however, that someone could have intentionally made the product appear to be flawed. So, one test for real objects is genuineness—that they are not faked or altered in some way. A second test is similar to one test for examples—to determine whether the object is representative. Imagine that a job applicant presents two writing samples to a prospective employer. These two samples are excellent, but everything else the applicant has written is of inferior quality. Thus, the real objects are not representative of the person's work. It would probably be wise to request additional samples of the person's work and/or to examine other types of evidence regarding the applicant's qualifications.

EVALUATING NONFACTUAL SUPPORT

Nonfactual support creates or strengthens interest and clarity. It also reinforces factual evidence. Indeed, factual evidence is not always superior to nonfactual support. Instead, nonfactual support is used for different reasons and should be evaluated by different standards. The authors of *In Search of Excellence* state that "American business has gotten mired in a swamp of economic and political woes." They go on to say that other countries are "now the islands of good news" (Peters and Waterman, 1982, p. 33). But they clearly do not mean that American business is literally in a swamp or that other countries are actually islands. Instead, the authors are being figurative.

Speakers use nonfactual support for clarity and interest, in the form of stories, hypothetical examples, literary quotes, figurative analogies, and so forth. The major criterion is appropriateness. This means that a speaker should (1) understand the difference between factual and nonfactual support and (2) avoid using nonfactual support when factual support is required.

Either factual or nonfactual support may persuade listeners and add clarity and interest to a presentation. Factual material establishes truth and validity, convinces listeners, or changes their minds. In contrast, nonfactual support more often makes ideas vivid and interesting. It helps get listeners more personally involved in the presentation. Thus, if Bob Trent wants his listeners to believe that American's computer products save money, he will need to offer facts that support his claim. If he wants to dispel a misconception about computers, he might tell a humorous story about someone who thought computers would someday take over the world.

EVALUATING REASONING

Reasoning is a matter of arriving at conclusions from data. Inadequate or erroneous data, or evidence, may invalidate your conclusions as a reasoner. But even the best and truest evidence does not guarantee that your reasoning is correct. Let's examine four common types of reasoning and learn ways to avoid making errors in their use. The four types are (1) reasoning by example, (2) reasoning by analogy, (3) causal reasoning, and (4) sign reasoning.

When you *reason by example*, you conclude that one or more examples represent a larger group, or population, and that what is true of the example will be true of any member of that population. A sales representative might tell customers that five people who recently purchased a new digital thermostat have enjoyed significant savings in their fuel bills. The assumption is, of course, that these five people are typical of those who have purchased the thermostat and that the same results can be expected by anyone else who purchases the product.

However, it may be that the five people used as examples are *not* typical of most people who have purchased this thermostat, and that actually there have been no significant fuel savings for the majority of purchasers. Thus, the most important criterion for reasoning by example is that the examples must be *typical* of the group they represent (see Ziegelmueller and Dause, 1975, pp. 113–114).

When you *reason by analogy*, you are drawing a conclusion based on a comparison of two or more items. An analogy may be either figurative or literal. In a *figurative analogy*, the items compared are *not* alike in most respects; however, some point of similarity is found. In a *literal analogy*, the items compared are similar or alike.

A supervisor might say, "John is the wolf stalking its prey when it comes to getting someone to do something for him." Obviously, there are few actual similarities between John and a wolf. But as a means of stressing that John is persistent, that he doesn't give up easily when he wants something from someone, the speaker has stressed a point of similarity with the way a wolf stalks its prey. Figurative analogies are more useful for aiding clarity, adding interest, or emotionalizing a point than for proof.

In another situation, one employee might say to another, "I know I'll get the promotion next month. For the past year I have done everything that Mary did before she was promoted. Since she got the promotion, so will I." This reasoning, like all analogous reasoning, depends on the likeness, or similarity, of the items being compared. If all conditions are the same, and if indeed the employee has done everything that Mary did, the promotion might come about as expected. But if there are important differences, the conclusion may be incorrect. For example, the company's financial picture may have taken a turn for the worse, so promotions might be denied. Perhaps Mary knew someone who had a great deal of influence and was responsible for a favorable decision regarding her promotion. If the speaker has no such assistance the outcome may be different—regardless of other similarities.

You use *causal reasoning* to conclude that the presence of one thing produces, or brings about, another thing or condition. You might start with the cause and reason to the effect, or you could begin with the effect and reason back to the cause. For example, an office manager might call a meeting and say, "If all this office socializing doesn't stop, we'll never get our paperwork processed each day." This person reasons that staff socializing (cause) will result in less paperwork getting processed (effect). The underlying assumption is that whenever workers socialize they accomplish less work.

A speaker might say that an increase in costly errors (effect) is due to recent reductions in the budget for employee training (cause). The conclusion is that an effort to save money has actually ended up costing money.

In order to evaluate causal reasoning in your presentations, apply the following criteria: (1) Is the asserted cause actually capable of producing the effect? (2) Are you omitting or ignoring multiple causes? (3) Are you mistaking coincidence for causality?

The first criterion asks you to consider whether something assumed or claimed as the cause is actually capable of producing the asserted or observed effect. For example, a person might claim to be able to perform a complex task after reading an article on the subject. Merely reading one article is probably not sufficient to enable the person to perform a difficult task successfully.

The second criterion, *multiple causality*, means that most effects are the result of more than one cause. For example, someone might assert that Japanese automobile manufacturers are successfully competing with American automobile manufacturers because Japan has lower wage scales. That might be one cause. Certainly, however, it is not the only cause, and it does not follow that lowering wages in the American automobile industry will solve the problem. Other causes might include differences between Japanese and U.S. trade policies, public perception of quality of the competing products, marketing techniques, and so forth. You should try to identify all major causes rather than assuming that there is only one.

The third criterion asks you to distinguish between causality and coincidence. In order for something to qualify as a cause, it must be clearly linked to the effect; that is, it must definitely produce the result. Coincidence, in contrast, is a mere side-by-side or circumstantial relationship in which a causal link is missing. For example, someone could become ill shortly after eating in the company cafeteria. At first it appears that eating in that cafeteria caused the illnesses. An investigation reveals, however, that others who ate the same food on the same day in the same cafeteria did not become ill. What seemed like a causal relationship was actually coincidental. This reasoning problem is referred to by the Latin expression *post hoc, ergo propter hoc*. An English translation is "after this, therefore because of this." The reasoner assumes that the event or condition that occurs first causes the subsequent event or condition. Coincidence is mistaken for causality.

Sign reasoning is related to causal reasoning. In sign reasoning, you assume that the presence of one thing indicates the presence of something else. If you are driving along in your car and see a sign for a railroad crossing, you can assume that there is a railroad crossing ahead. The sign suggests it, or points toward it. An economist might decide that the national debt, increasing consumer debt, and unfavorable trade balances point to a coming economic depression. These factors may not cause the depression, but they are indications, or signs, of its coming.

It is important to realize that sometimes an assumed sign relationship is invalid. You might assume that your instructor's gruff and generally unfriendly behavior is a sign that he or she is displeased with you or your work. A more careful observation might show, however, that your instructor behaves this way when bothered by personal problems. So, the behavior is not a sign of displeasure with you or your work at all.

Another problem with sign reasoning is that sometimes people focus on less important signs while ignoring more significant indicators. For example, if you were trying to select an apartment you might think an unusually low monthly payment and closeness to campus indicate that a certain apartment is a good choice. But if you fail to discover that the neighbors are noisy, that the apartment is infested by insects, and that the landlord refuses to keep it warm enough in the winter, you will miss important signs that it will not be a good choice.

There are, then, two basic tests for sign reasoning. First, it is a mistake to focus on one sign while ignoring others or while ignoring the various meanings of a sign. Second, it is important not to focus on signs that are less important while disregarding more important and meaningful indicators (see Ziegelmueller and Dause, 1975, p. 119).

ADDITIONAL REASONING PROBLEMS

There are additional reasoning errors that you should avoid in presentations. You should also be aware of these errors when listening to the speaking of others. Such errors are often referred to as *fallacies*. A fallacy occurs when someone's reasoning is incorrect and misleading.

One fallacy is called *ad hominem*. This means that the speaker attacks a person rather than dealing with that person's arguments. Consider a situation in which a manager in a corporation argues against a policy advocated by labor. Rather than responding to the argument, a labor spokesperson attacks the management representative as arrogant and totally unconcerned with the welfare of working people. Although this is a response, it doesn't deal with the issue per se.

Another common reasoning fallacy is *begging the question*: the speaker avoids dealing with a disputed issue by arguing another issue. For example, in a small group discussion, three members of the group repeatedly argue that the organization needs to raise money for purchasing new equipment. A fourth member then argues that what the organization needs is more dedication to its goals. This person is begging the question by ignoring the funding issue.

A third problem is called a *non sequitur*. This Latin expression means "it does not follow." A speaker who draws a conclusion that does not follow from the premise has committed a non sequitur. For example, a speaker might complain that salary increases have been smaller since the new manager took over, saying that the manager was responsible for the unsatisfactory raises. As discussed in relation to causal reasoning, there may be a number of causes for an effect; there may be reasons for the smaller raises that have nothing to do with the new manager.

Another fallacy is called *"you're another."* In this situation the speaker refuses to answer specific questions or charges and, instead, points out problems, inadequacies, and faults in the person raising the issues: "Ms. Schmidt has shown a lot of concern about a few small items in my expense account, but she failed to mention the time she went on company funds to a convention in Chicago and then spent an entire day going to the Art Institute and visiting with friends instead of attending meetings." Note that the speaker in no way addresses the charges about the expense account.

The fallacy called *arguing in a circle* means, essentially, that a person uses the argument or position being advocated as a reason for accepting it. For example, someone might say, "The complexity of a problem makes it impossible to solve because the utter complexity of it is too great to comprehend." Obviously, his reasoning moves in a circle.

Yet another way to avoid dealing with the relevant issue (and a means of throwing another person off guard) is to ask *loaded questions*. For example, a speaker might ask, "Are you willing to risk the future of the company and its employees on a proposal that only promises to make you look good to the "higher-ups"? Obviously, no one would want to answer "yes" to such a ques-

Table 11.1   REASONING FALLACIES

Fallacy	Nature	Correction
Ad hominem	Attacking the person instead of addressing the issue.	Deal with the issue.
Begging the question	Dealing with an issue not under discussion.	Stick to the issue being discussed.
Non sequitur	Reaching a conclusion that does not follow from the premise.	Make certain that the premise supports the conclusion.
"You're another"	Pointing out the faults of someone who mentions your faults.	Deal with the charges.
Arguing in a circle	Justifying a conclusion by restating the reason.	Separate conclusions from reasons.
Loaded questions	Asking questions which cannot be answered without harming the presenter.	Ask fair questions.
False choice	Excluding possible choices or solutions.	Discuss all viable choices.

tion. It is loaded against the person being asked to respond (see Chapter 4 for a detailed discussion of loaded questions).

Finally, speakers may attempt to provide *false choices*, suggesting, for instance, that there are only two alternatives when there are actually more than that. A speaker might say, "It's time to decide. We either accept this approach to advertising or lose our competitive edge in today's market." There may well be other ways to remain competitive (see Rieke and Sillars, 1984, pp. 85–86, and Sproule, 1980, p. 85).

The fallacies of reasoning we have discussed are listed in Table 11.1.

SUMMARY

- Support is anything that a speaker uses to back up or strengthen assertions. Support may be factual or nonfactual. Factual support consists of testimony, statistics, examples, and actual objects. The source of support material is where the material is found. Support may be in the form of evidence, values, and/or credibility.

- Reasoning is the process of arriving at a conclusion from data. It consists of the evidence (data), the claim (conclusion), and the thinking that justifies the move from data to conclusion. Reasoning and factual support are closely related.

- Nonfactual support enhances interest and clarity. It helps listeners to understand and to be more interested and involved in the presenter's message. Nonfactual support can consist of stories, hypothetical examples, literary quotations, figurative analogies, and so forth.

- A speaker can reason in four ways: by example, by analogy, by cause, and by sign. Examples should be typical. Analogies depend on similarities, so the presenter must beware of differences that void the comparison. Causal reasoning requires the establishment of a link between cause and effect. Sign reasoning is not always reliable;

the reasoner must be aware of conditions that render an assumed sign invalid and must be aware of multiple signs.

- Common fallacies include *ad hominem* (attacking the person instead of the issue); begging the question (arguing an issue not under consideration); *non sequitur* (arguing a conclusion that does not follow from the premise); "you're another" (arguing that the other person is guilty of unacceptable behavior); arguing in a circle (using the position advocated as a reason for accepting that position); asking loaded questions (asking questions in which all answers are damaging); and presenting false choices (limiting possible alternatives unrealistically).

QUESTIONS FOR REVIEW AND DISCUSSION

1. How do evidence and reasoning work together?
2. When is it acceptable, and even desirable, to use nonfactual rather than factual support?
3. How is the use of support and reasoning related to audience analysis and audience adaptation?
4. Why do some people think factual support is always persuasive?
5. How can a speaker possess unquestionable facts and yet use incorrect reasoning?
6. Under what conditions could a speaker reason correctly with false support material?

ACTIVITIES

1. Bring in editorials and letters to the editor from a magazine or newspaper. In class or in groups, analyze and evaluate their use of support and reasoning.
2. Write a brief paper in which you discuss your views regarding the ethics of emotional appeal.
3. Watch a political speech on television or videotape and then analyze and evaluate the use of support and reasoning.
4. Divide into small groups and create examples of each type of reasoning fallacy discussed in this chapter. Share them with the class.
5. Observe advertisements on television or videotape. Analyze them for use of support and reasoning.

Chapter
12

Organizing the Presentation

After reading and reviewing this chapter, you should be able to . . .

1. Define and explain the benefits of carefully organizing your presentation.

2. Compare the process of organizing a presentation to building a bridge.

3. Explain how the central idea is vital to the presentation.

4. Identify, explain, and give examples of six patterns of organization that can be used in preparing a presentation.

5. Explain the purpose of the conclusion and identify the five components essential to fulfilling that function in a successful presentation.

6. Identify the four subfunctions of an introduction and explain the role of each.

7. Explain the purpose of transitions and identify key parts of the presentation where transitions are needed.

8. Identify the function of an outline and explain four important outlining techniques.

When Bob Trent's department needs something that requires the under-standing, support, or approval of others—personnel, a budget increase, a new program, or a new policy—he determines what type of approach to use for organizing a presentation. The structure, or *organization*, of a presentation is the logical and strategic arrangement or sequencing of ideas in a clear, coher-ent, and unified order. Clarity and simplicity are principal goals. Bob needs to present his ideas in such a way that the audience can easily follow and un-derstand them.

Just as good impressions are important in the social setting, they are ex-tremely important in the business setting. Successful proposals are well-organized proposals, and well-organized proposals are generally successful proposals. Most listeners expect presentations to be well-organized. Thwart-ing their expectations may damage the speaker's credibility. McCroskey and Mehrley (1969) found that "serious disorganization and extensive nonfluen-cies seriously restrict the amount of attitude change a communicator can produce and substantially reduce the communicator's credibility" (p. 21). Curtis and Kline (1974) discovered that "an organized message promoted greater comprehension of the material by an audience than a randomly orga-nized one" (p. 49). Thus, you should not risk losing credibility with a poorly organized presentation. When the decision makers are in a position to pro-mote you, dismiss you, or in some other way affect your salary and/or career, it is even more important that you be credible. Carefully organizing your message is one way to project a favorable image.

Organizing a presentation is like building a bridge. In either situation, the builder needs to develop and connect three substructures (see Figure 12.1). The substructures of a bridge are the entrance, span, and exitway. The parts of a presentation are the introduction, body, and conclusion. Linking pins connect the bridge as a unified whole. The transitions are the linking pins of a presentation. You should begin organizing your message with the body or main substructure. A good way to begin is to select a central idea and major points to support it (Chapter 8 discussed the central idea). The central idea statement is the span of the presentation, and the main points are the sup-porting framework. Next, you should plan a conclusion, and finally, an intro-duction for the bridge (see Table 12.1). Speakers sometimes go about this process inappropriately, planning the introduction before really knowing what they are introducing.

The central idea is the heart of any presentation. Thus, the development of the body of a presentation begins with a careful scrutiny of that idea. In well-structured messages the central idea is supported by a few main points, generally two to five. You greatly assist your listeners by using no more than five main points. Moreover, minimizing the number of main points makes it

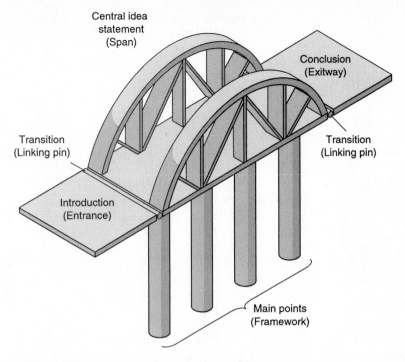

Figure 12.1 A presentation is structured like a bridge.

easier to master the material and enhances clarity and simplicity. A principle of information theory is that most people can only process five to nine "bits" of information (Miller, 1956). You achieve clarity by developing a unified, coherent, and relevant message. Howell and Bormann (1988) explain that the presenter can unify a message by "searching for and finding a central theme to which each element logically relates" (p. 62). This "central theme" is the thesis or central idea statement. Coherence "refers to how the various parts of the message cluster together" (Howell and Bormann, 1988, p. 62). You can best measure coherence by examining the finished product for a clear, unified overall design. And you can measure the relevance of ideas by looking at the relationship of all materials to the central theme. Discard irrelevant ideas (or file them for future use) unless you have a plausible rationale for inclusion of such material. For example, some tangential material might be useful in addressing peripheral questions.

Table 12.1   PURPOSE OF MAJOR ORGANIZATIONAL
COMPONENTS

Introduction: Preview the message
Body: View the message
Conclusion: Review the message

Keep your message concise and to the point. Needlessly belaboring ideas destroys the directness and succinctness important in achieving simplicity.

PATTERNS OF ORGANIZATION

Develop your main points on the basis of divisions dictated by the wording of the central idea statement, by the topic, and, occasionally, by the audience. For example, a passive audience might be activated by a problem-solution format that identifies a serious problem that threatens their security and a solution that reduces the threat. This systematic approach greatly enhances the unity, coherence, and relevance of the main points that support the presentation's central idea. Consistent use of an appropriate organizational pattern is the foundation of overall organization. Speakers frequently use chronological, spatial, topical, causal, and problem-solution patterns; the process of reflective thinking; and the motivated sequence. We will discuss these methods of organization. But remember that the patterns discussed in this chapter are only a few of numerous organizational schemes speakers can use for structuring their main points.

Chronological Pattern

You can use a chronological pattern when your purpose lends itself to a time sequence. The chronological pattern is more practical for informational briefings, but it can be adapted for persuasive proposals. When proposing a budget increase for his department, Bob Trent might begin by discussing the department's budget history; next, he could discuss the present budget; and, finally, he could discuss future needs for his program. Let's consider some examples:

Proposal: American Computer Systems should broaden its recruitment of personnel, because of growth patterns during the past few years.
  I. During the 1960s, employee recruitment centered around our headquarters in Missouri.
  II. During the 1970s and 1980s, employee recruitment expanded slightly to accommodate plants in Kansas and Iowa.
  III. As we prepare for the 1990s, our employee recruitment efforts should include all major universities and colleges throughout the Midwest.

Proposal: The Promotions and Advertising Department of American Computer Systems needs a higher budget commensurate with its expanded mission.
  I. Last year's budget of $200,000 was adequate for a department devoted only to product promotion.
  II. This year's budget of $250,000 was tight, because we expanded our mission to include market research, product research, and package research.
  III. Next year's budget must be increased to $600,000 because we will add copy costs, media costs, and customer motivation research.

Spatial Patterns

The spatial pattern is more practical for informational briefings, but it can be adapted for making persuasive proposals. For example, when the focal point of a presentation deals with promotion of products or services, thereby emphasizing the structure or function of items, it may prove useful to present ideas spatially.

> *Proposal:* American Computer Systems should broaden employee recruitment to universities within a 100-mile radius of plant locations.
> I. Current recruitment is restricted to colleges and universities in Missouri.
> II. New plant development at Lawrence, Kansas, warrants recruitment in several Kansas universities and colleges.
> III. Plant development in Ames, Iowa, warrants recruitment at several Iowa universities and colleges.

Topical Pattern

In the topical pattern, the main topic is divided into main points or categories. Often this involves listing the reasons which justify acceptance of the proposal.

The main points have no logical connection other than their relationship to the purpose, or major topic. At times, however, you might decide to arrange points in an order of importance determined by assessing the audience's level of interest or resistance.

Because of its applicability to practically any subject, purpose, or audience, the topical pattern is a useful method of presentational organization. For example, an advertising account executive might explain, in an initial presentation to Bob Trent, that her agency will successfully promote American's new computer product:

> *Proposal:* American Computer Systems should hire our advertising firm to promote the CX-1000 computer line.
> I. Our marketing group will thoroughly research all markets to determine the best strategy for reaching your potential customers.
> II. Our media group will determine the most effective use of your advertising dollars to reach your customers and potential customers.
> III. Our creative advertising group will create powerful, imaginative messages to entice these potential customers to buy your product.

Causal Pattern

Another way to arrange ideas is to discuss the causes of a problem and consider subsequent effects or results. You can also reverse the pattern, examining a known condition (effect) and then offering an explanation of its causes. Use this pattern cautiously, for there are seldom single causes or effects (Chapter 11 discusses multiple causality in detail). Moreover, you must watch out for false causes. Use this pattern only after careful analysis of causal relationships. The following are two examples of causal outlines:

Proposal: Steadman Manufacturing's agriculture division must lower costs to keep farm machinery prices consonant with the prices farmers receive for their products, so the company's sales do not drop.

Cause I. The cost of our raw materials and labor is increasing.

Cause II. The prices farmers receive for commodities have fallen.

Effect III. Farmers will be squeezed between rising machinery expenses and falling prices.

Proposal: There are monetary benefits to health club memberships for American Computer Supply's employees.

Cause I. Companies across the nation are losing millions of dollars' worth of time because of workers' illness.

Cause II. Absent workers' benefits must still be paid for, and additional costs are incurred in hiring replacement workers.

Effect III. Physically fit workers are absent far less frequently than unfit workers.

Effect IV. Physically fit workers have higher morale, more ambition, and better concentration and thus perform at higher productivity levels.

Problem-Solution Pattern

Dividing the topic into two main points is the simplest way to use a problem-solution pattern. The first point demonstrates or diagnoses the problem, and the second presents a way to solve the problem. Good solutions are practical, workable, and advantageous to the parties involved. This pattern lends itself especially well to persuasive proposals. Decision makers listen and respond positively when they can readily identify with a problem affecting their welfare, and they are likely to accept a practical, workable, and beneficial proposal. Look at the following examples:

Proposal: The financial crisis facing Steadman Manufacturing can be solved best by making a concerted effort on several fronts.

Problem I. Our agricultural customers will continue to face a financial crisis for the rest of the twentieth century.

Solution II. The crisis needs the joint action of three groups: farmers, public officials, and private corporations like ours.

Proposal: Our company should add employee referral to our recruiting methods.

Problem I. Our present recruiting methods are expensive, and the situation is aggravated by a high employee turnover rate.

Solution II. Employee referrals would help reduce recruiting costs and could reduce our high turnover rate through compatibility factors.

Proposal: The local school system should mainstream deaf students.

Problem I. The current State schools for the deaf provide a low-quality education for their students.

Solution II. Mainstreaming can provide quality education for the hearing-impaired.

The following proposal presents two main points that address dimensions of the problem, then a two-part solution to the problem. A problem-solution format may include more than one main point for both the problem and solution steps.

> *Proposal:* Using paid instructors instead of volunteers to teach the lower-level classes will dramatically reduce the problems of inadequate human resources and poor instruction that we are experiencing in the swimming program.
> Problem I. Our winter swimming program is in trouble because of poor instruction.
> Problem II. Hiring professionals is expensive.
> Solution III. We should use paid instructors instead of volunteers to teach the lower-level swimming classes.
> Solution IV. Raising course fees will offset the cost of hiring instructors.

Reflective Thinking Pattern

The process of reflective thinking discussed in Chapter 6 is another excellent format for developing a presentation. You will recall that the six-step pattern includes (1) definition and limitation of a problem, (2) analysis of the problem, (3) generation of possible solutions, (4) appraisal of suggested solutions, (5) selection of the best solution, and (6) implementation of the solution.

Suppose Bob Trent is receiving complaints from customers regarding the way they are treated by his sales staff. No matter who a customer is—an individual, a business, or a public firm—the future of American Computer Systems and the jobs and livelihoods of all people in the company depend on how well customers are treated. Bob knows he must address this problem quickly.

He decides to make a proposal to his superior, Carmen Garcia. First he holds a discussion session with his sales force, using as an organizational pattern the Dewey process of reflective thinking:

> *Proposal:* A customer relations training session is needed for all sales staff at American Computer Systems.
> Problem definition I. Customers are complaining about rude treatment by sales personnel at American.
> Problem analysis II. Some business firms report that sales personnel fail to listen before they talk.
> Possible solutions III. The sales staff suggested several solutions, including telephone training, practice in perception checks, listening training, and disciplinary interviews with noncompliant employees.
> Solution appraisal IV. Members of the group developed criteria and applied the criteria to the suggested solutions.
> Selection V. The group decided that listening training is the most effective means of solving the problem.
> Implementation VI. All sales personnel should attend a two-day training session on listening improvement.

Bob closed the presentation to Carmen Garcia by (1) stressing the importance of listening as an effective sales tool and (2) noting that if the sales staff does not contribute to the satisfaction of individual customers by utilizing good listening techniques, American may well lose the customers.

The Motivated Sequence

Alan H. Monroe (1939) developed the motivated sequence, which was based on the psychology of business sales (books on that subject used terms like *attention, interest, desire,* and *action*). Monroe and Ehninger (1967) defined the *motivated sequence* as a standard method of speech organization that uses a "sequence of ideas which, by following the normal process of human thinking, motivates an audience to respond to the speaker's purpose" (p. 265). The conventional divisions of a speech are the introduction, body, and conclusion, but the motivated sequence consists of five steps: (1) attention, (2) need, (3) satisfaction, (4) visualization, and (5) action (see Figure 12.2). Using these five steps can contribute to a successful business proposal. The functions of each step follow:

Step 1: Attention (getting attention)

Step 2: Need (showing the need, describing the problem)

Step 3: Satisfaction (satisfying the need, presenting the solution)

Step 4: Visualization (visualizing the results, if the proposal is accepted and if rejected)

Step 5: Action (requesting action and/or approval)

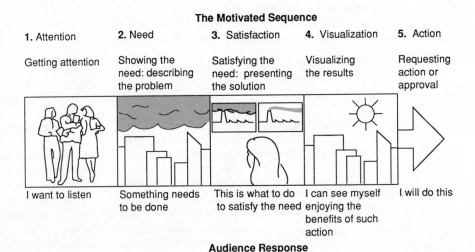

Figure 12.2 The motivated sequence. (*Source*: From B. E. Gronbeck, D. Ehninger, and A. H. Monroe, *Principles of Speech Communication*, 10th ed. Glenview, Ill.: Scott, Foresman and Company, 1988.)

The attention step typically functions as the introduction; the need and satisfaction steps constitute the body of the message (each step comprises a main point); and the visualization and action steps generally serve as the conclusion. Bob Trent could well use Monroe's motivated sequence for his important presentation to the Sento Group:

Proposal: The CX-1000 personal computer will provide services for the growing needs of the Sento Group.

Attention I. People who make decisions about computer equipment purchases need to know what systems to choose from, what software to buy, and whether a system can be updated for changing business needs.

Need II. Our needs analysis for the Sento Group suggests certain problems exist: many employees do not use the hardware and software available; several different generations of equipment and multiple types of software are in use; and there are problems with the printer interface.

Satisfaction III. The CX-1000 system from American Computer Systems addresses all these concerns. In addition, it can be updated through use of expansion slots as the Sento Group's business grows.

Visualization IV. Imagine all employees being involved in computerization, increasing their productivity, and producing more attractive final products.

Action V. Purchase the CX-1000 to meet your computer needs of today and tomorrow.

Proposal: The integration of police and fire services is an answer to budgetary and efficiency problems in municipal safety services.

Attention I. Integration of police and fire services is not a new issue. (It was first done successfully in 1911.)

Need II. Police and fire services are both faced with budget problems, demands for more and varied services, and layoffs.

Satisfaction III. One solution to the budgetary and efficiency problems of police and fire administrators is the integration of police and fire services.

Visualization IV. Significant benefits will accrue from either total or partial integration of these services.

Action V. Vote yes for the integration of these two public safety services.

Proposal: The polygraph should be adopted as a tool for screening potential police employees.

Attention I. Thirty percent of our current police department employees have committed a serious crime or have some type of psychological problem.

Need II. A poor selection process can seriously damage a police department.

Satisfaction III. Use of the polygraph can help us avoid such problems.

Visualization IV.
(negative accentuation) Some departments may prefer a traditional screening process and risk hiring police with criminal records.

Action V. Let's hire stable people and not former criminals in our police department.

Note that in the polygraph proposal, the visualization step focused on a negative rather than a positive result. The visualization step may stress the potential risk of *not* following the advocated proposal. In this step you can utilize contrast by painting a picture, or visualization, of the dangers of maintaining the status quo.

Climax Versus Anticlimax Organization

Climax and anticlimax arrangements order materials according to their relative size, strength, importance, or emotional impact. *Climax* schemes save major arguments for the end, the strongest appeal of the message; *anticlimax* schemes present them in a less forceful or less appealing part of the message (see Table 12.2). Whether to use a climax scheme or an anticlimax scheme is an important question.

In a study on retention of visually perceived messages, Doob (1953) had subjects read five short passages on various controversial issues. He found that items appearing first tended to be recalled more often and more quickly but with no more accuracy. Using "strong" and "weak" speeches on the same side of a topic, Cromwell (1950) found that subjects made significantly greater attitude shifts in the direction advocated by the speaker when messages were presented in a weak-to-strong (climax) pattern. Hovland, Janis, and Kelley (1953) added a new dimension to climax/anticlimax studies by hypothesizing (1) that "presentation of major arguments at the outset (anticlimax) will be most effective where the audience is initially little interested" in the message and (2) that other factors would be more important when advance attention was high. They also suggested that climax order would be most effective when issues were familiar to the audience and/or when the audience manifested deep concern (pp. 115–120).

Clark (1974) transmitted four short speeches via videotape, in different combinations based on "the pro/con and weak/strong dimensions" (p. 322). His hypothesis, that audience response is influenced by order, was not supported, but Clark inferred that "with one-sided persuasive messages, climax order is superior to anticlimax order in producing positive audience evaluation of messages" (p. 331). Moreover, he postulated that with a two-sided persuasive message, "climax order in the first side followed by anticlimax order

Table 12.2 CLIMAX/ANTICLIMAX ORGANIZATION

Scheme	Purpose
Climax order (key points stated last)	Use key ideas last for great impact. Accentuate key ideas this way when the issues are familiar to the audience or when the audience is very concerned.
Anticlimax order (key points and issues stated first)	Use key ideas first when audience has little interest in the issues.

in the second side is superior to any other arrangement in producing positive audience evaluation of messages" (p. 331).

Although the research findings on climax and anticlimax organization are helpful, you should exercise caution when generalizing from these studies, particularly since a fairly narrow range of message topics was used and most of the research is now dated.

When addressing an apathetic audience, you might begin with the strongest point as an attention-getting device. Or, you might reserve the point with the most impact (by virtue of strength, importance, or emotional impact) for last, to serve as a "clincher" or "kicker" to gain the support of the audience.

BEGINNING AND ENDING THE PRESENTATION

Every presentation, whether short or long, needs an introduction and a conclusion. The speaker previews the message for the audience at the beginning and reviews the message at the end. "Well begun is half done." A good, strong, crisp introduction is critical to setting a positive tone for the proposal. Moreover, a succinct but stirring exit is equally important for obtaining the support of the audience.

The Conclusion

The major purpose of the conclusion is to refocus your listeners' attention on the message. Generally, you should prepare the conclusion after preparing the body of the presentation and before preparing the introduction. This is because the conclusion is where you review the key "selling points" and ask for the "sale." The function of the introduction is more holistic—to introduce the entire presentation, including the conclusion.

The conclusion is largely a review. There are several components that should come together to fulfill this function:

1. Summarizing key points
2. Focusing on your theme and purpose
3. Reminding listeners of the urgency for the change
4. Providing listeners with a clear course of action
5. Asking for questions

The Summary   Since most people will only remember about 25 percent of what they hear (see Nichols and Stevens, 1957, p. ix), the value of reinforcement through summaries is clear. This may be the only time some listeners process the main ideas. Therefore, you should briefly repeat and drive home the main points. Baird (1974) discovered that inclusion of "a review produced significantly more comprehension than did inclusion of no summary whatsoever" (p. 127).

Reinforce the Proposal   After summarizing the main points, you should reinforce the heart of the proposal. Highlight the proposed product, process, plant, policy, or personnel changes, so that your listeners understand what you are asking them to support.

State the Urgency of the Change   Most proposals are made in response to a specific problem. The proposed change represents an attempt to solve the problem and to accrue significant benefits to the organization. Since humans tend to procrastinate, it is generally desirable to press for a decision while the issues are fresh. If immediate action is urgent, make this clear. However, never try to manufacture urgency. Keep in mind that you may be too close to an issue and hence lack objectivity. You can severely damage your reputation if you urge immediate action when there is no need for it; be judicious and realistic, to ensure you are not "crying wolf."

Propose a Course of Action   Asking for a sale or some particular action is a delicate step. You want to establish finality in a presentation, but your analysis of the audience may tell you not to press hard at this time. However, it is usually appropriate to request some kind of action—perhaps to ask the decision makers to study your handouts, to take a "straw vote," to get back to you in a few days, or to call you if they have further questions about your proposal. Remember that if you have done your homework and the proposal is a sound one, you should ultimately prevail.

Ask for Questions   Many sales and other desired audience responses are made or lost in the question-and-answer session. (Chapter 16 addresses this "addendum" to the conclusion.) Inviting questions may be risky, but try to view it as a necessary part of making presentations. The question-and-answer period is the time to listen for objections. Your ability to handle questions will reveal your confidence, character, and sense of professionalism as well as the soundness of your ideas.

THE INTRODUCTION

Use the introduction to preview the central idea of your presentation. This "courting period" may well determine whether your audience decides to listen to you. An effective introduction (1) gains favorable attention, (2) promotes friendliness and goodwill between the speaker and audience, (3) provides important reasons to listen, and (4) orients the audience toward the body of the message.

Gaining Favorable Attention

Before a speaker can "sell" an idea, he or she needs to attract favorable attention. Getting *attention*, or the process of selecting and sustaining a focus, can be difficult. You can attract attention by pounding your fist on a lectern. But the key is gaining *favorable* attention and sustaining it. Since people attend to stimuli in short bursts, the speaker's challenge is to attract and maintain the listeners' *favorable* attention throughout the presentation. Gaining attention can be compared to casting a net around a school of fish and pulling them into the boat. If the thrower's aim is off or the mesh is too large, the fish will escape. You must ensure that your "net" is adapted to the interests of the audience. You can employ several interest factors to secure favorable attention: intensity, movement, familiarity, novelty, humor, and suspense have high attention value. These factors, coupled with a brief, direct message in good taste, will help gain favorable attention.

Intensity   Everything else being equal, greater intensity attracts attention. A light, sound, smell, or object that is more intense than surrounding stimuli will attract attention.

For example, the North Star occasionally stands out in the sky because of the intensity of its light. Limburger cheese attracts attention because of its strong smell. Vivid words attract attention, particularly when contrasted with more traditional language. (Additional means of achieving striking effects through intense, vivid language are discussed in Chapter 13.) At the bicentennial celebration of Cornell University, former senator and onetime presidential hopeful Edmund Muskie used intense language in the introduction of his speech entitled "The Chains of Liberty":

> Someone once asked Lee Trevino what to do when it starts lightning on a golf course. "Hold up a five-iron and start walking," he said. "Even God can't hit a five-iron." In this two hundredth year of our federal union, the American political system has been moving through a lightning storm—and there aren't enough five-irons to go around. Some officials have taken hard hits. Some of our institutions have been jolted. And recent events have left flash-burns in the fabric that binds our society together. (Muskie, 1987, p. 4)

Motion   A moving object usually attracts more attention than a stationary object. An animated, dynamic, yet composed speaker will attract attention. A speaker having a clear plan of movement gives the audience a sense of progress. Nonverbal communication can provide movement in the delivery of a presentation. In a message to the Brevard Economic Development Council, Willard E. Rockwell, Jr., chairman of General Space Corporation, illustrated movement through vocal stress:

> I know that most of you share with me a deep concern for this country's future in space. And I know you share with me a common determination that we *will* have a future in space . . . and confidence that we will again lead the world in developing space for the benefit not only for our own citizens . . . but for future generations throughout the world. We *can* do it . . . and we *must* do it. The only alternative is that the Russians do it for us . . . and this is an alternative which, I submit, is unacceptable to the people of this country . . . and to every other civilized country. We cannot allow that to happen. Yet . . . most of us know that,

slowly but surely, it is happening. The Russians are making giant strides in space . . . at a time when we are virtually standing still. Not only are the Russians making rapid progress, but also the French, the Chinese and the Japanese. (Rockwell, 1986, p. 8)

Familiarity You can attract attention by referring to the familiar. In a technological age of rapid change, people often feel comfortable with the familiar. You can refer to members of the audience by name or to their positions, assignments, achievements, and frustrations, in order to make listeners feel that you are interested in and concerned about them. Used sparingly, the familiar is an effective way to attract and maintain favorable attention. Charles Wick, director of the U.S. Information Agency, used reference to the familiar in his introduction to a speech delivered to the U.S. Marine Correspondents Association:

> The story of the Marines is the story of America, from our independence to Iwo Jima, from Danang to the bunkers of Beirut. As correspondents, you have told thousands of stories of hardship, danger, valor and compassion. You have reported on wars with words and pictures. You have told the stories the way they were, and we are stronger today because you did. America still has wars these days, but recently they have only been wars of words and ideas. This evening, I want to talk about the war of ideas. While the weapons of hardware are a needed deterrent, in a confrontation, the loser will lose and the winner also will lose. Thus, the war of ideas is the only viable alternative. The United States Information Agency (USIA) is America's arsenal in the war of ideas. The Director of USIA is the principal adviser on foreign attitudes to the President, the Secretary of State and the National Security Council. USIA tells America's story to the world through public diplomacy, where government communicates directly with other peoples, today made more possible than ever through telecommunications. Cultural historian Marshall McLuhan perceived this nearly 20 years ago. He predicted that satellite technology would bring the world together in an electronic "global village." (Wick, 1985, p. 16)

Novelty Perhaps one reason for movie director Steven Spielberg's success is the novelty of his characters, both in appearance (*E.T.*) and in personality (*Gremlins*). A newspaper maxim is "when a dog bites a man, it's an accident; when a man bites a dog, it's news." That which is unique attracts attention. A circus or carnival offers unusual phenomena—a 500-pound person, the world's strongest man or woman, a flesh-eating amoeba, a five-legged calf. Contrast is one important type of novelty, for humans are drawn to contrast.

Movies like *Star Wars* carry uniqueness to an extreme; their striking characters certainly attract attention. At the same time, novelty for novelty's sake can be counterproductive. Speakers are advised not to appear in a gorilla suit or some other outlandish garb for the sake of gimmickry.

In their book *Contemporary American Speeches*, Linkugel, Allen, and Johannesen (1978) include a moving speech by Kathy Weisensel. Early in the speech, she discusses the differences between mental illness and mental retardation:

Let's extend that definition with a series of contrasts. Mental retardation is always permanent; mental illness is usually temporary. Mental retardation is subnormal intelligence; mental illness is distorted intelligence. Mental retardation involves deficient cognitive abilities; mental illness involves emotional impairment of cognitive abilities. Mental retardation is manifested early; mental illness may occur anytime in life. The mentally retarded person is behaviorally stable; it is the mentally ill person who is given to erratic behavior. The extremely mentally retarded person is submissive and mute; the extremely mentally ill person may be violent and criminally dangerous. Thus retarded people are retarded, and no more. We need no longer place them in pens with the criminally insane, as was the custom in medieval societies. (Linkugel, Allen, and Johannesen, 1978, p. 81)

The striking contrast of these conditions was particularly touching because Ms. Weisensel had just divulged to the audience that her older brother was mentally retarded.

Humor   Enjoyment enhances attention. Humor facilitates relaxation of both speaker and listener. It is essential, however, to follow some important guidelines when using humor:

1. Make sure the humor is relevant. Speakers often use humor that is unrelated to anything in the presentation. Irrelevant jokes or other means of humor are inappropriate.
2. Use humor in good taste. One of the quickest ways to attract *unfavorable* attention is to tell an off-color story that offends someone in the audience. Stay away from stories that are gender-based or ethnically based or that in some way may embarrass a member of the audience. If you poke fun at anyone, make yourself the butt of the joke. Peter Walters, chairman of British Petroleum Company, used humor in good taste when he poked fun at himself in the following story:

   Two old ladies were walking around a somewhat overcrowded English country churchyard, and came upon a tombstone on which was the inscription: "Here lies John Smith, an oilman and an honest man."
   "Good heavens!" said one lady to the other, "isn't it awful that they had to put two people in the same grave!" (Walters, 1988, p. 424)

Suspense   Creating an aura of mystery is a useful way to attract attention. The mystery of Stonehenge has attracted visitors for hundreds of years. Alleged sightings of the Loch Ness monster likewise attract hundreds of thousands of tourists. By introducing suspense into a story, you can rivet the audience's attention on your desired point. A speaker used suspense effectively in the following example:

I applaud you for your charitable accomplishments. But I am not here to appeal to that side of you. Rather I want to talk to you about another important people-oriented issue. I want to share with you some of my thoughts about this country's small businesses and the people who own and operate them. In particular, I want to discuss a grave and invidious—but unnecessary—threat that now confronts this nation's independent, small-business community. I call this peril, the "Europeanization" of American labor policy. (Sloan, 1987, p. 29)

Promote Friendliness and Respect

A second function of the introduction is to convey friendliness, sincerity, and sensitivity to any hostility or distrust in the audience toward you or your proposal. Assuring your listeners that you have honorable intentions and that you have their best interests at heart is quite important. In some cases, having someone else introduce you as the speaker can help to build goodwill. Often, however, you will be an employee or supervisor of those in attendance, so an introduction by another will be unnecessary or inappropriate. Regardless of the circumstances that bring you to the presentation situation, an introduction that attracts favorable attention will promote friendliness and respect between you and your audience. R. E. Allen, chairman of the board of American Telephone and Telegraph, promoted respect for the audience and for himself with the following opening statement:

> I come to this meeting not as a scholar of foreign affairs. I come as a businessman whose company is deeply involved in the international arena. On the one hand, by providing communications service that links the United States and some 250 nations and territories around the globe. And on the other hand, as a company that has offices or plants in some 35 countries and whose products are sold in some 100 countries, through joint alliances and distributors. (Allen, 1988, p. 484)

Provide a Reason to Listen

A proposal inherently suggests change. Nonetheless, people often view meetings and presentations as a waste of time. The attitude is "Why should I care?" or "Not another scheme to get my money or make my job more difficult!" Thus, as speaker, it is essential to make it clear that your proposal is vital to the audience members. Show them how the proposal will affect their health, property, reputation, security, loved ones, employment, or future, and you have a greater chance of effecting the desired change. The following introduction to a presentation advocating cremation established a reason to listen:

> In the five or so minutes while I am speaking with you twenty Americans will die and the families of those twenty Americans will be subjected to the third largest expenditure of their lives, outranked only by the cost of their homes and cars. (Curtis, 1974, p. 74)

This speaker pointed out that each listener will someday have to confront death, the loss of loved ones, and the major costs involved.

In Kathy Weisensel's speech, she established a compelling reason to listen:

One out of thirty-three persons is born mentally retarded. It is the most wide-spread, permanent handicap among children. It is among the least understood handicaps of adults. In Wisconsin alone, there are 120,000 retarded people. (Linkugel, Allen, and Johannesen, 1978, p. 80)

Orientation Statement

A strong introduction should provide a smooth *orientation*, or transition into the body of the presentation. Most commonly, this statement is the central idea of the presentation. Such a statement serves as a linking pin for bridging the gap from the introduction to the body of the presentation.

People seem inherently opposed to change "that affects their lives, especially if the changes are initiated by others" (Tubbs, 1988, p. 330). They resent intrusion on their time and on their ways of doing things. Changes in policies, processes, procedures, plants, and personnel are sometimes disruptive, annoying, and time-consuming. Thus, the introduction becomes a critical "courting period" for building your credibility as the speaker. By attracting favorable attention, by promoting friendliness and goodwill between yourself and the audience, by providing a reason to listen, and by orienting the audience to the body of the message, you can fulfill the function of an introduction—that of setting the stage or previewing the body of the presentation.

TRANSITIONS

Unless they have superhuman memories, listeners cannot review what you have said in a presentation the way they can reread pages or sections of an essay. Listeners cannot see punctuation marks, either, to help them distinguish one idea from another. Hence, speakers should provide transitions or connections that tell an audience where the presentation has been, where it is, and where it is going. *Transitions* are words or sentences that connect the segments or parts of a presentation. They are generally needed most at the completion of main ideas and as connecting links between major organization units (between the introduction and the body and between the body and the conclusion). Transitions also connect subpoints. Regardless of where they are needed, transitions serve three important purposes: (1) they indicate that an idea is completed; (2) they provide a link to the next idea; and (3) they preview a forthcoming idea.

Conveying that an idea is completed signals to listeners that the next idea is coming. A link to the next idea is often provided at the same time. Glenna Crooks (1986), director of the policy division of the American Pharmaceutical Association, spoke to the First Annual National Conference on Women's Health; she combined both transition purposes by saying, "So much for the theory of public policy. Let us turn now to . . . " (p. 759).

Sometimes transitions are used to announce the next idea or subtopic, or they may be used to preview all the main points (e.g., a partitioning transition in the introduction). Edmund Cornish (1980), president of the World Future Society, used a transition to partition main points in an address to the Better Housing League of Cincinnati: "So let's look now at six different scenarios suggesting how the family might develop in the years ahead" (p. 121).

When more than one person is involved in a presentation, transitions help to make the shift from speaker to speaker. If the total message is to have maximum impact, it is essential that the speakers emphasize how the several parts that are "tag-teamed" back and forth fit together; one speaker or the other must ensure that the links are made each time.

Strive for variety in transitions. Some stock phrases, such as *and, also,* and *since,* are acceptable; but one mark of a polished presenter is avoiding the use of the same few phrases. Remember that transitional phrases help your audience to shift gears, focus on your ideas, and summarize what you have said. In essence, transitions are linking pins that lead your listeners step by step through your presentation.

OUTLINING

The outline is to you, the speaker, what the blueprint is to a builder. The outline displays the analysis and arrangement of ideas in the presentation. It reveals at a glance the amount of supporting material you have collected and helps you assess its adequacy. The outline acts as a gauge of your preparation for anticipated objections to your proposal.

The audience seldom sees your outline. Its purpose is to serve *you.* There are no rigid rules, but there are common practices that promote clarity and unity in outlining. Let's illustrate with a right and wrong example of each practice.

Consistent Numbering System   Use a consistent numbering system. Although you are free to use whatever system you desire, it helps to understand a standard system. Ideas comparable in importance should be ranked on the same level. For example:

Wrong	Right
I. Our present recruiting methods are expensive, and the situation is aggravated by a high employee turnover rate.	I. Our present recruiting methods are expensive, and the situation is aggravated by a high employee turnover rate.
II. Having one recruiter away from the office is costly.	A. Having one recruiter away from the office is costly.
A. Average cost to the company for a recruiter is $400 per day.	1. Average cost to the company for a recruiter is $400 per day.
B. It may be quite costly if the recruiter is on an extended trip.	2. It may be quite costly if the recruiter is on an extended trip.
C. Employee turnover is significant.	

1. Our company loses 24 percent of our employees every year, which is 4 percent above the average.
2. Most of the employees that leave are younger employees.

B. Employee turnover is significant.
   1. Our company loses 24 percent of our employees every year, which is 4 percent above the average.
   2. Most of the employees that leave are younger employees.

Proper Indentation Indentation depicts the logical relation of ideas. The greater the importance of an idea, the closer it should be to the left-hand margin of the page. If a statement takes up more than one line, the second and succeeding lines should be indented to the beginning of the first line. Consider this example:

<table>
<tr><td align="center">**Wrong**</td><td align="center">**Right**</td></tr>
</table>

II. Employee referrals would help reduce recruiting costs and our high turnover rate.
A. Employee referrals would be less expensive than our current recruiting methods.
1. Recruiters would spend less time on the road.
2. Referrals would be less time-consuming to identify.
B. Employee referrals could lower turnover rates.
1. Referral applicants are usually well informed about the job beforehand by the employee that recommends them.
2. Referral applicants are usually more satisfied because they may have a better chance to be promoted, which increases earnings and enhances benefits.

II. Employee referrals would help reduce recruiting costs and our high turnover rate.
   A. Employee referral would be less expensive than our current recruiting methods.
      1. Recruiters would spend less time on the road.
      2. Referrals would be less time-consuming to identify.
   B. Employee referrals could lower turnover rates.
      1. Referral applicants are usually well informed about the job beforehand by the employee that recommends them.
      2. Referral applicants are usually more satisfied because they may have a better chance to be promoted, which increases earnings and enhances benefits.

Proper Subordination Items in the outline should be arranged in a hierarchy. Since a subordinate idea is a subdivision of a larger heading, it should fall below that heading in scope and importance. It should also support or explain the idea in the superior heading. For example:

<table>
<tr><td align="center">**Wrong**</td><td align="center">**Right**</td></tr>
</table>

I. Stress sufferers produce cues which can be detected by people around them.

I. Stress sufferers produce cues which can be detected by people around them.

A. Some of these signals are easily
seen by those around them.
  1. Irritability.
  2. Playing with pocket change.
  3. Stroking mustache or beard.
  4. Playing with hair.
  5. Clearing the throat frequently.
  6. Frequent yawning or sighing.
II. There are other cues which are not
recognized as easily, unless you
know the person's habits.
A. Increased or decreased eating.
B. Increased smoking.
C. Increased or decreased sleeping.
D. Compulsive gum chewing,
whistling, or laughing.
E. Reversal in behavior patterns.

A. Some of these signals are easily
seen by those around them.
  1. Irritability.
  2. Playing with pocket change.
  3. Stroking mustache or beard.
  4. Playing with hair.
  5. Clearing the throat frequently.
  6. Frequent yawning and sighing.
B. There are other cues which are
not recognized as easily, unless
you know the person's habits.
  1. Increased or decreased eating.
  2. Increased smoking.
  3. Increased or decreased sleeping.
  4. Reckless driving.
  5. Compulsive gum chewing,
  whistling, or laughing.
  6. Reversal in behavior patterns.

Single Units of Information Including items in one point defeats the purpose of good outlining. If you run two items together, the relationship each
bears to the other becomes blurred. The following illustrate the point:

Wrong

I. What is the Suzuki method? Children learn to play an instrument in
much the same way they learn
their own language. The ability to
learn is based on the environment.
Repetition is a learning reinforcement.
II. There are some general characteristics that describe this method. (1)
Individual lessons plus sessions are
included. (2) Reading is postponed
until technique on the instrument
is established. (3) There is emphasis on listening to recordings. (4)
Continuous review, reinforcement,
and performance of learned works
is stressed. (5) Cooperation rather
than competition among students
is emphasized. (6) Tonalization and
musical sensitivity are stressed.

Right

I. What is the Suzuki method?
A. Children learn to play an instrument in much the same way
they learn their own language.
  1. The ability to learn is based
  on the environment.
  2. Repetition is a learning reinforcement.
B. There are some general characteristics that describe this method.
  1. Individual lessons plus sessions are included.
  2. Reading is postponed until
  technique on the instrument
  is established.
  3. There is emphasis on listening
  to recordings.
  4. Continuous review, reinforcement, and performance of
  learned works is stressed.
  5. Cooperation rather than competition among students is
  emphasized.
  6. Tonalization and musical sensitivity are stressed.

Technical Plot   A full-content outline can include a technical plot. The *technical plot* is a tool for identifying the completeness and variety of the support you use to clarify, amplify, vivify, and prove your ideas. Gronbeck, Ehninger, and Monroe (1988) explain that a technical plot can help you determine the soundness of your ideas, the adequacy of supporting ideas, whether you have overused a particular form of support (see Chapter 11), and whether attempts at persuasion (see Chapter 10) are properly adapted to the audience and occasion (p. 145).

As you become more proficient in making presentations, you may choose not to write out complete technical plots. Keep in mind, however, that an inventory is always useful as a means of ensuring that you are using several forms of support.

Figure 12.3 shows a full-content outline, including technical plot (see left-hand margin).

Some presenters feel comfortable speaking from a full-content outline. Many speakers use an extemporaneous method; they distill the outline to key phrases and words. A flip chart is a streamlined outline—in essence, an enlarged series of note cards. Regardless of the form, effective outlines illustrate the principles of consistency, indentation, subordination, and simplicity.

```
                    ADOPTING A FLEXTIME PROGRAM

                      (PERSUASIVE PRESENTATION)

   Specific Purpose: After my presentation, I want my audience, the
        Board of Directors, to consider adopting a flextime program for
        our sales department personnel.

   Central Idea Statement: A flextime program could alleviate many
        problems currently plaguing our sales staff, with the results
        being very beneficial to all affected.

   Pattern of Order: Monroe's motivated sequence

   Attention Step

   Introduction: Good morning! Thank you all for this opportunity to
        speak with you today. One of my areas of responsibility as the
        sales department manager is monitoring problems of the sales
        department staff. As you know, our sales department has been
        plagued with a high degree of turnover, absenteeism, and
        tardiness. Today, I want to explain to you how the adoption of
        a flextime program would alleviate these problems and be very
        beneficial to our organization. If you have any questions during
        my presentation, I ask that you save them until the conclusion of
        my speech, at which time I will be more than happy to address them.


   Need Step     I. The sales department is presently experiencing three
                     serious problems.
   Technical Plot
                 A.  We presently have twelve people on our sales staff.
   Statistics        1.  Six are women with children at home.
   Statistics        2.  Two are single women.
   Statistics        3.  Four are men with children at home.

                 B.  Absenteeism and tardiness have been recurring
                     problems for this department.
   Statistics        1.  Employees miss, on the average, two days a month.
   Fact              2.  Employees are often tardy to work and must often
                         leave early because of family-related situations.

                 C.  Our employee turnover has been very high.
   Example           1.  Thus far this year, we have had to hire three
                         new employees to fill the twelve positions.
   Example           2.  In 1988, we had to refill five of the twelve
                         sales positions.
```

Figure 12.3 An outline for a presentation. (*Source*: from B. E. Gronbeck, D. Ehninger, and A. H. Monroe, *Principles of Speech Communication*, 10th ed. Glenview, Ill.: Scott, Foresman and Company, 1988.)

Satisfaction Step

II. A flextime program could alleviate the problems our sales
department is experiencing.

Testimony   A. According to <u>Management Review</u> magazine, flextime is
the generic term for flexible scheduling formats.

Explanation   1. Employees are required to work a "core" number
of hours.

Explanation   2. Beginning and ending hours of the workday are
"flexible"—the choice of the employee.

B. Flextime is becoming more widely accepted in the
United States and Europe.

Fact   1. Flextime was first introduced in Germany in 1967
to reduce rush hour congestion.

Fact   2. Control Data was the first major company in the
United States to adopt flexible hours.

Example   3. Other prominant U.S. companies that have adopted
flextime programs include Corning Glass Works,
IBM, Polaroid Corporation, Syntex Corporation,
Levi Strauss and the Wells Fargo Bank.

Testimony   4. According to the November, 1987 issue of
<u>Management Review</u>, variations of flexible
scheduling are now available to more than
one-fifth of the American work force, and
flextime is very popular in Europe also.

C. Flextime has been cited by <u>Public Personnel Management</u>
magazine to have several benefits.

Explanation   1. Flextime increases productivity.
Explanation   2. Flextime decreases absenteeism and turnover.
Explanation   3. Flextime enhances employees' satisfaction with work.

D. Our present sales staff's schedule could easily be
altered to accommodate a flextime program.

Fact   1. The sales department is open from 6:00 a.m. to
6:00 p.m.—the same business hours as the rest
of the company.

Fact   2. Salespeople within the sales department presently
work from 8:00 a.m. to 5:00 p.m.

Fact   3. Lunches of the sales staff are staggered, with
four salespeople taking lunch at the same time at
one-hour intervals between 11:00 a.m. and 2:00 p.m.

E. A flextime program would alter the current schedule
and provide much more flexibility.

Explanation   1. We would establish "core times" when employees
must be in the office, working.

Explanation   2. "Flexband" hours would be established around these
core hours, from which employees select starting
times, stopping times, and lunchtimes.

Explanation   3. Flextime would give employees flexibility regarding
when to begin to work and when to leave at the end
of the day. They would still work a full shift,
but they would have the part of the day most
valuable to them for themselves.

Figure 12.3 *(continued)*

	F.	The sales staff's job duties and responsibilities would easily accommodate a flextime program.
Testimony		1. According to <u>Business Week</u>, jobs that can be done on a project basis are best suited for flexible scheduling.
Explanation		2. Sales meetings, training sessions, telemarketing activities, and service calls would be conducted during the "core" hours.
Explanation		3. All paperwork and record keeping would be done by the sales staff during the "flexband" hours.

Visualization Step

	III.	The advantages of such a flextime program are very evident.
		A. Absenteeism and tardiness would decrease.
Statistics		1. Employees would have time to take care of personal and family problems.
		2. According to studies done at the University of Connecticut, companies surveyed reported a three-fourths reduction in absenteeism after adopting a flextime program.
		B. Turnover would decrease.
Explanation		1. Present turnover is high because of inflexible hours.
Explanation		2. Employees will be satisfied with their flexible hours.
		C. Job satisfaction and employee morale will be improved by flextime.
Testimony		1. According to Sheri South's article in the July, 1989, issue of <u>CA Magazine</u>, employee morale and job satisfaction increase after the implementation of a flextime program.
Testimony		2. According to Barney Olmsted's article in the November, 1987, issue of <u>Management Review</u>, employees have more positive feelings for a company that they believe wants to help them achieve a balance between their work life and family life.

Action Step

Conclusion:
As you can see, the flextime program I have illustrated today would reduce our present problems of a high degree of turnover, absenteeism, and tardiness. I understand that the board will meet again next Monday, at which time a vote will be taken to decide whether such a program will be implemented. I encourage you to adopt such a program, which has been very successful and beneficial to many companies across the United States and Europe. Are there any questions?

Figure 12.3 *(continued)*

BACKGROUND REFERENCES

Norwood, J. (1987, November). American workers want more--more work, that is. Across the Board, pp. 60-62.

Olmstead, B. (1987, November). (Flex)time is money. Management Review, pp. 47-50.

Owen, J. (1988, December). Work-time reduction in the U.S. and Western Europe. Monthly Labor Review, pp. 41-44.

Rowbotham, S. (1989, March). Flexi-Britain. New Statesman and Society, 13(62).

Sharratt, J. (1989). The impact of the information explosion on management innovation. Industrial Management and Data Systems, 3, 22-25.

South, S. (1989, July). The part-time party line. CA Magazine, pp. 36-42.

Summer hours and the issue of flextime. (1987). Personnel Journal, 66(8):25-26.

Time running out on 40-hour work week. (1987). Journal of Accountancy, 164(3):54.

Verespej, M. (1988). Part-time workers: No temporary phenomenon. Industry Week, 236(8):65-66.

Welter, T. R. (1988). The goal is working smarter, not longer. Industry Week, 236(8):65-66.

Where they flex. (1988, April). Inc., p. 128.

Wojahn, E. (1988, November). Bringing up baby. Inc., pp. 64-66, 70.

Figure 12.3 *(continued)*
(Special thanks to Michelle Merando, a student in presentational speaking class at Central Missouri State University.)

SUMMARY

- A well-organized presentation is a logical, strategic sequence of ideas in a clear, coherent, and unified structure. A well-organized presentation helps listeners to focus their attention and to understand and remember the message. Well-organized ideas are usually more persuasive.

- There are three substructures that must be unified into a fluid presentation. The core element, developed first, is the body of the message, which consists of the central idea and the main supporting points. The conclusion, developed next, restates the main points. The introduction, developed last, previews the message.

- There are several patterns of organization (chronological, spatial, topical, causal, problem-solution, reflective thinking, and motivated sequence) which contribute to the overall clarity, coherence, and unity of the presentation. The body is organized around a pattern of order that structures the proposal in detail.

- The conclusion should (1) summarize key points (review); (2) focus on the theme and purpose; (3) remind listeners of the urgency of the charge; (4) provide listeners with a clear course of action; and (5) ask for questions.

- The introduction, which previews the entire presentation, includes four critical functions: (1) gaining favorable attention, (2) promoting friendliness and goodwill between the speaker and audience, (3) providing important reasons to listen, and (4) orienting the audience toward the body of the message.

- Using intensity, movement, familiarity, novelty, humor, and suspense are basic ways to attract the attention of an audience, but the speaker must avoid the boomerang effect of gimmickry.

- Transitions are linking pins, or connections between the parts of a presentation. Transitions can (1) indicate that an idea has been completed, (2) provide a link to the next idea, or (3) preview a forthcoming idea.

- Using an outline, or blueprint of the presentation, aids in properly organizing a message. The outline helps the speaker assess the clarity, coherence, and unity of the planned presentation. Good outline practices include (1) consistent use of symbols, (2) proper indentation, (3) proper subordination, and (4) using single units of information. A technical plot can be used as part of the outline, to help check the completeness and variety of support.

QUESTIONS FOR REVIEW AND DISCUSSION

1. What are the benefits of carefully organizing a presentation?
2. How is organizing a presentation like building a bridge?
3. Describe six patterns that can be used in organizing a presentation.
4. What is the purpose of the conclusion? What are its five components?
5. What are the four subfunctions of an introduction? What functions do they serve?
6. What is the function of transitions? What guidelines are important to observe in the use of transitions?
7. What is the function of the outline as a presentation tool? Explain the four important practices of outlining.

ACTIVITIES

1. Study the presentations at the end of Chapter 8. Analyze the organizational structure of the outlines. What other patterns of development might have been used?

2. Go the library and find a book of quotations, such as *Bartlett's Familiar Quotations,* by John Bartlett; *Peter's Quotations: Ideas for Our Time,* by Laurence J. Peter; or *The Public Speaker's Treasure Chest,* by Herbert V. Prochnow and Herbert V. Prochnow, Jr. Locate the interesting quotations that could be used to begin presentations for the following proposals:

   Quality control

   Benefits of advertising

   Executive selection process

   Assessment centers

   Moonlighting

   Promotion practices

   Motivation

3. Using the topics suggested in Activity 2, write a complete body, conclusion, and introduction to a presentation. Develop a paragraph explaining the attention devices you will use in introducing your presentation.

Chapter 13

Stylizing the Message

After reading and reviewing this chapter, you should be able to . . .

1. List the four benefits of stylized messages.

2. Compare and contrast written and oral language styles.

3. Discuss characteristics of language that business presenters need to understand.

4. Contrast the use of pragmatic and unifying styles.

5. Define and explain the three characteristics of a stylized message— clarity, vividness, and appropriateness.

6. Identify and explain seven syntactical devices.

7. Differentiate among the use of metaphor, simile, and personification.

8. Identify and explain five suggestions for using style effectively.

*T*he following announcements appeared in church bulletins:

> This afternoon there will be a meeting in the south and north ends of the church. Children will be baptized at both ends.
>
> On Sunday, a special collection will be taken to defray the expense of the new carpet. All those wishing to do something on the new carpet, come forward and get a piece of paper.

As these examples illustrate, communicating clearly and accurately is not easy. Psalms 55:21 states, "The words of his mouth were smoother than butter, but war was in his heart; his words were softer than oil, yet were they drawn swords." It is no wonder that Burke said, "A great part of the mischiefs that vex this world arises from words" (Prochnow and Prochnow, Jr., 1977, p. 441).

On the positive side, Proverbs 25:11 says, "A word fitly spoken is like apples of gold in pictures of silver." While the right word "fitly spoken" may be difficult to capture, effective language facilitates making successful business presentations. In this chapter we will explore the potential of words to communicate and to confound. You will learn about the differences between oral and written style as well as how to use "schemes" of syntax and figures of speech. *Style* is "the individual manner in which a given person uses language" (Reid, 1982, p. 74), or, as Swift said, "how to use proper words in proper places." We will also explore some techniques of language important for business presentations.

BENEFITS OF USING STYLIZED LANGUAGE

Language style can be a significant factor in presentation. Certainly, style cannot replace content. All components of a message are important, but ideas are more important than the clothing in which they are garbed. You are working toward striking language that complements the message but does not upstage or distract from it. A study of style can provide several positive contributions to your effectiveness as a presenter:

1. A stylized message can be more *attention-getting*. By nature, a highly stylized message deviates from language norms. Hence, the elements of surprise and novelty are always elements of style (Jordan, Flanagan, and Wineinger, 1975). A stylized message can attract and maintain audience interest.
2. A stylized message can enhance *cognition or understanding* of the message (Mazza, Jordan, and Carpenter, 1972). The use of a metaphor

or a simile can facilitate understanding of a message. A complex idea may be conveyed more clearly with a figure of speech.

3. A stylized message can aid in *retention* of the message (Jordan, Flanagan, and Wineinger). Using various schemes of syntax or figures of speech can help the audience remember key elements of the message. Advertisers use slogans and novelty to facilitate retention and recall of their messages.

4. A stylized message can increase the *persuasive appeal* of the message (Siltanen, 1981; Reinsch, 1971; Bowers and Osborn, 1966). When attention is gained and maintained, the audience is more likely to understand and retain the message, and there is a greater probability the proposal will be accepted.

Hence, attention, cognition, retention, and motivation are significant by-products of incorporating the principles of language style.

ORAL STYLE VERSUS WRITTEN STYLE

When you speak of style you may think of clothing and various accessories to dress that make you a unique person. Like the fashion-conscious person, a presenter should have an attention-getting and memorable style. This is achieved particularly by using language that is clear, vivid, and appropriate. Additionally, you can stylize your language by using words and phrases that deviate from language norms. Such language differs from the way people normally arrange and choose words. Two ways to stylize everyday speech, which may lack luster and impact, are to rearrange word order and use different words.

Our English language follows conventions. Everyday sentences follow patterns: subject-verb (he fell); subject-verb-object (she hit the ball); or subject-verb-complement (Fred is a beast). Most of our sentences are declarative rather than interrogative.

Before exploring the nature of language, let's discuss some basic differences between oral and written style.

Oral Style Is Less Formal   Written language is more formal in structure and content than oral communication. Sentences are generally longer and more complex in written style. Words are also more likely to be multisyllabic. Oral communication, in contrast, is characterized by shorter sentences, fewer complex sentences, and simpler words. (Fewer than 100 words probably account for nearly 50 percent of the words most people use each day.) Oral style also uses more vernacular phrases and contractions than written style.

Oral Style Is More Repetitive   When reading printed text, you can stop to reexamine a passage, a sentence, or a word, and you can look up the definition of an unfamiliar word. When listening to oral communication, however, you do not have such luxuries (although sometimes people turn to a neighbor for confirmation of a word or thought, often at the expense of not following the speaker).

Oral style is much more redundant, and appropriately so. Speakers are admonished to "tell them what you are going to tell them, tell them, and tell them what you have told them." Speakers build in repetition to ensure that listeners attend to and understand the message. Recall that most people listen at about 25 percent efficiency (Nichols and Stevens, 1957, p. ix). Thus, redundancy is essential, especially when expressing complex ideas. It is important to state the thought, restate it, provide an example, and summarize the idea.

Oral Style Is More Personal   When you are speaking, you should look at the members of the audience, maintaining eye contact with them. In oral presentations we use many personal references (*I, my, we, you,* and *me*). In written communication we tend to use more impersonal pronouns (*one, he* or *she*).

Personal: *You* should enroll in a payroll deduction health program.

Impersonal: *One* should enroll in a payroll deduction health program.

The differences between oral and written style are a matter of degree. Formality in spoken language obviously varies with the situation. Public speeches generally are more formal than presentations. Ceremonial addresses are more formal than traditional informative or persuasive speeches. Compare the styles of two writers (e.g., Louis L'Amour and Stephen King, or Henry David Thoreau and Edgar Allan Poe) to see their distinctive traits. The speaking styles of George Bush and Jesse Jackson are different, as are those of Margaret Thatcher and Barbara Bush. The speaker's personality, the occasion, the subject, and the audience all affect the style of the language. Generally, however, oral style is more informal, more repetitive, and more personal than written communication.

THE NATURE OF LANGUAGE

Language Is Imprecise   It is no secret that communication is delicate. One reason people have trouble with this elusive process is that language is imprecise. As a speaker, you will have to consider both denotative and connotative meanings of words. The denotative meanings of a word are the literal or dictionary definitions of a word. The word *cow*, for example, is defined as "the mature female of wild or domestic cattle of the genus *Bos* or of any of the various animals the male of which is called the bull" (*Webster's Third New International Dictionary,* 1976). This straightforward definition provides a literal description (provided one is familiar with the meaning of *Bos*) of a cow.

Connotative meanings are even more imprecise. Connotative meanings are suggested to each listener by his or her own personal associations with an object or thing. When you think of a cow you may think of a walrus or a clumsy person. Or you may think of an Angus cow, a Jersey cow, or a glass of milk. The word may evoke an image of Bossy, your grandparents' milk cow. It might conjure images of horseflies biting the cows as your grandfather milked them.

A basic principle of communication is that meanings are in people, not in words (see Chapter 1). The imprecision of language challenges every speaker. Avoid the dangerous assumption that communication automatically occurs as intended. Words that are clear to the speaker may have a different meaning to members of the audience.

Language Is Powerful   Joseph Conrad said that with "the right word and the right accent," a person can move the world (Brussell, 1988, p. 447). Words are powerful. Throughout history, the power of words has started and ended wars. Words moved voters to send some politicians to Washington and to deny others the office they seek. The adage "Sticks and stones can break my bones but words can never hurt me" could not be further from the truth.

Words Have the Power to Create Images   The story is told of a vicar who asked a little boy his name:

> "Reginald d'Arcy Smif, sir," replied the boy with a grin. The vicar turned to the boy's father. "What made you give the boy a name like that?" he asked. "Cause I want 'im to be a professional boxer," returned the parent, "an' wiv a name like that he'll get plenty o' practice at school." (Prochnow and Prochnow, Jr., 1977, p. 129)

Presenters, like storytellers, have the power to create images. Your words and phrases make the listeners imagine profits and losses, new plants, more personnel, new procedures, corporate takeovers. The words you use stimulate images and meanings that can lead decision makers to reject the proposal outright, table the proposal, or implement your ideas immediately.

Words Have the Power to Affect Behavior   The words used to describe an object or action can affect our attitudes and feelings about it. Years ago, George Smathers, who was running in Florida for the United States Senate against the incumbent, Claude Pepper, used an accusatory intonation in his voice in a campaign speech that went something like this:

> Are you aware that Claude Pepper is known all over Washington as a shameless extrovert? Not only that, but this man is reliably reported to practice nepotism with his sister-in-law, and he has a sister who once was a Thespian in wicked New York. Worst of all, it is an established fact that Mr. Pepper before his marriage habitually practiced celibacy. Furthermore, Claude Pepper had the audacity to matriculate at our home state university in full view of a major portion of the student body. (*Time*, April 17, 1950, p. 28)

(Incidentally, George Smathers unseated the incumbent in that election.)

Word choices certainly influence attitudes about the object being sold. Funeral directors, for example, demonstrate great familiarity with words that "soften" attitudes about death. The term *remains* is used rather than *corpse* or *body*. Other "deathless" words include the following:

> Service, not funeral; Mr., Mrs., or Miss Blank, not corpse or body; preparation room, not morgue; casket, not coffin; funeral director or mortician, not undertaker; reposing room or slumber room, not laying-out room; deceased, not dead; autopsy or post-mortem, not post; casket coach, not hearse; shipping case, not shipping box; flower car, not flower truck; remains or cremated remains, not ashes; clothing, dress, suit, etc., not shroud; drawing room, not parlor. (Mitford, 1963, p. 62)

How do you react to the term *landfill* versus *city dump*? Which term is preferable—*old person* or *senior citizen*? Do you go to a *barber* or a *hairdresser*? Would you prefer to apply for a *supervisory position* or a *junior management position*? As presenters, your choice of words communicates some of your attitudes and can affect the attitudes of the decision makers.

If words did not have the power to influence behavior, there would be few, if any, salespeople, preachers, politicians, or teachers. Speeches and presentations are a means of influencing others to accept our predetermined goals. President Bush's inaugural address was a means to establish the goals for his presidency. Mikhail Gorbachev delivered a "landmark speech" in which he loosened the straitjacket of Kremlin ideology and announced a unilateral cut in his country's armed forces. Student leaders in various campus organizations emerge, are elected to offices, and affect other groups and units because of words. Words have an uncanny power to influence behavior because language is never neutral. As Kenneth Burke (1966) has stressed, all language, even our most scientific attempts to name and define without emotion, is in itself persuasive; our language reflects our attitudes (pp. 44–45). Would you tell a friend that his new outfit is "nice," "fantastic," "OK," "gorgeous," or "so-so"? When you ask a friend to dinner would you tell her that you plan to serve "seafood" or "dead fish"?

Obviously, word choice is directly related to a speaker's persuasive strategies. It makes sense to give careful thought to your words, realizing that they do indeed have an impact on your listeners' emotions and attitudes.

Charles Larson discusses two approaches to speaking style: *pragmatic style* and *unifying style*. Pragmatic style is appropriate when "persuaders . . . find it necessary to convince listeners who do not necessarily support their position. . . . Unifying persuaders" speak "to people who, in large measure, already believe what is going to be said" (Larson, 1989, p. 141).

Pragmatic speakers, as Larson describes them, use specific, concrete evidence. Listeners cannot as easily disagree with materials. In pragmatic speaking there is little idealism and much realism; the language itself is specific and concrete. The idea of this approach is to make it difficult for listeners to provide varying interpretations (Larson, p. 142).

Unifying speakers, however, face an audience that is already agreeable and supportive. The task is to inspire that audience, or as Larson expresses it, "to whip up enthusiasm and dedication or to give encouragement." Such speaking allows more general and more idealistic language. The speaking can be more emotional and visionary, and language can be more abstract and non-specific. There is probably less intellectualizing in this style than in pragmatic speaking (Larson, pp. 141–142).

Of course, a speaker is not restricted to either of the two extremes represented by the pragmatic and unifying styles. A speaker might use both styles, even in the same speech or presentation (Larson, p. 142). In Bob Trent's presentation on the need for listening instruction, some members of the audience will respond to pragmatic elements, others to unifying style. All members of this audience will expect concrete evidence and specific ideas. At the same time, since they are dedicated to the company and to the success of its training program, they will all be receptive to unifying elements such as idealism and emotional support.

USING LANGUAGE EFFECTIVELY

As a presenter, your challenge is to use words to convey the meanings you intend to communicate. However, communication is elusive. Rarely, if ever, does the listener process words—much less a message—exactly as the presenter intended. One poster is worded, "I know you think you understand what I said but what I said is not what I meant." Effective language is clear, vivid, and appropriate.

Clarity

Eisenberg explains that clarity in message transmission is a continuum:

> Clarity (and conversely, ambiguity) . . . arises through a combination of source, message, and receiver factors. Clarity exists to the extent that the following conditions are met: (1) an individual has an idea; (2) he or she encodes the idea into language; and (3) the receiver understands the message as it was intended by the source. In trying to be clear, individuals take into account the possible interpretative contexts which may be brought to bear on the message by the receiver and attempt to narrow the possible interpretations. Clarity, then, is a continuum which reflects the degree to which a source has narrowed the possible interpretations of a message and succeeded in achieving a correspondence between his or her intentions and the interpretation of the receiver. (Eisenberg, 1984, pp. 229–230)

The essence of using clear language is to select words that minimize ambiguity. As Bob Trent prepares his presentation, he should constantly ask, "What should I say to make my proposal clear to the board of directors?" He can use familiar, concrete words and clarify his style through signposting.

Use Familiar Words   If the words are not familiar to the audience, the message will not be clear. Why try to dazzle your audience with megasyllable words when simple words will convey the thoughts just as well? Why say, "I hesitate to articulate for fear I might deviate from the true course of rectitude" when a simple "I don't know" will do? Clarity was vital when a blip appeared suddenly on a ship's radar screen:

> "Tell that ship to change its course 15 degrees!" said the Admiral. The radio man did and the word came back on the radio, "You change your course 15 degrees." "Tell that ship that we're the U.S. Navy and to change its course 15 degrees," said the Admiral. The radio man did and the word came back again, "You change your course 15 degrees." This time the Admiral himself got on the radio and said, "I am an Admiral in the U.S. Navy. Change your course 15 degrees." The word came back over the radio, "You change your course 15 degrees, I am a lighthouse!" (Lamm, 1985, p. 4)

Technical language can be abstruse. Its use should be avoided or defined unless the decision makers are familiar with the terminology. Most companies use a great deal of technical language. Suppose you were employed as a consultant by a major airline. You might need to translate airline jargon into a layperson's language. One way to do this is to clarify by using an analogy. For example,

> A *tariff* is a schedule of rates or charges, like a motel schedule of prices that depends on number of beds, number in the party, TV, phone, and so on.

> *Fare construction units* are like stock market quotations, which fluctuate from day to day depending on supply and demand.

Use Concrete Words   For clarity, you need to free your language from ambiguity. Language is *ambiguous,* or nebulous, if it readily offers two or more interpretations to the listener. Language that is concrete is specific or more restricted in meaning. The word *stove* is more concrete (specific) than the term *heating device. Banana* is more concrete than *fruit. Thread* is more concrete than *sewing materials.* Concrete words usually communicate more clearly than abstract words. You may understand a written statement after reading it several times. But an obscure or ambiguous oral style almost always confuses listeners. They cannot turn back the pages and linger over abstract words—especially as they continue to process other ideas that you are presenting to them.

Peter Walters, chairman of British Petroleum Company, explained the benefits of trade relationships between the United States and Great Britain in spite of "internal demands for protectionism." He clarified this abstract subject as follows:

> And so far as foreign, direct investment is concerned, I believe that both the United Kingdom and the United States realize that, when this is motivated by the desire for profit and efficiency, it will produce extra opportunities from

> which everyone benefits. *"Two blades of grass where one blade grew before"* is a simple way of explaining it. Since foreign companies bring with them technological and managerial skills, capital investment and sometimes even access to foreign markets, they are able to open up opportunities which may not be open to domestic producers. [Emphasis added; Walters, 1988, p. 426]

By using a simple explanation—"two blades of grass where one grew before"—Walters showed the audience that wealth was not merely being transferred but was being created by foreign investment.

Signposting   Clarify your style by making it easy for listeners to follow your thinking. Clear presenters chart where they are going, providing signposts along the way and letting listeners know when a destination is reached. Richard Munro, chairman and chief executive officer of Time, Inc., used signposting in "The Five Commandments of Free Enterprise," a speech he delivered at a dinner in Tampa, Florida:

> So in the true spirit of free enterprise, I've left five commandments for you. You decide for yourself what it takes to make the system work, because in the end that's precisely what the system is all about: deciding for yourself.
>   . . . That said, let's get on with business. Commandment number one: Thou shalt not covet thy neighbor's goods.
>   . . . Which brings me to my second commandment: Quality talks; everything else shall walk.
>   . . . But everyone . . . should be aware of this third commandment: If you want the golden eggs, then thou shalt not cook the golden goose.
>   . . . I'll give you commandment number four: Thou shalt not be an idiot.
>   . . . My fifth commandment: Thou shalt not just stand there, thou shalt go for it.
>   . . . Free enterprise isn't an abstraction. It's you and I. It's our determination to compete and to help others compete. . . . Constantly enlarging the golden circle of opportunity . . . willingly reaching out to those once excluded from our national dream. . . . Always remembering that when we're at our best, we're unbeatable. (Munro, 1988, pp. 233–235)

Munro previewed where he was going, provided signposts along the way, and concluded with a rousing note of optimism.

Vividness

Good style is lively and vivid. Vivid language appeals to the senses and makes an indelible impression: it helps you to *see, hear, touch, taste,* and *smell* images and ideas.

We can "see" what one speaker describes: "The computer screen is replacing the blast furnace as the symbol of America at work" (Ong, 1988, p. 471). We can "hear" the stirring thoughts expressed by another speaker:

> It's good to have more people living significantly longer—I hope to be one of them. But when it's a social good, it's an economic time bomb. We can count its

ticks, second-by-second. If we're prudent, we won't sit on our hands and wait for it to blow up. . . . But government alone couldn't defuse our 21st-century demographic time bomb. (Schreyer, 1988, p. 404)

"Seeing" and "feeling" are linked in another passage:

To focus the space telescope closer, the vast Pacific Ocean is now seen as not a chill and distant barrier that separates us, but a means of transportation and communication that links us forever together and to all the other nations and territories that depend on the Pacific Ocean for commercial trade, cultural interchange and economic development. The Pacific Rim is a new conception of that linkage, and amongst all its diversity of peoples, it is clear that Japan and the United States have the capacity to lead them to higher reaches of economic prosperity, political stability, and technological and intellectual fulfillment. The Pacific Rim is itself a marvelous exhibit of new historic explosive economic change: witness resurgent Taiwan and depressed Vietnam. (Posvar, 1988, p. 405)

Touch, taste, and, to a degree, smell are combined in Munro's vivid comments about his third commandment:

If you want the golden eggs, then thou shalt not cook the golden goose. . . . Where regulations are concerned, it means government must be honest about its tendency to excess. You know the story. Government wrings the golden goose's neck, plucks its feathers, boils it, and then forms a national commission to investigate why the bird is no longer laying eggs. (Munro, 1988, p. 233)

Vivid sight and taste imagery also were cleverly wedded together by W. C. Fields in one of his many famous lines: "I always keep a supply of stimulant handy in case I see a snake—which I also keep handy" (Adams, 1969, p. 97).

Vivid language patterns can also be enhanced through the use of figures of speech and syntactic devices discussed later in this chapter.

Appropriateness

On a recent trip to Europe, a businessman and his wife, along with hundreds of other successful financial advisors and their spouses, met a distinguished lady who was introduced by an executive vice-president of a large insurance company as "your very duke-ess" rather than "her grace, the duchess." Needless to say, members of the audience were embarrassed, amused, and shocked by this social blunder. Imagine how offended the duchess must have been by this inappropriate effort.

An appropriate style uses language that is adapted to the decision makers and the specific occasion for the presentation. It is difficult to discuss appropriateness without discussing clarity and vividness. Language that is clear and vivid may yet be inappropriate if it offends the taste or sensibility of the listener. Slang and vulgarity, for example, should generally be avoided in presentations. Such language can be expressive, but it may not elicit a positive response from the audience.

Appropriate language also establishes a direct personal relationship with the audience. Use words like *I, we, mine, you, yours,* and *ours* frequently in

Table 13.1   USING LANGUAGE EFFECTIVELY

Goal	Strategy
To make your language clear you should:	Use familiar words.
	Use concrete words.
	Use signposting.
To make your language vivid you should:	Use words that appeal to the listeners' senses.
To make your language appropriate you should:	Avoid words that are in poor taste.
	Use words that are personalized.
	Use words that are direct.

your presentation style. A direct approach is coupled with a touch of humor in the following statements:

> *I* am delighted to address this distinguished organization and to see a number of longtime colleagues here. *I* am particularly happy that the Chairman of the American Council on Science and Health, Dr. Stephen Sternberg, from Memorial Sloan-Kettering Hospital, and the Council's Associate Director, Dr. Edward Remmers, were able to attend this morning so that *I* can turn over all the tough questions you may address to me to them. [Emphasis added; Whelan, 1987, p. 57]

Another speaker used clear, vivid, and appropriate language to establish a personal relationship with the audience:

> *I* came here to talk with you today about what *I* consider the number one economic issue for the 1990s and beyond: not the twin budget and trade deficits *we* hear about, but a shortfall even more fundamental to *our* economic future. That's the savings gap, and what it means for America's next century.
>
> But first, let me say a few words about the recent crisis of confidence in the financial markets.
>
> For many of *us*, certain days stand out vividly. If *we're* old enough, Pearl Harbor. The day President Kennedy was shot. And now, October 19, 1987.
>
> In my business, that was a day when people could forget their diets—they sweated off ten pounds. Black Monday shocked Wall Street. It stunned the nation. It was scary. It was sobering. [Emphasis added; Schreyer, p. 403]

The power of clear, vivid, and appropriate language can help you create images, influence attitudes, and affect behavior (see Table 13.1). Let's explore specific means of stylizing language.

LANGUAGE STRATEGIES

When republican vice-presidential candidate Dan Quayle debated democratic vice-presidential candidate Lloyd Bentsen in 1988, Senator Quayle made a point of comparing his senate experience with that of John F. Kennedy. Senator Bentsen responded by saying, "I knew Jack Kennedy well. Jack Kennedy was a friend of mine. Senator, you are no Jack Kennedy." All the major networks chose to excerpt or highlight these lines from the hour-long debate.

What makes a certain portion of a speech or presentation memorable and quotable? What techniques do speech writers and advertisers use to give language color and style? Memorable style deviates from language norms in terms of word arrangement (syntax), word choice, and/or figures of speech. There are at least seven techniques of syntax that can be used to provide arresting language arrangement.

Omission

Using a scheme of *omission* means we streamline language to the "bare bones." Omission means using only essential words or phrases. Newspaper ads, telegraphed messages, and slogans use a minimum of words: "Say it with flowers," "Buckle up for safety," "Fifty-four forty or fight," "Remember the Alamo," are all examples of the scheme of omission.

During World War II, a navy captain of a destroyer used omission in the following succinct message to command headquarters: "Sighted sub—sank same." Rather than cabling "Today we spotted a submarine, engaged it in battle, and sank it," the captain reported only the essential data to his supervisors.

Advertisers are masters of omission. Television ads usually include background music that complements the message. After appropriate conditioning, the prospective buyer fills in the words every time the music is played. "Coke is it" and "Just say no" are but two of scores of messages we unconsciously know because of effective advertising strategies.

Inversion

Another technique is to *invert,* or reverse the normal word order of a phrase or sentence. "When it rains, you may become depressed" is reversed—the normal order is "You may become depressed when it rains." The majority of our sentences are declarative, so one way to utilize inversion effectively is to ask a question. A *rhetorical question* contains its own answer. In a presentation, the speaker may ask rhetorical questions or questions designed to involve the decision makers. For example, during his presentation Bob Trent may ask the board of directors for some information simply to get or maintain their attention; he may ask others to determine whether the audience needs further details in order to understand his proposal. After his proposal, Bob might ask a summary question: "Do you have any questions regarding the services American can provide to support employee training on this computer equipment?" The inverted structure of this question accentuates the message—the services American Computer Systems offers.

Suspension

In many jokes and stories, a "catchword" is retained or *suspended* until the end of the story. This creates suspense and keeps the listeners' attention. A few years ago, advertisers came up with the now-famous phrase "Things go better with Coca-Cola." The key word comes last. The stylized version is a memorable advertising tool.

Antithesis

The word *antithesis* means "opposite." A sentence structure using the scheme of antithesis will balance two opposing phrases to heighten their differences for listeners. The sentence often will use parallel structure:

> If guns are outlawed,
> only outlaws will have guns.

> It's not the size of the dog in the fight,
> it's the size of the fight in the dog.

> It's nice to be important,
> but it's more important to be nice.

A character in the play *Inherit the Wind*, which depicts the so-called Scopes monkey trial, used antithesis in a well-known statement:

> I am more interested in the Rock of Ages than I am in the Age of Rocks. (Gassner, 1958, p. 429)

Stanley C. Gault (1988), chairman of the board and chief executive officer of Rubbermaid Incorporated, combined the schemes of inversion and antithesis in a speech at a marketing conference: "So to this group would I ask: Does marketing have a future in America? And does America have a future in marketing?" (p. 208).

Obviously, use of antithesis is not restricted to any particular group. It is used by advertisers, politicians, religious leaders, and business people who want their presentations to have dramatic appeal.

Repetition

The presenter who uses *repetition* uses the same key word or phrase several times for emphasis. One of the most effective addresses of the twentieth century, Martin Luther King's "I Have A Dream," derives its power partly from use of repetition. In one segment, Dr. King repeated "I have a dream," the key theme of the speech. The following excerpt illustrates this use of repetition:

> I say to you today, my friends, so even though we face the difficulties of today and tomorrow, *I still have a dream*. It is a dream deeply rooted in the American dream . . .

I have a dream that one day this nation will rise up and live out the true meaning of its creed: "We hold these truths to be self-evident; that all men are created equal."

I have a dream that one day on the red hills of Georgia the sons of former slaves and the sons of former slave owners will be able to sit down together at the table of brotherhood; *I have a dream—*

That one day even the state of Mississippi, a state sweltering with the heat of injustice, sweltering with the heat of oppression, will be transformed into an oasis of freedom and justice; *I have a dream—*

That my four little children will one day live in a nation where they will not be judged by the color of their skin but by the content of their character; *I have a dream today.*

I have a dream that one day down in Alabama, with its vicious racists, with its governor having his lips dripping with the words of interposition and nullification, one day right there in Alabama little black boys and black girls will be able to join hands with little white boys and white girls as sisters and brothers; *I have a dream today.*

I have a dream that one day every valley shall be exalted, every hill and mountain shall be made low, and rough places will be made plane and crooked places will be made straight, and the glory of the Lord shall be revealed, and all flesh shall see it together. [Emphasis added]

Stanley Gault repeated the theme of competitiveness in a marketing address:

Now for the "not so good news" . . . and the reasons why the word *competitiveness* has become the buzzword in political and business circles. "We must make America *competitive* again," says the Speaker of the U.S. House of Representatives.

"*Competitiveness* will be our #1 priority," says the chairman of the Senate Finance Committee.

The President's State of the Union Address said, "We'll be proposing steps to restore American *competitiveness.*"

A press release by the AFL-CIO said, "We must seek a more *competitive* America."

So, we have quite a bandwagon rolling. Everyone's suddenly in favor of *competitiveness.* [Emphasis added; Gault, p. 207]

Parallelism

Parallelism is a stylistic device that uses the same word or root word to begin several sentences or phrases. Parallelism, like repetition, punctuates or emphasizes key words, but in parallelism the key word or phrase is generally at the beginning of the sentence or the beginning of a new thought. Richard Munro used parallelism effectively in "The Five Commandments of Free Enterprise" when developing his fourth commandment—"Thou shalt not be an idiot." He introduced the parallel structure by quoting Lee Iacocca's advice to graduating seniors at the Massachusetts Institute of Technology a few years ago: " 'Don't get worried or depressed,' he told them. *'Get mad'* " [emphasis added; p. 235]. Munro then picked up the "get mad" theme himself:

Get mad about the national debt. . . . *Get infuriated* about annual deficits. . . . *Get incensed* about the fact that . . . there are 23 million illiterates. . . . *Get livid* about the growing shortage in skilled, trained workers. . . . And when you're smoking with savage indignation, *get involved.* [Emphasis added; Munro, p. 235]

Alliteration

Alliteration uses the same sounds (usually initial consonants) in two or more neighboring words or syllables for striking or novel effect (e.g., "miles meandering through the mazy moor"). Alliteration can add rhythm and cadence to a thought. The slogan "Fifty-four forty or fight" uses omission and alliteration simultaneously, as does "Better buy Buick." For a more stately example, consider Edward M. Kennedy's "Address to the Democratic National Convention" in 1980: "And we can be proud that our party stands *p*lainly, *p*ublicly and *p*ersistently for the ratification of the Equal Rights Amendment" [emphasis added; p. 716].

Another example comes from George Meany's 1980 address to the AFL-CIO: "The shifting, changing economic policies established by the administration have, without exception, failed because they were *ill*-advised, *ill*-considered, *in*effective and *in*equable" [emphasis added; p. 166].

The seven techniques of language style—omission, inversion, suspension, antithesis, repetition, parallelism, and alliteration—can serve you well in your efforts to craft memorable, moving presentations (see Table 13.2). If you were to ask most people age 35 or older what President John F. Kennedy's most memorable statement was, more likely than not, they would respond, "Ask not what your country can do for you; ask what you can do for your country." This quote is easy to remember because it integrates so many of the syntax techniques we have discussed.

Table 13.2 SCHEMES OF SYNTAX

Technique	Function
Omission	Uses short words and phrases that often become slogans.
Inversion	Reverses the expected order of words and phrases; statement often becomes a question.
Suspension	Places a key word at the end of the phrase or sentence for effect.
Antithesis	Develops a parallel structure balancing one part or clause of a sentence with another.
Repetition	Repeats a key idea or word several times for effect and emphasis.
Parallelism	Keys on the same initial word or phrase several times for emphasis.
Alliteration	Repeats consonant sounds in two or more neighboring words or syllables for striking effect.

The sentence uses omission: the obvious subject for that sentence, "you," is omitted. It also uses inversion. In conversation we would typically say "do not ask" rather than "ask not." This combination of omission and inversion makes the opening very striking.

Kennedy also used suspension. The key idea, or message, was "ask what you can do for your country." A reversed sentence structure would have been more lackluster: "Ask what you can do for your country, not what your country can do for you."

Kennedy also used antithesis and parallelism. Two clauses are employed, balancing each other with parallel language keying each of the two thoughts: "Ask not what your country can do for you; ask what you can do for your country."

Kennedy also used the scheme of repetition. This 17-word sentence uses *only 8 words.* A form of the word *you* is used four times; *country, ask, what, can, do,* and *for* are each used twice. It would be difficult for most of us to construct a 17-word sentence that used only 8 different words. Try it!

Finally, Kennedy used alliteration in the words *ask, can* and *country.* The "k" sound is repeated three times at even intervals, with three words in between.

USING FIGURES OF SPEECH

Figures of speech can be used in addition to schemes of syntax to stylize a presentation. A figure of speech deviates from language norms by using words in nontraditional ways. Figures of speech serve as means to achieve impact when conveying ideas to decision makers. Figures of speech include metaphors, similes, and personification.

Metaphors

Metaphors are used to make implied comparisons. Broadly speaking, anytime you use a word to convey a meaning not normally carried by that word, you are using a metaphorical device. If you take an exam and say "I really bombed the test," you are using a metaphorical term to describe how poorly you performed.

In a speech at Westminster College in Fulton, Missouri, Winston Churchill referred to the Russian military defense as an "iron curtain." Journalists readily picked up this metaphor in the newspapers. Like Churchill, presenters today use metaphors to paint vivid images in the minds of the listeners. In a presentation on bank failures, Clarke noted that "one benefit of the lull in Washington between Christmas and the reconvening of Congress is that it gives all of us the opportunity to do those things we don't seem to have the time to do when the *gang of 535* are in town" [emphasis added; p. 290].

William Schreyer (1988) used a novel metaphorical device when he observed, "Government alone couldn't defuse our 21st-century *demographic time bomb*" [emphasis added; p. 404]. Elizabeth M. Whelan, discussing the "Health Hoax and a Health Scare," provided a vivid description of an operating room used for tobacco-related maladies: "A thoracic surgeon on my Board refers to his operating room as *'Marlboro Country'* " [emphasis added; p. 58]. Stanley C. Gault used a series of metaphors to illustrate the fruits of aggressive marketing: "There may be some question as to whether or not the U.S. can ever be the *'800-pound gorilla'* it was in the past . . . but if we combine our capabilities and *'Yankee Peddler'* tenacity . . . we're going to get more than our share of the *peanuts* [emphasis added; p. 209].

Similes

Like a metaphor, a *simile* draws a comparison. A simile is more obvious than a metaphor: it is signaled by the words *like* or *as*. For example,

She has teeth *like stars*.

He is *as sly as a fox*.

Her office area is *like a zoo*.

Used sparingly, similes can "spice" a presentation to make it more vivid and interesting. Robert Clarke closed his speech on bank failures with a simile:

Dealers will sometimes take cracked and broken pottery and glue it back together so skillfully that the flaws don't show. One test to see if a piece has been repaired that way is to plunge it into a bucket of cold water. If it has been cracked, the crack will reappear. If it has been broken, it is likely to fall apart. For a bank, a depressed economic environment is *like a bucket of cold water.* [Emphasis added; Clarke, p. 292]

In a speech entitled "The Real Cause of Inflation: Government Services," Herbert Richey noted

Those early complaints caused by the initial capital shortage are *like the hiss of the safety valve on a boiler.* The economy is signaling that it cannot grow any faster, that the pressure is dangerously high. Trying to "stimulate" the economy with new money at such times is *like "fixing" your boiler* by *throwing more coal on the fire* and *shutting off the safety valve.* [Emphasis added; Richey, 1977, pp. 387–388]

Richey's use of the word *boiler* to represent the volatility of the economy is vivid. The extended comparison, discussing the boiler and the safety valve, made the simile even more vivid.

Personification

Personification attributes human qualities to inanimate objects. Like the metaphor or simile, if used skillfully and sparingly, personification can help you achieve a lasting impression. However, overly used, personification becomes trite and labored. In discussing "Hope, Fear, and Technology," Michael Marien (1984) used personification sparingly and effectively: "High-tech is *riding high in the saddle,* and will surely continue to do so, at least for the near future" [emphasis added; p. 139]. Obviously, high technology does not ride. *People* do these things. However, this unusual language, which has inanimate objects engaging in these activities, makes striking points that listeners can visualize.

SUGGESTIONS FOR USING STYLE EFFECTIVELY

The syntax schemes we have discussed—omission, inversion, suspension, antithesis, repetition, parallelism, alliteration, metaphor, simile, and personification—can pay huge dividends by adding novelty, interest, and impact to your message. Here are some suggestions for using style in practical ways:

1. Do not overstylize. Integrate stylistic devices, but use restraint. Too much novelty can distract from the content of the message if the audience focuses on the language rather than on the content of the presentation.
2. Consider using stylistic devices when developing your opening sentences, statements of major ideas, and conclusions. These are critical elements. The audience needs to give "100 percent plus" attention during the introduction, the development of main points, and the conclusion. Again, "well begun is half done." You can also use these techniques when presenting key ideas and when calling for support in the conclusion.
3. Use short, ordinary words in unique ways. You can use long words to lend style to language, but short words help effective and efficient listening. When a technical term is too abstruse or cumbersome, use a figure of speech to convey the idea.
4. Stylize to economize. When sentences or phrases become too long or complex, consider recasting the sentences using antithesis or suspension. Also consider using omission or repetition of key thoughts essential to understanding the complexity of a long sentence.
5. Observe others' use of style. As you listen to radio and television and read newspapers, magazines, and trade journals, look for effective stylized messages. Watch the evening news and listen for impressive figures of speech or other effective stylistic devices. Note that speakers consistently use inversion (in the form of questions) when they want an immediate audience response.
6. Practice stylizing your messages. Actively explore ways to incorporate the various stylistic techniques into your presentations. You probably already know the functional value of omission when you want someone to do something (e.g., "Come here" rather than

"Please come into my office," "Stop" rather than "Please cease and desist in what you are about to do"). Incorporate other stylistic devices as well to work for you in your business presentations.

SUMMARY

- You can use words in different ways to maximize the positive impact of your language. It is challenging to communicate what you mean. Language is powerful; words have the power to create images and to influence behavior.

- Judiciously used, stylized language can make presentations more attention-getting, easier to understand and retain, and more persuasive.

- Presenters may want to adopt pragmatic style, using specific, concrete evidence, to persuade a resistant audience. They may use the unifying style for an agreeable audience that needs to be moved to action.

- Speakers must always strive for clarity. Effective language uses concrete, specific words as well as words that are vivid and appropriate.

- There are differences between oral and written communication. Oral language is more informal, more repetitive, and more personal than written style.

- Schemes of syntax include omission, inversion, suspension, antithesis, repetition, parallelism, and alliteration. Figures of speech, such as metaphors, similes, and personification, deviate from language norms, using word choices that vary from traditional ways of expressing thought. Five suggestions for stylizing a message are: (1) do not overstylize; (2) consider using stylistic devices when developing opening sentences, statements of major ideas, and conclusions; (3) use short, ordinary words in unique ways; (4) stylize to economize; and (5) observe others' use of style. Figures of speech, like other stylistic devices, serve as a means of achieving positive impact when presenting proposals to decision makers.

QUESTIONS FOR REVIEW AND DISCUSSION

1. Discuss four benefits of stylized messages.
2. What are the differences between written and oral language styles?
3. Identify and explain characteristics of language that business presenters need to understand.
4. How do pragmatic and unifying styles differ?
5. Explain why presenters need to use words that are clear, vivid, and appropriate.
6. Discuss seven syntactical devices speakers can employ.
7. How are metaphors, similes, and personification used?
8. Describe five ways presenters can use style effectively.
9. How can Bob Trent stylize his proposal to the Sento Group? Follow the sample ideas, utilizing Monroe's motivated sequence from Chapter 12.

ACTIVITIES

1. The following phrases are from successful presentations, speeches, or statements. Compare and contrast each of these phrases with a more commonplace way to express the same thoughts.

   A man's legs should be long enough to touch the ground.

   National purse has no bottom.

   Washington's gang of 535.

   Model T Health.

   Economic suicide.

   The souls of young people are . . . spiritually unclad.

   Remember the Alamo.

   Speak softly and carry a big stick.

2. Find examples of the use of omission, inversion, suspension, antithesis, repetition, parallelism, and alliteration in issues of *Vital Speeches of the Day* or in other contemporary or historical sources.

3. Look through magazines or monitor radio or television advertisements for the use of attention-catching language. Identify the category of stylistic devices the source is using.

Chapter 14

Multimedia Support

After reading and reviewing this chapter, you should be able to . . .

1. Describe the multimedia options open to a presenter.

2. Discuss the advantages and disadvantages of various multimedia options.

3. Indicate how to overcome resistance to using common multimedia aids.

4. Select multimedia aid(s) appropriate to a given presentation.

5. Apply "ten commandments" for successful multimedia aids.

6. Construct a multimedia aid script and use an audio track.

*B*ob Trent wants to impress the Sento Group with his product line. He seeks to highlight their computer needs, show how American Computer Systems' products can meet those needs effectively, and emphasize how American's computers are cost-effective for Sento. Multimedia aids will support his effort. Bob realizes that good visuals are a "must." They are not a substitute for good presentation content, and they need to be clear, legible, and accurate. Aids must be prepared well in advance.

Once a presenter like Bob Trent has outlined what he or she intends to say, it is time to consider using multimedia aids. *Multimedia aids* are external sensory materials which a speaker employs (beyond spoken words, feelings, and bodily actions) to clarify, amplify, or vivify a message. Regardless of how well a presenter prepares content and polishes delivery skills, people in the audience will be inattentive from time to time. Effective presenters repeatedly attempt to renew audience interest and attention. Multimedia aids can help significantly in this regard.

WHY USE MULTIMEDIA AIDS?

Media aids, writes Munter (1982), "add interest, variety, and impact—and remain in the memory longer than words" (p. 98). Such aids are appropriate in most business settings. People learn and retain the most through observation—85 percent of the data you gather and retain is from sight and sound (Smith, 1984, pp. 51–52). One review of research findings stated that visual aids increase comprehension by 200 percent in teaching; visual aids improve retention by 14 to 38 percent; and visual aids can reduce (by up to 40 percent) the time needed to clarify a single concept in a business presentation (Cothran, 1989, pp. 4–8). Obviously, there are pros and cons to the use of each type of multimedia aid for a particular audience. Overall, however, there are good reasons to employ multimedia aids.

One salient reason is that well-chosen and relevant multimedia aids *command attention*. The unusual qualities of a display, the vivid colors on a chart, the unique shape of an object, the timbre of a particular sound, all may serve to gain attention and to renew interest in ideas being presented. Complete attention can be held for only seconds and has a very short "half-life." Multimedia aids can be used effectively to control listener attention through visual and oral stimuli.

All presenters should strive to gain and maintain the involuntary attention of their audience. *Involuntary attention* is the type of attention that is given without conscious effort. *Voluntary attention* is attention that takes conscious effort. It is difficult to maintain involuntary attention, but it can be renewed over time. Bostrom (1988) tells us, "Your goal as a speaker is to get your listeners' attention without having to ask for it. In other words, you would like their attention to be involuntary" (p. 174). Obviously, voluntary attention is much better than no attention at all. Multimedia aids can be of significant help in creating and sustaining attention.

Attention is selective. People focus on particular stimuli and disregard other stimuli. You may type at your computer while watching television. A particularly interesting set of stimuli originating from the television may entice you to turn and watch it. Later, an idea comes to you that you want to write down, and you forget about the television program. You are practicing selective attention.

As mentioned in Chapter 12, some stimuli provide us with heightened awareness. Intensity, large size, repetition, duration, bright colors, motion, change, and contrast are psychophysical attention factors. The term *psychophysical* refers to the interaction between psychological processes and physical stimuli (Bostrom, pp. 175–176). Combining these factors in the form of multimedia aids can help significantly in maintaining a level of involuntary attention in a presentation.

Multimedia aids may also be used *to clarify ideas.* Words are sometimes insufficient to communicate ideas. The proverbial picture is worth a thousand words; the addition of visual and additional auditory or sensory input can convey difficult concepts and help provide clearer mental pictures. Complex messages, in particular, are enhanced by multimedia aids. Anderson (1966) showed that a combination of spoken and pictorial presentations could have more impact on complex topics than spoken messages alone. Listeners remembered the content of the presentations far longer when pictures were used in presentations (pp. 499–505). The addition of visual and auditory input can complement the spoken words.

Directly related to clarity is the notion of abstraction. Words, by their nature, are abstractions. They are understood on the listener's terms. A successful presenter attempts to focus and control the levels of abstractions perceived by an audience. Multimedia aids can focus attention and greatly increase clarity. They do so by *greatly reducing the level of abstraction.* A simple chart or picture, for example, can focus attention in a way that words alone often can not. Seiler (1971) noted in his summary of research conclusions that visual aids "add clarity to the message, increase attention, improve listener comprehension, reduce stage fright, enhance message organization, and improve communication effectiveness generally" (pp. 174–175).

Presenters who use visuals are perceived more favorably than those who do not. Seiler concluded, "Apparently, visuals do add credence to a speaker and thus become a form of support that strengthens a speaker's acceptability by his audience" (p. 183). Presenters who use visuals are perceived as more persuasive, more credible, and more interesting than those who do not use visual support (Cothran, 1989, pp. 4–8).

Business executives, by necessity, are information processors. Perhaps this has led to a reliance upon so-called "left brain" thought processes. Visual and auditory multimedia aids may stimulate a broader integration of brain function and encourage further development of mental creativity. The client may see more possibilities for the presenter's ideas when multimedia aids are employed. The utilization of *more than one channel of communication* can be a plus for attention and creative thinking.

Another reason to use media aids relates to Western culture itself. Audiences have become increasingly visually oriented. Foss (1982) noted, "Ours is a visual age. The image seems to have taken over the written word as we are confronted more than ever before with other forms of visuals in our everyday lives: photographs, posters, pamphlets, billboards, images on television and film" (p. 55). Perhaps Foss would agree that written words are, indeed, visual. The move to a more multisensory orientation in our society has not reduced the importance of hearing to human understanding. However, many children have been raised on the visual, as well as auditory, stimuli of television, interactive electronic games, and the computer, with its visual display terminal. All this has contributed to a more visually oriented culture. In other words, Western culture has developed an *expectation of visual enhancement* in communication. Audiences may not be impressed as favorably when a presentation is composed exclusively or primarily of spoken words.

The eye is capable of registering a tremendous amount of data. The receptor systems of sight are equipped to transmit millions of "bits" of information to the conscious and/or unconscious mind. Neglecting this visual potential for enhancing a presentation is like choosing a second-best approach or attempting to compete with one hand tied behind your back. It may be concluded that it is *harder not to watch a multimedia aid than not to listen to a speaker.*

The presentation can be made "user-friendly" by the use of multimedia aids. Hence, *actively involving the client* can be a good multimedia strategy in a business presentation. Allowing a prospective client to operate a product can be one of the best and surest means of acquainting that person with the product's salient features. Sales of interactive games support the idea that people of all ages enjoy personal involvement. "Computer shyness," especially among middle-aged people, can be overcome successfully through guided, directed involvement. According to Howell and Bormann (1988), "A rough rule-of-thumb is that the increase in audience interest and learning is roughly proportional to the amount of audience activity" (p. 176).

When multimedia aids supplement rather than substitute for a business presentation, they are excellent devices. Effective multimedia aids are more than note cards. They are the salt and spice necessary to make presentations vivid and memorable.

WHY SOME PRESENTERS DO NOT USE MULTIMEDIA AIDS

There are many reasons why multimedia aids should be used in business communication. Often, however, business presenters let their relatively minor concerns about multimedia aids preclude their use. How can we overcome the problem of multimedia avoidance?

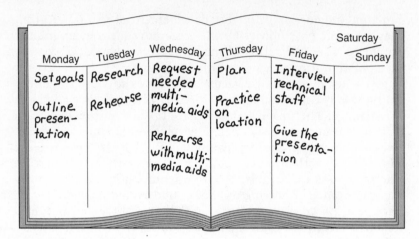

Figure 14.1 A calendar.

One reason for not using multimedia aids is that *it takes time to plan and prepare them.* Actually, it may be that people do not think about integrating media aids into a presentation until it is too late to develop them adequately. The presenter might brainstorm in advance regarding appropriate multimedia aids and utilize a calendar plan for their timely development. The calendar itself becomes a media aid for the presenter in the planning process. *What* must be done, *when,* and *by whom* can be plotted on the calendar and checked regularly (see Figure 14.1). You can solve the time problem by discussing ideas with in-house or contracted media specialists, then following up with concrete plans.

Many presenters have what may be termed a *verbal bias.* They simply do not think of using a multimedia aid; they concentrate solely upon verbal content. Awareness of this preference is the first step toward using media.

Another reason for limited use is that many speakers are *untrained in the use of multimedia aids.* These people may remember the times they have seen equipment fail to function properly. A projector bulb can go out and leave an indelible negative memory. Media equipment does require advance practice for confidence and precise operation. It is important that the presenter be in control of the multimedia aids rather than allowing the aids to control the presentation! The more complex the multimedia aids, the more practice is necessary.

Another concern is the notion that *employing multimedia aids takes too much time.* The wish to present as much information in the shortest period of time may appear to rule out a multimedia approach. However, multisensory stimuli have the potential to better shape images and focus attention on the crucial data. Using a team approach can help overcome time concerns—one person handles the multimedia aids, and the presenter is free to ensure verbal continuity. In fact, if carefully constructed, more information can be presented by the use of multimedia aids in the same amount of time. For example, Bormann et al. note that a television commercial "uses music,

Table 14.1   SUGGESTIONS FOR POSITIVE USE OF MULTIMEDIA AIDS

Perceived problem	Possible solutions
Multimedia aids take too much time to prepare.	Brainstorm in advance, and use a calendar.
Presenters are untrained in use of multimedia aids.	Practice at the scene in advance with the equipment you will use.
Multimedia aids take up too much presentation time.	Cover many ideas with a single multimedia aid.
Multimedia aids are gimmicks.	Use professionally prepared and carefully planned multimedia aids.

sound effects, dramatized segments, dance, graphs, charts, testimonials, animation, flip charts, and camera tricks to catch the audience's attention and make a point clearly and quickly." The oral presentation is an organizational message "that grew out of similar pressures and has adapted many of the multimedia techniques of television and film to the needs of managers" (pp. 203–204).

Some speakers avoid multimedia aids because of *cost*. Visuals for a presentation can be expensive. If professional artwork is not available within the organization and must be contracted, the expense can climb rapidly. However, with some attention to neatness, a business presenter can prepare attractive and functional multimedia aids for only a few dollars. For example, simple transparencies can be made with acetate and a marking pen. The decision to purchase an expensive computer presentation graphics system depends on volume (Smith, 1989, p. 10). Considering the potential return from the investment in visual aids, in most cases it is money well spent.

There is a notion, perhaps as a result of gimmicks on television commercials, that media aids are little more than elements in a "dog and pony show." Some fear that the "flash" of technology distracts audiences from what is truly important. Style may substitute for substance. However, carefully constructed multimedia aids highlight and extend the substance of a given message.

Table 14.1 summarizes positive suggestions for overcoming negative stereotypes about using multimedia aids.

In reality, well-developed and tailored multimedia aids complement the presenter's concern for an audience. Multimedia aids must be targeted to the specific situation (audience and circumstances). Decision makers recognize the effort that goes into preparing these aids. When used properly, multimedia aids serve as a kind of a positive "calling card" for the presenter.

TYPES OF MULTIMEDIA AIDS

Multimedia aids may be either *abstract* or *tangible*. Abstract multimedia aids are two-dimensional; tangible aids are three-dimensional. A drawing is an abstract aid, and a working model is a tangible aid. Abstract multimedia aids can help clarify the verbal message. Tangible aids may be animate or inanimate. Some animate objects are much easier to control than others. Plants, for example, are easier to control than most animals, including humans.

A model of an inanimate object can emphasize or minimize particular features. It can be smaller or larger than the actual object. Models can demonstrate a process; they are not frozen in time. Models can be taken apart. Models can eliminate irrelevant features and focus attention on the factors under discussion.

More time and effort may be required in removing tangible objects from audience attention—they need more handling than projected images. A speaker must integrate dimensional multimedia aids into the presentation without allowing them to dominate it.

SELECTION OF APPROPRIATE MULTIMEDIA AIDS

Select multimedia aids with an eye toward what is appropriate. Decisions regarding appropriateness should be made (1) after analysis of the audience (see Chapter 9); (2) after consideration of the time available for the presentation; (3) with an understanding of the space and configuration of the room; and (4) with an understanding of the difficulty of placing multimedia equipment in the room (electrical outlets and lighting controls).

Smith (1984) asserts that audiences prefer the horizontal format to the vertical. When listeners shift their expectations from the horizontal to the vertical, the speaker's points can get lost (p. 72). Make multimedia aids large and legible. Eliminate all unnecessary materials.

A presenter should also consider the appropriate level of formality when selecting and integrating multimedia aids. Knowing the personal preferences of the audience and analyzing the context will help. The types of multimedia aids used partially establish the formality of the presentation. For example, it is less formal to draw transparencies with the audience present than to prepare them in advance.

Each multimedia aid has its strengths and weaknesses. The presenter should inventory the possibilities of each available aid. Bob Trent reviewed the pros and cons of several multimedia aids to decide which ones he would use to support his presentation.

Videotape Recordings   In real estate sales, the modern camcorder or more sophisticated video devices can aid business presentations. An agent can send out-of-town clients a videotape that introduces the community and highlights some aspects of the area, along with an introduction to and promotion of the real estate agency. For a particular individual, the agent could include a few listings in the client's price range—perhaps an exterior shot and a feature focus of the kitchen and family room. The tape might conclude with a broker or sales agent informally welcoming new clients to the city.

Once the client arrives for an on-site visit, the agent can make a more thorough business presentation before going to inspect property. Here the salesperson interacts with the prospect and uses multimedia aids to show a variety of listings within the client's range of financing and interests.

Note how this type of business presentation minimizes the wear and tear on homeowners, prospective buyers, and agents. Effective presentational techniques and multimedia aids make it possible to show selected properties without leaving the office.

The disadvantages of using video include the initial expense for the proper equipment and the time required to record and edit the videotape. The tape itself is inexpensive and can be used again and again. The prices of hand-held camcorders are competitive. Several models have character generators: information can be superimposed on the visual image. This ability to overlay data on the visual has additional possibilities for the business presentation.

Multiple monitors or large-screen projections should be provided for large audiences. Various recording formats require different types of playback equipment. An on-site test of equipment is recommended.

Professional productions cost more. However, the lower prices of camcorder and monitor/playback equipment now on the market have made professional-quality multimedia aids a viable option for business presentations.

At Sue Derkman's suggestion, American Computer Systems made an on-location videotape featuring an interview with a satisfied customer. The tape demonstrates an application similar to Sento's needs for a personal computer network and presents good testimonials from satisfied product users. Bob Trent decided the tape would be a valuable sales aid for his presentation.

A camcorder in use. (Joel Gordon)

Modern computer-generated drawings can show depth and great detail. When such technology is available, it makes for an excellent visual presentation. Kringle and Schaff (1989) add, "The videodisc appears to be ready. Although it failed to catch fire in its debut 10 years ago, it has since gained acceptance in a different form—as the compact disc" (p. 6). The potential for interactive video presentations is here today.

Projected Images   There are a variety of ways to project images during a business presentation. *Opaque projectors* enlarge and display images from a nontransparent source—a picture or chart from a book or photograph. Such devices are bulky, and the room must be very dark for a sharp projection. The presenter must consider sight lines, since the large projector must be placed directly in front of the viewers.

Bob Trent decided that he could not darken the room sufficiently to use an opaque projector.

Transparency projectors (overhead projectors) provide flexibility for presenters. They are inexpensive and offer an almost infinite number of possibilities. A presenter can overlay transparencies in order to show additive processes. Presenters can project vivid colors onto a screen while controlling detail. Transparency projectors have few limitations. They are versatile, and they are not particularly expensive or bulky (some are the size of a briefcase). For these reasons, business presenters use transparency projectors widely.

An opaque projector in use. (Photo by Chris Walker for the Chicago *Tribune*)

However, some attention must be paid to focusing and setting the distance from the screen for appropriate magnification of the data.

Sutherland (1989) indicates, "A big projection screen carries a certain dramatic punch. Smaller monitors, on the other hand, stand up better in brighter environments. Windows need not be shaded. Room lights can stay up full—or need be only slightly dimmed. The first question, therefore, is not *what*, but *where*" (p. 17). Obviously, permanent presentation facilities are advantageous.

Bob Trent decided to use a transparency projector to detail specific features of the CX-1000 personal computer.

Slide projectors offer potential and flexibility for business presentations. They project 35-millimeter slides onto a screen. The presenter can synchronize multiple projectors. Slides are capable of showing great detail, from simple charts to pictures of actual objects.

The presenter needs to allow time for film development and proper mounting. The projector itself must be set up a considerable distance from the screen, and sight lines may be a problem. Rear projection, where possible, can eliminate this difficulty.

A transparency projector in use. (University of Colorado; photo by Arnold Ogden)

Bob decided he did not need to use a slide projector this time. Two multimedia aids would suffice for a short presentation.

Additional Representations   Through a variety of means, including videotape, opaque projections, transparencies, and 35-millimeter slide projections, speakers can use abstract representations in the business setting. In addition speakers can display charts on an easel; use a chalkboard; use flannel graphs; use markers on newsprint; use flip charts; use computer graphics; and so on. Abstract representations help the presenter make salient points in a business presentation.

Visual images include graphs (bar, line, and pie types); drawings; tables; and pictures. When using any graph, consider whether the images are large enough for all the audience members to see.

Bob considered showing a bar graph on the transparency projector to illustrate the relative cost-effectiveness of American's computer line compared to competing systems.

A 35-millimeter slide projector in use. (Courtesy Eastman-Kodak)

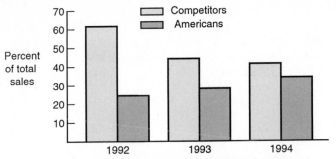

Projected market shares for American Computer's
XT-1000 as compared to those of strongest competitor

(a)

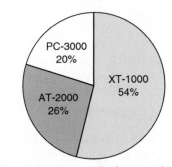

Percent of computer sales by computer type
for American Computer in previous fiscal year

(b)

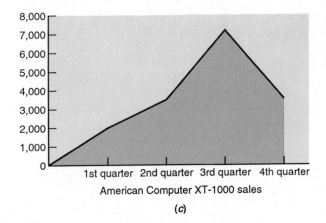

American Computer XT-1000 sales

(c)

Figure 14.2(a) Bar graph; (b) pie graph; (c) line graph.

Color ink jet printers driven by modern color graphics software can provide vivid pictures. The speaker can give a copy to each member of an audience. Blackboard-sized electronic copyboards can save what a speaker writes or draws during a presentation and then output copies at the touch of a button. Each of these options comes at a considerable price. However, their use is relatively simple and the visuals are excellent.

SPECIAL CONSIDERATIONS

Pointers, especially unobtrusive telescoping pencil-sized ones, may help you to focus attention. Turning toward the audience, point with the arm nearest the multimedia aid or screen. Unfortunately, pointers seem to invite the presenter to "play with them" unconsciously. Put them away when not in use. It is better to point out an object on a screen rather than on the surface of an overhead transparency. There is less chance of blocking sight lines and of scratching the surface of the transparency.

Each type of multimedia material has a specific potential for communicating a particular kind of information. Some two-dimensional displays are more formal than others. Writing on a flip chart as you speak is more informal than projecting 35-millimeter slides or carefully developed transparencies.

Placement of multimedia aids is an important consideration. It is better to keep the speaker as the focus of audience attention, when possible. Remember, most projectors are oriented toward the screen, and the line of projection must be clear. Equipment for other displays and presentations may be placed at about a 45-degree angle and slightly to one side of the audience. In this way the speaker remains the center of attention and can direct the audience to multimedia aids when appropriate. Obviously, protecting the line of sight and presenting clear visuals are the two most important considerations.

Presenters must guard against the overuse and/or misuse of any multimedia aid. Some audience members find chalkboards dull unless the speaker uses colored chalk. Others think colored chalk is "artsy" or in poor taste. Also, it is easy for the presenter's body to block the board. (The same is true for other display devices.) Chalkboards will not serve well for large audiences, but they are satisfactory for many presentations where brief notations are required.

SCRIPTS

Sometimes you can improve the quality of multimedia aids by developing a script and audio tracks. Script writing can be fun and challenging. After completing the general plan of the presentation and laying out the visuals in preliminary form, you can address any necessary scripting. Audio tracks provide novel stimuli that can renew attention during the presentation. Choose a person with an announcer-quality voice to speak the lines.

Kenny (1982) discusses five steps in the script-writing process: (1) review your objectives; (2) set your theme; (3) research your subject; (4) organize your information; and (5) write your script (pp. 86–95).

Reviewing your objectives should take only a few minutes, but be sure that the direction of the script corresponds with the objectives. The theme of the presentation is the basic, underlying argument to establish the case for the purchase of your product, idea, or service. Speakers frequently restate a theme in slightly different words during the script. Research gives the text authenticity and depth. You'll need to be prepared to answer questions beyond the script. Furthermore, research will help you make a stronger case. Organize your information strategically—for example, in a pattern like Monroe's motivated sequence (see Chapter 12). You want your presentation to (1) get attention; (2) establish a clear need for your product; (3) show how the product can meet the need; (4) help the audience visualize the product in operation; and (5) exhort action (for example, encourage the clients to purchase the product). Using these guidelines will make script writing an easy last step.

Bob Trent knows that multimedia aids can help his audience focus their thinking in the direction he desires. Models, diagrams, charts, and graphs add depth to the repertoire of multimedia aids he can use in conveying ideas to his audience. In addition to increased retention, multimedia aids help maintain attention, reinforce ideas, add realism, save time, help organize the presenter, and build presenter confidence. Now that Bob has made his selection of multimedia aids, he needs to review how to use the aids most effectively.

TEN COMMANDMENTS FOR USE OF MULTIMEDIA AIDS

1. *Select multimedia aids because they are the single best way to present the information desired.* Do not choose multimedia aids simply because their use is expected or because of content problems in the presentation. Instead, use multimedia aids purposefully to complement your message.
2. *Base the selection of multimedia aids on careful analysis of the audience, the occasion, and the context of the presentation.* Consider the degree of formality, the nature of the audience, and the site of the presentation. For example, if you cannot control the lighting in a room, do not use certain types of projectors, such as the opaque projector.
3. *Choose multimedia aids that you can integrate easily into the flow of the presentation.* Sensational or overly complex aids defy attempts at clarity and conciseness. Aids cluttered with detail may serve more to distract and confuse the auditors rather than to focus attention and renew interest.

4. *Select and construct all multimedia aids carefully.* Multimedia aids should represent the presenter well. Select vivid, pleasantly contrasting colors. Make certain that all multimedia aids are appropriate for the time, audience, and occasion. Multimedia aids should reflect taste, effort, and coordination with all aspects of the presentation.

5. *Make multimedia aids clear and concise.* Bar graphs are excellent for statistical comparisons. They present information vividly and concisely. Keep in mind the "C I O" principle—keep aids clear, interesting, and organized. Check the size of each visual aid (in the context of its use) to make sure that it adds to the presentation.

6. *Keep all multimedia aids out of sight until it is time to present them.* Aside from projectors, which must be placed properly in advance, avoid placing any aid where it can distract your listeners. When displayed too soon, aids lose their impact.

7. *Avoid "talking" to the multimedia aid(s).* Beginning presenters have a tendency to "talk" to their multimedia aids. It is as though the aids contain a magnet, drawing the speaker's attention away from the task of monitoring audience feedback. The speaker should always present ideas directly to the audience, reading and adapting to listeners' feedback.

8. *Keep the multimedia aids out of the listeners' hands.* Unless you plan for members of the audience to handle or operate equipment, keep objects and materials out of their hands. Handouts compete for attention with the presenter. The person passing it, the person receiving it, and the person who will receive it next are affected. Save any handout materials until the presentation is complete or until you reach the point in the presentation where physical contact with the multimedia aid will not destroy attention.

9. *Explain multimedia aids clearly and concisely.* Forecast what your listeners will see or hear, and then let them experience the multimedia aid. Without specific explanation (highlighting), the entertainment function of a multimedia aid may obscure its information value. Enjoyment rather than increased attention often is the net result.

10. *Be prepared to regain attention after using multimedia aids.* You can increase your volume and speaking rate, move in relation to a stationary background, and quickly restore lights to their original intensity.

SUMMARY

• Use multimedia aids to add interest, aid listeners' memory and renew their attention, and add variety to a presentation. Multimedia aids clarify ideas and reduce abstractness. Visual aids meet the needs of a visually oriented culture, and multimedia aids provide an opportunity to involve a potential client with the product or service.

- Some presenters who shun multimedia aids do so because they are biased toward verbal communication. Others think the aids take too much time to prepare. Some presenters are untrained in the use of multimedia aids, and some presenters view them as frivolous. With proper planning, presenters can minimize negative factors and maximize the many advantages of employing multimedia aids.

- Multimedia aids can be formal or informal, animate or inanimate, two-dimensional or three-dimensional. The newer forms include camcorders and computer graphics; the more traditional aids include projectors, charts, and the blackboard. Using scripts and audio tracks can improve the quality of multimedia aids.

- Select multimedia aids after careful analysis of the audience and occasion. Keep some guiding principles in mind, and use multimedia aids when (1) they are the best way to present images and information; (2) they complement the content of the presentation; (3) they do not interrupt the flow of the presentation; (4) they are carefully constructed; (5) they are clear and concise; (6) they are kept out of sight until needed; (7) you do not "talk" to the aids; (8) they are kept out of the hands of listeners; (9) they are explained well to the audience; and (10) you are prepared to regain lost attention.

QUESTIONS FOR REVIEW AND DISCUSSION

1. List at least three good reasons for presenters to use multimedia aids.
2. What can be done to overcome inexperienced presenters' reluctance to use multimedia aids?
3. What are the basic types of multimedia aids?
4. What should be done to ensure the selection of the most appropriate multimedia aids for a particular business presentation?
5. What are the ten commandments for use of multimedia aids?

ACTIVITIES

1. Describe what multimedia aids you think Bob Trent should select for his computer sales presentation to the board of directors of the Sento Group. Carefully consider the *why* of your selection.
2. In Bob Trent's presentation, which multimedia aids would underscore an air of formality, and which aids would contribute to an aura of informality?
3. Observe a presentation; then make a careful analysis of which multimedia aids contributed most and which contributed least. How could multimedia aids be used to improve the presentation?
4. Suppose that you were to speak to your city council regarding a hazardous traffic situation. Which multimedia aids would you choose? Give your reasons for selecting or not selecting each option.

Making and Evaluating Your Presentation

Chapter
15

Delivery of the Message

After reading and reviewing this chapter, you should be able to . . .

1. Define communication apprehension and explain what happens to your body as a result of the anxiety you feel.

2. Identify and explain several ways to manage communication apprehension.

3. Identify and explain three goals of good delivery.

4. Compare and contrast the benefits and liabilities of four different delivery formats.

5. Identify and explain the criteria for effective posture, movement, gestures, eye contact, and appearance.

6. Identify and explain the functions that gestures serve.

7. Describe the four functions of eye contact in a presentation.

8. Identify and explain seven characteristics of effective vocal delivery.

*P*erhaps one of the most anxious moments in the life of any presenter is that "moment of truth" when the decision makers are assembled in the boardroom and the convener signals that it is time to present the proposal. Bob Trent has planned his presentation; the delivery of the message is but one more step in the process of making the sale. But is it really that simple? No! Speakers seem to have a universal impulse to panic when they hear the phrase "Ladies and Gentlemen, it gives me great pleasure to introduce . . . " (Fill in your name.)

MANAGING COMMUNICATION APPREHENSION

The apprehension you feel prior to giving a presentation is common. Several years ago the Speech Communication Association reported the results of a survey by Bruskin and Associates (1973), which asked American adults to rank the most tension-producing events in their lives (p. 4). This survey indicated that the number one fear of most Americans is speaking in public. Incredibly, a majority of the respondents found speaking before a group more frightening than a variety of tension-producing items, including height, insects, financial problems, deep water, sickness, and even death (see Table 15.1).

Most people are apprehensive about many communication tasks—speaking in a group, conducting interviews, meeting new people, and engaging in social activities. The terms *stage fright* and *communication apprehension* imply that those experiencing such reactions are abnormal. Actually, this common reaction to challenging situations is experienced by musicians, ath-

Table 15.1 THE TOP 12 TENSION-PRODUCING ITEMS

1. Speaking before a group
2. Height
3. Insects
4. Financial problems
5. Deep water
6. Sickness
7. Death
8. Flying
9. Loneliness
10. Dogs
11. Driving a car
12. Darkness

letes, and actors, as well as those engaged in oral communication. You should not feel abnormal if you do experience such anxiety.

It may be more appropriate to view this phenomenon as performance apprehension. Regardless of the labels you attach, what is important is how you deal with it. Several findings and observations should provide some comfort to the new presenter:

1. Performance apprehension is common.
2. Presenters can confront apprehension by understanding its causes.
3. Adequate preparation is the best way to minimize apprehension.
4. Apprehension is difficult for audiences to detect.
5. Some physical involvement can help defuse apprehension.
6. Some apprehension can be useful.
7. Realize that listeners want you to do well (this includes your instructor).
8. Relax and visualize success.

Performance Apprehension Is Common

It is no secret that performance apprehension is commonplace even among very successful speakers and presenters. Actress Carol Burnett was afraid of speaking in public—and so was Abraham Lincoln (Masterson, Beebe, and Watson, 1989, p. 330). Most of you experience speaker's anxiety too. It may be helpful to understand some of the factors that cause you to react as you do.

McCroskey (1984) defines communication apprehension as "an individual's level of fear or anxiety associated with either real or anticipated communication with another person or persons" (p. 79). Bradley (1986) defines stage fright as "a normal form of anxiety, or emotional tension, occurring in anyone confronted with a situation in which the performance is important and the outcome uncertain" (p. 382).

Understand the Causes of Apprehension

When you are confronted with an anxiety-producing situation, as when making an important proposal, your body goes into action. Your adrenal gland pumps adrenalin into your system. Adrenalin is an amazing stimulant. It restores vitality to your muscles and increases their responsiveness. Its other effects are described graphically by Bradley:

> Large quantities of sugar are released into the blood from the reserves in the liver and insulin is released from the pancreas to convert the sugar into energy, giving the body greater strength to cope with physical problems. Numerous red corpuscles are discharged into the bloodstream from the spleen. Breathing is quickened, thus bringing in more oxygen and expelling the carbon dioxide more rapidly. The pulse rate speeds up so that more fresh blood arrives at the muscles, the heart, the brain, and the central nervous system with larger quantities of oxygen. Blood is diverted away from its normal process of picking up digested

food from the stomach and the intestines to transport throughout the body and is now directed to the muscles, heart, brain and central nervous system to provide these organs with greater oxygen and energy. (Bradley, 1986, pp. 384–385)

Because of these dramatic changes in your body, you may experience a queasy feeling in your stomach (commonly called "butterflies"). Dryness of the mouth ("cottonmouth") is caused by more rapid breathing. Every manifestation of the anxiety you are experiencing has a physiological explanation.

Try to think of these reactions as helpful to your delivery. As blood is pumped to the brain, you become capable of thinking more clearly and more rapidly. Your increased energy level produces a more dynamic delivery. Thus, because of apprehension, speakers such as Bob Trent *can* perform at a greater level of effectiveness. It is also possible for apprehension to be debilitating, if uncontrolled. But viewing your apprehension as an ally can enhance your outlook and confidence.

Preparation Defuses Anxiety

There is no substitute for thorough preparation as a way to reduce and control speech anxiety. Of course, preparation goes beyond a mastery of the material. It includes a thorough analysis of the audience, including anticipation of questions and appropriate responses. Preparation also includes a thorough rehearsal of your delivery. If possible, practice at least once in the place where you will later deliver the presentation. (Bob Trent might want to make one practice presentation in the Sento boardroom, if possible.) Speakers budget at least one hour of preparation (including research, review of objectives, proposal development, and practice) for each minute of delivery. If you are not thoroughly prepared, you will naturally be more anxious about what you are going to say, how you are going to organize the message, and what the reaction from the audience might be. Thorough preparation is the sensible way to minimize performance anxiety and maximize the probability of success.

Apprehension Is Not Obvious

The severely anxious presenter usually fears that his or her apprehension is painfully evident to everyone in the audience. Actually, most physiological reactions are internal. The audience becomes aware of tension only when the speaker acknowledges it. Avoid such admissions, since they detract from the subject and draw attention to your anxiety. Take comfort in knowing that your anxiety is hidden by the thorough preparation that allows you to exude confidence and composure. And, if you are nervous, never apologize.

Physical Involvement Helps

When anxiety strikes, some presenters grasp the speaker's stand and hang on for dear life; some clasp their hands together or stuff them into their pockets to mask the trembling. These actions are counterproductive. A better plan is to step away from the stand for some freedom of movement as you emphasize your main points. Couple that physical movement with gestures that describe, enumerate, and/or punctuate the ideas you express. By channeling nervous energy into physical activity, you can propel some of the pent-up energy into the presentation; this "bleeds off" the extra energy and adds a dynamic quality to your message.

A word of caution: avoid engaging in random movements to defuse anxiety. *Good delivery enhances the message. Poor delivery distracts from it.*

Controlled Apprehension Can Be Useful

Instead of trying to eliminate communication apprehension, learn to control it. A useful means of accomplishing this is to concentrate on communicating. Become idea-centered, not self-centered. Speakers who are self-conscious rather than idea-conscious worry about everything *except* effective communication. When you are concerned about conveying the message, self-centered questions fall by the wayside. Speakers who ask "How do I look?" "Is my nervousness showing?" or "Does the audience like me?" are asking self-centered questions. In contrast, questions like "Are these decision makers hearing and understanding what I am saying?" "Are they 'buying' my ideas?" "Are there points needing further emphasis?" or "What feedback am I receiving and how should I adjust to it?" suggest that the speaker is concentrating on communicating a message to the listeners. By concentrating on communicating with your audience, you will channel your nervous energy into the effective delivery of ideas.

Listeners Want You to Do Well

Most decision makers want the speaker to make a successful presentation. This thought gives Bob Trent comfort. Few events are more unpleasant than a boring or embarrassingly poor presentation. The audience generally is composed of busy executives who spend much of their time in meetings. They want to be stimulated, challenged, entertained, and moved, rather than bored and resigned to suffering through an anxiety-ridden presentation. Even an audience hostile to your ideas seldom enjoys watching you suffer from communication apprehension. They, like most listeners, want you to speak well.

Relax

"Relax" is easy to say but hard to do. But successful presenters remind themselves that they have earned the right to speak. They have done their homework. They have completed the steps of preparation: their objectives are clear; the audience has been analyzed; a central idea has been determined; main points have been planned; evidence has been identified and collected; an outline has been developed; and the presentation has been rehearsed, preferably at least once in the meeting room for the presentation. Like an athlete thoroughly prepared and eager for the game to begin, a speaker can best use the last few minutes to relax and visualize success. Relaxation exercises, such as deep breathing or tensing and relaxing muscle groups, may be helpful.

Another good way to control physical tension prior to making a presentation is to interpret it positively. An accomplished skier views the slopes from the top of the mountain as an exciting challenge, in spite of a pounding heart and "butterflies"; a seasoned presenter can derive as much excitement from making presentations as a skier who successfully executes moguls on a steep ski run. You, too, can see making a presentation as a pleasurable opportunity to communicate ideas.

THE IMPORTANCE OF DELIVERY

Although it makes no sense to think of a presentation without content, the effectiveness of any presentation depends heavily on the ability of the speaker to deliver the content to the listeners through verbal and nonverbal symbols. Words, the voice, physical actions, and multimedia aids are the means by which presenters reach their listeners. Content represents the goal; delivery represents the means. They are both important in effective speaking. We discuss content in other chapters in this book; in this chapter we focus on delivery.

Goals of Delivery

Consider three basic goals when striving for effective delivery:

1. Be natural, direct, and sincere.
2. Minimize distractions.
3. Maintain interest and variety.

Be Natural, Direct, and Sincere   The presenter whose delivery is calm, composed, natural, and direct, and who conveys a sincere belief in the integrity of the proposal, will probably be viewed as credible and effective. Successful salespeople stress the importance of believing in their product or service. Sincerity should be a natural part of delivery, a by-product of believing in your product.

Convey Ideas Without Distraction   If audience members comment primarily on your polished delivery—the grace and ease with which you moved; the rich, oratorical quality of your voice; or your fluid, sweeping gestures—you may have attracted more attention to what you did or how you expressed yourself than to the content of the message. In fact, it may well be that one of the best compliments a listener can give the speaker is to say, "I didn't notice your delivery." This means that the delivery did not overshadow or detract from the ideas. If delivery calls attention to itself, the message usually suffers. And if the message suffers, the presenter probably fails to achieve his or her objective. Hence, the goal of delivery is to convey ideas with a minimum of distractions. Good delivery does not call attention to itself.

Maintain Interest and Variety Listeners commonly complain, "the speaker was boring." In comparing characteristics of effective and ineffective speeches, Monroe (1937) discovered that the first six factors that student audiences identify with ineffective speakers are delivery-related: (1) a monotonous voice, (2) stiffness, (3) lack of eye contact with the audience, (4) fidgeting, (5) lack of enthusiasm, and (6) weak voice. Monroe discovered that audiences like (1) direct eye contact, (2) alertness, (3) enthusiasm, (4) a pleasant voice, and (5) physical activity. Clearly, listeners desire that speakers maintain interest and variety in the delivery as well as the content of the message.

TYPES OF DELIVERY

One of the first decisions Bob Trent needs to make as he plans his presentation is the choice of delivery format. Possible formats include (1) reading from a prepared manuscript, (2) delivering a memorized presentation, (3) delivering the presentation impromptu, and (4) making an extemporaneous presentation. You should be familiar with the characteristics of each style so you can make a decision as to which delivery format best fits your purpose.

Reading from a Manuscript Bob might want to use a *manuscript style* because he thinks it is safe. After all, he can write out his presentation exactly as he plans to say it and then read the message to his audience. Although this method may provide Bob the security of knowing he will not leave out or forget part of his message, few people read aloud well enough to make this approach truly effective. Most people, especially busy executives, do not like to be read to. The speaker might as well photocopy the presentation and let each of the members of the audience read it for themselves in the privacy of their own offices. As pointed out in Chapter 13, there are significant differences between oral and written styles. Speech is more informal, more personal, more direct, and more redundant than written communication. For effective manuscript delivery, the presentation must be written out in a speaking style and the speaker must be able to sound as though he or she is speaking normally, not reading.

Think about the problems of a presenter who is reading a written message and happens to look up to see shaking heads, quizzical looks, or frowns. What if the success of the presentation hinges on spontaneous response to such feedback? The necessary eye contact is impossible, since the speaker's eyes are on the manuscript. Page turning also distracts audience attention.

Memorized Delivery   Initially it may appeal to Bob Trent to *memorize* his presentation. Since reading the presentation has significant disadvantages, he might memorize the message word for word. Freed from the manuscript, Bob will have more eye contact with the audience. However, a careful analysis suggests some disadvantages. For example, the presenter is even more likely to notice negative feedback from the audience—pained expressions, quizzical looks, and the desire to challenge ideas. The need to respond to such feedback will be immediately apparent, but the memorized message is "static" and inflexible. Any deviation from the memorized script would invite disaster. Departing from a memorized message and then trying to get back into the flow proves difficult indeed. Moreover, most memorized presentations *sound* memorized, conveying a stilted, artificial tone. Only the most accomplished orator can make a memorized presentation seem natural and spontaneous.

Impromptu Speaking   An *impromptu* presentation is delivered without any preparation or rehearsal ("off the cuff"). Advantages of impromptu delivery include not having to spend hours in formal preparation, far less formality in speaking style, and maximum opportunity to establish eye contact and direct interaction with listeners.

Sometimes impromptu presentations are necessary because of time constraints, emergency situations, or other circumstances that demand a "Johnny-on-the-spot" to respond at that moment. Some speakers are unusually capable of "thinking on their feet," and some are experienced in giving presentations that can be adjusted to various circumstances. But most impromptu presentations lack the research base, organization, audience adaptation, time control, and polish essential to success.

Responding to listeners' questions (see Chapter 16) is an impromptu format, even though the wise presenter makes every effort to anticipate questions the audience members are likely to ask. Although different situations may require different approaches, some generalizations hold true for impromptu speaking:

1. *Anticipate the situations.* Anticipate when you may be called upon to speak. Most impromptu situations are not a complete surprise. A friend who prizes your judgment may drop by to ask your advice on a matter. You may be called upon in a fraternity or sorority business meeting to discuss membership problems because you chaired the membership drive last year. Sometimes you know that the chairperson has a tendency to call upon others to speak "off the cuff." When you can predict that you are likely to be called upon, you can formulate a response in advance, and your impromptu presentation will be more effective.
2. *Respond confidently.* When called upon to speak, you have little choice but to say something. If the topic is beyond your realm of experience or expertise, decline with a polite but firm resolve. Whether you choose to decline or address the topic, do not hesitate. Either decline, ask for a moment to collect your thoughts, or respond. Which-

ever option you choose, act confident and try to maintain a positive, professional image.

3. *Present a thesis early.* Draw upon the guidelines presented in Chapters 8 and 12 for selecting a thesis statement. Begin by identifying the essence of the point you want to make. You may want to begin by saying, "I strongly support this idea, for three reasons," or "I see several problems with this idea." Presenting your central idea early suggests that you are certain of your position; be provisional only when you are uncomfortable with taking a strong stance.

4. *Provide supporting data.* Once you have identified your thesis, you need to provide reasons for your point of view. You can use one of the patterns of organization identified in Chapter 12. Generally, a topical pattern is easiest to develop. As with any presentation, you will be clearer and more persuasive when you provide supporting data to clarify, amplify, and prove your central idea.

5. *Do not "wear out" your invitation to speak.* Sage advice for impromptu speaking is to "stand up, speak up, and shut up." Impromptu speakers often begin with an apology, which creates a negative first impression. No one expects an impromptu speech to be polished. But impromptu speakers often stammer in low tones that no one can hear, and they tend to ramble on without focus. You need to identify a central idea, quickly select a pattern of organization, develop your position, and make your points.

Remember, if you are forewarned about a speaking assignment, take the time to prepare. The impromptu style appeals only to the indifferent speakers, lazy speakers, and "high rollers" who love to risk their image and/or future.

Extemporaneous Speaking Speech communication experts recommend *extemporaneous* speaking for most occasions. When delivering a presentation extemporaneously, the speaker usually works from a storyboard or from a written outline reduced to speaking notes. The exact wording is not memorized or written out verbatim.

A speaker could use note cards or a key word outline. Some people like to make up a loose-leaf booklet with pictures, graphs, statements, and so on that accentuate key points in the presentation. This type of aid is most appropriate in a one-on-one or one-to-few setting. Extemporaneous speakers often use a flip chart that includes key ideas to serve as a "public note card" for the audience as well.

The extemporaneous style is informal and conversational. This style conveys to the audience that the presentation literally is being created as they listen to it. Since audiences prefer a spontaneous presentation to a "canned" one, this style adds interest and excitement, particularly when coupled with multimedia aids that augment and highlight key ideas and concepts. An extemporaneous message also allows flexibility for adapting to the feedback provided by the audience. In fact, the carefully prepared, yet flexible extemporaneous presentation easily lends itself to the interactive style typical of

Table 15.2   PRESENTATION FORMATS

Format	Characteristics
Manuscript	The presentation is written out, then read from the prepared text.
Memorized	The presentation is memorized and is presented without notes.
Impromptu	The presentation is made without advance notice.
Extemporaneous	The presentation is made with advance notice. It is outlined and prepared carefully. Main ideas are generally committed to memory, but the exact wording of the message is not.

presentational settings. Bob Trent selected the extemporaneous style because it does not have most of the disadvantages of the manuscript, memorized, and impromptu formats and it promotes a well-organized and interesting presentation which can be delivered in a dynamic and direct manner (see Table 15.2).

VISUAL DELIVERY TOOLS

How can you best capitalize on the extemporaneous style? Consider the two categories of delivery elements at your disposal—visual and vocal communication. In addition to multimedia support (covered in Chapter 14), several other visual elements can enhance effective delivery of a presentation. They include (1) posture, (2) movement, (3) gestures, (4) eye contact, (5) facial expression, and (6) personal appearance.

Posture

Posture refers to your carriage. Posture sometimes reflects upon your credibility as a speaker. The positions of your head, feet, and shoulders, especially, are central to good posture. The audience may associate careless posture with sloppy ideas. Good posture does not mean a military stance. The feet should be positioned a comfortable distance apart with your weight evenly distributed. The head and body should be erect, which tells decision makers that you are alert, energetic, and confident. Standing with your shoulders slouched or your body draped across a speaker's stand, as if you lack the energy to stand alone, communicates neither vitality nor interest to the audience. We know that facial and vocal cues play a significant role in expressing emotions; the posture of the speaker conveys the intensity of the emotions.

The size of the audience, the informality of the setting, and your own comfort zone will in large measure dictate your speaking stance. Some speakers feel at ease sitting on the edge of a table; others enjoy sitting at a table with the audience; and others, when there are only one or two audience members, enjoy sitting in a casual configuration, such as around a coffee table. Regardless of the environment, the speaker's posture should reflect a positive interest in the presentation situation and attention to the speaking conventions expected for the occasion.

Movement

Movement is an easily abused delivery tool. While some movement is desirable, you should not pace aimlessly about. Conversely, you do not want to exhibit the other extreme of appearing to have your feet nailed to the floor. Movement may be incorporated into the presentation as long as it does not detract from the message. Movement should always serve a purpose. For example, it might be appropriate to move forward as you introduce a new idea, or backwards when you reject an idea. You can move toward a flip chart you are using to illustrate an idea. Movement comes best between ideas, not during the development of an idea. Your movement should complement, or correspond to, the verbal content of the message; that is, change position when you change ideas. Motions should not appear aimless or overly theatrical.

Also keep in mind your proximity to the audience. Hall (1959) identified four zones of communication interaction. *Intimate distance,* from bodily contact to $1\frac{1}{2}$ feet, is appropriate for a presentation to one person you know well, especially if you use a portfolio and/or other visuals that you must share at a close distance. *Personal distance* is in the range of $1\frac{1}{2}$ to 4 feet. This zone is more appropriate when there are at least two listeners and visuals are restricted in size. *Social distance* is within the range of 4 to 12 feet. This is the usual distance for most group decision making. In decision-making groups of this size, speakers often use a flip chart or an overhead projector so listeners can focus on enlarged visuals. Most presentations take place in this zone. *Public distance* extends from 12 feet on out. Presentations to large audiences occur in this zone.

Barriers also affect a speaker's movement. Lecterns, rows of chairs, portable chalkboards, elevated stages, projected visuals, smoking and nonsmoking seating, or the need to use a microphone can impede the speaker. When such barriers separate you from your listeners, attempt to move closer to the audience. Even subtle movement, such as leaning toward the audience, conveys a desire to interact with the listeners and, at the same time, can increase a sense of trust between speaker and audience.

Gestures

As in private conversation, gestures serve as means for the presenter to emphasize, describe, and enumerate. Yet many speakers who gesture easily and naturally when conversing informally find it awkward and uncomfortable to gesture before an audience.

You have undoubtedly observed a variety of awkward gestures. Some speakers lock their hands behind their backs in "parade rest" fashion. Others place them in front of their bodies in a "fig leaf clutch." Another common pose is to place one hand on the hip in a "broken wing" pose, or even both hands on the hips in a "double broken wing." Although there is nothing inherently wrong with any of these gestures, speakers sometimes use them for security rather than for enhancing their communication with the audience. When such gestures dominate a speaker's delivery they become distracting to the audience.

Keeping your hands in your pockets may convey a secure, comfortable, and casual image, but who can resist the temptation to rattle loose change or keys? Such noise may prove distracting and thus detrimental to your message. Do you grasp the podium until your knuckles turn white? Do you tap a pencil or pointer on any available surface? Videotaping your delivery may help you discover some of your distracting gestures. Another way is to ask someone to watch you rehearse and then critique your gestures.

If you are not sure what to do with your hands, you might begin by letting them hang naturally at your sides. The secret is to keep them apart so that they are free for (1) pointing, (2) dividing, (3) describing, (4) approving, (5) rejecting, and (6) emphasizing ideas in your presentation.

- *Pointing.* Using your hand as a pointer is a useful way to reinforce or clarify what you are saying. A telescoping pointer extends your reach, so you can draw your listeners' attention to an item on a flip chart or screen.
- *Dividing.* Dividing gestures partition a message into components, like a cook cutting a pie into serving portions. The fingers of your dominant hand are extended as if you were preparing for a handshake, with the palm held perpendicular to the floor, and with a karatelike motion you "divide" or set apart an idea for consideration. But try not to fall into a routine axe-chopping pattern.
- *Describing.* Describing gestures help the audience to visualize an object or concept. Saying an object is 18 inches wide while holding your hands approximately that distance apart is a natural way to complement and stress the verbal component of your message. Using your hands to describe a new widget that your company plans to produce helps the audience to picture that object.
- *Approving.* Extending your open hands invites the audience to support or approve of an idea or proposal. Again, it is important to monitor your gestures to ensure you are not sending a signal incongruent with the intended message.
- *Rejecting.* You can extend one or both hands outward with the palms toward the audience to ask for the rejecting of a course of action, or to convey the need for caution when implementing a proposal.
- *Emphasizing.* Some gestures add emphasis to a message. Raising three fingers as you state "I have three points to make" serves to reiterate

your verbal statement. Shaking a tightly clenched fist stresses the importance of a point. Television newscasters sometimes use their hands to emphasize a point; they may also emphasize key ideas by nodding their heads.

Gestures should work for you, not against you. Their purpose is to emphasize and strengthen verbal messages, not to detract from them. The following list suggests how:

1. *Relax.* Gestures should be relaxed. Tense, rigid gestures can create an unpleasant mood or climate during the presentation. Fluid, relaxed gestures create a professional climate essential to quality decision making. Prerehearsed gestures come across as telegraphed and choppy.
2. *Use appropriate gestures.* Gestures should be appropriate. Gestures obviously should not be obscene, unprofessional, awkward, or stilted.
3. *Vary your gestures.* Gestures should be varied. Beware of stereotypic gestures, such as clasping the hands at the beginning of each presentation. People are creatures of habit, and it is easy to fall into a mindless use of gestures.
4. *Make obvious gestures.* Gestures should be obvious, not oblique. Some presenters make subtle gestures that are masked by the lectern. Some seem to forget their hands are in their pockets. Gesturing with an elbow while the hands are buried gives a "wounded duck" look.
5. *Time your gestures.* Gestures should be timed to coincide with the verbal message. When you say you want to make three points, gesture simultaneously rather than before or after the statement.
6. *Regulate your gestures.* Gestures should be regulated. Adapt the use of gestures to the size of the audience. If the proximity of the audience places you in the intimate zone rather than the public zone, limit the expanse of your gestures. Presenting to a small audience in a casual setting requires more subtle gestures.
7. *Make natural gestures.* Gestures should be natural. The "fig leaf clutch" is not professional. Dramatic, sweeping gestures are appropriate for a theatrical performance but appear unnatural in a presentation. Remember that one of the nicest compliments you can pay a presenter is that you did not notice the delivery.

Eye Contact

Eye contact is a vital part of effective delivery. Bob Trent knows that eye contact serves at least four important functions: (1) establishing and maintaining credibility, (2) monitoring audience feedback, (3) sustaining audience interest, and (4) regulating the communication channel.

Establishing and Maintaining Credibility Eye contact definitely affects speaker credibility. Beebe (1974) discovered that increased eye contact enhances "the listener's perception of the speaker's credibility" (p. 24). He noted that moderate eye contact (approximately 50 percent of the time) and high eye contact (approximately 90 percent) greatly increased the perceived honesty of the speaker (pp. 21–25). In fact, Beebe observed that speakers with less than 50 percent eye contact are viewed as less friendly, uninformed, inexperienced, and possibly dishonest! Since credibility typically fluctuates throughout a presentation, it is essential that speakers guard against negative perceptions caused by an absence of eye contact.

Monitoring Audience Feedback   Eye contact also allows the speaker to monitor audience feedback. Failure to maintain close eye contact weakens or destroys a vital link with your audience. Feedback enables a speaker to observe audience response and to adapt to it. Hence, eye contact helps presenters to achieve their objectives by adjusting to audience needs.

Sustaining Audience Interest   Failure to maintain eye contact tells listeners that you are not interested in them. Listeners process message content better when the speaker maintains more than 50 percent eye contact (Beebe, 1978). Your audience members will learn more when they perceive that you are interested in them.

Regulating the Communication Channel   Eye contact also tells others that the communication channel is open. Eye contact indicates that the speaker welcomes interaction. Lack of eye contact suggests, among other things, preoccupation with other matters.

Since eye contact facilitates effective communication, Bob Trent should establish eye contact with his audience before he speaks. He should walk to the front of the room, pause to establish eye contact with each member of the audience, and then begin his presentation.

As he speaks, he should renew eye contact with each listener. Such visual exchange suggests that Bob is interested in each person in his audience. Merely sweeping the audience from side to side, like a security camera in a bank, is undesirable. Bob wants all the members of the decision-making body to feel that he is speaking directly to them and that he will respond to any feedback.

Facial Expression

Facial expressions play a key role in conveying the presenter's emotions and attitudes. Speakers should carefully communicate the kinds of emotional responses they believe are appropriate. Sometimes a large part of the message is delivered through facial expressions. The face is capable of an incredible number of blends of expression. Our faces display six primary emotions: happiness, surprise, sadness, fear, disgust, and anger (Knapp, 1980, p. 167).

Obviously, Bob Trent should not rehearse his emotions. If his listeners know him well, efforts to contrive facial expressions would probably backfire.

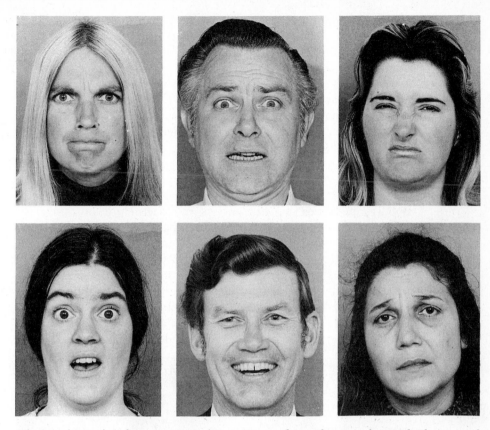

The six basic facial expressions. (From *Unmasking the Face* by Paul Ekman and Wallace V. Friesen. Englewood Cliffs, N.J.: Prentice-Hall, 1975)

If Bob prepares well, sincerely desires to communicate, and "loses himself" in an effort to reach his audience, his facial expressions will be natural.

Personal Appearance

Another visual element in presentations is the speaker's personal appearance. Since most listeners have expectations about the way a business presenter should look, audience analysis can provide information as to how the speaker should dress. Presentation styles, situations, audiences, and settings vary so much that it is difficult to prescribe a particular dress code. J. T. Molloy's two books, *New Dress for Success* (1988) and *The Woman's Dress for Success Book* (1978), provide some guidelines for business dress. Still, an appropriate wardrobe depends upon climate, custom, culture, and the nature of the client. Client expectations in a sports organization may differ from those in a Fortune 500 company.

Your personal appearance—dress, grooming, length and style of hair, jewelry, and so on—affects audience responses to you, especially during the opening moments of your presentation. As the audience adjusts to you and you adjust to the audience, a greater measure of tolerance may develop. You can increase the odds of acceptance by following some guidelines: (1) when in doubt, dress conservatively; (2) mirror the dress of the audience; and (3) it is better to overdress than to dress more casually than most audience members. If the men are all wearing suits and ties and the women are all wearing dresses or suits, you should not dress casually. You should dress as well as, or slightly better than, the best-dressed member of the audience.

VOCAL DELIVERY

Bob Trent realizes that his voice is an extremely important delivery tool. He knows that many audience members believe that they can tell a lot about him from his voice. The film *My Fair Lady* was about one person's attempt to change another's vocal characteristics. Age, occupation, status, education, regional origin, and income range are but a few of the variables people may infer from the voice. A speaker's credibility is affected by the listeners' attitudes toward his or her voice. Vocal delivery affects (1) the ability to be understood and (2) the ability to maintain audience interest.

Components of vocal delivery include rate, pause, pitch, volume, quality, pronunciation, and articulation. Presenters who use each of these dimensions effectively can increase their success with various groups and individuals.

Rate

A fast rate of speech usually suggests excitement and vitality; a slow rate tends to signal calm and confidence. When you speak rapidly, however, your listeners may feel that you are disregarding their ability to keep up with your ideas (even though they can comprehend speech more rapidly than you can talk).

Likewise, from the listener's viewpoint a slow rate sometimes suggests a lack of interest and preparation. Your rate of delivery should be governed, in part, by the complexity of the material being presented and the familiarity of the audience with the proposal's content. For example, technical material may be difficult for some people but relatively easy for technicians familiar with the concepts. When ideas are new and/or complex, you should slow down delivery; when the ideas are familiar or relatively easy to understand, you can increase your rate. Most speakers tend to talk at a rate of 125 to 150 words a minute. Listeners can process information at a thinking rate of at least 400 to 800 words a minute. Thus, your listeners generally can think faster than you speak, but there is a considerable difference between a listener simply keeping up with you and thoroughly understanding the material. When presenting key ideas it is important to slow the rate to facilitate comprehension.

There is no ideal rate, but you may have observed that presenters sometimes speak too rapidly—perhaps because of time constraints, personality factors, or communication apprehension and the desire to finish a presentation as soon as possible.

It is a good idea to tape-record your presentation and ask someone to assess your speaking rate for interest and understanding. Since it is not difficult to vary your rate of delivery, this can be an excellent way to add variety and interest to your presentation.

Pauses

Speakers can vary their rate by pausing. People often use the generally undesirable vocalized pause—*uh, er, mmm, ah*—but they may neglect the silent pause. Pausing between words, ideas, or sentences adds emphasis to your message. A pause before a word can heighten suspense. Pausing after a thought gives decision makers time to savor the material and reflect on it. You may find it awkward, at first, to include pauses in your delivery because the silence seems like an eternity. Actually, the time lapse seems longer to you than it does to the audience. With some practice you can feel comfortable with pauses. But remember whenever you pause to avoid filling the gap with verbal fillers (*ah, so, you know,* etc.).

Pitch

Pitch helps speakers create variety. Your vocal pitch is how high or low your voice sounds on the musical scale. A lack of pitch variety, or monotone delivery, often produces a highly ineffective presentation. To some people, monotone delivery is intolerable, regardless of what the speaker says.

Everyone has a habitual pitch range. This is our range during normal conversation. This pitch is determined by the rate at which our vocal chords vibrate. The faster the vibration, the higher the pitch, and the slower the vibration, the lower the pitch. Men's vocal chords generally vibrate more slowly than women's, so men have a lower vocal pitch.

Inflection results from raising or lowering the pitch as words or sounds are produced. Your use of inflection colors the meanings of your words. Raising the pitch can signal that you are asking a question; lowering the pitch denotes finality. When you want to communicate excitement, your pitch normally rises. When you desire to convey calmness, you lower your pitch. Thus, inflection, the combining of pitch with words and sounds, helps communicate your emotional state. Good speakers use considerable variation in their inflection. (Listen to play-by-play descriptions by a good sports commentator.) As you get involved in your subject and in reaching your audience, your inflection will change naturally.

Volume

Beginning speakers sometimes speak too softly. Adequate volume is a fundamental objective of delivery. Inadequate volume frustrates listeners. Volume is determined by the amount and force of air passing through the voice box, or larynx. The force depends on the diaphragm, a muscle in the upper abdomen which forces the air from the lungs through the larynx.

Since your voice will sound louder to you than to your listeners (your ears are closer to your mouth than their ears are), it is important to seek the aid of others to determine whether you are speaking loudly enough. If there are any doubts, ask the people furthest from you whether they can hear you. Other factors affect your volume, including environmental noise and the amount of emphasis you want to place on key ideas or phrases. Ceiling or furnace fans, air conditioners, noise from your multimedia aids, and interaction between members of the audience are but a few of the distractions you may need to overcome. Increased volume, coupled with a slower delivery rate, can help your audience to hear and understand your message. Keep in mind that you can emphasize points by lowering your volume as well as by raising it; decreasing the volume while maintaining an audible level of delivery can also attract and maintain audience attention.

Voice Quality

Each voice is unique; so, like fingerprints, no two voices are alike. That which causes your voice to differ from others is voice quality. Quality figures prominently in the general impression your voice makes on listeners. You have all heard voices that sounded melodious, resonant, lusty, rich, harsh, thin, breathy, hoarse, or gravelly. If you suspect that listeners think your voice quality is distracting or irritating, consult a speech pathologist, but beware of making a judgment based solely on your own analysis of your voice. Others may hear your voice differently—you hear your own voice partially through bone conduction, while others hear your voice exclusively through sound waves in the air. Two suggestions may help improve your vocal quality: (1) maintain adequate breath support, and (2) try to stay relaxed while speaking. Tension can produce a harsh-sounding voice.

Pronunciation

Mispronouncing words can damage your credibility. Common pronunciation errors are listed in Table 15.3. People need all the help they can get in correcting pronunciation errors. Consult a dictionary if you are in doubt about the correct pronunciation of a word. One of the authors heard a nursing student refer to a hernia as a "hi-renni," a fetus as a "festus," and a womb as a "whamb." Such mispronunciations might well destroy a patient's confidence in this nurse.

Articulation

Good articulation is a matter of producing speech sounds clearly and distinctly. One of the quickest ways to kill audience interest and respect is to mumble. Never talk with gum in your mouth, and don't chew on a pencil;

Table 15.3 COMMON PRONUNCIATION ERRORS

1. *Omission.* One or more sounds are sometimes omitted from the following words. Check a dictionary for correct pronunciation, then pronounce the words "correctly" but with the appearance of easy naturalness.

belong	interesting	pumpkin
candidate	Italy	regular
cemetery	laboratory	superintendent
chocolate	library	suppose
couldn't	mirror	surprise
diamond	municipal	temperature
dictionary	particular	understand
figure	perhaps	usual
generally	poem	violent
geography	police	when
government	privilege	which
governor	probably	why
intellectual		wouldn't

2. *Addition.* Sounds are commonly added to the following words. Again, check a dictionary for correct pronunciation.

across	elm	often
athlete	evening	parliament
athletics	film	pincers
attacked	grievous	salmon
column	height	subtle
draw	idea	sword
drowned	law	statistics

3. *Substitution.* Sounds are sometimes changed in the following words. (For example, a radio announcer shouted that the fans at a football game were "jubulant," and later he said that the players were covered with "prespiration.") For some words, the terms *right or wrong* do not apply; in these cases, decide which pronunciation is preferable in your cultural environment.

accept	experiment	larynx
accessories	futile	percolator
almond	genuine	persist
apparatus	gesture	perspiration
breaches	get	prelude
catch	guarantee	presentation
character	hearth	pronunciation
children	hero	ration
coupon	heroine	relevant
creek	horizon	spontaneity
culinary	hundred	status
cupola	instead	substantiate
data	iodine	syrup
discretion	irrelevant	tedious
docile	jubilant	vigilant

Table 15.3   (*continued*)

4. *Accent.* People often have problems with where the stress falls in the following words. Look them up in the dictionary, and when there is a choice, decide which pronunciation is preferable in your community and cultural surroundings. Note that in many of the words, the vowel in the last syllable is properly pronounced "uh."

abdomen	comparable	irrefutable
acclimated	contractor	pretense
admirable	despicable	program
adult	dirigible	recess
allies	divan	research
Arab	exquisite	resources
aspirant	finance	robust
assiduity	grimace	romance
autopsy	hospitable	vagary
cement	inquiry	vehement

Source: Adapted from *Developing your speaking voice* by John P. Moncur and Harrison N. Karr, pp 262–263. Copyright © by John P. Moncur and Harrison N. Karr. Reprinted by permission of HarperCollins Publishers.

having anything in your mouth seriously impairs the clarity of your speech. (Table 15.3 lists commonly misarticulated words.)

REHEARSING YOUR PRESENTATION

Mere knowledge of techniques does not ensure that you will deliver your presentations effectively. Speakers practice making their presentations to "murder boards" and/or other critical observers. Review the suggestions made in Chapter 8 as you prepare for delivery of your presentation. Allow enough time for a series of rehearsals and the development of the necessary speaking aids. The environment for the presentation rehearsal should be as authentic as possible. Meaningful rehearsal should build confidence, increasing the probability of success through effective delivery of the message.

SUMMARY

- The way you deliver the presentation affects your credibility and the impact of your message. Use a delivery style that is natural, direct, and sincere; minimize distractions; and maintain interest and variety.

- Four types of delivery are reading from a prepared manuscript, memorizing, impromptu speaking, and extemporaneous speaking. The extemporaneous format is generally preferred; this style works best when you reduce an outline or a storyboard to a brief set of notes or highlights on a flip chart.

- There are several factors to consider for effective delivery of a presentation. Posture, movement, and gestures should be relaxed, purposeful, natural, and adapted to the expectations of the audience. Eye contact helps establish and maintain credibility, monitor feedback, sustain audience interest, and regulate the communication channel. Facial expressions communicate emotions to the audience. An audience analysis should identify appearance and dress expectations.

• Vocal cues also communicate emotions to the audience. Appropriate volume, articulation, and pronunciation help the audience understand the message. Other variables—vocal pitch, inflection, rate, and voice quality—affect the listeners' perception of the speaker.

• Speakers must rehearse their presentations carefully.

QUESTIONS FOR REVIEW AND DISCUSSION

1. What are some ways to control communication apprehension?
2. Describe, compare, and contrast four different delivery formats.
3. Why is extemporaneous delivery the preferred delivery format?
4. What functions do gestures serve?
5. List the ways you can make your gestures, posture, movement, and appearance more effective.
6. What are the four functions of eye contact in a presentation?
7. Describe several characteristics of effective vocal delivery.

ACTIVITIES

1. Videotape one of your messages during a rehearsal or the actual presentation. Critique the tape, focusing on delivery. Write an analysis of the strengths and weaknesses of your vocal and nonverbal delivery, based upon the principles and suggestions presented in this chapter.
2. Attend a business presentation as an observer or as a participant. Pay particular attention to the speaker's delivery. Write a critique of the speaker's use of posture, movement, gestures, eye contact, facial expression, appearance, and vocal cues. If you were a consultant to the presenter's supervisor, what advice would you give?
3. In making your next presentation, experiment with some different delivery techniques. After experimenting with these new dimensions to your style, write a report about what you liked and what you did not like. What risks did you take? Do you hope to retain any of the results in your new repertoire of delivery techniques?

Chapter 16

Responding to Audience Concerns

After reading and reviewing this chapter, you should be able to . . .

1. Indicate the various reasons why audience members ask questions during a presentation.

2. Recognize how questions serve as opportunities to check whether the audience understands and accepts the speaker's proposal.

3. "Field" questions and respond in a positive manner.

4. Audit nonverbal cues to help determine how the audience is responding to a presentation.

5. Handle difficult and hostile questions.

6. Control questions so that they are relevant to what is being presented.

*S*elling is vital to success in our society. People secure gainful employment because they have "sold" employers on the advantages of hiring them instead of others. Everything produced is intended to be sold. Anyone who wants to sell an idea or a product must inform people of its value and instill a desire to purchase the item or accept the idea. Perhaps the art of making a successful sales presentation was described best by five-and-dime store king F. W. Woolworth, who was said to have observed that he did not sell, but he made it easy to buy (*Royal Bank Letter*, 1983, p. 4). Bob Trent must make American Computer Systems' products easy to buy or he will not be a successful sales team leader.

In order to accomplish his task, Bob must be prepared to respond to questions and objections. In fact, one of the most important aspects of an effective business presentation is the way in which questions and objections are answered. Question-and-answer sessions can be more important than the presentation itself. Too often presenters have a negative attitude toward these sessions. Rather than feeling that questions will *wreck* a presentation, good presenters "should look on questions as an opportunity. They should cast aside W-R-E-C-K and concentrate on the R-E-C, seizing an opportunity to Repeat, Emphasize, and Clarify" (Smith, 1984, p. 154).

It is likely that careful "reading" of nonverbal feedback from the audience will indicate that one or more people may be unsure about something. Conscientious attention to nonverbal cues gives the presenter a chance to ask for questions. Overcoming the objections of others is a necessary part of sales presentations.

Bob Trent realizes that a sales presentation without objections is most likely a presentation without a sale. People who voice no reservations about needing the product or services offered, and who have no questions about the price or the quality of service after the sale, probably are not interested in the product or service. Sales trainer Tom Hopkins (1982) terms objections "rungs of the ladder of success" and notes, "They [champion salespeople] know they've reached the Klondike and are digging for gold when they start hearing objections. . . . It's when they don't get objections that they're really worried" (p. 187).

An *objection* is a question or a statement that indicates a client wants more information. Many objections are stated politely, but others come with shades of negativism. Objections may be serious or minor. Minor objections may signal a simple need for personal attention or interaction. Major objections obviously indicate the need for careful, thorough answers.

People ask questions for a wide variety of reasons: a need to achieve a better understanding, to secure personal attention, to show what they know, to make their own point clear, or to set up a later question or objection.

"Whatever their reason," writes Smith (1984), "it's not the rationale behind the question, but how you handle it that's important" (p. 156).

Real estate agents know that minor objections often reveal that at least one party to a presentation feels the discussion is moving too rapidly. If there are more serious objections, the sales agent may not have done an effective job of "qualifying" the client. Qualifying the client is a type of audience analysis: How much money can the client spend on a down payment? How much money will a bank lend the client? What monthly payment can the client afford? If the property does not meet these conditions, the most skilled presenter cannot make a sale.

The way the presenter meets the first question or objection sets the tone for further interaction. For example, a speaker who ignores verbal and/or nonverbal feedback, or whose tone of voice reveals annoyance with a question, is less likely to succeed. More importantly, this speaker is neglecting an opportunity to help a decision maker understand more fully.

Some questions imply negative evaluations that can easily put the presenter on the defensive. An anxious speaker may make statements that will be regretted later. When you practice delivering your presentations, allow your colleagues occasionally to interrupt the planned flow of information with questions.

PRINCIPLES

The following 16 suggestions will help presenters like Bob Trent handle questions and objections effectively:

1. *Realize that overcoming objections helps to make presentations successful.* Silent, unquestioning listener's may be uninterested listeners. People ask questions and raise objections when they are interested and attentive. Remember that even unconscious nonverbal cues can suggest annoyance with a question. Using video recordings to observe your practice sessions will help you to detect and minimize the use of such negative cues. Thus, through practice you can learn to create an atmosphere that openly encourages feedback.

2. *When listeners ask questions or raise objections, they provide the presenter with a valuable opportunity.* The listeners' specific verbal feedback clarifies the nonverbal clues the presenter observes. The presenter can tailor his or her responses to the needs and concerns of the individuals in the audience.

3. *Presenters need to practice handling questions and objections.* Answering questions and objections well is a skill that can be learned. Many professional presenters spend as much time preparing to answer questions as they do preparing the presentation itself.

   One of the authors of this text served as a sales trainer for an agribusiness corporation. This position involved numerous presentations to teach new salespeople how the company's management wanted its "sales pitches" made to farm families across the country. The trainer had to spend hours learning about the products, fielding questions at farm shows, and, ultimately, conducting practice sessions before company researchers and employees, who fired off question after question. All of this took place *prior* to making actual training presentations. The preparatory sessions provided excellent opportunities for growth and development.

4. *Announcing in advance that questions are welcome will encourage listeners to respond.* The presenter can stress that questions are welcome and can encourage the audience to write down issues or concerns as they occur. Asking "What questions do you have?" may be better than "Do you have any questions?" This approach assumes that listeners will have questions. Providing paper and pencils further underscores receptivity to questions.

   Sometimes it is not possible to field questions during the presentation. In these cases, it is desirable to mention that a question-and-answer session will follow later.

5. *Be willing to wait for the first question.* Each audience has its own "personality." Some are anxious to get into dialogue; others are slow to start but will ultimately raise relevant concerns and questions. It is not easy to endure silence, but recognizing that silence works on the audience as well as the presenter can make such quiet moments more positive. Eventually, questions probably will come. If there are no questions, you might decide to "prime the pump." If you are certain that your listeners can benefit (most often they can), you may begin to "unfreeze" the audience by asking questions yourself. Bob Trent might ask, "I understand that one of your greatest needs is for computer access for multiple users. What specific problems have you had?" or "Do you all agree that modem access for home use would be advantageous?" Such questions might open communication channels. Once you handle the first question professionally, others are likely to follow. If there are no other questions, it may be time to close.

6. *Keep answers brief.* Answering with just a "yes" or "no" would stifle dialogue—but don't use a question as an excuse for making another presentation. Keep answers short and simple. A clear answer and a reason or example to support it should suffice.

7. *Use the technique of restating questions and objections before responding.* This process can avoid or minimize misunderstanding. Listen to questioners actively and carefully. Watch nonverbal cues. By repeating the questions, you demonstrate that you are not avoiding listeners' questions and objections. You also give yourself a moment to organize your thoughts. You want to understand what the questioner intended to ask. Restating ensures that you actually address the question that was asked.

8. *There is no such thing as a "dumb" question.* Listeners' questions deserve the presenter's attention. Expressing appreciation for questions asked and concerns raised will create a positive atmosphere. Using the questioner's name in the acknowledgment further compliments the audience member who speaks out and encourages further participation.

   A question rarely, if ever, deserves a "put-down." Any humorous or sarcastic responses should be at the expense of the presenter, not the questioner. Sarcasm and humor at the questioner's expense might win a battle for the presenter, but they will lose the war. Losing the audience probably means losing the sale.

9. *Observe nonverbal behaviors.* Initially, establish eye contact with the person who asked the question. Then gradually shift to include others present. Conclude your response by looking directly back at the questioner. Try to decide whether the questioner appears satisfied with your response. You may need to ask whether you have answered the question satisfactorily. You should not do so, however, when the answer clearly is "no." When the questioner is unsure, unsatisfied, or upset, you may wish to ask him or her to "hold on" for a few more moments as you complete your answer. Then invite additional responses.

   You should also monitor your own nonverbal "language" as you answer objections and questions. Are you crossing your arms in what could be considered a defensive posture? Are you shifting your weight from one foot to the other, suggesting that you are unsure or overly anxious? Strive for an impression of attentive interest and relaxation rather than defensiveness or defiance.

10. *Exhibit patience in meeting objections and answering questions.* If a person is genuinely unsure about something, or his or her thinking has taken a negative direction, take a few moments to deal with the concerns. Impatience may save you time but will reduce chances for a sale. In the long run, patience saves time. A good rule is to listen carefully before responding. Then patiently deal with additional questions. Should one or more people appear to take sadistic pleasure in skewering and roasting you, patience is your best ally. Eventually, many other audience members may begin to identify with and support you.

11. *If you don't know the answer or are not at liberty to answer, say so.* The more important the question, the more desirable it is to promise to find the answer and get back to the questioner at a specific time. Never intentionally give an inaccurate or incomplete answer. If possible, call upon a qualified member of your team to respond. This often enhances your credibility.

   Unless you are trying to avoid answering, the audience will respect your explanation that you cannot answer certain questions.

You should not discuss trade secrets, information that denigrates a competitor, matters under litigation, and so forth.

12. *Try not to allow a few people to dominate the questioning.* A few outspoken individuals can destroy the flow of a presentation by asking a lot of self-serving questions. One way to deal with this problem is to announce in advance that time will be set aside for questions. Another technique is to anticipate such questions rhetorically and answer them in the presentation. You might say, for example, "You may wonder how this is possible. Let me explain." While such strategies serve, in part, as a control over unwanted questioning by one or a few people, they should not be used when listeners ask unique, relevant questions.

   If some people persist in asking questions despite your best efforts, Paul Timm (1981) rightly advises, "You may suggest that you'll get together with them after the presentation to clarify things" (p. 164).

13. *Insist that questions be relevant to the topic under discussion.* Again, it may be a good idea to advise a questioner that you will be happy to talk over other concerns after the presentation. Since you are responsible for controlling the time, it is important not to permit one or a few people to get the discussion off track.

14. *Do not "plant" questions in the audience in advance.* Presenters may fear that questions will not materialize from their audience. They may decide to ensure that questions and concerns are raised by "planting" questions with an audience member or two. This may produce the desired questions and responses, but it is not a good idea to use this tactic. Ethical considerations discourage it; such a strategy produces contrived and deceptive communication, not honest, spontaneous discussion.

   When no one asks questions, you might start the discussion yourself by bringing up the questions frequently asked by others or questions that you thought of when planning the presentation. If this does not produce further interaction, close the question-and-answer period.

15. Generally, *encourage questions during the presentation.* This is easier with small audiences. Exceptions to this advice are obvious. For example, listeners often raise points that you or another presenter will discuss later. You may tell an audience, "Let me put you 'on hold' with that question, if I may. That topic will be addressed later, and I will be happy to come back to your question then. Ok? Thank you." This way premature questions or concerns may be postponed to a more appropriate time.

   Reserving time for questions at the end may be appropriate, but it can be anticlimactic. If the presentation peaks properly at the end, motivation will be the highest at that point. Additional objections that emerge then may diminish your chances of success. All in all, it is better to encourage questions throughout the presentation.

16. *Treat objections as questions.* A presenter should not try to "defeat" a listener by overturning objections; the best technique is to treat objections as requests for more information. "As objections are raised, regardless of the kind of prospect you have, all the way from the gullible to the hostile," writes Zig Ziglar (1984), " . . . we first of all should act delighted about the objection and assure the prospect this objection is not going to be a problem when he has seen the remaining portion of the presentation (*objections thrive on opposition, but they die with agreement*)" (p. 273). An alternative is to provide an answer to the objection at the time it is raised, after restating the objection as a simple question.

Objections can be removed one by one. For example, letters from satisfied clients may remove doubts about service. Evidence that the price is competitive, that the product is unique, or that the price will soon go up may remove doubts about the value of the product.

NEGATIVE SITUATIONS

At times presenters encounter obviously hostile questions and objections directed at them, their products, or their services. You know when you are being "put on the spot." *Loaded questions* are calculated to evoke emotional responses—they use words like *mother, God, country,* or *flag.* "You wouldn't vote against the U.S. Constitution and the Bill of Rights, would you, in opposition of gun control?" is a loaded and leading question. Another form of loaded question is the *dilemma* question. "I understand that your company made record profits from its sales last year and yet has a very poor service record. Is that an example of incompetence or mismanagement?" can hit you hard and produce almost instant defensiveness. From the questioner's point of view, the strategy may be simply to see how the presenter handles stress. An appropriate response to this question would be to say "Neither" and to thank the questioner for pointing to the company's success in sales and for the opportunity to speak about recent innovations made in customer service.

"Hypothetical horribles" are questions that extend a point made in the presentation to an extreme. For example, a member of the audience may seek to derail Bob Trent by asking, "Assuming that we would purchase your computer hardware and software, wouldn't this put more than half of our managers and staff out of work in three or four years?" Bob might respond by saying "Computers have created more jobs than they have replaced, industrywide," "It might be that the agency is 'overmatched' with routine work now and could use the computers to reduce the work load." Bob might have data to support a stronger statement: "Computers have increased the morale at the vast majority of installations; and, given the narrow profit margin in this and many contemporary business settings, those who do not adopt a multiuser computer operation may lose market position soon," or, "It might be that no person would have employment in that sector of the company without the new computer installation." These hypothetical responses are plausible explanations for addressing what initially seems to be a damaging question. Provided Bob remains calm and can think on his feet, he has every chance of doing well.

As mentioned, questions sometimes contain *loaded language.* Imagine that a listener says, "It seems like you insurance types want to sell us high-sales-commission programs rather than what is best for us or what we can afford. Isn't that the case here?" A reasonable response might include some of the following concepts: "I think I can identify with some of what you are thinking here. However, that simply isn't the case. [This language serves as a transitory bridge to your answer.] As an insurance broker, I can offer a very wide variety of plans. I selected this plan for its low cost to your company and because of the following benefits. [Develop benefits here.] I learned long ago that it is better to please clients than to make a 'killing' on one sale or account. Our loading factor on this policy, by industry standards, is extremely competitive, and the performance experience is quite high. I really feel that your company can ill afford not to have a policy like the one we are discussing."

Handling difficult questions or objections can be fun. Avoid defensiveness and keep a sense of humor. Some presenters may find it effective to question the questioner playfully. "I'll bet you have been sitting there thinking up that 'killer question' for 20 minutes, haven't you, Bill? Let me make you a deal. If I answer that question, you'll buy lunch for everyone here, right?" Humor can reduce any tension in yourself and the audience before you respond to an objection or question. Of course, you must be careful in making light of a serious objection in a hostile audience situation.

Conditions are barriers that clients perceive as standing between them and buying services or products. The main motive for qualifying clients in advance is to determine whether there are conditions that render sales impossible. The presenter needs to know in advance whether the client can afford a product or service, whether the audience can make an independent purchase decision, whether the company's credit record is good, and so forth. Even a skilled presenter may discover a hidden condition during a presentation. Hopkins (1982) advises, "When that happens treat it like an objection [a request for more information]. That is, try to break it down, it's a condition, and you'll need to develop the ability to swallow hard and then quickly and courteously disconnect from that prospect who, you've just discovered, can't buy" (p. 188).

Rarely does it pay to argue or to resort to anger and sarcasm. Winning arguments is much easier than winning over prospects. Don't leave a client with only one way to get even with you—that is, by not giving you business. Always allow clients room to "save face." Psychologically, it may be better to accept the client's negative feelings and to deflect them bit by bit over time than to counter them directly.

There is an art to turning an irrelevant, inane, or insincere objection or question into a relevant, measured, and sincere one. As long as listeners remain in dialogue with you, consider what is being said by their behavior: they are interested and want to go ahead. They simply would not keep on asking and objecting if they didn't want what is being presented.

SUMMARY

- Handling questions and objections properly is an important consideration in effective business presentations. Questions and objections indicate interest in the products or services being discussed. Members of an audience ask questions for a variety of reasons, and handling questions successfully is really the art of handling people well.

- There are 16 guidelines relevant to handling questions and objections: (1) Realize that overcoming objections helps to make presentations successful. (2) When listeners ask questions or raise objections, they provide the presenter with a valuable opportunity. (3) Presenters need to practice handling questions and objections. (4) Announcing that questions are welcome in advance will encourage listeners to respond. (5) Be willing to wait for the first question. (6) Keep answers brief. (7) Use the technique of restating questions and objections before responding. (8) There is no such thing as a dumb question. (9) Observe nonverbal behaviors. (10) Exhibit patience in meeting objections and answering questions. (11) If you don't know the answer or are not at liberty to answer, say so. (12) Try not to allow a few people to dominate the questioning. (13) Insist that questions be relevant to the topics being discussed. (14) Do not "plant" questions in the audience in advance. (15) Encourage questions during the presentation. (16) Treat objections as questions.

- There are productive ways to handle negative situations, including loaded questions, hypothetical questions, and loaded language. Conditions (barriers that clients perceive to stand between them and buying) may be treated as questions as well.

QUESTIONS FOR REVIEW AND DISCUSSION

1. Why should a presenter consider a question, or even an objection, a positive indication?

2. What does it mean to say that the way the first question or objection is met will set a tone for further interaction or will indicate that the presenter really is not open for questions?

3. What steps should a presenter take to get ready to handle questions and objections?

4. How can the presenter control the situation so that questions flow freely and yet time is managed properly?

5. How can the presenter handle hostile objections or questions?

6. What are "hypothetical horribles" and "dilemma questions," and how should they be handled?

ACTIVITIES

1. If you have had sales experience, choose a product or service that you have offered for sale, but about which you have little information. Prepare a list of questions and objections that you would have difficulty answering. Take the list to someone who can answer. Observe how this person responds, verbally and nonverbally, to your questions and concerns.

2. Consider what questions you would ask the authors regarding material in this chapter. Imagine how the authors might handle the questions or objections to your satisfaction. How would you answer your own questions?

3. Reflect on a presentation that you have heard recently. Analyze the way questions and objections were handled by the presenter(s). Make a list of ways in which each presentation could be strengthened. Consider why you did or did not buy the service or product offered.

Chapter 17

Evaluating Your Presentation

After reading and reviewing this chapter, you should be able to . . .

1. Analyze and evaluate the presentations of others.

2. Evaluate your own presentations.

3. Apply one or more systems of criticism to your own presentation.

4. Analyze and use audience feedback as part of the evaluation process.

*E*valuating a speech or presentation is part of a larger process called *speech criticism*. Some people think of criticism as faultfinding or making negative statements about something or someone. It is actually a matter of analyzing and evaluating something (a speech, literary work, movie, etc.) for the purpose of increasing understanding, enhancing appreciation, or assisting in the improvement of the work. The evaluations rendered may be positive, neutral, or negative.

THE NATURE OF EVALUATION

Analysis involves the examination of a message: its content, purpose, support, audience, and social context (Campbell, 1972, pp. 14–21). You might informally analyze a message, or you might do a formal, systematic analysis of the work. Essentially, analysis is a matter of identifying and examining the components of the work that you are criticizing.

Evaluation, in contrast, is the process of making a judgment. Again, this judgment may be positive or negative, or it may be mixed. When you evaluate a message you are making a decision about its *value* or *worth*. Such a decision may represent nothing more than your personal reaction ("That speech was boring"). Or, the judgment may result from a systematic analysis and application of a set of evaluative standards. You might judge another's work or your own work. This chapter will focus on the latter.

THE IMPORTANCE OF EVALUATION

There are at least two reasons why you can benefit from learning to evaluate your own presentations thoroughly and effectively. First, if you evaluate your presentations *prior* to their actual delivery, you will stand an excellent chance of preventing problems. Second, understanding how to evaluate your presentations will enable you to do a better job of understanding what worked and what failed in the delivery of your presentations, so you can improve future presentations.

When Bob Trent has completed his preparation of an important presentation, he analyzes and evaluates his work. He can make changes that will improve the presentation and its chance for success. He might find ways to improve the flow of ideas, the wording of his message, the types of arguments and evidence used, and so forth. Making such changes and improvements would not be possible if Bob did not have the knowledge, desire, and ability to be critical of his work prior to its presentation.

After Bob has delivered his presentation, it is important for him to judge its effectiveness. Did he accomplish his goals? What did he do well, and what could he have done better? These are the kinds of questions that self-evaluation of his presentation can help him to answer. Such evaluation will, of course, help him to improve future presentations. Before he can do that, however, he needs to learn how to evaluate his work after he has presented it to an audience.

STEPS IN EVALUATION

There are four important steps that Bob can follow to criticize his presentations: (1) developing a positive attitude toward the criticism of his work, (2) analyzing his presentation, (3) interpreting the major elements of his presentation, and (4) evaluating, or judging, his presentation. (For an extensive discussion of these steps, see Cathcart, 1981.)

Developing a Positive Attitude

It is not easy for Bob to criticize his own work. During the process of thinking through and preparing a presentation, he becomes attached to his work. After all, it represents hours of hard effort. It contains *his* thoughts and *his* ideas. In effect, Bob strongly identifies with his work. It represents who he is as a person and as a professional. Given this kind of personal ownership, it is hardly surprising that Bob finds it difficult to be objective enough to evaluate his work stringently. It is much easier for him to approve of the finished presentation.

In spite of this normal tendency not to be critical of your work, it is important for you to develop a positive attitude toward self-criticism. You should begin by realizing that the very best effort to prepare a presentation does not eliminate the need for improvement and polish. Essentially, you can learn to approach your work with the attitude that it can be improved, that effective communication requires analysis, evaluation, and revision. With a little effort, you *can* develop such a positive attitude.

Try to realize and keep in mind the purposes and importance of effective presentations. Since presentations are given to specific audiences for definite purposes, everything that you can do to improve your presentations prior to their delivery will work to your advantage. Also, learning to be critical of your work after you have presented it will enable you to avoid mistakes in the future and to improve subsequent presentations.

Analyzing Your Presentation

Analysis is a matter of breaking the presentation into its components: (1) the purpose, (2) the audience, (3) the support, (4) the reasoning, (5) the organization, (6) the language, and (7) multimedia aids. You should examine each of these components carefully, both prior to the delivery of the presentation and after presenting it.

As a presenter, you need to have a clear idea of your *purpose*. But it is also important for you to make certain that your presentation develops, supports, and effectively conveys that purpose to your audience. You want to examine your presentation in order to determine whether it does what you want it to do. For example, if you want to convince your listeners to approve your idea for a new product, everything in the presentation should move in that direction. If one part of the presentation dwells on an existing product without relating it to the new idea in any way, you might make a change.

You might have more than one purpose. For example you may want your listeners to adopt your idea, but you also want them to view you as a dedicated team player. Hence, you should make certain that you relate the discussion of the product to indications that you are that team player. You might need to add or delete specific points, support, or language.

The *audience* is closely linked to your purpose. Thus, you need to examine every part of your presentation in relation to both audience and purpose. Review exactly what you want to achieve and then analyze the audience in order to determine whether the purpose is appropriate. You also should carefully review your analysis of the audience, making certain that it is as accurate as possible. This analysis will enable you to make necessary changes in the purpose or in the presentation itself. After the delivery of your presentation, additional use of audience analysis will help you to determine ways in which the presentation succeeded or failed.

Support material is anything, either factual or nonfactual, that you use to back up your positions (see Chapter 11). In order to analyze your support, you must carefully review your use of statistics, examples, and real evidence. You should apply the tests discussed in Chapter 11. Also, make certain that your support is appropriate to your arguments, purpose, and audience.

Determine whether the nonfactual support in your presentation adds interest or clarifies and reinforces the factual support that you use. You need to be sure that the support material is appropriate for your audience. Larson (1989) discusses unifying and pragmatic styles that can help you to make these decisions (pp. 141–144; see Chapter 13). A hostile audience generally requires more factual support and more concrete language than an accepting, supportive audience.

Analysis of your *reasoning* extends naturally from the analysis of support material. Keep in mind that people reason with support material in order to establish conclusions. As discussed in Chapter 11, reasoning is the process of drawing conclusions from data. Identify each type of reasoning you use, and apply the appropriate tests for each type. For example, Bob Trent might identify his uses of reasoning by example, cause, and sign, making certain that he reasons clearly, accurately, and logically in each case.

You need to determine whether the *organizational pattern* of your presentation is both accurate and appropriate. Checking for accuracy is a matter of comparing your organization with the steps called for by that pattern. For example, if you use Monroe's motivated sequence, analyze your outline to see that you have followed each of the five steps and that they actually develop the attention, need, satisfaction, visualization, and action components (see Chapter 12 for a thorough discussion of Monroe's motivated sequence and other patterns of organization).

The appropriateness of an organizational pattern depends on the audience. For example, if the audience is strongly opposed to Bob's purpose, he will not employ a structure which states the purpose early in the presentation and then presents reasons for acceptance. Instead, a problem-solution approach is more appropriate. Again, examining the organization of a presentation beforehand will improve effectiveness. Analyzing it afterward can help the presenter decide why the presentation worked, or did not work, as desired.

When analyzing the *language* in your presentation, you review such ordinary but highly important factors as correctness (the right word for the idea or concept), clarity (language that helps your listeners understand what you want to communicate), and appropriateness (language that fits the subject, the audience, and the occasion). Chapter 13 provides an extensive discussion of these factors. You should always keep these factors in mind in your work, both before and after its presentation.

When analyzing the effectiveness of your multimedia aids, make certain that your audio and visual materials are integral to your presentation; make sure they can be heard and seen by all your listeners; and make sure they do not detract from the effectiveness of your presentation (see Chapter 14). Again, prior analysis can prevent problems, and analyzing your use of these devices after you have made a presentation can help you to improve future presentations.

Interpreting the Major Elements of Your Presentation

This step in the evaluative process is not really separate from analyzing your presentation. Think of it, instead, as a continuation of the analysis function. As you analyze, you also interpret the material in your presentation. According to Cathcart's approach to criticism, interpretation involves examining your motives, examining audience responses, examining the situation, and applying a system of criticism (Cathcart, 1981, pp. 77–103).

Your *motives* relate to why you behave as you do. Behind the choices you make lie your past experiences, values, beliefs, needs, and so forth. Cathcart (1981) states that speech critics should attempt to understand the speaker's background as a means of better understanding his or her values, beliefs, and attitudes (p. 79). But you, as a critic of your own work, can do the same. You can examine *your* values, attitudes, and beliefs in order to understand why you made the choices you made and, also, to decide whether you want to change those decisions in subsequent presentations. For example, Bob Trent realized that he included certain information in a presentation to show how much he knows to a particular listener. He decided, after careful interpretation of his own motives, that the information really did little to help his listeners understand the point he was trying to make. Therefore, he decided to omit that information in the future.

Interpreting *audience responses* ties into your analysis of the presentation after you deliver it. An effective presenter is vitally concerned with audience responses. Sometimes such responses are quite clear. Bob Trent made a specific proposal to a group of five key decision makers in his organization, and they immediately rejected his proposal by a vote of 4 to 1. Of course, he knew what the response was. But he did not know why his listeners responded as they did. Bob asked for feedback from one of those listeners, and he discussed the meeting with his supervisor, Carmen Garcia, seeking input as to why the proposal was rejected. Carmen was in a position to obtain feedback that Bob could not acquire. Finally, Bob reviewed his presentation in order to determine where and how it could have been improved. He followed the steps of evaluation that we are examining in this chapter.

The *situation* may strike you as being the same as the audience. However, although the audience is definitely part of the situation, other important factors are involved. There might be personnel problems within the organization, for instance, that are so significant and pressing as to have an important impact on your listeners. In a situation not involving such problems, the same listeners might respond quite differently.

Other factors in the situation might have an impact on your presentation. Political, social, and economic events can affect the listeners and/or their organization. During a serious economic recession, for example, your listeners may react more conservatively or more reluctantly to a proposal requiring an investment of funds in an uncertain market area. In a company that has secured a significant government contract, or that has healthy profits, your listeners might be more receptive to a risky proposal.

As a presenter attempting to evaluate your own work, it is important that you interpret such situational factors and the impact they might have on your presentation. When Bob Trent discovers that a particular word, idea, or proposed action clashed with his listeners' needs or values, he omits it or changes the way or the order in which he presents it.

You need to know about the various *systems of criticism* you can use in interpreting your work. On the one hand, you are not attempting to function as a formal critic; on the other hand, however, the application of a system of a criticism to your work is a legitimate and important activity. In this discussion we do not attempt to explore all possible systems but will present basic systems that you can easily apply to your presentations. Like other aspects of criticism, these systems can be used both before and after the delivery of a presentation.

Karlyn Campbell divides critical interpretation into three basic systems. She calls them (1) traditional rationalism, (2) psychological criticism, and (3) dramatistic criticism (pp. 24–38). Each of these can provide you with a starting point for analyzing and interpreting your work. And, as indicated in the next section of this chapter, these systems can form the basis for evaluating your presentation.

Traditional rationalism begins with the assumption that human beings are essentially rational. Thus, a speech or presentation that is prepared correctly and logically should be effective. This approach considers listeners to be judges who can analyze the parts of a presentation and render a decision accordingly. This means that you must research your subject carefully, making certain the ideas, support, and reasoning are clear, accurate, and logical. It also means that you should organize your ideas in a reasonable, easy-to-follow manner. Your organization should, above all, help your listeners to understand and retain the content of your presentation. You should cast your ideas in language that is clear, correct, and appropriate. You should strive to deliver the presentation effectively, employing vocal variety, proper pronunciation, and so on, as well as appropriate gestures and facial expressions and posture that corresponds to and enhances the verbal message. If you handle all these elements effectively, your presentation should convince the listeners.

Psychological criticism is concerned with the motives and needs of your audience. This approach operates under the assumption that speeches and presentations are designed for and presented to listeners. Thus, an effective presentation is one that involves accurate audience analysis, effective audience adaptation, and the accomplishment of the speaker's purpose in relation to the audience. The most important element, then, is *effects*, or *results*. The way to interpret a speech or presentation is to determine how well the presentation achieved its purpose with regard to the audience. Every aspect of your preparation involves the management of ideas, arguments, evidence, and reasoning so as to appeal to your listeners' motives. Critically, you try to interpret the elements of the presentation in relation to their impact on your audience.

The *dramatistic approach* is based on the rhetorical theory of Kenneth Burke (1962). Burke's theory rests on the symbol-using, symbol-misusing capacity of humans. Through language, which Burke views as a *mode of action*, people shape others' attitudes as well as their own. Through the process of "identification" (uniting with others while acknowledging differences), people engage in "strategies" (conscious or unconscious efforts) that will overcome their separation from other people, without denying individuality and personal differences. The key to Burke's theory is that much speaking aims at overcoming separation between humans and groups of humans. As Campbell indicates, this approach involves examining groups, or series, of speeches rather than isolated, individual presentations (p. 37). For example, Bob Trent might analyze several of his presentations, attempting to see how well he succeeded in bringing about cooperation and unity. James Andrews (1983) states that effective criticism can be accomplished by the careful examination of one speech or presentation, but "genre" criticism denoting "a similar grouping or species" is "a search for generalities that can be made about discourses in such matters as purpose, style, form, types of proof, and the like (p. 59)." Table 17.1 summarizes the three systems of criticism.

Table 17.1 SYSTEMS OF CRITICISM

Approach	Emphasis	Primary basis for evaluation
Traditional rationalism	The speech or presentation	Accuracy, truth, structure
Psychological criticism	The audience	Effects or results
Dramatistic criticism	The audience and the speaker	Cooperation, understanding, unity

Evaluating the Presentation

Evaluation, or judgment, flows directly from the process of interpretation. Each of the three general critical systems suggests a particular approach to evaluation. This does not mean that you cannot combine these approaches, nor does it mean that they do not share common elements. You should decide which approach is best for your presentation and the circumstances in which you will deliver it. You can apply an evaluative system to your presentation both before and after its delivery. In the first case, you attempt to predict its success in light of the analysis and interpretation you have used. In the second case, you use what you learn to better prepare future presentations.

When using traditional rationalism, you should remember that facts and reasoning are subject to disagreement—that "the truth" is not always easy to determine or agree upon. It is also possible that people's perception of truth varies from one situation to another. For example, Bob Trent might decide that one audience will view a weakness in his proposal as insignificant but another audience will be more alarmed. Thus, he will spend more time discussing how the weakness can be overcome when he addresses the second audience.

As a critic of your own work, you can apply the truth criterion to your presentations, but you might want to use elements from the following two standards as well.

In psychological criticism, the major standard of evaluation is the effect: does the presentation obtain the desired result, or results, from the audience? If Bob Trent convinces his listeners to accept a new policy, he can conclude that he gave an effective presentation. If Bob's listeners reject his policy, he will conclude that his presentation was not effective.

This standard clearly applies to evaluation done *after* the delivery of your presentation. As you analyze your presentation *prior* to its presentation, you might interpret it in light of audience, topic, types of arguments and appeals, and so on, for the purpose of *predicting* its effectiveness. Later, you can see how accurate your initial evaluation was.

Like traditional rationalism, psychological evaluation has limitations. A presentation may be only one of a number of factors that affects an audience. A seeming success or failure may have little or nothing to do with the presentation itself. Multiple effects may be difficult to identify or explain. Also, it is sometimes difficult to know what actually constitutes effectiveness. Although the majority of listeners may reject Bob's proposal, the one person who accepts it may eventually have more influence than the others. It is true, too, that failure may not be what it appears to be. As a presenter, Bob may plant ideas in the minds of his listeners that, in combination with other facts and events, may *eventually* bring about a change in their thinking.

When attempting to determine the effects of a presentation, you will have to find out how your listeners will respond to your effort. You can do this formally, through the use of pre- and posttesting. Unfortunately, this may not be practical, so you will often have to use less formal means: (1) You can seek feedback from key listeners, such as your supervisor, or you can ask for the opinion of a friend or colleague who heard the presentation. (2) You can look for specific outcomes which will indicate whether you were effective (a favorable vote, a contract, a sale, etc.). (3) You can observe other behaviors and nonverbal responses in the audience. Listen to comments about your presentation. Pay attention when others report what audience members have said about your presentation.

Dramatistic criticism can help you predict and observe how well you succeeded in establishing identification, or lessening the distance between you and your listeners. As in psychological criticism, you must have a means of learning whether identification is accomplished. If feedback and responses reveal increased understanding and unity between you and your listeners, you can assume that you were at least partially successful. Bob Trent might discover that he has opened lines of communication with his listeners, that they are more willing to communicate with him than previously; audience feedback suggests changed attitudes toward him and his ideas. Even if they do not agree with Bob, the quality and quantity of interaction have increased, and this might lead to significant progress in the future.

In dramatistic criticism, evaluation is based more on changes in relationships and interaction than on specific outcome such as a successful sale or adoption of a proposal. Again, better relationships may lead to desirable outcomes, but that is secondary. In dramatism your goal is to have a successful presentation by increasing the understanding and unity between you and your listeners. By learning to detect such changes you will have a valuable way to evaluate your presentations.

ANALYZING FEEDBACK

One important factor in evaluating your presentations is feedback from your listeners. As discussed in Chapter 1, feedback consists of any message, verbal or nonverbal, that your listeners send back to you in relation to your message. Such feedback might be given to you directly and immediately, but it might also come to you indirectly or after a period of time has passed. For example, Bob Trent invites his listeners to ask questions both during and after his presentations. The audience also provides nonverbal feedback as he speaks. Additionally, any decisions rendered will be direct and powerful feedback. Later, too, Bob's supervisor or colleagues might make comments about his presentation. More indirectly, his status and progress in the organization may be, at least partially, a response to his speaking.

Listeners typically give three types of feedback: positive feedback, negative feedback, and neutral feedback. Regardless of when or how the feedback is presented to you, it will probably fall into one of these three categories.

Positive feedback is an expression of agreement, acceptance, or reinforcement of your efforts as a presenter. It may relate to any part of your message as well as to the entire effort. It does not necessarily mean that listeners agree with you. For example, one listener might tell you that you did an outstanding job of gathering data and explaining your position clearly, but that person may not accept your proposal in the end. Such a positive response can be quite valuable by telling you that you can do well without overtly succeeding. Positive feedback encourages you to do well and rewards your efforts.

Negative feedback consists of either verbal or nonverbal feedback which provides statements of disagreement, disapproval, and rejection. Clearly, this is not as desirable or enjoyable as positive feedback. Listeners may ask leading questions, express outright disagreement, frown, or even laugh derisively at your statements; your supervisor might complain about some aspect of your presentation; or the response from the group may be negative.

As undesirable as it may seem, however, negative feedback can be useful. Your task is to learn from it. Try to respond to it by asking questions: why are people responding negatively, and what should you do differently in future presentations? It is also useful to ask for additional feedback from those who give you negative comments. If a supervisor told you that your presentation was not effective, you might ask what particular areas needed improvement. Reflecting a positive response to negative feedback can help you more than reacting angrily.

Neutral feedback is a more controversial concept than positive or negative feedback. *Any* feedback can be perceived or interpreted as positive or negative. Neutral feedback is neither positive or negative. It is, instead, used to seek clarification or additional explanation. For example, a listener might tell Bob Trent that he or she does not understand one of Bob's explanations. This listener is merely asking for more information and explanation. Rather than trying to treat such feedback as either positive or negative, Bob takes it at face value and provides that additional information. Feedback can help the presenter avert misunderstanding and improve communication. When listeners provide feedback, they are actively participating with you in the communication process.

There are useful ways to respond to feedback: (1) Regard feedback as an aid to assessing and improving the effectiveness of your speaking. (2) Try to respond directly and specifically to feedback, without anger. (3) Encourage your listeners to provide feedback both during and after your presentations. (4) Pay attention to feedback from all sources, attempting to discern patterns or repeated messages. If many listeners have the same response, that may be significant. (5) Use feedback in conjunction with the other means of analyzing, interpreting, and evaluating your presentations discussed in this chapter.

SUMMARY

- Learning to analyze and evaluate your presentations both before and after their delivery will contribute significantly to your growing competence as a presentational speaker. Self-criticism provides you with an important means of maximizing your chances for success by enabling you to avoid problems before they occur and/or by improving the quality of future presentations.

- Speech criticism is the process of evaluating your presentation. It involves two basic steps: analysis and evaluation. Analysis consists of examining the presentation's content, purpose, support, audience, and social context. Evaluation is the process of making a judgment about your presentations. Analysis and evaluation of your presentations will help you improve them prior to their delivery and will help you improve future presentations.

- Steps in evaluating your presentations include (1) developing a positive attitude, (2) analyzing your work, (3) interpreting the major elements of your presentations, and (4) judging the effectiveness of your work.

- There are three basic systems for interpreting and evaluating your presentations: traditional rationalism, psychological criticism, and dramatistic criticism. Traditional rationalism emphasizes technical aspects of presentations and calls for a judgment of the truth or accuracy of a presentation. Psychological criticism emphasizes the audience and calls for an evaluation of how the presentation affects the audience. Dramatistic criticism stresses the interaction of speaker and audience and calls for an assessment of whether the presentation brings people together and creates understanding and unity.

- Another way to evaluate your speaking is to utilize audience feedback. Feedback is any verbal or nonverbal communication from listeners, sent back to the speaker in response to the message. You can maximize your ability to use feedback by (1) regarding it as a useful tool for evaluation, (2) responding directly to it without anger, (3) encouraging listeners to give you feedback, (4) paying attention to all sources of feedback, and (5) using feedback in conjunction with other elements of analysis and evaluation.

QUESTIONS FOR REVIEW AND DISCUSSION

1. Why is it important to evaluate your presentations?
2. Explain the difference between analysis and evaluation.
3. How could a presenter *combine* aspects of the three systems of criticism (traditional rationalism, psychological criticism, and dramatistic criticism)?
4. What is the nature and importance of feedback?
5. Discuss major strengths and weaknesses or problems with each of the three systems of criticism (traditional rationalism, psychological criticism, and dramatistic criticism).
6. Why do you think people have trouble learning to criticize their own speaking?

ACTIVITIES

1. Locate a collection of speeches. Select a speech that interests you and decide how you would analyze and evaluate the speech in accordance with the material in this chapter.

2. Make a classroom presentation and specifically invite feedback from your listeners.

3. Interview a person whose job requires him or her to make numerous presentations. Ask how this person evaluates presentations.

4. Select a speech criticism text and read sample critiques. Find examples of the types of criticism discussed in this chapter.

5. Attend a meeting or speech in which questions will be permitted. Observe how speakers respond to feedback.

Bibliography

Chapter 1

Birdwhistell, R. (1955). Background to kinesics. *ETC., 13,* 10–18.

Conrad, C. (1990). *Strategic organizational communication* (2nd ed.). New York: Holt, Rinehart and Winston.

DePaulo, B. M., and Rosenthal, R. (1979). Ambivalence, discrepancy, and deception in nonverbal communication. In R. Rosenthal (Ed.), *Skill in nonverbal communication* (pp. 204–248). Cambridge, MA: Oelgeschlager, Gunn & Hain.

DePaulo, B. M., Zuckerman, M., and Rosenthal, R. (1980, Spring). Humans as lie detectors. *Journal of Communication, 30,* 129–139.

DeVito, J. A. (1988). *Human communication: The basic course* (4th ed.), New York: Harper & Row.

Eckman, P. (1965). Communication through nonverbal behavior: A source of information about an interpersonal relationship. In S. S. Thompkins and C. E. Izard (Eds.), *Affect, cognition, and personality* (pp. 390–442). New York: Springer.

Mehrabian, A. (1968). Communication without words. *Psychology Today, 11,* 53.

Pace, R. W., and Faules, D. F. (1989). *Organizational communication* (2nd ed.). Englewood Cliffs, NJ: Prentice-Hall.

Yukl, G. (1981). *Leadership in organizations.* Englewood Cliffs, NJ: Prentice-Hall.

Chapter 2

Blake, R. R., and Mouton, J. S. (1964). *The managerial grid.* Houston, TX: Gulf.

Blake, R. R., and Mouton, J. S. (1985). *The managerial grid III: The key to leadership excellence.* Houston, TX: Gulf.

Cathcart, R., and Gumpert, G. (1986). I am a camera: The mediated self. *Communication Quarterly, 34,* 89–102.

Cooley, C. H. (1983). *Human nature and the social order.* New Brunswick, NJ: Transaction Books.

Curtis, D., Winsor, J., and Stephens, R. (1989, January). National preferences in business communication. *Communication Education, 38,* 6–14.

DeVito, J. A. (1989). *The interpersonal communication book.* New York: Harper & Row.

Dwiggins, C. (1986). Sharing management: Three ethical scenarios. *Journal of Business Ethics, 5,* 213–218.

Filley, A. C. (1975). *Interpersonal conflict resolution.* Glenview, IL: Scott, Foresman.

Gibb, J. (1961). Defensive communication. *Journal of Communication, 11,* 141–148.

Goss, B., and O'Hair, D. (1988). *Communication in interpersonal relationships.* New York: Macmillan.

Herzberg, F. (1966). *Work and the nature of man.* New York: Collins.

Herzberg, F. (1968). One more time: How do you motivate employees? *Harvard Business Review, 46,* 53–56.

Herzberg, F. (1987a). One more time: How do you motivate employees? *Harvard Business Review, 65,* 109–120.

Herzberg, F. (1987b). Workers' needs. *Industry Week, 234,* 29–32.

Joiner, C., Jr. (1985). Making the "Z" concept work. *Sloan Management Review, 26,* 57–63.

Kreps, G. L. (1986). *Organizational communication.* New York: Longman.

Maslow, A. H. (1954). *Motivation and personality.* New York: Harper & Row.

McGregor, D. (1985). *The human side of enterprise.* New York: McGraw-Hill.

Mead, G. H. (1967). *Mind, self and society.* Chicago: University of Chicago Press.

Myers, G., and Myers, M. (1988). *The dynamics of human communication* (5th ed.). New York: McGraw-Hill.

Ouchi, W. G. (1981). *Theory Z.* New York: Avon Books.

Powell, J. (1969). *Why am I afraid to tell you who I am?* Niles, NJ: Argus Communications.

Schutz, W. (1966). *The interpersonal underworld.* Palo Alto, CA: Science and Behavior Books.

Schutz, W. (1967). *FIRO-B* (1977 ed.). Palo Alto, CA: Consulting Psychologists Press.

Chapter 3

Argyle, M. (1975). *Bodily communication.* New York: International Universities Press.

Becker, S. L., and Ekdom, L. R. V. (1980). That forgotten basic skill: Oral communication. *Association for Communication Administration Bulletin, 33,* 12–25.

Cathcart, R. (1981). *Post communication: Rhetorical analysis and evaluation* (2nd ed.). Indianapolis: Bobbs-Merrill.

Dale, E., O'Rourke, J., and Bamman, H. (1971). *Techniques of teaching vocabulary.* Palo Alto, CA: Field Education Publications.

DiSalvo, V., Larsen, D. C., and Seiler, W. J. (1976). Communication skills needed by persons in business organizations. *Communication Education, 25,* 269–275.

Floyd, J. J. (1985). *Listening: A practical approach.* Glenview, IL: Scott, Foresman.

Johannesen, R. L. (1971). The emerging concept of communication as dialogue. *Quarterly Journal of Speech, 57,* 373–382.

Johnson, J. D. (1971). A survey of listening programs of a hundred major industries. In S. Duker (Ed.), *Listening: Readings* (pp. 288–301). Metuchen, NJ: Scarecrow Press.

Knapp, M. L. (1978). *Nonverbal communication in human interaction* (2nd ed.). New York: Holt, Rinehart and Winston.

Knapp, M. L. (1980). *Essentials of nonverbal communication.* New York: Holt, Rinehart and Winston.

Moore, B. C. J. (1977). *Introduction to the psychology of hearing.* Baltimore: University Park Press.

Murch, G. (1973). *Visual and auditory perception.* Indianapolis: Bobbs-Merrill.

Nichols, R. G., and Stevens, L. (1957). *Are you listening?* New York: McGraw-Hill.

Norman, D. A. (1968). Toward a theory of memory and attention. *Psychological Review, 75,* 522–536.

Rogers, C. R., and Farson, R. E. (1969). Active listening. In R. C. Huseman et al. (Eds.), *Readings in interpersonal and organizational communication* (pp. 480–496). Boston: Holbrook Pres.

Rogers, C. R., and Roethlisberger, F. J. (1952). Barriers and gateways to communication. *Harvard Business Review, 30,* 46–52.

Rubin, D. (1983). *Teaching reading and study skills in content areas.* New York: Holt, Rinehart and Winston.

Spearitt, D. (1962). *Listening comprehension: A factoral analysis, 76.* Melbourne: Australian Council for Educational Research.

Sperry Corporation. . . . Your personal listening profile (pamphlet).

Steil, L. K., Barker, L., and Watson, K. W. (1983). *Effective listening: Key to your personal success.* Reading, MA: Addison-Wesley.

Treisman, A. M. (1969). Strategies and models of selective attention. *Psychological Review, 79,* 282–299.

Tyson, P. D. (1982). A general systems approach to consciousness, attention, and mediation. *Psychological Record, 32,* 491–500.

Weaver, C. H. (1972). *Human listening.* Indianapolis: Bobbs-Merrill.

Werner, E. K. (1975). *A study of communication time.* M.A. thesis, University of Maryland–College Park.

Wolvin, A. D., and Coakley, C. G. (1982). *Listening.* Dubuque, IA: Wm. C. Brown.

Chapter 4

Arthur, D. (1986). Preparing for the interview. *Personnel, 63,* 37–49.

DeVito, J. (1988). *Human communication: The basic course* (4th ed.). Harper & Row.

Downs, C. W., Smeyak, G. P., and Martin E. (1980). *Professional interviewing.* New York: Harper & Row.

Hugenberg, L. W., and Yoder, D. D. (1985). *Speaking in the modern organization: Skills and strategies.* Glenview, IL: Scott, Foresman.

Stewart, C. J., and Cash, W. B., Jr. (1988). *Interviewing principles and practices* (5th ed.). Dubuque, IA: Wm. C. Brown.

Chapter 5

Avery, R. D., and Champion, J. E. (1982). The employment interview: A summary and review of recent research. *Personnel Psychology, 35,* 281–322.

Bolles, R. N. (1988). *A practical manual for job-hunters and career changers.* Berkeley, CA: Ten Speed Press.

Downs, Cal W., Smeyak, G. Paul, and Martin, Ernest. (1980). *Professional interviewing.* New York: Harper & Row.

Haynes, Marion G. (1978). Developing an appraisal program. Part I. *Personnel Journal, 57,* 14–19.

Hopper, R. (1977). Language attitudes in the employment interview. *Communication Monograph, 44,* 346–351.

Infante, Dominic A., and Gorden, William I. (1987, Summer). Superior and subordinate profiles: Implications for independent-mindedness and upward effectiveness. *Central States Speech Journal, 38,* 73–80.

Karren, Ronald J., and Nkomo, Stella M. (1988, April). So, you want to work for us. . . . *Personnel Administrator, 33,* 88–90.

Koontz, Harold. (1971). *Appraising managers as managers.* New York: McGraw-Hill.

Lunn, Terry. (1987, December). A scientific approach to successful selection. *Personnel Management 19,* 43–45.

Maier, Norman R. F. (1976). *The appraisal interview: Three basic approaches.* La Jolla, CA: University Associates.

McEvoy, Glenn M., Buller, Paul F., and Roghaar, Steven R. (1988). A jury of one's peers. *Personnel Administrator, 33,* 94–96.

Stewart, Charles J., and Cash, William B., Jr. (1988). *Interviewing principles and practices* (5th ed.). Dubuque, IA: Wm. C. Brown.

Chapter 6 Note

Portions of this chapter are adapted from Curtis, D. B., Mazza, J. M., and Runnebohm, S. (1979). *Communication for problem solving.* New York: Wiley.

Chapter 6

Argyris, C. (1964). *Integrating the individual and the organization.* New York: Wiley.

Barker, L. L., Wahlers, K. J., Watson, K. W., and Kibler, R. J. (1991) *Groups in process* (3rd ed.). Englewood Cliffs, NJ: Prentice-Hall.

Bormann, E. G., and Bormann, N. C. (1988). *Effective small group communication.* Edina, MN: Burgess.

Curtis, D. B., Mazza, J. M., and Runnebohm, S. (1979). *Communication for problem solving.* New York: Wiley.

Dewey, J. (1910). *How we think.* Boston: Heath.

Doyle, M., and Straus, D. (1976). *How to make meetings work: The new interaction method.* New York: Berkley.

Fisher, B. A. (1980). *Small group decision making.* New York: McGraw-Hill.

Fisher, B. A., and Ellis, D. G. (1990). *Small group decision making.* New York: McGraw-Hill.

Gouran, D. S. (1969, August). Variables related to consensus in group discussion of questions of policy. *Speech Monographs, 36,* 387–391.

Hirokawa, R. Y. (1983, Summer). Group communication and problem-solving effectiveness: An investigation of group phases. *Human Communication Research, 9,* 291–305.

Hirokawa, R. Y., and Pace, R. (1983, December). A descriptive investigation of the possible communication-based reasons for effective and ineffective group decision making. *Communication Monographs, 50,* 363–379.

Janis, I. L. (1972). *Groupthink* (2nd ed.). Boston: Houghton-Mifflin.

Kreps, G. L. (1990). *Organizational communication* (2nd ed.). New York: Longman.

Likert, R. (1961). *New patterns of management,* New York: McGraw-Hill.

Mintzberg, H. (1980). *The nature of managerial work.* Englewood Cliffs, NJ: Prentice-Hall.

Naisbitt, J. (1984). *Megatrends: Ten new directions transforming our lives.* New York: Warner Books.

Osborn, A. F. (1957). *Applied imagination.* New York: Scribner's.

Parnes, S. J. (1967). *Creative behavior guidebook.* New York: Scribner's.

Sattler, W. M., and Miller, N. E. (1968). *Discussion and conference* (2nd ed.). Englewood Cliffs, NJ: Prentice-Hall.

Seibold, D. R. (1979). Making meetings more successful: Plans, formats and procedures for group problem-solving. *Journal of Business Communication, 16*(4), 3–20.

Shaw, M. (1981). *Group dynamics: The psychology of small group behavior* (3rd ed.). New York: McGraw-Hill.

Sommer, R. (1965). Further studies of small group ecology. *Sociometry, 2*, 337–348.

Tubbs, S. L. (1988). *A systems approach to small group interaction* (3rd ed.). New York: Random House.

Zarda, A. (1982). *Making groups effective.* San Francisco: Jossey-Bass.

Chapter 7

Auger, B. Y. (1972). *How to run better business meetings.* AMACOM, A Division of American Management Associations.

Benne, K. D., and Sheats, P. (1948, Spring). Functional roles of group members. *Journal of Social Issues, 4*, 41–49.

Brilhart, J. K., and Galanes, G. J. (1989). *Effective group discussion* (6th ed.). Dubuque, IA: Wm. C. Brown.

Davies, K. R. (1988, July). Getting your meetings' worth. *The Rotarian, 153*, 12–13.

Delbecq, A. L., Van de Van, A. H., and Gustafson, D. H. (1975). *Group techniques for program planning: A guide to nominal group and Delphi processes.* Glenview, IL: Scott, Foresman.

Doyle, M., and Straus D. (1976). *How to make meetings work: The new interaction method.* New York: Berkley.

Ewbank, H. L. (1968). *Meeting management.* Dubuque, IA: Wm. C. Brown.

Fisher, B. A., and Ellis, D. G. (1990). *Small group decision making: Communication and the group process.* New York: McGraw-Hill.

Goldberg, A. A., and Larson, C. E. (1975). *Group communication.* Englewood Cliffs, NJ: Prentice-Hall.

Jay, A. (1976, March–April). How to run a meeting. *Harvard Business Review, 54*, 43–57.

Mosvick, R. K., and Nelson, R. B. (1987). *We've got to start meeting like this.* Glenview, IL: Scott, Foresman.

Ross, R. S. (1989). *Small groups in organizational settings.* Englewood Cliffs, NJ: Prentice-Hall.

Royal Bank Letter. (1984, Sept./Oct.). Royal Bank of Canada, Issn. 0229-0242, vol. 65(5).

Seibold, D. R. (1979). Making meetings more successful: Plans, formats and procedures for group problem-solving. *The Journal of Business Communication, 16*(4), 3–20.

3M Meeting Management Team. (1987). *How to run better business meetings.* New York: McGraw-Hill.

Tropman, J. E., and Morningstar, Gersh. (1985). *Meetings: How to make them work for you.* New York: Van Nostrand, Reinhold.

Chapter 8

Bormann, E. G., Howell, W. S., Nichols, R. G., and Shapiro, G. L. (1982). *Interpersonal communication in the modern organization* (2nd ed.). Englewood Cliffs, NJ: Prentice-Hall.

Dance, F. E. X. (1987, November). What do you mean by presentational speaking? *Management Communication Quarterly, 1*(2), 260–271.

Hugenberg, L. W., Owens, A. W. II, and Robinson, D. J. (1988). *Simulations for business and professional communication* (3rd ed.). Dubuque, IA: Kendall/Hunt.

Mager, R. F. (1962). *Preparing instructional objectives.* Belmont, CA: Fearon.

McLuhan, M. (1964). *Understanding media.* New York: McGraw-Hill.

Chapter 9

Beiswinger, George L. (1979, Fall). Why corporations stifle creativity. *Business and Society Review, 31,* 59–61.

Duncan, Hugh Dalziel. (1968). *Communication and social order.* London: Oxford University Press.

Dutton, Richard E. (1972, November). Creative use of creative people. *Personnel Journal, 51,* 818–822.

Folger, Joseph P., and Poole, Marshall Scott. (1984). *Working through conflict: A communication perspective.* Glenview, IL: Scott, Foresman.

Galbraith, John Kenneth. (1968). *The new industrial state.* New York: Mentor Books.

Goldhaber, Gerald M. (1983). *Organizational communication* (3rd ed.). Dubuque, IA: Wm. C. Brown.

Grossman, Stephen R. (1982, June). Training creativity and creative problem-solving. *Training and Development Journal, 36,* 62–68.

Holleran, Brian P., and Holleran, Paula R. (1976). Creativity revisited: A new role for group dynamics. *Journal of Creative Behavior, 10,* 130–137.

Janis, Irving (1967). *Victims of groupthink: A psychological study of foreign decisions and fiascoes.* Boston: Houghton-Mifflin.

Kiefer, Charles, and Stroh, Peter. (1983, April). A new paradigm for organization development. *Training and Development, 37,* 26–35.

Lawler, E. E. III. (1982). Drives, needs and outcomes. In D. A. Nadler, M. L. Tushman, and N. G. Hatvany (Eds.), *Managing organizations: Readings and cases.* Boston: Little, Brown.

Littlejohn, Stephen W. (1983). *Theories of human communication* (2nd ed.). Belmont, CA: Wadsworth.

Lynch, Dudley, and Gorovitz, Elizabeth Shey. (1982, August). Brain strategies: Applications for change and innovation. *Training and Development, 36,* 62–67.

Maslow, Abraham H. (1968). *Toward a psychology of being* (2nd ed.). Princeton, NJ: Van Nostrand Reinhold.

Maslow, Abraham H. (1970). *Motivation and personality* (2nd ed.). New York: Harper & Row.

McGinnis, Michael A., and Ackelsberg, M. Robert. (1983, Summer). Effective innovation management: Missing link in strategic planning? *The Journal of Business Strategy, 4,* 59–66.

Mettal, Walter G. (1977). Cybernetics, general systems, and creative problem-solving. *Journal of Creative Behavior, 11,* 53–66.

Nadler, D. A., and Lawler, E. E. III. (1982). Motivation—A diagnostic approach. In D. A. Nadler, M. L. Tushman, and N. G. Hatvany (Eds.), *Managing organizations: Readings and cases*. Boston: Little, Brown.

Ouchi, William G. (1981). *Theory Z*. New York: Avon Books.

Parnes, Sidney J. (1977). CPSI: The general system. *Journal of Creative Behavior, 11*, 1–11.

Patton, Bobby R., and Giffin, Kim. (1978). *Decision-making group interaction* (2nd ed.) New York: Harper & Row.

Poole, M. S., and Hirokawa, R. Y. (1986). Communication and group decision-making: A critical assessment. In R. Y. Hirokawa and M. S. Poole (Eds.), *Communication and group decision-making*. Beverly Hills, CA: Sage.

Putnam, L. L. (1986). Conflict in group decision-making. In R. Y. Hirokawa and M. S. Poole (Eds.), *Communication and group decision-making*. Beverly Hills, CA: Sage.

Raudsepp, Eugene (1983, April). 12 vital characteristics of the creative supervisor. *Supervision, 45*, 14–26.

Rehder, Robert R., and Porter, James L. (1983, December). The creative MBA: A new proposal for balancing the science and the art of management. *Business Horizons, 26*, 52–54.

Schuster, John. (1987, July). Tune in. *Corporate Report/Kansas City, 16*, 12.

Watson, Charles E. (1983, December). Managerial mind sets and the structural side of managing. *Business Horizons, 26*, 21–27.

Chapter 10

Aristotle. (1984). *The rhetoric and the poetics* (W. R. Roberts and I. Bywater, Trans.). New York: The Modern Library.

Berko, R. M., Wolvin, A. D., and Curtis, R. (1983). *This business of communication*. Dubuque, IA: Wm. C. Brown.

Bitzer, L. (1968, January). The rhetorical situation. *Philosophy and Rhetoric, 1*, 1–12.

Bryant, D. C. (1953). Rhetoric: Its functions and its scope. *Quarterly Journal of Speech, 34*, 401–424.

Burke, K. (1969). *A rhetoric of motives*. Berkeley: University of California Press.

Burns, J. M. (1978). *Leadership*. New York: Harper & Row.

Cronkhite, G. (1969). *Persuasion: Speech and behavioral change*. Indianapolis: Bobbs-Merrill.

Fellows, H., and Ikeda, F. (1982). *Business speaking and writing*. Englewood Cliffs, NJ: Prentice-Hall.

Hauser, G. A. (1986). *Introduction to rhetorical theory*. New York: Harper & Row.

Hirokawa, R. Y., and Poole, M. S. (Eds.). (1986). *Communication and group decision-making*. Beverly Hills, CA.: Sage.

Iacocca, L. (1984). *Iacocca: An autobiography*. New York: Bantam Books.

Johannesen, R. L. (1983). *Ethics in human communication* (2nd ed.). Prospect Heights, IL: Waveland Press.

Keast, W. R., and Streeter, R. E. (Eds.). (1956). *The province of prose*. New York: Harper Brothers.

Kiefer, C., and Stroh, P. (1983, April). A new paradigm for organizational development. *Training and Development, 37*, 26–35.

Larson, C. U. (1989). *Persuasion: Reception and responsibility* (5th ed.). Belmont, CA: Wadsworth.

Maslow, A. H. (1968). *Toward a psychology of being* (2nd ed.). Princeton, NJ: Van Nostrand Reinhold.

Maslow, A. H. (1970). *Motivation and personality* (2nd ed.). New York: Harper & Row.

McCroskey, J. C., and Young, T. J. (1981, Spring). Ethos and credibility: The construct and its measurement after three decades. *Central States Speech Journal, 32*, 24–34.

Minnick, W. (1957). *The art of persuasion*. Boston: Houghton Mifflin.

Nadler, D. A., Tushman, M. L. and Hatrany, N. G. (1982). *Managing organizations: Readings and cases*. Boston: Little, Brown.

Naisbitt, J. (1982). *Megatrends*. New York: Warner Books.

Norman, D. A. (1968). Toward a theory of memory and attention. *Psychological Review, 75*, 522–536.

Richards, I. A. (1965). *The philosophy of rhetoric*. New York: Oxford University Press.

Rieke, R. D., and Sillars, M. O. (1984). *Argumentation and the decision making process* (2nd ed.). Glenview, IL: Scott, Foresman.

Rosenblatt, S. B., Cheatham, T. R., and Watt, J. T. (1982). *Communicating in business* (2nd ed.). Englewood Cliffs, NJ: Prentice-Hall.

Simons, H. W. (1986). *Persuasion: Understanding, practice, and analysis* (2nd ed.). New York: Random House.

Weaver, R. M. (1971). Language is sermonic. In Richard L. Johannesen (Ed.), *Contemporary theories of rhetoric: Selected readings*. New York: Harper & Row.

Chapter 11

Campbell, K. K. (1982). *The rhetorical act*. Belmont, CA: Wadsworth.

Cronkhite, G. (1969). *Persuasion: Speech and behavioral change*. Indianapolis: Bobbs-Merrill.

Ehninger, D. (1974). *Influence, belief, and argument: An introduction to responsible persuasion*. Glenview, IL: Scott, Foresman.

Eisenberg, A. M., and Ilardo, J. A. (1980). *Argument: A guide to formal and informal debate* (2nd ed.). Englewood Cliffs, NJ: Prentice-Hall.

Freeley, A. J. (1981). *Argumentation and debate: Reasoned decision making* (5th ed.). Belmont, CA: Wadsworth.

Infante, D. A. (1988). *Arguing constructively*. Prospect Heights, IL: Waveland Press.

Peters, T. J., and Waterman, R. H., Jr. (1982). *In search of excellence: Lessons from America's best-run companies*. New York: Harper & Row.

Rieke, R. D., and Sillars, M. O. (1984). *Argumentation and the decision making process* (2nd ed.). Glenview, IL: Scott, Foresman.

Sproule, J. M. (1980). *Argument: Language and its influence.* New York: McGraw-Hill.

Toulmin, S. (1958). *The uses of argument.* Cambridge, England: Cambridge University Press.

Ziegelmueller, G. W., and Dause, C. A. (1975). *Argumentation: Inquiry and advocacy.* Englewood Cliffs, NJ: Prentice-Hall.

Chapter 12

Allen, R. E. (1988, June 1). Commitments sought require commitments kept. *Vital Speeches of the Day, 54,* 484.

Baird, J. E., Jr. (1974, Summer). The effects of speech summaries upon audience comprehension of expository speeches of varying quality and complexity. *Central States Speech Journal, 23*(2), 119–127.

Clark, A. J. (1974, Summer). An explanatory study of order effect in persuasive communication. *The Southern Speech Communication Journal, 39,* 322–332.

Cornish, E. (1980, December 1). The family and its home in the 1980s. *Vital Speeches of the Day, 47,* 120–124.

Cromwell, H. (1950, June). The relative effect on audience attitude of the first versus the second argumentative speech of a series. *Speech Monographs, 17,* 105–122.

Crooks, G. M. (1986, October 1). How to make a difference: Shaping public policy. *Vital Speeches of the Day, 52,* 756–760.

Curtis, D. B. (1974). *An experimental study of the effects of message organization.* Unpublished doctoral dissertation, University of Missouri–Columbia.

Curtis, D. B., and Kline, J. A. (1974). Effects of message organization in attitude change, comprehension and retention. *Missouri Speech Journal, 5,* 44–53.

Doob, L. W. (1953). Effects of initial serial position and attitude upon recall under conditions of low motivation. *Journal of Abnormal and Social Psychology, 48,* 199–205.

Gronbeck, B. E., Ehninger, D., and Monroe, A. H. (1988). *Principles of speech communication* (10th ed.). Glenview, IL: Scott, Foresman.

Hovland, C. I., Janis, I. L., and Kelley, H. H. (1953). *Communication and persuasion.* New Haven, CT, and London: Yale University Press.

Howell, W. S., and Bormann, E. (1988). *The process of presentational speaking* (2nd ed.). New York: Harper & Row.

Linkugel, W. A., Allen, R. R., and Johannsen, R. L. (1978). *Contemporary American speeches* (5th ed.) (pp. 80–83). Dubuque, IA: Kendall/Hunt.

McCroskey, J. C., and Mehrley, R. S. (1969, March). The effects of disorganization and nonfluency on attitude change and source credibility. *Speech Monographs, 335,* 13–21.

Miller, G. A. (1956). The magical number seven, plus or minus two: Some limits on our capacity for processing information. *Psychological Review, 63,* 81–97.

Monroe, A. H. (1939). *Principles and types of speech* (rev. ed.). New York: Scott, Foresman.

Monroe, A. H., and Ehninger, D. (1967). *Principles and types of speech* (6th ed.). Glenview, IL: Scott, Foresman.

Muskie, E. S. (1987, October 15). The chains of liberty. *Vital Speeches of the Day, 54,* 4–7.

Nichols, R. G., and Stevens, L. (1957). *Are you listening?* New York: McGraw-Hill.

Rockwell, W. F., Jr. (1986, October 15). The future of the U.S. space program: Our well-being as a nation. *Vital Speeches of the Day, 53,* 8–10.

Sloan, J. (1987, October 15). The American folly of courting "Europeanization." *Vital Speeches of the Day, 54,* 29–31.

Tubbs, S. L. (1988). *A systems approach to small group interaction.* New York: Random House.

Walters, P. (1988, May 1). America: A new home for B. P. *Vital Speeches of the Day, 5,* 424–427.

Wick, C. Z. (1985, October 15). The war of ideas: America's arsenal. *Vital Speeches of the Day, 52,* 16–21.

Chapter 13

Adams, A. K. (1969). *The home book of humorous quotations.* New York: Dodd, Mead.

Bartlett, J. (1980). *Familiar quotations* (15th and 125th anniversary ed.). Boston: Little, Brown.

Baruch, R. M. (1980, January 15). Lifestyle revolutions in the television age. *Vital Speeches of the Day, 46,* 209–213.

Bowers, J. W., and Osborn, M. M. (1966, June). Attitudinal effects of selected types of concluding metaphors in persuasive speeches. *Speech Monographs, 33*(2), 147–155.

Brussell, E. E. (1988). *Webster's new world dictionary of quotable definitions* (2nd ed.). New York: Websters' New World.

Burke, K. (1966). *Language as symbolic action.* Berkeley: University of California Press.

Clarke, R. L. (1988, March 1). Bank failures. *Vital Speeches of the Day, 54,* 206–209.

Eisenberg, E. M. (1984, September). Ambiguity as strategy in organizational communication. *Communication Monographs, 51*(3) 227–242.

Florida—anything goes. (1950, April 17). *Time,* p. 28.

Gassner, John. (1958). *Best American plays fourth series 1951–1957* (edited). New York: Crown Publishers.

Gault, S. C. (1988, January 15). Today's marketing mission. *Vital Speeches of the Day, 54,* 206–209.

Jordan, W. J., Flanagan, L. L., and Wineinger, R. W. (1975, Spring). Novelty and recall effects of animate and inanimate metaphorical discourse. *Central States Speech Journal, 26*(1), 29–33.

Kennedy, E. M. (1980, September 15). Address to the Democratic National Convention. *Vital Speeches of the Day, 46,* 714–716.

Lamm, R. D. (1985, October 15). Time to change course. *Vital Speeches of the Day, 52,* 4–6.

Larson, C. (1989). *Persuasion: Reception and responsibility* (5th ed.). Belmont, CA: Wadsworth.

Linkugel, W. A., Allen, R. R., and Johannsen, R. J. (1978). *Contemporary American speeches* (5th ed.) (pp. 365–370). Dubuque, IA: Kendall/Hunt.

Marien, M. (1984, December 15). Hope, fear and technology. *Vital Speeches of the Day, 51,* 137–142.

Mazza, I., Jordon, W., and Carpenter, R. (1972, Winter). The comparative effects of stylistic sources of redundancy. *Central States Speech Journal, 23*(4), 241–245.

Meany, G. (1980, January 1). The trade union movement. *Vital Speeches of the Day, 46,* 164–166.

Mitford, J. (1963). *The American way of death.* Greenwich, CT: Fawcett.

Munro, J. R. (1988, February 1). The five commitments of free enterprise. *Vital Speeches of the Day, 54,* 233–235.

Nichols, R. G., and Stevens, L. A. (1957). *Are you listening?* New York: McGraw-Hill.

Ong, J. D. (1988, May 15). Workplace 2000—managing change. *Vital Speeches of the Day, 54,* 471–473.

Posvar, W. W. (1988, April 15). U.S.-Japanese relations in a global perspective. *Vital Speeches of the Day, 44,* 405–408.

Prochnow, H. V., and Prochnow, H. V., Jr. (1977). *The public speaker's treasure chest* (3rd ed.). New York: Harper & Row.

Reid, L. (1982). *Speaking well* (4th ed.). New York: McGraw-Hill.

Reinsch, N. L., Jr. (1971, June). An investigation of the effects of the metaphor and simile in persuasive discourse. *Speech Monographs, 38*(2), 142–145.

Richey, H. S. (1977, April 15). The real cause of inflation: Government services. *Vital Speeches of the Day, 33,* 386–389.

Schreyer, W. A. (1988, April 15). Financing America's future. *Vital Speeches of the Day, 54,* 403–405.

Siltanen, S. (1981, Fall). The persuasiveness of metaphors: A replication and extension. *The Southern Speech Communication Journal, 47,* 67–83.

Walters, P. (1988, May 1). America: A new home for B.P. *Vital Speeches of the Day, 54,* 424–427.

Whelan, E. M. (1987, November 1). Health hoax and a health scare. *Vital Speeches of the Day, 54,* 57–61.

Chapter 14

Anderson, J. (1966). More on the equivalence of statements presented in various media. *AV Communication Review, 16,* 499–505.

Bormann, E. G., Howell, W. S., Nichols, R. G., and Shapiro, G. L. (1982). *Interpersonal communication in the modern organization.* Englewood Cliffs, NJ: Prentice-Hall.

Bostrom, R. (1988). *Communicating in public: Speaking and listening.* Santa Rosa, CA: Burgess.

Cothran, T. (1989, July). The value of visuals. *Presentation Technologies,* 4–8.

Ehninger, D., Gronbeck, B., McKerrow, R., and Monroe, A. (1986). *Principles and types of speech communication* (10th ed.). Glenview, IL: Scott, Foresman.

Foss, S. (1982). Rhetoric and the visual image: A resource unit. *Communication Education, 31*(1), 55–66.

Howell, W., and Bormann, E. (1988). *The process of presentational speaking.* New York: Harper & Row.

Kenny, M. (1982). *Presenting yourself.* New York: Wiley.

Kringle, P., and Schaff, D. (1989, September). Interactive training beginning to produce. *Interactive Technologies,* 5–6.

Munter, M. (1982). *Guide to managerial communication* (2nd ed.) (p. 98). Englewood Cliffs, NJ: Prentice-Hall.

Seiler, W. (1971). The conjunctive influence of source credibility and the use of visual materials. *Southern Speech Communication Journal, 37*(2), 174–185.

Smith, J. (1989, July). Presentation graphics: Do you build or buy? *Presentation Technologies,* 10–12.

Smith, T. (1984). *Making successful presentations: A self-teaching guide.* New York: Wiley.

Sutherland, D. (1989, July). Projecting with authority. *Presentation Technologies,* 16–19.

Chapter 15

Beebe, S. A. (1974, January). Eye contact: A nonverbal determinant of speaker credibility. *Speech Teacher, 23,* 21–25.

Beebe, S. A. (1978). Effects of eye contact, posture, and vocal inflection upon credibility and comprehension. *Australian Scan, 7–8,* 57–69.

Bradley, B. E. (1986). *Fundamentals of speech communication* (4th ed.). Dubuque, IA: Wm. C. Brown.

Bruskin & Associates. (1973, December). *Spectra* (A survey conducted by R. H. Bruskin & Associates). Annandale, VA: Speech Communication Association.

Hall, E. T. (1959). *The silent language.* New York: Doubleday.

Knapp, M. (1980). *Essentials of nonverbal communication.* New York: Holt, Rinehart and Winston.

Masterson, J. T., Beebe, S. A., and Watson, N. H. (1989). *Effective speech communication.* Glenview, IL: Scott, Foresman.

McCroskey, J. C. (1984, March). Communication apprehension and accumulated communication state anxiety experiences: A research note. *Communication Monographs, 51,* 79–84.

Molloy, J. T. (1976). *New dress for success.* New York: Warner Books.

Molloy, J. T. (1978). *The woman's dress for success book.* New York: Warner Books.

Monroe, A. H. (1937). *Measurement and analysis of audience reaction to student speakers' studies in attitude change.* Bulletin of Purdue University Studies in Higher Education No. 22. West Lafayette, IN: Purdue University.

Chapter 16

Hopkins, Tom. (1982). *How to master the art of selling.* New York: Warner Books.

The science of selling. (1983, Nov./Dec.). *The royal bank letter, 64*(6). Royal Bank of Canada.

Smith, Terry C. (1984). *Making successful presentations: A self-teaching guide.* New York: Wiley.

Timm, Paul R. (1981). *Functional business presentations.* Englewood Cliffs, NJ: Prentice-Hall.

Ziglar, Z. (1984). *Secrets of closing the sale.* New York: Berkley Books.

Chapter 17

Andrews, J. R. (1983). *The practice of rhetorical criticism.* New York: Macmillan.

Burke, K. (1962). *A grammar of motives and a rhetoric of motives.* New York: Meridian Books.

Campbell, K. K. (1972). Critiques of contemporary rhetoric. Belmont, CA: Wadsworth.

Cathcart, R. (1981). *Post communication: Rhetorical analysis and evaluation.* Indianapolis: Bobbs-Merrill.

Larson, C. U. (1989). *Persuasion: Reception and responsibility* (5th ed.). Belmont, CA: Wadsworth.

Name Index

Subject Index